THE HISTORY OF LANGUAGE LEARNING AND TEACHING
VOLUME I
16TH–18TH CENTURY EUROPE

LEGENDA

LEGENDA is the Modern Humanities Research Association's book imprint for new research in the Humanities. Founded in 1995 by Malcolm Bowie and others within the University of Oxford, Legenda has always been a collaborative publishing enterprise, directly governed by scholars. The Modern Humanities Research Association (MHRA) joined this collaboration in 1998, became half-owner in 2004, in partnership with Maney Publishing and then Routledge, and has since 2016 been sole owner. Titles range from medieval texts to contemporary cinema and form a widely comparative view of the modern humanities, including works on Arabic, Catalan, English, French, German, Greek, Italian, Portuguese, Russian, Spanish, and Yiddish literature. Editorial boards and committees of more than 60 leading academic specialists work in collaboration with bodies such as the Society for French Studies, the British Comparative Literature Association and the Association of Hispanists of Great Britain & Ireland.

The MHRA encourages and promotes advanced study and research in the field of the modern humanities, especially modern European languages and literature, including English, and also cinema. It aims to break down the barriers between scholars working in different disciplines and to maintain the unity of humanistic scholarship. The Association fulfils this purpose through the publication of journals, bibliographies, monographs, critical editions, and the MHRA Style Guide, and by making grants in support of research. Membership is open to all who work in the Humanities, whether independent or in a University post, and the participation of younger colleagues entering the field is especially welcomed.

ALSO PUBLISHED BY THE ASSOCIATION

Critical Texts
Tudor and Stuart Translations • New Translations • European Translations
MHRA Library of Medieval Welsh Literature

MHRA Bibliographies
Publications of the Modern Humanities Research Association

The Annual Bibliography of English Language & Literature
Austrian Studies
Modern Language Review
Portuguese Studies
The Slavonic and East European Review
Working Papers in the Humanities
The Yearbook of English Studies

www.mhra.org.uk
www.legendabooks.com

EDITORIAL BOARD

Chair: Professor Jonathan Long (University of Durham)
For *Germanic Literatures*: Ritchie Robertson (University of Oxford)
For *Italian Perspectives*: Simon Gilson (University of Warwick)
For *Moving Image*: Emma Wilson (University of Cambridge)
For *Research Monographs in French Studies*:
Diana Knight (University of Nottingham)
For *Selected Essays*: Susan Harrow (University of Bristol)
For *Studies in Comparative Literature*: Duncan Large
(British Centre for Literary Translation, University of East Anglia)
For *Studies in Hispanic and Lusophone Cultures*:
Trevor Dadson (Queen Mary, University of London)
For *Studies in Yiddish*: Gennady Estraikh (New York University)
For *Transcript*: Matthew Reynolds (University of Oxford)

Managing Editor
Dr Graham Nelson
41 Wellington Square, Oxford OX1 2JF, UK

www.legendabooks.com

The History of Language Learning and Teaching

VOLUME I

16th-18th Century Europe

Edited by
Nicola McLelland and Richard Smith

LEGENDA

Modern Humanities Research Association
2018

Published by Legenda
an imprint of the Modern Humanities Research Association
Salisbury House, Station Road, Cambridge CB1 2LA

ISBN 978-1-78188-698-4 (HB)
ISBN 978-1-78188-369-3 (PB)

First published 2018

All rights reserved. No part of this publication may be reproduced or disseminated or transmitted in any form or by any means, electronic, mechanical, photocopying, recording or otherwise, or stored in any retrieval system, or otherwise used in any manner whatsoever without written permission of the copyright owner, except in accordance with the provisions of the Copyright, Designs and Patents Act 1988, or under the terms of a licence permitting restricted copying issued in the UK by the Copyright Licensing Agency Ltd, Saffron House, 6–10 Kirby Street, London EC1N 8TS*, England, or in the USA by the Copyright Clearance Center, 222 Rosewood Drive, Danvers MA 01923. Application for the written permission of the copyright owner to reproduce any part of this publication must be made by email to legenda@mhra.org.uk.*

Disclaimer: Statements of fact and opinion contained in this book are those of the author and not of the editors or the Modern Humanities Research Association. The publisher makes no representation, express or implied, in respect of the accuracy of the material in this book and cannot accept any legal responsibility or liability for any errors or omissions that may be made.

Trademark notice: Product or corporate names may be trademarks or registered trademarks, and are used only for identification and explanation without intent to infringe.

© *Modern Humanities Research Association 2018*

Copy-Editor: Richard Correll

CONTENTS

	Acknowledgements	ix
	Introduction — Establishing HoLLT: The History of Language Learning and Teaching NICOLA MCLELLAND AND RICHARD SMITH	1
1	The Historiography of Modern Language Teaching: From National Views to a European Perspective MARCUS REINFRIED	20
2	French Didactics in Late Medieval and Early Modern England: Thinking Historically about Method RORY G. CRITTEN	33
3	Teaching Agreement: A Case Study in the Language Pedagogy of Two Humanist Treatises on Syntax from Early Modern England ANNELI LUHTALA	52
4	The Use of Dialogues in Teaching Foreign Languages (Sixteenth Century): Circulations and Adaptations of Berlaimont's *Dictionarium* (1556) in Spain, the Netherlands, and England JAVIER VILLORIA-PRIETO AND JAVIER SUSO LÓPEZ	67
5	Histoire de quelques règles de prononciation pour savoir lire le français: de Berlaimont (1527) à Reixac i Carbó (1749) MARC VIÉMON	83
6	Latin Schoolbooks in Late Seventeenth-Century Finland SUVI RANDÉN	96
7	Teaching Czech in a Plurilingual Community in the Age of Enlightenment: The Case of František Jan Tomsa ALENA A. FIDLEROVÁ	110
8	Native Tongues and Foreign Languages in the Education of the Russian Nobility: The Case of the Noble Cadet Corps (1730s–1760s) VLADISLAV RJÉOUTSKI	129
9	Veneroni en Espagne: l'*Explicación de la gramática francesa* (Madrid, 1728) d'Antoine Courville MANUEL BRUÑA CUEVAS	145

10 Giuseppe Baretti's Multifarious Approach to Learning Italian in
   Eighteenth-Century Britain   156
   VILMA DE GASPERIN

11 Londres et les britanniques dans l'ancienne grammaticographie du
   Portugais Langue Étrangère (XVIIe–XIXe siècles)   173
   MARIA DO CÉU FONSECA

   Index   192

ACKNOWLEDGMENTS

Every chapter in this collection has been submitted to blind (i.e. anonymized) peer-review by at least two readers. We sincerely thank all those who read and commented on earlier drafts of chapters for their very helpful comments. We also acknowledge gratefully the generous support of the A. S. Hornby Educational Trust and, above all, the support of the Arts and Humanities Research Council network grant that led to the production of these three volumes [AH/J012475/1]. We owe a special debt of gratitude to Louis Cotgrove, our editorial assistant on this project. Finally, we thank the editors at Legenda, in particular Graham Nelson, and our contributors for their commitment and forbearance during the complex process of bringing this three-volume collection to publication.

INTRODUCTION

Establishing HoLLT: The History of Language Learning and Teaching

Nicola McLelland and Richard Smith[1]

The History of Language Learning and Teaching as a Field of Study

In this introduction, we set ourselves two tasks. First, as this three-volume collection marks the culmination of our AHRC-funded project 'Towards a History of Modern Foreign Language Teaching and Learning' (AH/J012475/1), we reflect on the emergence of an international community of scholarship focused on what has come to be called — following McLelland and Smith (2014a) — the History of Language Learning and Teaching (HoLLT), and we describe how this is becoming established as a newly emerging interdisciplinary, intercultural and plurilinguistic field of enquiry. Second, we outline what the present collection contributes to this developing field, and how it helps indicate future directions of research.

These three volumes, following on from McLelland and Smith (2014a) and Smith and McLelland (2018a), represent the first time that a substantial collection of research studies in the field of history of language learning and teaching has been published in an English-dominant country. Relevant studies have appeared in several countries over the years, most consistently in the area of French as a second/foreign language, but there has not, until recently, been a recognizable discourse community of historians of language learning and teaching communicating together across both language and geographical borders.

As we explain more fully below, there are biases of focus over the three volumes which reflect their origins in a UK-based research network project, albeit one with strong connections to Continental Europe. Almost all the chapters started life as papers at a conference we organized in July 2014 at the University of Nottingham.[2] The conference was the last of a series of three events which were designed to bring together potentially interested UK-based academics and teacher educators in the field of modern foreign language teaching with some of those we knew in Continental Europe who were already doing relevant historical research. The conference followed on from two smaller workshops in the previous two years (at the Universities of Nottingham and Warwick, respectively), which themselves led to the publication of McLelland and Smith (2014a) and Smith and McLelland (2018a), respectively. Thus, with only a few exceptions (to be explained further below), the chapters in this collection were not commissioned for purposes of coverage but represent instead an illustrative sample of original, in-depth studies in the broad field of HoLLT, reflecting the specialist interests of those who heard about and chose to present papers at the conference at the time.

Nevertheless, we hope that both the substantial amount of research on display here and our arrangement of chapters across the three volumes will encourage the kind of 'transnational comparison of factors of language teaching and learning' which is mentioned as a desideratum by Reinfried (this volume). As Reinfried points out, the juxtaposition of papers can provoke 'new insights [...], even though such links are not usually made explicitly by the authors of papers themselves'. In the interests of moving beyond possible silos in research, we have deliberately avoided either a country- or a language-based arrangement of papers, instead taking a broadly chronological approach. Following this introduction and the similarly meta-historical chapter by Reinfried, Volume I contains studies of language learning and teaching in sixteenth- to eighteenth-century Europe, from French didactics in late medieval and early modern England (Critten) to the early grammatography of Portuguese as a foreign language (Fonseca). Although these two book-end chapters focus on England, the overall geographical and linguistic range is wide, extending from Russia in the east to Spain in the south-west of Europe, and taking in Latin, Czech and Italian as well as French and Portuguese. Similarly, Volume II (*19th–20th Century Europe*) begins and ends with issues relating specifically to French language learning in England (Cohen, Daniels) but covers a variety of European languages and settings overall, including, for example, German in Spain (Marizzi) and English in Germany (Giesler, Doff). The chronological focus of Volume III (*Across Cultures*) is also on the nineteenth and twentieth centuries, but with a thematic arrangement which similarly mixes target languages and regions. Part I contains papers on 'The Place of Culture in Language Teaching', mainly in early to mid-twentieth-century Germany and England, while Part II consists of chapters on 'Language Learning beyond Europe', from Arabic learning by nineteenth-century visitors to Egypt (Mairs) to the late twentieth-century 'wave' of secondary school Japanese studies in New Zealand (Harvey). Overall, the scope of this collection is deliberately broad, with contributions covering aspects of the history of language learning and teaching in Western Europe (the majority), but also Eastern Europe, Africa, China, Japan, India, the USA and New Zealand.[3]

Part I of Volume III particularly foregrounds an often only implicit thread running through the history of language teaching, even though it is one whose effects can outlast learners' knowledge of the language itself: the teaching of culture, whether this be 'high' or 'everyday' culture, and of cultural values (Risager 2007). Culture has to date received relatively little explicit attention in the historiography of language teaching, which has tended to focus more on tracing the historical development of methods (although see McLelland 2015a: 249–334). It was partly for this reason that we adopted the theme of 'Connecting Cultures' for our conference, to invite a focus on this important area of language teaching (history), at the same time as highlighting needs to connect the different traditions, or 'cultures' of language teaching themselves, across different regions and languages. The relevance of historical research into culture teaching is clearly articulated by Klippel (Vol. III), who argues that the foundation for the ways in which English-speaking cultures are represented in today's English language textbooks in Germany were already laid in the late nineteenth century. On the other hand, there have been changes in approach which illuminate shifting perceptions of self and other: Raisz's analysis of debates on cultural representation in German English-language teaching after World War II is illuminating in this respect (Vol. III), while Sharp's study of 'cultural readers' of the 1920s and 1930s for German learners of English (in the same volume) reveals a focus on representations of the English or British (generally conflated!) in an era before mass migration, on the basis of their Celtic, Anglo-Saxon, Viking and Norman heritages, which now seems archaic. Both Byram and Schleich (Vol. III) are interested in language learning in the context of internationalism and internationalization. Schleich's study of the International Scholars' Correspondence network — a pen-friend service run for school pupils in Germany, France, Britain and the USA in the period before World War I — reflects a belief (to some extent explicitly pacifist) in the power of a 'standing army of correspondents' who would help promote peace and understanding between nations. Comparative studies of cultural representations like that of Wegner (Vol. III), who compares the representation of German culture to school pupils learning the language in twentieth-century England and France, are relatively rare, but can be particularly fruitful. Wegner shows how differing aims of modern foreign language teaching in England and France reveal 'specific politics and ideologies as well as traditions and changes in educational goals', differences that are determined by national rather than common European concerns, such as the concern in France with analysis of Germany as the 'enemy' (until after World War II) and a greater focus on Germany's culture heritage, compared with an emphasis in England both on overcoming insularity and on economic interests, reflected in a greater emphasis on communicative skills. 'Interculturality' is brought to the fore in this collection, then, both as topic and as a characteristic of the range of authors and contexts assembled here.

With some exceptions, however, scholars brought together in the general area denoted here by 'HoLLT' have not until now tended to view it in the unified form we have been arguing for, since it has not hitherto 'existed' as a disciplinary space. (It is therefore not surprising to find that the authors in this collection do not yet refer much to work outside the domains — different language or area traditions, or, more typically, different disciplinary formations — they themselves identify with.) Nevertheless, whereas in previous work we have referred to 'building' the field of HoLLT, we now wish to explain how the publication of this book can be seen to mark, or at least accompany, its *establishment*. For overviews of previous research in the area see McLelland and Smith (2014b), McLelland (2017, chapter 2) and Smith and McLelland (2018b). Here, we merely note that what pre-existed HoLLT as a newly unified — or unifying — field of enquiry was a set of separate centres or strands of research, for example the history of French teaching, or history of English studies in Germany, coalescing around a particular learned society in the first case (SIHFLES: see below) or universities (Augsburg; the Ludwig-Maximilians-University, Munich; Bremen) in the second case, or involving separate pieces of work in separate disciplines, with researchers working very much in isolation from one another. We note the existence, based in France, but with wider reach, of SIHFLES (*Société Internationale pour l'Histoire du Français Langue Etrangère ou Seconde*); in Italy, CIRSIL (*Centro Interuniversitario di Ricerca sulla Storia degli Insegnamenti Linguistici*); in Spain, SEHEL (*Sociedad Española para la Historia de las Enseñanzas Lingüísticas*); and in Portugal APHELLE (*Associação Portuguesa para a História do Ensino das Línguas e Literaturas Estrangeiras*). In the Netherlands, the Peeter Heyns Society has been in existence for the past twenty years, while in Germany the Matthias-Kramer Society was founded in 2013, though on the back of several decades of work by a number of German scholars. Independently of our own efforts, most of these different centres of research had already been coming together to some extent. For example, SIHFLES, CIRSIL, SEHEL, APHELLE and the Peeter Heyns Society held joint conferences in Spain (Granada, 2008) and Italy (Gargnano, 2011), yielding themed journal issues that to some extent transcended language or geographical boundaries: on multilingualism in European language teaching (Fernández Fraile and Suso López 2009) and on women in the European history of language learning and teaching (Finotti and Minerva 2012), respectively. Our funded network was in part inspired by these first steps already taken on the European continent, and our 2014 conference — to our knowledge, the first ever conference on the history of language learning and teaching held in the UK — was designated the third in this series of joint initiatives. As a UK base for this collaboration, we drew on the further support of the Henry Sweet Society for the History of Linguistic Ideas, itself founded in 1983.

For fuller discussion of the benefits of establishing HoLLT on a sound basis as an 'overall, language-independent yet language-*interdependent*, geographically discrete and yet geographically intertwined' field of study (Smith and McLelland 2018b: 4), we refer the reader to McLelland and Smith (2014b), and Smith (2016). Here, we merely reiterate two key points. The history of language learning and teaching has, like any historical enquiry, its intrinsic value: recovering our shared past. At a basic and practical level, also, knowledge or — in the absence of knowledge — *assumptions* about language learning in the past underpin the understanding of language teaching today: its place in society, its teachers and learners, its methods, its assessment. There are key questions relating to all of these at any time, but especially so now, at a crucial moment when modern language learning is generally acknowledged to be in crisis in the UK[4] and in other English-dominant nations, and where the learning of languages other than English in other parts of the world is similarly under pressure.[5] To repeat the argument advanced by Smith (2016: 76), 'historical evidence is needed as a basis on which to build appropriate reform efforts [...]. Historical research into applied linguistic antecedents [and, we would add here, foreign language teaching antecedents more widely conceived] can place present-day conceptions [..] in perspective and reveal their historically constituted limitations'. Largely for this reason, we see developing historical awareness as a keystone in language teacher education (see Smith and McLelland 2018b) and in language education reform (Smith and Imura 2004).

As we shall argue more fully below, HoLLT also has a potentially powerful role to play when it intersects with the critical examination of histories of colonialism, missionary work and postcolonial experience, whose legacies continue today, not least in the area of ELT (English Language Teaching).[6]

In our previous publications, we have written of 'building the history of language learning and teaching' (McLelland and Smith 2014a, 2014b), and of establishing what Smith (2016) has termed 'Applied Linguistic Historiography'. These previous contributions have been concerned with arguing for the establishment of a new field (in the former case) and discussing appropriate methods of inquiry (in the latter case). Alongside these more or less scholarly reflections, we have also been engaged in a project to build HoLLT in practical terms, first by means of the two workshops and the conference which gave rise to most of the papers here, then followed by the establishment in 2015 of a research network with much wider reach (the AILA Research Network on History of Language Learning and Teaching (www.hollt.net), which has itself organized two international events, with the next planned for summer 2018. The publication of this set of three volumes will, we trust, serve to place HoLLT even more firmly on the disciplinary map.

In further justification of the idea that, partly as a result of these efforts, HoLLT is becoming 'established' or 'disciplinarized', we structure the remainder of this introductory chapter according to the following themes: HoLLT in relation to the overt intention of our original network project — generating interest in historical research among modern language specialists in Britain and the English-speaking world; HoLLT and the History of ELT; HoLLT in Europe; HoLLT beyond Europe, including colonial and postcolonial relationships; and, finally, historiographical and interdisciplinary achievements in advancing the field of HoLLT.

HoLLT and Modern Languages in Britain and the English-speaking World

Apart from the history of teaching of culture, highlighted above, these three volumes can be seen to establish two further areas as important domains of research within HoLLT: first, HoLLT in Britain and the English-speaking world more generally, and, second, HoLLT with regard to ELT.

With few exceptions, chiefly focused on the early modern period, Britain — like the rest of the English-speaking world — has had very little history of researching HoLLT, and has been slow to begin to emulate earlier work in (especially) France and Germany.[7] Notwithstanding the pioneering work in the history of English language teaching by Howatt (1984; 2nd edn with Widdowson, 2004), more recent work by Smith (e.g. 1999, 2003, 2005, 2009), and, for languages other than English, by McLelland (2015a, 2017), basic research with primary sources has been limited, especially for the period since about 1800, both about language learning in Britain, and about learning English as a foreign language.

Our collection helps fill gaps in both these hitherto under-researched areas. Indeed, one of our intentions in bringing scholars from abroad to events in the UK in 2012–14, including the conference which gave rise to this publication, was, precisely, to stimulate interest in historical research in Britain. Given that there *are* a number of papers by UK-based researchers in this collection, we feel we succeeded, to an extent, in this aim, even though more than half the research studies in the collection as a whole were carried out by researchers based outside Britain. Thirteen of the chapters deal with language learning in Britain: these range from Critten's study of French learning in the medieval period and Luhtala on Latin in sixteenth-century England to Italian in the early modern period (Gasperin) and Portuguese in the seventeenth to nineteenth centuries (Fonseca), all in Volume I;[8] and, in Volumes II and III, Latin, French and other languages in the nineteenth (Cohen, Kirk, Lorch), early twentieth (Ashby and Przedlacka, Byram, Martinez, Wegner) and later twentieth centuries (Daniels, Scott and, again, Wegner). The chapters about Britain in these volumes signal, then, a growing interest in Britain's language learning history, and McLelland (2017) — the first overarching history of language learning and teaching in Britain — benefited tremendously from, and cites fully, the research of many of the contributors to the present collection.

Nevertheless, lacunae remain, not just in terms of chronological spread but also in areas of focus. The study of representing a 'target' culture — the 'hidden curriculum' of language teaching (Byram 1989: 1) — has been a prominent focus in recent language pedagogy (e.g. Byram 1993, 2008, Risager 2006, 2007), but one that has barely been matched by historical studies (Wegner (1999) and McLelland (2015a: 249–334), are exceptions that, thus far, have only proved the rule). More primary research on the social history of language learning and teaching in the twentieth century is also needed, extending the work of scholars such as Cohen (1996, 1999, and Vol. II here) for French in the eighteenth and nineteenth centuries. So, too, there is a need for critical analysis of the complex history of assessment, akin to that undertaken for ELT by Weir et al. (2013) and Weir and O'Sullivan (2017).[9] There is also further work to be done on the history of bilingual and supplementary languages education, or the presence of these languages in our societies risks erasure from history.[10] Finally, there is also a need for comparative work on languages advocacy and policy. Comparisons across the devolved nations of Britain are a first desideratum, but there are also lessons to be learned from comparisons with other Anglophone countries and beyond. Here our collection invites comparison among Anglophone countries as far apart as the USA (Bale) and New Zealand (Harvey), but also within the devolved nations of the United Kingdom (Scott on Scotland, Daniels on England). It is interesting to see a decline in languages study in places as far apart as Scotland and New Zealand, as well as the complaints about a lack of coherent policy from both Scott and Harvey. Even if, as Reinfried (this volume) observes, such connections are not yet obvious to contributors in this collection themselves, their juxtaposition here for the first time will, we hope, encourage greater awareness of points of comparison and contrast in future work.

As to what value HoLLT might have for future advocacy and policy-making, Bale's and Martinez's studies of advocacy for Spanish in the USA and in Britain are striking. Bale concludes that, in the USA in the first half of the twentieth century, making the case for Spanish on pragmatic grounds failed. The dramatic decline of German from American schools was not just the result of World War I, but was part of 'general homogenization' towards a 'single national identity', where Spanish could no more find an easy way in than could German. As for the UK, Martinez's study shows that public interest in promoting a language was not always matched by individual demand — Spanish was often introduced on the basis of its anticipated utility to learners, only to be dropped later owing to lack of demand. The words of E. W. J. Jackson in the early 1920s, cited by Martinez, are telling: 'Of course [firms] would consider the ability to deal with such correspondence [in Spanish] an asset in any clerk they employed, but as far as I am able to gather it is an asset they are not willing to pay for'. A prescient echo through time, too — as Britain embarks on compulsory language learning in primary schools from age eight — is the concern about shortage of expertise expressed a century ago in 1917 by the President of the Board of Education, that with regard to the teaching of Spanish, 'it is too soon to say whether the supply of competent teachers will be adequate' to meet the desire of many Local Education Authorities to introduce Spanish more widely (Martinez, Vol. II).

HoLLT and the History of English Language Teaching (ELT)

The decline of modern languages in the UK charted by Daniels and Scott (Vol. III) is matched by the rise of English Language Teaching (ELT), which in turn goes hand in hand with declining interest in learning languages *other* than English in many parts of the world beyond Britain too. Given this seemingly inexorable rise of ELT, it is striking that while there has been a scholarly society dedicated to research into the history of French as a foreign or second language for more than twenty-five years (cf. Besse 2014), there is, as yet, no such equivalent for the history of ELT, and there has been comparatively little research into the history of the learning and teaching of English as a foreign language (cf. Howatt and Smith 2014, Linn 2016: 13–14) beyond certain centres. The fact that Volumes II and III of this collection contain a number of chapters in the area of history of English learning and teaching (nine in all) gives rise to hopes for further development. Partly, this may be promoted by the way the collection brings to a wider readership work which has been going on for a number of years in some German universities (particularly at Ludwig-Maximilians University, Munich, under the leadership of Friederike Klippel until her retirement in 2015) (Klippel, Schleich, Sharp, Ruisz, all Volume III); and at the University of Bremen (Doff, Giesler, Volume II, Hethey, Volume III). Much of this work relates to the nineteenth century, when English first began to come into the curriculum in the developing school system in Germany. As Doff makes clear, the development of education for girls, and the way English was taught to them, had a significant influence on overall methodological developments towards teaching practical language skills and not (so much) *about* the language. Focusing particularly on schooling in Bremen, Giesler provides insights into another way in which relatively practical goals became incorporated into school curricula, this time in a manner seeming to prefigure present-day interest in teaching language through content. In Volume III, while Klippel provides a broad overview of eighteenth- and nineteenth-century textbooks and their cultural contents, Sharp subjects textbooks from the 1920s to particular examination, from the same cultural perspective. Sharp, Hethey and Ruisz all highlight and explain the influence of a particular way of viewing culture — *Kulturkunde* — which was prevalent in the 1920s and 1930s and which continued to have influence after the Second World War.

One further centre where the history of English language teaching has begun to develop is at the University of Milan, as represented in this collection by Pedrazzini and Nava (both, Vol. II). Their chapters complement one another in the way they explore a relatively recent period of history (the 1980s and 1990s) when communicative language teaching spread around the world and was adopted and adapted in different ways in different countries. These studies of different geographical contexts (Germany and Italy) for the learning and teaching of English correspond well with the call in Howatt and Smith (2014) for studies of English teaching history which are grounded in local realities and which might thereby serve as a necessary counterweight to the centre to periphery methods-based narratives which pervade the field of ELT and dominate teacher education worldwide (see also Hunter and Smith 2012).

India is another context in which research into the history of English teaching has been developing (cf. Sridhar and Mishra 2016), and Dixit and Padwad in their chapter (Vol. III) draw lessons for current English language education policy from an overview of national curricular developments since Independence. The focus of this work, as of most of the chapters concerned with the history of English teaching in these volumes, is on relatively recent history, as may seem to befit the recency of its rise when compared with French and Italian, at least in European contexts. Nevertheless, the learning and teaching of English has a longer history in former British colonies like India, while 'local' histories of ELT have hardly begun to be uncovered outside a few countries (represented in this collection by Germany and Italy). The historiography of English language learning and teaching worldwide is evolving, but there are many lacunae, and we hope that these volumes will help stimulate more interest in History of ELT around the world.

HoLLT in Europe

Much research in the area of HoLLT has tended to be nationally based, whether focusing on the history of teaching a particular national language (e.g. French; cf. Besse, 2014) or the history of language learning and teaching in a particular country (e.g. Svanholt 1968 on Denmark; Hulshof et al. 2016 on the Netherlands). Our *Language & History* special issue (McLelland and Smith 2014a), which brought together state-of-the-art overviews of the histories of teaching French, German, Spanish, and English was a first step towards overcoming these disciplinary boundaries; our special issue of *The Language Learning Journal* containing histories of language learning traditions in particular countries or regions — Britain, France and Switzerland, Germany, the Low Countries, Portugal and Spain — has been another (Smith and McLelland 2018a).

In the present collection, our broadly chronological approach again juxtaposes chapters dealing with different geographical areas and language traditions. We hope that, in this way, readers will be helped to discover significant similarities and differences across languages, across language learning traditions, and through time. The shared experience of the Reform Movement in Europe, c. 1880–1920, is one area of convergence, highlighted as a common reference point in a number of studies here, including Linn (Vol. II) and Schleich (Vol. III), who, in their respective studies of early periodicals and pen-friend networks, each highlight Europe-wide developments. Another, much earlier, trans-European phenomenon is the common recycling of dialogue books across languages and borders in the medieval and early modern periods — see the contributions by Cuevas, Viémon, and Villoria and Suso, in Volume I. Their careful textbook analyses add, too, to our understanding of language learning as part of a shared European cultural history and European book trade, with materials adapted and re-printed for new audiences. For example, we know that Veneroni's *Maître italien* (Paris 1768) enjoyed widespread transmission through France, the Netherlands, Germany and England. However, Cuevas shows in his chapter here that Courville's *Explicación de la gramática francesa* (Madrid, 1728) — previously viewed as a work in its own right — is no more than a translation into Spanish of the introduction of Veneroni's work, an introduction to grammar intended 'pour les dames et ceux qui ne scavent pas le Latin', thus adding a Spanish chapter to the complex reception history of this single text.

The cross-Europe traffic in language learning materials is also illustrated by Viémon's study, tracing the transformation of pronunciation rules from Berlaimont (1527) to Reixac i Carbó (1749). Villoria and Suso López take another small part of this complex Berlaimont tradition, with its point of origin in a 1556 edition of Berlaimont's *Dictionarium*, to present examples of the variety of adaptations of dialogues, re-used in publications in sixteenth-century Spain, England and the Netherlands, in texts ranging from vocabularies and dialogues to full manuals, adapted in very different ways for different age groups, for men and women, and in different parts of Europe. Just as Courville translated Veneroni's introduction to grammar for women, so too some of the reception of Berlaimont texts involved repackaging them as materials especially suited to women and girls as learners. Baretti, too, was writing, at least in part, for girls like the lively young Miss Hetty named as his pupil in his dialogues (see de Gasperin, Vol. II). (The place of gender in the European history of language teaching is examined in two other contributions in Volume II: Doff's study of English-language education for girls and women in nineteenth-century Germany, noted above, and Cohen's illuminating study of gendered attitudes to oral proficiency in nineteenth-century England.)[11] Such recycling underlines that publishing language manuals and textbooks was a business, and they were as subject to the publisher's desire to turn a profit as any other book. Thus, the (often unacknowledged) recycling of materials was not just a feature of the pre-modern period. The nineteenth century saw a renewed blossoming of patented 'Methods' that promised sales trading on recognized 'brands', some of whose history can be traced through the contributions in this collection too: Thimm's method applied to Arabic features among the sources examined by Mairs (and see McLelland 2015b for its application to Chinese); Fonseca (Vol. II) finds an 1883 Ahn manual for English speakers to learn Portuguese;[12] Ahn and Ollendorff were adapted for Greek learners of French (Mytaloulis), and the main focus of Mytaloulis's attention — a textbook for Greek learners of French — is itself a re-purposing of a manual first written for French learners of English, complete with culturally specific references to London's Vauxhall Gardens. Untangling the complex relationship between patented methods like those of Ahn, Ollendorff and Thimm and their imitations remains a research desideratum, and one that would require international cooperation. Its interest lies not just in accurate cataloguing for book historians, but also in promising insights into the diffusion of beliefs about language learning and teaching through time and space, for many adaptations and imitations maintained only certain aspects of the innovations and improvements touted by their originators.

There are also themes traceable over long periods of time in this collection. One case in point is the place that grammar should have in teaching children, a persistent issue, whether for fifteenth-century Latin in England (Luhtala), modern languages in seventeenth-century Finland (Randen), Italian in eighteenth-century England (de Gasperin) or languages in early twentieth-century Russia (Protassova). Another aspect of this is the way 'modern' approaches are shown clearly to have antecedents in previous experience — Content and Language Integrated Learning (CLIL) in nineteenth-century Germany, for example (Giesler, Vol. II), or monolingual methods, more generally, in medieval and early modern England (Critten, Vol. I).

Building on previous thematic work on language learning in Europe as alluded to above, then, the papers in this collection help support our contention, expressed in Smith and McLelland (2018a: 4), that 'the task of developing a (unified) European history of language learning and teaching seems to be becoming steadily more possible'.

HoLLT beyond Europe; Colonial and Postcolonial Relationships

The present collection differs in scope from McLelland and Smith (2014a) and Smith and McLelland (2018a) in that we have deliberately sought to extend its range beyond the European focus of those two collections. Reinfried (this volume) celebrates the headway made in moving from national perspectives to a European perspective on HoLLT, but it needs to be recognized that Europe itself was a colonial force beyond its borders, and language learning in the colonial encounter remains significantly under-researched. The structuring of the three volumes (with the first two focused on Europe, and only Part 2 of the third moving 'beyond Europe') is certainly itself Eurocentric, but the structure is centrifugal in aspiration, reflecting our desire to promote research in and into areas of the world outside Europe, whilst acknowledging some of the important work already in existence (e.g. Vigner 2000 on the teaching and learning of French in the French empire, Sanchez-Summerer 2011, 2012 on French in Palestine; Rokkaku 1988 on Japanese language teaching in China).

Part 2 of Volume III offers case studies of language learning in colonial contexts in both directions: colonialists learning about the culture of the colonized space in question, and those colonized learning the colonialists' language — Europeans learning Arabic (Mairs), Westerners learning Chinese (Gianninoto); but also Chinese learning German (McLelland), German in Cameroon (Boulleys), English in post-independence India (Dixit and Padwad), language-learning in Jordan (Odeh and Zanchi). There are also cases of non-European colonial and postcolonial relationships (Japanese learning Chinese in the chapters by Chang Zou and Yang Tiezheng); and new forms of influence, including explicit cultural diplomacy alongside economic influence: Spanish in the USA (Bale), French in Jordan (Odeh and Zanchi) and the learning of Japanese in New Zealand (Harvey). The number of chapters dealing with HoLLT beyond Europe is relatively small, and are in some cases first steps into very unfamiliar territory for European scholars of language learning, but our intention is that they will help open up the field of HoLLT beyond its historical Eurocentric biases, this being a major aspiration of the ongoing HoLLTnet network, noted above, under the auspices of AILA (L'Association Internationale de Linguistique Appliquée).

For example, the insights provided into language learning traditions in Asia in Volume III suggest some new avenues for research into both the learning of non-European languages and of language learning beyond Europe. The contributions by Chang Zou, Yang Tiezheng and McLelland all bring to light approaches to language learning in early twentieth-century China and Japan that are — while influenced by Western ideas — quite different to the contemporary European traditions of the time (cf. Rokkaku 1988), while Gianninoto's examination of materials for learning Chinese unearths an early instance of corpus-driven vocabulary selection in language teaching, with a very early case of a corpus of over a million characters being used to guide character selection and arrangement in Martin's (1897) *Analytical Reader* of Chinese.

The potential of comparative studies becomes apparent if we look across some of the studies in this collection to examine assumptions about the colonized 'other'. Prendergast advises his imagined learner of the Indian language Telugu to 'divest himself of the habit of omitting every word which may, either classically or logically, be deemed superfluous. These standards are altogether inapplicable in the East'. (Prendergast 1872: 174, cited by Lorch, Vol. II). Whatever the truth of the matter for Telugu, the claim was applied to the whole of the undifferentiated 'East' — but contradicts similarly sweeping rules of thumb for English learners of Chinese: 'It is a safe rule [...] to begin by cutting out all superfluities. It [i.e. what one wants to say] should, in fact, be treated as one would treat a telegraphic message' (Hillier 1907: 44, cited in McLelland 2015b: 134–35). Britain's colonial subjugation of other parts of the world was, then, reflected in the language English speakers were given to use with the colonized in these settings: in the teach-yourself Arabic manuals discussed by Mairs (Vol. III), in some of Prendergast's manuals (Lorch, Vol. II), and in manuals of Chinese (McLelland 2015b).

Interdisciplinary and Historiographical Achievements

We end by considering the progress made in establishing HoLLT not just in terms of coverage but also with regard to methodological and interdisciplinary historiographical advances. Our contributors to this collection include practitioner-researchers (former language teachers such as Daniels), teacher educators (Byram and others), phoneticians (Ashby and Przedlacka), specialists in the history of linguistics (Linn and others) and specialists in individual languages (for example, Luhtala for Latin, and many others). Although all the authors share an allegiance to primary sources, relatively few (Cohen, Rjéoutski, and others) are historians by primary training; many more engaged in HoLLT were originally trained in another primary discipline and have come to history later. The present collection therefore provides models of historical research which will be useful to those starting out in this field or seeking to move beyond the range of approaches with which they are most familiar. The collection illustrates the potential of widening the range of methodological approaches in the historiography of language learning and teaching, as well as the potential of a wider range of sources, and given the disparate backgrounds of those working in HoLLT, this is an area where we have much to learn from one another.

The fact that some authors have come to history relatively recently from a main concern in other areas broadens the range of research **methodologies** available to all, to mutual benefit. In particular, some chapters in this collection show a clear social scientific influence, evident in their explicitness about epistemological assumptions and about method. Criado introduces an applied linguistic approach, adopting a framework for textbook analysis that is heavily influenced by current second language acquisition theory. Similarly, Scott's framework for analysis of recent language education policy in Scotland is influenced by work in the field of language policy research. Compared to more traditional historiographical work, top-down (relatively theory-driven) approaches, though skilfully handled in these cases, can run risks of anachronism (as well as of ignoring evidence which does not fit a particular 'model'), but they may also be more readily seen to have higher relevance value — that is, to be easily readable and/or acceptable — within the disciplines from which they derive methodologies, since they adopt models or methodological approaches which are already familiar within those disciplines.

Meanwhile, other studies in this collection illustrate the range of **sources** at our disposal, and how to interpret them. For the medieval and early modern periods in Europe, **teaching materials** themselves are often the only available sources for the history of learning and teaching languages, as Klippel notes in her contribution (Vol. III): 'Treatises on language teaching were relatively rare — Seidelmann (1724) is an early example [...] Journals dealing with educational matters only began to be published in the late eighteenth century'. Teachers' handbooks (as exploited by Hidden, Vol. II) do not pre-date the Reform Movement of the late nineteenth century. However, textbooks have been in use for many centuries and, for many periods, they 'are the historian's most valuable source' (Klippel, Vol. III). Several studies in our collection exemplify the value of examining such teaching materials as primary sources. Critten, for example, argues that surviving fifteenth-century materials can be interpreted as evidence of monolingual target-language teaching of French in late-medieval England. He concludes with a plea against a teleological approach to HoLLT: the present-day focus on using the target language in the classroom is not the high-point of steady improvement, but merely the latest in a series of stages in a history of continuities and discontinuities. Luhtala also offers a close analysis of materials for teaching Latin in pre-Humanist and Humanist materials for English learners of Latin. Taking a seemingly minor point of detail — teaching the rules of 'concord' (agreement) — she shows how Humanists sought to move away from Scholasticism to simplify the teaching of grammar for young learners, but also demonstrates that some pre-Humanists had already been working towards that goal, with simple catechistic questions to teach, for example, how to recognize the subject and object.

In the era before treatises and journals, prefaces to language textbooks might often be the only opportunity to set out and critique ideas on language learning and teaching. Textbook **paratexts**, indeed, can be as informative as the texts themselves, such as the 'Essay on the Proper Method for Teaching and Learning that Language' by Chambaud (1750), a French teacher in England who introduced targeted grammar exercises in teaching language some decades ahead of Meidinger (1783) (see McLelland 2017: 95–99). So, too, **annotations and inscriptions** in textbooks may tell us something about who used them and how, as Mairs (Vol. III) demonstrates with regard to Arabic phrasebooks. The materials produced by learners themselves can also be valuable sources — a specialized case in point is that of the letters produced by pen-friends and examined as part of Schleich's study of the so-called 'International Scholars' Correspondence' network of the early twentieth century (Vol. III; see also Schleich 2015).

A number of our contributors have responded to the call (first made by Stern 1983: 87, 114, echoed by Smith 1999: 3 and McLelland 2015a: 7) for **detailed biographical studies** of figures in HoLLT. Fidlerová's study (Vol. I) of the career and work of the writer, translator and textbook author František Jan Tomsa (1751–1814) provides an insight into the complexity of teaching a language in a multilingual context such as the Austro-Hungarian Empire. Fidlerová argues for the potential polyfunctionality of Tomsa's works, suggesting that Tomsa's publications may have had a role not just as manuals for German-speaking learners of Czech as a foreign language, but also in promoting Czech to those who were first-language speakers of the language but had not been educated in it, and so contributing to currents of linguistic patriotism at the time. In Volume II, Provata examines the history of teaching French in Greece through the case of the author Ioannis Carassoutsas (1824–1873), while Lorch's close examination of the biography of Thomas Prendergast (1806–1886) offers clues as to why this former civil servant in India, himself never a language teacher, took it into his head during his retirement in Cheltenham to develop his own 'Mastery Method' of language learning. Like Lorch, Mairs (Vol. III) reveals the potential of close biographical study of textbook authors to take us beyond 'the words on the page'. As Mairs observes, her answer to the question of how 'an Arabic-German bilingual who died in Austria in 1876 [came] to be the author of an English guide to self-instruction in Arabic that was published after his death in 1883 [...] tells us much about the language publishing business in the late nineteenth century.'

Both McLelland (2015a: 8–10) and Smith (2016) have argued for attention to be paid to a wider variety of primary sources, and the present collection offers some exemplary demonstrations of how recent research is increasingly able to do so. Ashby and Przedlacka's chapter in Volume II is a case study for the role of **material culture** — in this case technological objects themselves — to assess the role of history of technology in language teaching. They offer a sober assessment of the claims made for sometimes outlandish phonetic equipment to transform the learnability of languages. While the supposed utility of the equipment served to justify the funding of phonetics laboratories, their assessment suggests that the claims were the first of a whole series of promises to revolutionize language teaching via technological innovations (radio, television, language laboratories, computers) with less impact than expected.[13]

Linn (Vol. III) — matching the emergence of periodical studies as a field of enquiry in the last few decades (cf. the newly founded *JEPS: The Journal of European Periodical Studies*) — turns his attention to the emergence of the first **specialized journals** and their role in the development of a modern language teaching community of practice, before, during and after the so-called Reform Movement of the late nineteenth and early twentieth centuries. Linn shows how a journal such as *Phonetische Studien* (from 1894 known as *Die neueren Sprachen*) provided language scholars and teachers with a vehicle through which to give voice to modern foreign language teaching as an independent discipline.

Rjéoutski's work on language learning in eighteenth-century Russia (Vol. I), Turcan's history of French in Moldavia (Vol. II), and Martinez' study of efforts to encourage Britons to learn Spanish in the nineteenth and first half of the twentieth century (Vol. II) all draw on unpublished papers preserved in **government archives**. Rjéoutski finds details of army cadets' language learning in the Russian State Archive for the History of the Armed Forces. Turcan was able to use minutes of meetings relating to school curricula, teacher training, and the preparation of teaching materials in Moldavia. Martinez similarly draws on rich material preserved in the UK National Archives, including Board of Education minute papers and records of school inspections, including classroom observations; similar files exist for other languages under the same reference (ED12 in the National Archives; note also ED24) but are still under-explored, except for Russian (cf. Muckle 2008: 260). Martinez also draws on newspaper reports and correspondence, as does Bale (Vol. III), in his study of advocacy for Spanish teaching in the USA in the first half of the twentieth century. Both Bale and Martinez are thus able to compare (and to some extent contrast) the uptake of Spanish classes with the **public discourse about its value** — an important dimension in the history of language teaching and learning in the twentieth century and beyond. **Official published reports and guidelines** on language learning are similarly valuable sources for understanding both the reality of and the hopes attached to language learning. Besides Extermann (Vol. II) and Wegner (Vol. III) in this collection, see in particular Byram's (Vol. III) examination of the Leathes Report (1918), and Cohen's (Vol. II) reading of the Clarendon and Taunton reports (1864, 1868), showing the very gendered perception — with influence, she argues, on the overall status — of 'oral' ability. As Cohen puts it, her evidence shows 'that the history of the "oral" and its meanings can be a means of identifying ideas and shifts in language education since the eighteenth century'. Indeed the status of the 'oral' remains relevant today in the contested territory between teaching language skills and modern languages as a 'discipline'.

For more recent times, **oral history** testimony can also be a valuable source, including, for example, our interview with John Trim, shortly before his death in 2013, and reproduced in Smith and McLelland (2014). The limitations of first-memory reminiscence are commented upon by Daniels (Vol. II), but the potential value of oral history data for triangulating with other sources has also been shown in this collection (Pedrazzini, Scott, Vol. II).

Conclusion

At the beginning of this Introduction we described HoLLT as a 'newly emerging interdisciplinary, intercultural and plurilinguistic field of enquiry'. The chapters in our three-volume collection — contributed by a combination of both established experts and scholars new to the territory — accurately represent the status of this still-emerging field, whose researchers come from different language backgrounds and from normally separate disciplines. In combination, as we hope we have shown, they offer a basis from which to explore further the territory of HoLLT in the Anglophone world, in Europe, and — we very much hope — increasingly in other parts of the world too, to scholarly benefit and to the practical benefit of language education professionals and policy-makers. While far from the last word in the history of language learning and teaching, the contributions in our collection exemplify a range of methodological and theoretical approaches, establish the field of HoLLT, and so also map out some of the paths that can lead towards more comparative and 'global' histories of language learning and teaching in the future.

References

AYRES-BENNETT, WENDY, and HELENA SANSON (eds). Forthcoming. *Distant and Neglected Voices: Women in the History of Linguistics* (Oxford: Oxford University Press)

BECK-BUSSE, GABRIELE. 1999. *Grammatik für Damen: Zur Geschichte der französischen und italienischen Grammatik in Deutschland, England, Frankreich und Italien (1605–1850)* (Habilitationsschrift FU Berlin)

——2014. *Grammaire des dames, Grammatica per le dame: Grammatik im Spannungsfeld von Sprache, Kultur und Gesellschaft* (Frankfurt: Peter Lang)

Besse, Henri. 2014. 'La Société Internationale pour l'Histoire du Français Langue Étrangère ou Seconde (SIHFLES), ou vingt-cinq ans d'investigations historiographiques sur l'enseignement/apprentissage du français langue étrangère ou seconde', *Language & History* 57.1: 26–43

British Academy (report prepared by Teresa Tinsley). 2013a. *Languages: The State of the Nation* (London: British Academy)

—— 2013b. *Lost for Words: The Need for Languages in UK Diplomacy and Security* (London: British Academy)

—— 2014. *Born Global: Rethinking Language Policy for 21st Century Britain. A policy research project into the extent and nature of language needs in the labour market. A summary of interim findings* (London: British Academy)

—— 2016. *Born Global: A British Academy Project on Languages and Employability* (London: British Academy). Available online at: <http://www.britac.ac.uk/policy/Born_Global.cfm>

British Council. 2017. *Languages for the Future: Which Languages the UK Needs Most and Why* (London: British Council). Online at <https://www.britishcouncil.org/organisation/policy-insight-research/research/languages-future>

Byram, Michael (ed.). 1989. *Cultural Studies in Foreign Language Education* (Clevedon: Multilingual Matters)

—— 1993. *Germany: Its Representation in Textbooks for Teaching German in Great Britain* (Frankfurt am Main: Diesterweg)

—— 2008. *From Foreign Language Education to Education for Intercultural Citizenship: Essays and Reflection* (Clevedon: Multilingual Matters)

Chambaud, Lewis. 1750. *A Grammar of the French Tongue. With a prefatory discourse, containing An Essay on the Proper Method for Teaching and Learning that Language* (London: printed for A. Millar, at Buchanan's-Head over against Catharine-Street in the Strand). [Available online through ECCO]

Cohen, Michèle. 1996. *Fashioning Masculinity: National Identity and Language in the Eighteenth Century* (London: Routledge)

—— 1999. 'Manliness, Effeminacy and the French: Gender and the Construction of National Character in Eighteenth-Century England', in *English Masculinities, 1660–1800*, ed. by Tim Hitchcock and Michèle Cohen (London: Longman), pp. 44–61

Fernández Fraile, María Eugenia, and Javier Suso López (eds). 2009. *Approches contrastives et multilinguisme dans l'enseignement des langues en Europe (XVIe-XXe siècles)*. Special issue: *Documents pour l'histoire du français langue étrangère ou seconde*, 42, online at <https://dhfles.revues.org/150>

Finotti, Irene, and Nadia Minerva (eds). 2012. *Voix Féminines: Ève et les langues dans l'Europe moderne*. Special issue: *Documents pour l'histoire du français langue étrangère ou seconde*, 47–48, online at <https://dhfles.revues.org/3112>

Gamarra Aragonés, Ana I. 2000. *Mujeres y lenguas extranjeras para el comercio en el XIX español* (Madrid: Editorial Complutense)

Glück, Helmut. 2002. *Deutsch als Fremdsprache in Europa vom Mittelalter bis zur Barockzeit* (Berlin: de Gruyter)

Havinga, Anna, and Nils Langer. 2015. *Invisible Languages in the Nineteenth Century* (Frankfurt: Peter Lang)

Howatt, A. P. R. 1984. *A History of English Language Teaching* (Oxford: Oxford University Press). 2nd edn 2004 with H. G. Widdowson

—— and Richard Smith. 2014. 'The History of Teaching English as a Foreign Language, from a British and European Perspective', *Language & History*, 57.1: 75–95

Hüllen, Werner, and Friederike Klippel (eds). 2000. *Holy and Profane Languages: The Beginnings of Foreign Language Teaching in Western Europe* (Wiesbaden: Harrassowitz)

HULSHOF, HANS, ERIK KWAKERNAAK and FRANS WILHELM. 2016. *Geschiedenis van het taalonderwijs in Nederland: Onderwijs in de moderne talen van 1500 tot heden* (Groningen: Uitgeverij Passage)

HUNTER, DUNCAN, and RICHARD SMITH. 2012. 'Unpackaging the Past: "CLT" through ELTJ Keywords', *ELT Journal* 66.4: 430–39

KLIPPEL, FRIEDERIKE. 1994. *Englischlernen im 18. und 19. Jahrhundert: Die Geschichte der Lehrbücher und Unterrichtsmethoden* (Münster: Nodus)

KOK ESCALLE, MARIE-CHRISTINE, and MADELEINE VAN STRIEN-CHARDONNEAU (eds). 2006. *Langue(s) et religion(s): une relation complexe dans l'enseignement du français hors de France XVIe-XXe siècle*. Special issue: *Documents pour l'histoire du français langue étrangère ou seconde*, 37, online at <https://dhfles.revues.org/57>

LANVERS, URSULA, and JAMES A. COLEMAN. 2013. 'The UK language learning crisis in the public media: a critical analysis', *The Language Learning Journal*, 45.1: 3–25

LINN, ANDREW. 2016. *Investigating English in Europe: Contexts and Agendas* (Berlin: De Gruyter Mouton)

——NEIL BERMEL and GIBSON FERGUSON. 2015. *Attitudes towards English in Europe: English in Europe* (Berlin: De Gruyter Mouton)

LOMBARDERO CAPARRÓS, ALBERTO. 2016. 'La influencia de Franz Ahn en España: ¿Mero éxito editorial o verdadero tráfico de ideas lingüísticas?' [Paper presented at SIHFLES conference 'Innovations pédagogiques dans l'enseignement des langues étrangères: perspective historique (XVIe–XXIe siècles)', University of Algarve, 7–9 July 2016]

LORCH, MARJORIE PERLMAN. 2016. 'A Late 19th-Century British Perspective on Modern Foreign Language Learning, Teaching and Reform: The Legacy of Prendergast's "Mastery System"', *Historiographia Linguistica*, 43.1/2: 175–208

MCLELLAND, NICOLA. 2015a. *German through English Eyes: A History of Language Teaching and Learning in Britain, 1500–2000* (Wiesbaden: Harrassowitz)

——2015b. 'Teach Yourself Chinese — How? The History of Chinese Self-Instruction Manuals for English Speakers, 1900–2010', *Journal of the Chinese Language Teachers Association*, 50.2: 109–52

——2017. *Teaching and Learning Foreign Languages in Britain: A History* (London: Routledge)

——2018. 'The History of Language Learning and Teaching in Britain', *The Language Learning Journal*, 46.1: 6–16

——and RICHARD SMITH (eds). 2014a. *Building the History of Language Learning and Teaching*. Special issue of *Language & History*, 57.1, with an introduction by the editors. 116pp.

——and RICHARD SMITH. 2014b. 'Introduction: Building the History of Language Learning and Teaching (HoLLT)', *Language & History* 57.1: 1–9

MUCKLE, JAMES. 2008. *The Russian Language in Britain: A Historical Survey of Learners and Teachers* (London: Routledge)

PRENDERGAST, THOMAS. 1872. *The Mastery of Languages* (London: Longmans, Green)

RISAGER, KAREN. 2006. *Language and Culture: Global Flows and Local Complexity* (Clevedon: Multilingual Matters)

——2007. *Language and Culture Pedagogy: From a National to a Transnational Perspective* (Clevedon: Multilingual Matters)

ROKKAKU, TSUNEHIRO 六角恒廣. 1988. *Tyūgokugokyōikushi no Kenkyū* 中国語教育史の研究 [*A Study of the History of Chinese Language Education*] (Tokyo: Tōhō Syoten 東方書店)

SANCHEZ-SUMMERER, KARÈNE. 2011. 'Les catholiques palestiniens et la langue française (1870–1960): une langue des minorités devenue minoritaire?', *Documents pour l'histoire du français langue étrangère ou seconde*, 45: 17–42

——2012. 'Le triptyque "Langue — Education — Religion" dans les écoles missionnaires françaises de Jérusalem en Palestine ottomane et mandataire'. *Sociolinguistica: International Yearbook of European Sociolinguistics*, 25: 66–80

SANSON, HELENA. 2014. 'Simplicité, clarté et précision: Grammars of Italian 'pour les dames' and Other Learners in Eighteenth- and Early Nineteenth-Century France', *Modern Language Review*, 109.3: 593–616

SCHLEICH, MARLIS. 2015. *Geschichte des internationalen Schülerbriefwechsels: Entstehung und Entwicklung im historischen Kontext von den Anfängen bis zum Ersten Weltkrieg* (Münster: Waxmann)

SCHRÖDER, KONRAD. 1980, 1982, 1983, 1985. *Linguarum recentium annales: Der Unterricht in den modernen europäischen Sprachen im deutschsprachigen Raum*, 4 vols (1500–1700; 1701–1740; 1741–1770; 1771–1800) (Augsburg: Universität Augsburg)

SEIDELMANN, CHRISTIAN FRIEDRICH. 1984 [1724]. *Tractatus Philosophico-Philologicus de Methodo Recte Tractandi Linguas Exoticas Speciatim Gallicam, Italicam et Anglicam*, facsimile and translation by FRANZ-JOSEF ZAPP and KONRAD SCHRÖDER (Augsburg: Universität Augsburg)

SMITH, RICHARD. 1999. *The Writings of Harold E. Palmer: An Overview* (Tokyo: Hon-no–Tomosha)

—— (ed.). 2003. *Teaching English as a Foreign Language, 1912–1936: Pioneers of ELT*, 5 vols (Abingdon: Routledge)

—— (ed.). 2005. *Teaching English as a Foreign Language, 1936–1961: Foundations of ELT*, 6 vols, with General Introduction (pp. xv–cxx) (Abingdon: Routledge)

—— 2009. 'Claude Marcel (1793–1876): A Neglected Applied Linguist?', *Language & History*, 52.1: 171–82

—— 2016. 'Building "Applied Linguistic Historiography": Rationale, Scope and Methods', *Applied Linguistics*, 37.1: 71–87

—— and MOTOMICHI IMURA. 2004. 'Lessons from the Past: Traditions and Reforms', in Makarova, V. and T. Rodgers (eds), *English Language Teaching: The Case of Japan* (Munich: Lincom Europe), pp. 29–48

—— and NICOLA MCLELLAND. 2014. 'An Interview with John Trim (1924–2013) on the History of Modern Language Learning and Teaching', *Language & History*, 57.1: 10–25

—— and NICOLA MCLELLAND (eds). 2018a. *Histories of Language Learning and Teaching in Europe*. Special issue: *The Language Learning Journal*, 46.1

—— and NICOLA MCLELLAND. 2018b. 'Guest Editorial: Histories of Language Learning and Teaching in Europe', *The Language Learning Journal*, 46.1: 1–5.

SMITH, GERALD HUMPHREY, GRAHAM MARTIN and WILLIAM HEDLEY. 2010. *Professionally Speaking: The Chartered Institute of Linguists Centenary, 1910–2010*: Chartered Institute of Linguists. Available for purchase from the Institute.

SRIDHAR, M., and SUNITA MISHRA. 2016. *Language Policy and Education in India: Documents, Contexts and Debates* (Routledge India)

STERN, H. H. 1983. *Fundamental Concepts of Language Teaching* (Oxford: Oxford University Press)

SVANHOLT, O. 1968. *Bøger og Metoder i Dansk Fremmedsprogsundervisning: En Historisk Fremstilling*. [*Books and Methods in Danish Foreign Language Teaching: An Historical Account*] (Copenhagen: Det Schønbergske Forlag)

VIGNER, GÉRARD (ed.) 2000. *L'Enseignement et la diffusion du français dans l'empire colonial français. 1815–1962*. Special issue: *Documents pour l'histoire du français langue étrangère ou seconde*, 25

WEGNER, ANKE. 1999. *100 Jahre Deutsch als Fremdsprache in Frankreich und England: Eine vergleichende Studie von Methoden, Inhalten und Zielen* (Munich: iudicium)

WEIR, CYRIL J., IVANA VIDAKOVIC and EVELINA DIMITROVA-GALACZI. 2013. *Measured Constructs: A History of Cambridge English Examinations, 1913–2012* (Cambridge: Cambridge University Press)

——— and BARRY O'SULLIVAN. 2017. *Assessing English on the Global Stage: The British Council and English Language Teaching, 1941–2016* (Sheffield: Equinox)

ZWARTJES, OTTO. 2012. 'The Historiography of Missionary Linguistics', *Historiographia Linguistica*, 39.2–3: 185–242

——— RAMÓN ARZÁPALO MARÍN and THOMAS C. SMITH-STARK (eds). 2009. *Missionary Linguistics (IV) Linguistica Misionera IV: Selected Papers from the Fifth International Conference on Missionary Linguistics, Merida, Yucatan, 14–17 March 2007* (Amsterdam: Benjamins)

Notes to the Introduction

1. This project has been a jointly conceived and led one from the start, and this introduction is likewise a collaborative effort. The order of authors is alphabetical only.
2. 'Connecting Cultures? International Conference on the History of Language Teaching'. The conference was supported by the Henry Sweet Society for the History of Linguistic Ideas, SIHFLES (Société internationale pour l'histoire du français langue étrangère ou seconde), APHELLE (Associação Portuguesa para a História do Ensino das Línguas e Literaturas Estrangeiras), CIRSIL (Centro Interuniversitario di Ricerca sulla Storia degli Insegnamenti Linguistici), PHG (Peeter Heynsgenootschap) and SEHEL (Sociedad Española para la Historia de las Enseñanzas Lingüísticas).
3. Indeed, three chapters in Volume III — those by Rachel Mairs, Vera Boulleys, and Jeff Bale — were not originally presented at the conference but were separately invited, to broaden the geographical coverage of the collection.
4. See Lanvers and Coleman (2013) for a recent analysis of the public discourse of a language learning crisis, and several reports by the British Academy (2013a, 2013b, 2014, 2016) and by the British Council (2017).
5. The Council of Europe's 'mother tongue + 2' policy — the aspiration that pupils should learn two languages in addition to their own language — is at least in part an attempt to maintain diversity in language learning in the knowledge that, for the majority of pupils on the European Continent, the first foreign language offered in schools will be English. On attitudes to English in Europe in the face of this reality and in the face of domain loss to English (e.g. in higher education), see Linn et al. (2015).
6. Cf. Kok Escalles and Van Strien-Chardonneau (2006), which includes contributions examining the religion-mediated teaching of French in Palestine, Egypt, and Turkey; cf. also the growing historiography of Missionary Linguistics, e.g. Zwartjes et al. (2009), Zwartjes (2012).
7. Note especially the journal dedicated to the history of teaching French as a foreign language, *Documents pour l'histoire du français langue étrangère ou seconde*, already publishing for over a quarter of a century (see Besse 2014), and key studies by German scholars such as Schröder (1980–1985), Klippel (1994), Hüllen and Klippel (2000), Glück (2002).
8. Given that Britain is not famed for its language learning prowess, past or present, it is striking to note that London was productive as an early centre for publication of Portuguese learning materials, with the first being published in 1692 — see Fonseca (Vol. II).
9. See now also McLelland (2017: 127–73) on Modern Languages assessment in Britain.
10. Cf. Havinga and Langer (2015) on the problem of 'invisible' languages in historical sociolinguistics and social history.
11. For more on questions of gender in HoLLT, see Beck-Busse (1999, 2014), Gamarra Aragonés (2000), Finotti and Minerva (2012), Sanson (2014), McLelland (2017: 53–61) and Ayres-Bennett and Sanson (forthcoming, on women in the history of linguistics more widely, but including the history of women's language teaching and learning).
12. Note also the reception of Ahn in Spain discussed by Lombardero Caparrós (2016).
13. On the history of technology in language teaching, see McLelland (2017: 107–14).

CHAPTER 1

The Historiography of Modern Language Teaching: From National Views to a European Perspective

Marcus Reinfried

Regional or national descriptions served as a starting point for the historiography of foreign language teaching. However, from the first half of the twentieth century on, international developments were integrated into historical studies. In a multi-volume work, the French linguist Ferdinand Brunot analysed the diffusion of the French language inside Europe. During the second half of the century, the internationalization of such investigations was strengthened by Louis Kelly, who included consideration of various languages in his (European and Northern American) history of foreign language teaching (Kelly 1969). Finally, at the end of the twentieth century, a history of foreign language didactics by Jean-Antoine Caravolas was published (in three volumes). This reference work constituted a considerable step forward, although it does not reflect the close international interconnectedness of developments in a wholly adequate way. Over the last few decades, several comprehensive collections of source material have also been published and half a dozen international societies that promote studies of the history of foreign language teaching have been founded. These have provided essential preliminary work which will permit the undertaking of larger joint projects in the future. Thus, differences and common features between European countries and regions can gradually start to be described. This chapter concludes with the presentation of a 'Model of teaching and learning factors in a foreign language classroom' which can indicate how key practical and theoretical factors play a role and can be applied in historical analysis as *tertia comparationis*.

The Usefulness of Historiography for a Better Understanding of the Contemporary Teaching and Learning of Foreign Languages

Over the last few decades, foreign-language learning and teaching has become a very large and important pedagogical field. It includes millions of language learners and teachers throughout Europe.[1] In previous centuries foreign-language learning was, generally, reserved for the privileged sectors of populations but it has become an increasingly important aspect of intercultural communication during the modern age. Like other intercultural phenomena, it has gained in prominence as a topic in social and cultural history in the last few years.

In addition to the general interest value of the history of language teaching and learning, it is also relevant for diachronic linguistics and for the history of linguistics. The grammars of the past reflect the language norms of the periods of their origin, and they also reflect the contemporaneous state of linguistic description and explanation. The development of linguistic knowledge has often taken place in the context of language teaching, and there have been many mutual influences.

Last but not least, there is a third domain to consider: the didactics of foreign and second language teaching, which constitute an important part of teacher education. In this field, an interest in the past is not yet deeply developed, but the teaching of foreign languages is only explainable from a historical perspective. In a given lesson, the choice and arrangement of the teaching elements can certainly be explained, partially, by the teaching situation and the reciprocal influences of factors such as objectives, contents, methods and media.[2] They interact, as some features of the teacher and the learners do.[3] But objectives, contents and methods are also always strongly connected with traditions and with corresponding cultural settings and assumptions. Knowledge of the origins of these concepts (for example, the communicative approach or intercultural learning) and of their development enables a deeper understanding of the whole teaching situation. In this sense, diachronic explanations constitute a necessary supplement to synchronic explanations.

History of ideas provides one way into the understanding of key concepts in the field of teaching and learning of foreign languages. Additionally, however, social history can explain why ideas arise in teaching contexts at particular times: there are contingencies that can be analysed even when there is no causal connection (in a strong sense) between the world of ideas and the social domain of language teaching. Social history can, for example, help us understand why the communicative approach appeared at a moment when learning populations became larger: practical and pragmatic objectives gained relevance when the number of pupils learning languages increased in many European countries.

The usefulness of historiography for a better understanding of the contemporary teaching and learning of foreign languages can easily be proven. Nevertheless, the description and analysis of the past do not yet have equivalent recognition to that of other, more established, research disciplines concerned with the teaching and learning of foreign languages. We live in modern societies in which, although political and cultural historiography are certainly institutionalized, many special fields are also more or less excluded from thorough and systematic historical review. However, as the German philosopher Odo Marquard (2003) says, 'Zukunft braucht Herkunft' — you have to understand origins and background in order to develop the future. And important progress in our specialized, but nonetheless large field of research has been achieved during the past few years. This fact may be improving the reception that scholars in this area receive. As I shall describe below, some important collections of sources have been compiled over the last decades and a great deal of research work has already been carried out.

The Beginning of Historiography of Foreign Language Teaching and the First Comprehensive Studies

International connections and interrelations are occasionally noticed by attentive researchers who are members of international societies (see below) when successive papers at conferences complement one another and a transnational comparison of factors of language teaching and learning is thereby enabled. This can lead to new insights in the mind of the listener, even though such links are not usually made explicitly by the authors of papers themselves. But before I focus in the sections that follow on interconnections within Europe,[4] there is a need to recognize that an international historiography has necessarily to build on previous national research.

Research into the history of language teaching began with investigations in Germany, at the end of the nineteenth century, during the Reform Movement. Most of the supporters of the Reform Movement were younger teachers, but there were also a few university professors who committed themselves to this teaching reform. Wilhelm Viëtor, the author of the well-known pamphlet *Der Sprachunterricht muß umkehren!* [*The Teaching of Languages Must Start Afresh!*], gained a chair at the University of Marburg. His colleague Edmund Stengel was a professor of Romance languages and literatures at the same university. In 1890, Stengel edited a bibliography of 625 French grammars which had been written or printed between 1400 and 1800.

Stengel was assisted in this project by forty lecturers and grammar school teachers who searched in university libraries throughout Germany and noted bibliographical references, including the numbers of editions. Stengel (1890/1976: 1–2) had, as he mentioned at a conference held in Dresden, the intention to use his bibliography for two purposes: a linguistic history of the descriptive grammars of French and a history of the teaching techniques of this foreign language.

Thus, from the beginning we have two different perspectives: on the one hand the linguistic perspective, and on the other hand the didactic perspective with elements of cultural and social history. Stengel himself was mainly interested in the beginnings of the grammaticography of French and in the development of descriptive categories. The specific problems of teaching and learning French as a foreign language in Germany were not his particular interest, but he at least recognized that these aspects were worth considering for special scientific research.

The first articles about the history of French as a foreign language were written by Karl Dorfeld, a teacher in a German grammar school, in the 1890s. They were printed as an appendix to a *Schulprogramm*, the annual report of a *Gymnasium* in Giessen (Dorfeld 1892), and as a contribution to a pedagogical manual edited by Wilhelm Rein (Dorfeld 1896). Dorfeld gives much information about references for the teaching of French in the early modern age, mentions the duration of the language learning and the number of weekly lessons, and gives detailed descriptions of the curricula and the exams. Some activities like speech exercises, translation and letter-writing are described in detail.

In the first decade after the turn of the nineteenth century, the methodological confrontation between the partisans of the Reform Movement and their opponents faded, and a mixed, more eclectic approach gained acceptance in Germany. The contemporary diversification of language teaching increased interest in the development of different teaching methods. Several articles appeared which addressed method variations from a historical perspective, some of these even in handbooks for trainee teachers (cf. Reinfried 2013: 207–08).

In 1914, a relatively extensive doctoral thesis about approaches in grammars of French between the sixteenth and eighteenth centuries was published. Albert Streuber, the author of this work, analysed approximately two hundred grammars used in the German-speaking territories. He distinguishes between the deductive, inductive and mixed approaches, although these technical terms are not precisely defined in his thesis. Nonetheless, we can see that for Streuber the deductive approach is not only characterized by the presentation of grammatical rules, but also by the primacy of written competence, whereas the inductive approach starts from a text or at least a sentence and is focused, rather, on oral communication. These two approaches relate to the two main methodological traditions from 1500 to 1800: the deductive approach based on grammatical consciousness and the knowledge of rules, often called the approach 'per praecepta', and the imitative approach beginning with the reading of dialogues or simple narrative texts, often called the approach 'ex usu', which allowed only a very measured input of grammar at beginner level (cf. Reinfried 2014: 259–60; Berré and Besse 2012: 68–69; Weller 1980: 146, 149–50).

After the First World War, some other important studies on the history of teaching languages appeared in Germany (cf. Reinfried 2013: 209–10), but the first comprehensive books addressing a national development over several centuries were published in the UK, the Netherlands and France. Kathleen Lambley's monograph (1920) describes the development of the teaching of French in England from the thirteenth to the beginning of the eighteenth century, when the Stuart period came to an end. The spread and developing status of the French language, which was mainly spoken by the nobility, are thoroughly described. This excellent book puts the emphasis on social contexts, tutors and the teaching material.

Another monograph, less well-known, but worth mentioning, is the study by Kornelius-Jacobus Riemens (1919) about the teaching of French in Holland from the sixteenth to the nineteenth centuries. This is a doctoral thesis written in French which was supervised by two professors of French philology teaching at universities in the Netherlands. This work focuses mainly on the foundation and development of the so-called *écoles françaises* [French schools] for boys and for girls,[5] and on description of the teachers and their social conditions.

The Beginnings of International Research: Brunot and Kelly

Riemens was also in touch with professors at the Sorbonne in Paris. Among them was Ferdinand Brunot, the author of a monumental work titled *Histoire de la langue française* [*History of the French Language*], of which nine volumes were published during his lifetime. Brunot was a linguist and a philologist, but completely uninterested in the description of languages as a system (unlike de Saussure and the many structuralists who followed him). He was a left-wing Republican and, as a historian, particularly focused on the social context, with all the educational and national ideals and ambitions which were typical of the period in which he lived, the French *Troisième République*. For all these reasons, he was especially interested in the unification and spread of the French language inside and outside of France, which he describes accurately and in a very detailed fashion.

The work contains many relevant facts about different periods: the fifth volume (Brunot 1966) describes the establishment of French as a foreign language in England, the Netherlands and Germany in the seventeenth century, while the eighth volume (1967) deals mainly with the eighteenth century and with the institutionalization of French teaching in various other European countries. In this volume, 161 pages (531–691) are dedicated to the status of the French language in the German-speaking countries alone. The eleventh volume (1969) describes the changing image of France and the French language during the French Revolution. It analyses the significance of the émigrés to the supply of teachers of French and refers to many sources on language policy in the occupied countries during the Napoleonic Era.

In the historiography of teaching foreign languages, these contributions by Ferdinand Brunot, written between the beginning of the twentieth century and 1938, the year of Brunot's death, represented a new, scientific kind of approach. Previously, the object of research had been, in principle, limited to 'one foreign language in one country'. Although Brunot's interest is restricted exclusively to French, he integrates many countries in his research. In this sense, he extends the research approach which had been dominant at the beginning of the twentieth century. Partly, this new approach of Brunot is due to the fact that, for some parts of his *Histoire de la langue française*, he takes the perspective of examining language *exportation*, whereas the dominant focus until then had been on state schools, in other words on language *importation*. However, there was another difference between Brunot and the majority of the other researchers I have already mentioned: Brunot was primarily interested in the social contexts that have supported, impeded and marked the French language. He described, for example, the appearance of 'Francomania' in the nobility and the middle classes (Brunot 1966: 169–77, 376–77; 1967: 609–16); he analysed the role of the Protestant refugees (1967: 149–55, 185–88, 219–21, 238–42, 332–52, 531–47), and the role of French literature and of the French theatre as conveyors of French culture and language (1967: 166–70, 211–22, 552–57, 573–81, 587–93; 1969: 114–17); and he described stereotypical perceptions of the French language (1967: 648–61; 1969: 55–72). Brunot's work was a landmark for the historiography of foreign and second language teaching and a first step towards an international perspective, although still limited to the French language.

A further step was taken in 1969, when Louis Kelly, a researcher based in Canada at the time, published a book that covered twenty-five centuries of language teaching in one volume. The division of the chapters in the book is partially inspired by key terms in the didactic compendium *Language Teaching Analysis* by William Mackey (1965). First, the teaching of vocabulary, grammar and of the basic communicative skills is described diachronically; then the evolution of variants of selection and progression of learning objectives are analysed; finally, the media and the psychological and linguistic background of the previously described methodological techniques are historically examined. The advantages of the book are that it is based on many primary and secondary sources — altogether 1400 printed publications — and it integrates the teaching of ancient languages into the historical description. Its disadvantages are that it is partially over-eclectic, that the social context and sometimes the ideas influencing methodological techniques or forms of media are not always clearly explained, and that the space of teaching foreign languages in Europe and in North America is perceived as a whole without differentiation between countries or areas. *25 Centuries of Language Teaching* was, however, an important step towards an international historiography of language teaching and still belongs to the basic literature for researchers in this field.

Collections of Source Material

During the second half of the twentieth century, beginning with Kelly, the concentration on French in the historiography of foreign language teaching diminished. Between 1980 to 1985, Konrad Schröder published *Linguarum recentium annales*, four volumes containing three thousand short excerpts from German secondary literature, including on the teaching of English, Spanish and Italian, arranged in chronological order, from the sixteenth to the eighteenth centuries. The excerpts give information on the publication of grammars and textbooks, the conditions of employment of foreign language teachers, the circumstances of modern language teaching in schools and the ways in which foreign languages were used. Not only do the common languages like French, Italian, English and Spanish appear in these *Annales* but also foreign languages that were rarely learnt in Germany, like Portuguese, Hungarian or Arabic. The second important collection of source material, again compiled by Konrad Schröder, was a biographical dictionary in six volumes (1991–99). This contains 3800 articles about foreign language teachers who lived in German-speaking countries between 1500 and 1800.

Another important collection of source materials, also focusing on Germany but with a multilingual orientation, was edited by Herbert Christ and Hans-Joachim Rang (1985). It contains the curricula in state schools and timetables showing numbers of lessons for different languages, from the eighteenth century to 1945. These curricula enable comparison of the learning objectives in different periods, indicating the expected communicative competences and grammatical and cultural knowledge in different school years. Some curricula also give methodological hints for teachers or information about recommended fictional literature for the advanced courses of instruction in a foreign language.

Other collections of source materials are anthologies of papers and excerpts from didactic or linguistic books concerning the history of language teaching. A voluminous example is the documentation of the Reform Movement edited by A. P. R. Howatt and Richard Smith (2002). These five volumes contain texts in German, English and French and focus on the origins of the didactic and phonetic ideas expressed in central, western and northern Europe at the end of the nineteenth century. As the Reform Movement was a very influential development, spreading in different ways and at different times to many countries (also in southern Europe), the texts could be used as a basis for a European research project.

Worth highlighting, also, is the reference book *Insegnare il francese in Italia* edited in 1991 by Nadia Minerva and Carla Pellandra. This is an analytical bibliography of eight hundred grammars and textbooks for the teaching of French published between 1625 and 1860. This *repertorio* was established under similar conditions to the bibliography of Edmund Stengel. As it is an analytical bibliography, the authors provide information about the grammatical metalanguage: Italian, French or Latin. They also list the grammatical aspects included, with the number of pages for each: pronunciation rules, orthography, morphology and syntax. Complementary components like dialogues, vocabulary lists, lists of phrases, anthologies of texts, introductions to familiar or commercial correspondence and exercises are also mentioned. This allows very interesting comparisons to be made between different periods.

Historical Societies for the Teaching and Learning of Foreign Languages

From the 1980s on, in many European countries, there have been a certain number of available publications about the history of language teaching — even if there has still been an excess of very specialized papers and a lack of comprehensive descriptions at a national level. In general, the interest in history of language teaching has been greater among exponents of Romance languages than among representatives of the English language. The long tradition of French language teaching, especially, which had already been at the centre of the historiography of foreign language teaching at its beginning, has attracted quite a few researchers. In 1987, the *Société Internationale pour l'Histoire du Français Langue Etrangère ou Seconde* (*SIHFLES*) was founded in Paris. The Society gathered many members in Italy and in Spain, some in Germany, in Belgium, in the Netherlands and other European countries, but only very few beyond Europe. Through its regular organization of at least one conference every year inside or outside France, it has contributed to a thorough exploration of the field of foreign language teaching and learning. The fifty-seven numbers of the review *Documents pour l'histoire du français langue étrangère ou seconde* published in the twenty-nine years of the existence of the society contain about 10000 pages and consist of a treasure house of multifaceted knowledge, presented from varying international, mainly European, perspectives. Approximately thirty issues of *Documents* can be downloaded free of charge from the internet [http://journals.openedition.org/dhfles].

SIHFLES might have inspired the creation of other networks of researchers in the field of teaching foreign languages. In Italy, around ninety researchers formed a very active society, CIRSIL (*Centro Interuniversitario di Ricerca sulla Storia degli Insegnamenti Linguistici*). In CIRSIL Anglicists, Germanists and Romanists work together. In Spain, SEHEL (*Sociedad Española para la Historia de las Enseñanzas Lingüísticas*) was founded, and in Portugal APHELLE (*Associação Portuguesa para a História do Ensino das Linguas e Literaturas Estrangeiras*). In the Netherlands the Peeter Heyns Society has been in existence for the past twenty years, and in Germany the Matthias-Kramer Society was founded in 2013. In the United Kingdom, the Henry Sweet Society, founded already in 1984 and devoted to the history of linguistic ideas, has recently developed more of a connection with the history of foreign language teaching.

From Caravolas to the Description of Mutual Impacts between European Countries

Another very important step forward has been the three-volume history of foreign language didactics written in French by Jean-Antoine Caravolas (1994, 2000), a multilingual Greek who acquired Canadian nationality some decades ago. He has covered the historical developments between 1450 and 1800 in many European countries. When he began his research in the 1980s, the internet did not exist and the inter-library loan system between Canada and Europe was restricted, so he had to travel throughout Europe to visit many libraries, even though little of this research was supported by grants.

One characteristic of the comprehensive study by Caravolas is that it includes information on the teaching of Latin and is not limited to the teaching of particular modern languages. The principal uniqueness of the three volumes, however, is that they attempt to survey the development of language teaching in a range of European countries. Nevertheless, each country (or sometimes cluster of countries) is represented as a more or less isolated entity. The common features of European development are not highlighted, with influences, dependencies and common time shifts being only rarely integrated into the analysis.

But this is what a Europe-wide historiography will need to do in the future. For example, there could be investigation of the way, in the late Middle Ages, foreign language tuition became available in England, in the Netherlands and in the leading Italian and German commercial towns and then, in the sixteenth and seventeenth centuries, the teaching of vernacular languages expanded to France, to Spain and Portugal, to the Scandinavian countries and to Poland (cf. Reinfried 2014: 255–58). Investigating the origins and transnational development of methodological ideas and texts used for language teaching is also important. In the seventeenth century, some methodological remarks in grammars or other schoolbooks used in different European countries suggest a certain raising of didactic consciousness. However, the grammar-based deductive approach, predominant in elementary instruction, was not connected with practical use of the foreign language. In the eighteenth century, language learning *ex usu* began to be propagated as a progressive approach to language acquisition and received extensive theoretical justification by French pedagogues like Noël-Antoine Pluche. The concept of a 'natural' education arose in other European countries as well. In Germany, the Philanthropinum, a reform school where a natural approach to language teaching was tried out, was founded in Dessau in 1774. Thus, a precursor of the direct method was invented. Nine years later, Johann Valentin Meidinger, a language tutor in Frankfurt, published a *Practical French Grammar* in which he combined short grammar lessons with intensive exercises. This coursebook became a bestseller and was imitated in Great Britain, Italy and Sweden. The grammar-translation method, founded by Meidinger and improved by other authors of practical grammars, spread in the nineteenth century across many European countries, while the holistic teaching via the senses of the 'Philanthropists' was at first confined to primary schools, from where it was transferred to secondary schools by precursors of the modern language Reform Movement in the middle of the nineteenth century. Finally, the direct method spread to other European countries by the turn of the twentieth century (Reinfried 2014: 261–63, 267–68) in a process displaying a complex evolution which has not yet been precisely researched in all its interactions and international influences, although the monograph of María Eugenia Fernández Fraile and Javier Suso López (1999: 365–91) contains much interesting information about the direct method and its theoretical background in Spain. Other members of the SIHFLES have also described more details of the method in further countries.

Common and Differing Aspects in the European History of Foreign Language Teaching and their Modelling

The common and the differing aspects in the history of language teaching in different countries or regions must also be clarified. Werner Hüllen (2005: 14, 60, 72) describes the era of early language teaching, until the end of the eighteenth century, as largely influenced by a pan-European tradition, whereas he characterizes the following era, with a shift in focus to state schools, as the era of 'national traditions' (Hüllen 2005: 73). This can be understood as meaning that the early era was rather homogenous whereas the later era was more heterogeneous, but this viewpoint does not convince me. I agree with Hüllen that the Latin grammars in the sixteenth century were still influenced by the early grammars of Donatus and Priscian and that the deductive method of teaching Latin greatly influenced the deductive method of teaching modern languages. The widespread 'Buchfamilien', as Hüllen (2005: 50) calls the series of similar books then available across Europe, contributed to a certain homogenization as well: the *Dialogues* and the dictionary of Noël de Berlaimont, for example, which were printed in one volume, had approximately one hundred editions in a dozen languages (ibid.: 54–57). The *Orbis Pictus* of Comenius even had 244 re-editions in fifteen languages (Reinfried 1992: 38). But these homogenizing influences were altogether limited.

In the seventeenth century a huge number of grammars and textbooks had already been published, and in the eighteenth century the number of printed books for foreign language teaching may have reached its peak. Stengel (1890: 69–122) lists for the latter era 377 grammars for the French language alone. Seventy per cent of the books in the eighteenth century had only one edition; the number of copies for one edition was usually (apart from bestsellers) between one and two thousand at that time. Thus, the eighteenth century was characterized by a great variety of books, and the diversification of the content of lessons increased with the diversification of learner groups, including more frequently now girls and even elderly people (cf. Kuhfuß 2014: 450–56). As a whole, the early era of modern language teaching before the French Revolution was in fact more heterogeneous than the two last centuries in which, starting with Meidinger, great methodologies spread throughout many European countries, with the grammar-translation method and the direct method, as suggested above, representing major pan-European approaches.

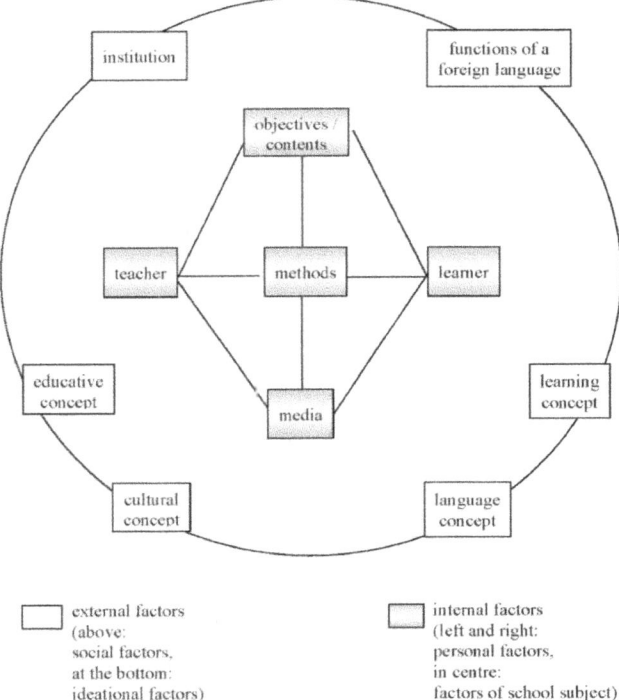

FIG. 1.1: Model of teaching and learning factors in a foreign language classroom (Minerva and Reinfried 2012: 16)

Figure 1.1 presents a model of key teaching and learning factors. In its centre are represented objectives, contents, methods and media (cf. also footnote 2). These factors have been coordinated more thoroughly from the modern age onwards, with the Age of Enlightenment having sharpened consciousness of needs for rationalization of teaching.

At a theoretical meta-level, educative, learning, cultural and language concepts (bottom of Figure 1.1) began to arise in the eighteenth and nineteenth centuries.

Important educational concepts were, for example, formal, practical and cultural general objectives. The main learning concepts, already existing in a theoretically elaborated form in the eighteenth century, were the approaches *ex usu* and *per praecepta*. Important cultural concepts developing from the Reform Movement onwards have been (and partially still are) the teaching of geographic and historical *realia*, the description of 'national character' in the context of teaching about a target culture, everyday-life cultural studies, and intercultural learning. The detailed analysis of the variants of culture pedagogy in the last four decades carried out by Risager (2007: 39–188) provides interesting insights into assumptions and important orientations in this domain. The language concepts above all relate to choices between the written or oral language and, from the twentieth century onwards, also to the exclusion or inclusion of language varieties. The historical development and determinants of the predominance at a given time of these concepts have not been analysed in depth so far, particularly at a broad European level. This could, then, constitute a useful framework for an international historiography of language teaching and learning.

Bibliography

BERRÉ, MICHEL, and HENRI BESSE. 2012. 'Méthodes, techniques d'enseignement du français comme L2: éléments pour une réflexion historiographique', in *Histoire internationale de l'enseignement du français langue étrangère ou seconde: problèmes, bilans et perspectives*, ed. by Marie-Christine Kok Escalle, Nadia Minerva, and Marcus Reinfried, Recherches et applications, 52 (Paris: Clé International), pp. 62–77

BRUNOT, FERDINAND. *Histoire de la langue française* (Paris: Colin, 13 vols.), V: *Le Français en France et hors de France au XVIIe siècle* (1966); VIII: *Le Français hors de France au XVIIIe siècle* (1967); XI: *Le Français au dehors sous la Révolution, le Consulat et l'Empire*, 2 vols (1969)

CARAVOLAS, JEAN-ANTOINE. 1994. *La Didactique des langues*, 2 vols (Montréal: Presses de l'Université de Montréal; Tübingen: Narr), I: *Précis d'histoire I. 1450–1700*; II: *Anthologie I: A l'ombre de Quintilien*

——. 2000. *Histoire de la didactique des langues au siècle des Lumières: précis et anthologie thématique* (Montréal: Presses de l'Université de Montréal; Tübingen: Narr)

CHRIST, HERBERT, and HANS-JOACHIM RANG (eds). 1985. *Fremdsprachenunterricht unter staatlicher Verwaltung: Eine Dokumentation amtlicher Richtlinien und Verordnungen*, 7 vols (Tübingen: Narr), I: *Einleitung und Orientierung*; II: *Allgemeine Anweisungen für den Fremdsprachenunterricht*; III: *Neuere Fremdsprachen I*; IV: *Neuere Fremdsprachen II*; V: *Alte Sprachen*; VI: *Prüfungsbestimmungen für den Fremdsprachenunterricht*; VII: *Der Fremdsprachenunterricht in Stundentafeln*

DORFELD, KARL. 1892. *Beiträge zur Geschichte des französischen Unterrichts in Deutschland. Beilage zum Programm des Großherzoglichen Gymnasiums in Gießen 1891/92* (Giessen: Keller)

——. 1896. 'Französischer Unterricht, geschichtlicher Abriß', in *Encyclopädisches Handbuch der Pädagogik*, ed. by Wilhelm Rein, 7 vols (Langensalza: Beyer, 1896-99), II, 395–419

FERNÁNDEZ FRAILE, MARÍA EUGENIA, and JAVIER SUSO LÓPEZ. 1999. *La enseñanza del francés en España (1767–1936). Estudio histórico: objetivos, contenidos y procedimientos* (Granada: Método Ediciones)

HOWATT, A. P. R., and RICHARD C. SMITH (eds). 2002. *Modern Language Teaching: The Reform Movement*, 5 vols, I: *Linguistic Foundations*; II: *Early Years of Reform*; III: *Germany and France*; IV: *Britain and Scandinavia*; V: *Bibliographies and Overviews* (London: Routledge)

Hüllen, Werner. 2000. 'Ein Plädoyer für das Studium der Geschichte des Fremdsprachenunterrichts', *Zeitschrift für Fremdsprachenforschung*, 11: 31–39
——. 2005. *Kleine Geschichte des Fremdsprachenlernens* (Berlin: Schmidt)
Kelly, Louis G. 1969. *500 B.C.–1969* (Rowley, MA: Newbury)
Klippel, Friederike. 2000. 'Zum Verhältnis von altsprachlicher und neusprachlicher Methodik im 19. Jahrhundert', *Zeitschrift für Fremdsprachenforschung*, 11: 41–61
Koordinierungsgremium im DFG-Schwerpunkt 'Sprachlehrforschung' (ed.). 1983. *Sprachlehr- und Sprachlernforschung: Begründung einer Disziplin*, Tübinger Beiträge zur Linguistik, 221 (Tübingen: Narr)
Kuhfuss, Walter. 2014. *Eine Kulturgeschichte des Französischunterrichts in der frühen Neuzeit. Französischlernen am Fürstenhof, auf dem Marktplatz und in der Schule in Deutschland* (Göttingen: V & R unipress)
Lambley, Kathleen. 1920. *The Teaching and Cultivation of the French Language in England during Tudor and Stuart Times With an introductory chapter on the preceding period* (Manchester: Manchester University Press)
Mackey, William Francis. 1965. *Language Teaching Analysis* (London: Longman)
Marquard, Odo. 2003. *Zukunft braucht Herkunft: Philosophische Essays* (Stuttgart: Reclam)
Mejer, Lene, Sadiq Kwesi Boateng, and Paolo Turchetti. 2010. 'More students study foreign languages in Europe but perceptions of skill levels differ significantly', *Eurostat: Statistics in Focus*, 49/2010 <http://www.uni-mannheim.de/edz/pdf/statinf/10/KS-SF-10-049-EN.PDF> [accessed 8 May 2015]
Minerva, Nadia, and Carla Pellandra (eds). [1]1991, [2]1997. *Insegnare il francese in Italia: repertorio analitico di manuali pubblicati dal 1625 al 1860*, Heuresis, 3; Strumenti, 5 (Bologna: CLUEB)
Minerva, Nadia, and Marcus Reinfried. 2012. 'Les Domaines à explorer et l'évolution historique', in *Histoire internationale de l'enseignement du français langue étrangère ou seconde: problèmes, bilans et perspectives*, ed. by Marie-Christine Kok Escalle, Nadia Minerva, and Marcus Reinfried, Recherches et applications, 52 (Paris: Clé International), pp. 14–28
Pellandra, Carla. 2007. *Le radici del nostro mestiere: storia e storie degli insegnamenti linguistici*, Quaderni del CIRSIL, 3 (Bologna: CLUEB)
Reinfried, Marcus. 1992. *Das Bild im Fremdsprachenunterricht: Eine Geschichte der visuellen Medien am Beispiel des Französischunterrichts* (Tübingen: Narr)
——. [5]2007 [1989]. 'Geschichte des Fremdsprachenunterrichts: Ein internationaler Überblick über die Literatur', in *Handbuch Fremdsprachenunterricht*, ed. by Karl-Richard Bausch, Herbert Christ and Hans-Jürgen Krumm (Tübingen and Basel: Francke), pp. 622–26
——. 2013. 'L'Historiographie de l'enseignement du français langue étrangère en Allemagne: un abrégé de son évolution.', in *Usages et représentations du français hors de France: 25 ans d'études historiques au sein de la SIHFLES*, ed. by Marie-Christine Kok Escalle and Karène Sanchez-Summerer (=*Documents pour l'histoire du français langue étrangère ou seconde*, 50), pp. 205–21
——. 2014. 'European History of Romance Language Teaching', in *Manual of Language Acquisition*, ed. by Christiane Fäcke (Berlin and Boston: de Gruyter), pp. 255–73
Riemens, Kornelius-Jacobus. 1919. *Esquisse historique de l'enseignement du français en Hollande du XVIe au XIXe siècle* (Leiden: Sijthoff)
Risager, Karen. 2007. *Language and Culture Pedagogy. From a National to Transnational Paradigm*, Languages for Intercultural Communication and Education, 14 (Clevedon: Multilingual Matters)
Schröder, Konrad (ed.). 1980-85. *Linguarum recentium annales: Der Unterricht in den modernen europäischen Sprachen im deutschsprachigen Raum*, 4 vols (Augsburg: Universität Augsburg), I (1980): *1500–1700*; II (1982): *1701–1740*; III (1983): *1741–1770*; IV (1985): *1771–1800*

—— (ed.). 1989–99. *Biographisches und bibliographisches Lexikon der Fremdsprachenlehrer des deutschsprachigen Raumes, Spätmittelalter bis 1800*, 6 vols (Augsburg: Universität Augsburg), I (1989): *Buchstaben A bis C — Quellenverzeichnis*; II (²1991): *Buchstaben D bis H — Erste Nachträge zum Quellenverzeichnis*; III (1992): *Buchstaben I bis Q*; IV (1995): *Buchstaben R bis Z – Zweite Nachträge zum Quellenverzeichnis*; V (1996): *Nachträge und Ergänzungen Buchstaben A bis K*; VI (1999): *Nachträge und Ergänzungen Buchstaben L bis Z — Dritte Nachträge zum Quellenverzeichnis*

SCHULZ, WOLFGANG. 1965. 'Die Theorie: Unterricht: Analyse und Planung', in *Unterricht: Analyse und Planung*, ed. by Paul Heimann, Gunter Otto, and Wolfgang Schulz (Hannover: Schroedel), pp. 13–47

STENGEL, EDMUND. 1976 [1890]. *Chronologisches Verzeichnis französischer Grammatiken vom Ende des 14. bis zum Ausgange des 18. Jahrhunderts nebst Angabe der bisher ermittelten Fundorte derselben*, ed. with an appendix by Hans-Joachim Niederehe, Amsterdam Studies in the Theory and History of Linguistic Science, 3rd ser., 8 (Amsterdam: Benjamins)

STREUBER, ALBERT. 1914. *Beiträge zur Geschichte des französischen Unterrichts im 16. bis 18. Jahrhundert, Part I: Die Entwicklung der Methoden im allgemeinen und das Ziel der Konversation im besonderen*, Romanische Studien, 15 (Berlin: Ebering)

SUÁREZ GÓMEZ, GONZALO. 2008. *La enseñanza del francés en España hasta 1850. ¿Con qué libros aprendían francés los españoles?*, ed., intro. and annotated by Juan F. García Bascuñana and Esther Juan Oliva (Barcelona: Promociones Publicaciones Universitarias)

WELLER, FRANZ-RUDOLF. 1980. 'Skizze einer Entwicklungsgeschichte des Französischunterrichts in Deutschland bis zum Beginn des 19. Jahrhunderts', *Die Neueren Sprachen*, 79: 135–61

Notes to Chapter 1

1. At the time of writing (2015), the population of the European Union is about 508 million people. Precise information about the number of foreign-language learners is difficult to come by. However, in 2008, already 93% of students at lower secondary level and 83% of students at upper secondary level were learning at least one foreign language in the EU (Mejer, Boateng and Turchetti 2010: 4, Table 2).
2. Objectives, contents, methods and media can be considered the four central aspects of teaching analysis and lesson planning; they play a crucial role in the modelling of teaching situations, for example for the Berlin School of General Didactics (Schulz 1965: 23). They also need to play a key role in any model of relevant teaching and learning factors for historical analysis (cf. Figure 1.1, in the section below titled 'Common and Differing Aspects in the European History of Foreign Language Teaching and Their Modelling').
3. Systematic analysis of regulating factors, which is the main task for *Sprachlehr-* and *Sprachlernforschung* ('empirical language teaching and learning research' (cf. Koordinierungsgremium 1983: 31)), also represents a relevant objective for the historiography of foreign-language teaching and learning.
4. The 'European perspective' adopted in my paper is of course not meant to imply — in a Eurocentric sense — any low opinion of historical or historiographical developments in non-European contexts but simply reflects the sphere of work I have myself been concerned with.
5. In the *écoles françaises*, pupils (often belonging to merchant families) initially learned how to read and write in their Dutch mother tongue. The central focus of lessons then changed to French, which was understood and spoken by the majority of the Dutch upper and middle class in this era. Increasing emphasis was placed in higher grades on arithmetic for boys and the teaching of good manners, needle- and housework for girls (Riemens 1919: 89–119).

CHAPTER 2

French Didactics in Late Medieval and Early Modern England: Thinking Historically about Method

Rory G. Critten

Recent commentators on the history of French education in medieval and early modern England argue that translation played a major part in the instruction of the language across both periods. In contrast, this chapter demonstrates that the prevalence of the technique in medieval French teaching is difficult to prove and that monolingual methods of instruction are equally likely to have been pursued, perhaps especially by those French teachers about whom we know the most, the Oxford *dictatores*. The argument highlights the sensitivity of both medieval and early modern teachers to the shifting material, linguistic, social, and geopolitical conditions that shaped the requirements of their students and defined the possibilities for instruction. As such, it illustrates the usefulness of a history of language learning and teaching that considers method as the product of a series of localized responses to particular teaching situations as well as of a teleological process of refinement and reform.

Introduction

In the Introduction to his *Esclarcissement de la langue francoyse* (London, 1530; *ESTC* S104266), John Palsgrave begins by itemizing the difficulty experienced by English learners of French:

> The diffyculte of the frenche tong / whiche maketh it so harde to be lerned by them of our nation / resteth chefely in thre thynges / In the diuersyte of pronunciation / that is betwene vs and them / in theyr analogie and maner of congruite / where in they be moche more parfyte and exquisyte than we be / and moche more approche towardes the parfection of the latin tong / than we do / And thyrdly in theyr propertes of spekyng where in theyr phrasys be dyfferent frome ours / and letteth vs / that thoughe we schulde gyue worde for worde / yet the sens shulde moche differ betwene our tong and theirs. (sig. [A6]v)[1]

Palsgrave goes on to offer some initial notes on these issues, each of which is treated in progressively greater detail over the course of his tripartite grammar of French. Particularly striking is Palsgrave's handling of the last of the problems that he identifies, French syntax, for while numerous French language teaching and reference texts survive from the later Middle Ages — including wordlists, verb tables, collections of model letters and dialogues, and grammatical and spelling treatises — syntax is a topic that these texts do not address systematically or in detail.[2]

For example, Palsgrave includes in his Introduction a few opening remarks on the topic of the Middle French conjunctive pronoun *en*: 'Somtyme in affyrmation they put *En* / before the verbe / more than we haue in our tong in the same sentence / as for He is fledde / they saye *Il s_en_ est en fuy*' (sig. [C5]^r; underlining added). The *Esclarcissement* proceeds by stages, gradually introducing its readers to more complex forms of grammatical explanation. Thus Palsgrave comes back to *en* in his second book, where we are told among other things that often the word 'signifieth nothyng / but onely as a signe of affirmation / vsed rather to make the sentence more fulle in sounde to the eare / than for any necessite' (II: sig. 46^r). Then, returning to the matter for the last time in his third book, Palsgrave rounds out his exposition of this grammatical and stylistic phenomenon by referring to authoritative writers of French. Thus, we read, *en* is more frequently deployed by writers of verse than 'in comen speche' and, in particular, by Jean de Meun and Alain Chartier (III: sigs 131^{r-v}). At the same time as the authority of these writers is assumed, Palsgrave reveals himself to be an interested chronicler of language change and a keen judge of other writers' attempts to rationalize French. The thirteenth- and fifteenth-century poets Jean de Meun and Chartier are said to use *en* 'more oftenner than suche as write aboute this tyme' (III: sig. [131]^v), and the discussion ends with a quibble regarding the usage of another poet, Jean Lemaire de Belges, who was a rough contemporary of Palsgrave:

> Whereas Johan le Mayre writeth the indiffynite inducatyue *ie men fouys*, I do nat alowe that orthographie / for *ie fouys*, signyfyeth I digge / and cometh out of *fodio*, where *ie men fuys*, cometh out of *fugio*, except Johan le Mayre dyd it to make a difference bytwene the present and the indiffynite / but as I haue afore declared it is non inconuenyent that they be lyke in their first persons. (III: sig. [133]^v)

In his sourcing and evaluation of authoritative examples for the various grammatical propositions that he advances, Palsgrave partakes of the new Humanist practices of philological investigation. The author deliberately aligns the *Esclarcissment* with this project in his Introduction, where he claims that by adding a third book to his study that expands upon his second he was 'folowyng the order of Theodorus Gaza / in his grammer of the Greke tonge' (sig. A3^r). Originally published in Venice in 1495, Gaza's grammar enjoyed a good reputation throughout sixteenth-century Europe; Erasmus made a partial translation of it in the 1510s (cf. Pizzi 1953). Palsgrave was personally acquainted both with Erasmus and with Thomas More and he has been credited with adapting their pedagogical ideas in his own teaching.[3] Of particular relevance in this regard is Palsgrave's *Ecphrasis anglica in comoediam Acolasti* (London,

1540; *ESTC* S105662), a schoolroom parallel text edition of William Fullonius's neo-Latin play *Acolastus*

> translated into oure englisshe tongue, after suche maner as chylderne are taught in the grammer schole, fyrst worde for worde, as the latyne lyeth, and afterwarde accordynge to the sence and meanyng of the latin sentences: by shewing what they do value and counteruayle in our tongue. (sig. [A1]ʳ)

In the Epistle addressing this work to Henry VIII, Palsgrave laid out his priorities as a teacher, chief among which was his aim by means of his translations 'perfectly to open the diuersities of phrases betwene our tonge and the latyn' (sig. [A4]ʳ). While an explicit reference to this contrastive pedagogic approach is missing in the *Esclarcissment*, we have already seen that in this earlier work Palsgrave proposed to elucidate French through comparison with English. He also repeatedly makes clear his conviction that translation into the target language is one of the main ways in which he anticipates that his readers will improve their knowledge of French. For example, having learned the basic precepts outlined in his Introduction, Palsgrave writes that:

> the lernar may than by the helpe of my tables by his own study be able to translate any matter or sentence he wyll / out of our tong in to frenche / and so incontynente accustome hym to haue thyr commen speche / whiche by this meanes with a lytell study is sone attayned vnto. (sig. [C6]ʳ)

As part of a broader movement that has sought to highlight points of continuity between the Middle Ages and the early modern period, historians of French didactics have begun to look for evidence of the teaching of French via translation prior to the publication of the *Esclarcissement*. This approach garners justification both from Palsgrave's statement of his intention to proceed 'takyng light and erudition' (sig. A2ʳ) from the work of his predecessors and through comparison with the medieval practices of Latin instruction out of which the Humanists' own pedagogy grew by a process of development and reaction. It has, however, led to a narrowing of the perspective on medieval French education in England that this chapter proposes to correct by focusing on some of the monolingual modes of instruction that the extant teaching and reference texts might have supported. While I argue for broader recognition of the diversity of late-medieval language instruction, I also make the case for a more serious consideration of the material, linguistic, social and geopolitical conditions within which French education in England took place before the institutionalization of modern language instruction. It is hoped that the outcome will be a better sense not only of what historical practices of French instruction might have been like but also of the ways in which thinking historically about method necessarily problematizes popular narrative accounts of developments in language teaching and learning.

The Medieval Evidence and its Interpretation

The latest discussions of the history of French education in medieval England have focused on one manuscript: Oxford, Magdalen College MS 188.[4] This is a large

(345 × 220mm) parchment book that dates to the second quarter of the fifteenth century. It owes its interest for historians of French didactics first to the small anthology of teaching and reference texts compiled in its opening quire (fols 1ʳ–8ᵛ). These include (1) a treatise on French spelling that is given the title *Orthographia gallica* by its most recent editor, R. C. Johnston (1987); (2) a trilingual vocabulary list giving the words for numbers, the days of the week, the months, holidays, and other sundry items in French, English, and Latin; and (3) a fragment of a treatise on letter writing in French accompanied by two sample letters. The second, much longer portion of the manuscript (fols 9ʳ–102ᵛ) contains an incomplete copy of the *Somme le roi*, a popular compendium of catechetical texts compiled by one Friar Laurent at the request of King Philip III of France in 1279–80.⁵ The particular attraction of this portion of the book for students of the French of late-medieval England lies in the partial glossing of its French text in both Latin and English.

In the first of a series of studies addressing this codex, Andres Max Kristol proclaimed it 'un grand manuscrit didactique' (1998: 185, cf. Kristol 2000, 2001a). Kristol's experience of cataloguing the extant French teaching and reference texts had persuaded him that, on their own, these works could not have provided sufficient grounding in French to enable a learner otherwise ignorant of the language to begin producing sophisticated utterances (1998: 177–78). In the trilingual *Somme le roi* Kristol saw a much-needed complement to the orthographic and morphological rules provided in the other French teaching and reference texts that he knew; it contained, he suggested, an implicit course in French syntax whereby the marked closeness of the Magdalen translator's English and Latin renderings of the French text were designed to highlight points of difference between Latin, French and English sentence structure.

Noting that in Continental French the *ne ... pas* structure had become the standard (i.e. not emphatic) negating formula by the fourteenth century, for example, Kristol (1998: 191–92) suggested that the Magdalen translator deliberately overdid the negation in the English and the Latin versions of his French source text in order to draw attention to the split structure. Thus in the following citation, the Latin and English translations replicate the French split negative and, in so doing, reinforce the negation in their original, giving the sense 'not at all' for the French 'not' (*not ... in eniwyse* in English and *non ... quovismodo* in Latin). The extract is taken from the rendition of the Ten Commandments with which the Magdalen copy of the *Somme le roi* opens. Throughout Magdalen 188, the French text of the *Somme* is given in a larger, more formal script than are the Latin and English translations; I give it here in bold:

> Thou shalt not take in eniwyse the name of god in vayn
> tu non assumas quovismodo nomen dei in vanum
> **Tu ne prendras pas le noun dieu en vain.**
> (Magdalen 188, fol. 9ᵛ)

Later in the same essay, Kristol (1998: 192–93) posited that by offering a studied variety in his rendering of the problematic Middle French word *en*, the Magdalen translator provided an implicit commentary on the uses of a grammatical feature of

French that might pose difficulties for English learners. In the following citations, the use of *en* as an indefinite pronoun (cf. Modern French *on*) is at stake. In the first passage it is rendered by *unus* in Latin and *oon* in English and subsequently by an indefinite pronoun in Latin (*quis*) and by a personal pronoun in English (*he*); in the second, it is rendered by a plural form in Latin (*faciunt*) and an indefinite pronoun in English (*me*[n] *dooth*). The extracts are taken from the account of the sins of the tongue that Friar Laurent attaches to his rendition of the Seven Deadly Sins (the Magdalen copy of the *Somme le roi* ends incompletely with this text). They treat the swearing of oaths and the pain that this causes Christ:

Or whan that oon by hotith certaynly that thynge that he knowith not if he may it fulfille
Vel quando unus promittit certitudinaliter hoc quod quis nescit si hoc poterit ad implere
Ou quant l'en promet certainement ce que l'en ne set ce l'en purra a complir.
(Magdalen 188, fol. 99^r)

these rentyn hym more smal than me dooth an hogge in the bocherye
Sed isti ipsum dilacerant magis minutim quam faciunt porcum in macello
mes cist le depiecent plus menuement qu'en ne fet le porcel en la boucherie.
(Magdalen 188, fol. 100^r)

Thus, Kristol argued, the reader is introduced to the English and Latin forms for which French substitutes its indefinite pronoun.[6]

More recently, Christel Nissille has expressed scepticism regarding Kristol's claims as to the Magdalen translator's didactic intent. Instead, she views the variety of translation strategies deployed in the rendering of particular aspects of the French source text as evidence of the translator's attempts to get to grips with the unfixed and changing nature of the French of late-medieval England (Nissille 2014: 155–58). Judging that an instructor might choose to draw out the points that Kristol assumes were deliberately planted there, Nissille does not abandon Kristol's theory of the manuscript's use in group teaching, but she does admit to some trouble imagining its deployment in the French language classroom (2014: 159). This difficulty is understandable since it is far from certain that the book's first application was didactic.

Ralph Hanna (2005) has identified a series of running titles added to Magdalen 188 as being in the hand of John Dygon, a recluse at the Carthusian monastery of Sheen (Surrey) who moved there towards the end of his life, in 1435. It is possible that Magdalen 188 got caught up in the traffic of books between Sheen and the Bridgettine community at Syon across the Thames: Marilyn Oliva (2009) and William Rothwell (2001b) have stressed the continuing importance of French in England's late-medieval nunneries in other contexts, and the catechetical items anthologized in the *Somme le roi* might have been deployed in the basic instruction of the women at Syon, for whom Sheen's monks produced other edifying compilations, as Vincent Gillespie (2008) and Paul J. Patterson (2011) have shown. Since Hanna (2005: 136–37) counts Magdalen 188 among those books most likely to have been acquired by Dygon during his reclusion, however, it seems at least equally probable that its early application was private. During his secular life, Dygon must have acquired basic clerical skills, including a facility in French, in the pursuit of the legal training that he is known to have completed at Oxford (cf. Hanna 2005: 128–29). It seems plausible that he obtained Magdalen 188 with a view to brushing up his French in his retirement. Thus Hanna (2005: 140) concludes that, although Dygon is not the manuscript's main scribe, Magdalen 188 'looks very much like an exercise combining both piety and foreign language practice'. In any case, Dygon's Carthusian profession and his status as a recluse at Sheen would normally have precluded his involvement in any kind of organized classroom teaching there.

Nissille (2014: 122–30) cites Hanna's work on Dygon's hand in Magdalen 188 and considers a variety of uses to which the manuscript might have been put before settling on her identification of the book as a 'manuel de langue' with a classroom application. Where the trilingual text of Magdalen 188 fosters a comparative approach to language study, she suggests, it links the practice of French instruction in medieval England with contemporaneous Latin teaching via the translation of *vulgaria*, that is, via the translation into and out of Latin of short, sample sentences.[7] At the same time, on Nissille's interpretation, Magdalen 188 would appear to adumbrate the procedures of comparative Humanist language pedagogy (Nissille 2014: 94–95). Thus Magdalen 188 is assumed to constitute a *passerelle* or little bridge that links each of these sets of trends; if the manuscript is unique in its combination of French teaching materials and a trilingual reading text, this is interpreted not as a potential indicator of the idiosyncratic interests of its first known owner, but as a demonstration of the 'silence des sources' (Nissille 2014: 8). Certainly, many of the surviving medieval books that contain language teaching and reference materials also contain sample texts that appear to have been selected with a view to providing reading practice. Brian Merrilees (1990) has demonstrated the popularity of the collocation of grammatical and reading materials in manuscripts containing Old and Middle French texts written to teach Latin, and Nissille herself (2014: 282–97) provides a useful account of the extant English manuscripts containing French teaching and reference materials that confirms the popularity of this mode of compilation among those books. Some of the reading texts in the manuscripts Nissille examines are, moreover, provided with glosses of greater or lesser completeness in Middle English, suggesting that an appetite for works prepared or adapted in this fashion extended beyond the walls of Dygon's reclusorium. In the extant manuscripts of Walter de Bibbesworth's *Tretiz*, for example, the French text of this verse vocabulary is often accompanied by Middle English glosses, and the *Femina*, a fifteenth-century adaptation of the *Tretiz*, is glossed throughout.[8] Nevertheless, Nissille's supposition regarding the capacity of Magdalen 188 to illuminate historical French didactics remains doubtful, not only because it relies on absent evidence but also because the motivations shaping the production of individual manuscript books are often difficult to grasp, even if broad patterns in the compilation of codices now containing French and Latin teaching and reference materials can be discerned.

The extant English manuscripts containing French teaching and reference materials have the appearance of having been put together for a variety of reasons. A few of these codices preserve what look to be student notes. In this category we might count Cambridge, University Library MS Additional 8870, a legal notebook that has been described by J. H. Baker (1989) and whose third quire contains various subject-specific teaching and learning resources in French and Latin. Other books containing French teaching materials may perhaps be collections assembled by instructors themselves. Because their texts contain apparent references to an identified medieval French teacher, this is the function accorded to two early fifteenth-century manuscripts, London, British Library MS Additional 17716 and Cambridge, Trinity College MS B. 14. 40, by Merrilees and Beata Sitarz-Fitzpatrick in their edition of the *Liber Donati* (1993: 1–2), a medieval French grammar transmitted in these codices. But the identification of these books as works compiled by learners or more advanced users of the language remains largely conjectural, and there will inevitably be some slippage between these categories among the total corpus of manuscripts containing French teaching and reference materials. Indeed, it is often difficult to ascertain whether a book that would appear to lend itself to teaching was in fact used in a pedagogic context or whether it was produced with the intention of collecting together an anthology of reference texts that may or may not have been previously used to teach the language to the manuscript's commissioner. In this connection, it is salutary to recall A. P. R. Howatt and H. G. Widdowson's general observation that before the nineteenth century most learners of modern languages studied 'on their own' (2004: 2).

While manuscripts can tell us a good deal about the kinds of French that medieval English users of the language desired to master, they provide only limited information about the means by which they attempted to acquire it. Moreover, Howatt and Widdowson's statement encourages us to realize that it may be unwise to think about the medieval and early modern history of modern language teaching as constituting anything so uniform as a continuous tradition: the first practices of French teaching in England are likely to have been multiple and disconnected. The remainder of this chapter focuses principally on the situation of medieval French teaching about which the most is currently known: the schools of the Oxford *dictatores*, a group of teachers existing on the fringes of the late-medieval University who taught French and Latin alongside the skills required in order to perform a variety of basic legal and commercial functions. The guiding conviction here is that Palsgrave's adaptation of Humanist language teaching practices to French education supports a mode of instruction that is fundamentally different to that pursued by these medieval teachers (and, as we shall see, by several of Palsgrave's sixteenth-century peers). Whereas the *dictatores* developed content-driven curricula that were geared to the acquisition of certain professional skills, in his *Esclarcissement*, Palsgrave designed a more language-driven course whose primary aim was to facilitate learners' access to the riches of contemporary French literature.[9] Where Palsgrave afforded signal importance to translation in his French instruction, I shall argue that consideration of the extant medieval French teaching and reference materials suggests that they were eminently suitable to support monolingual teaching methods, including dictation and drills, as well as the targeted practice of specialized uses of the spoken and written language.

French in the Classrooms of the *Dictatores* and Beyond

Some organized French instruction did exist in late-medieval England. The instructor with whom Merrilees and Sitarz-Fitzpatrick associate the manuscripts of the *Liber Donati* listed above is William Kingsmill (fl. 1420–50), who, along with his predecessor, Thomas Sampson (fl. 1370–1409), is known to have taught French privately in late-medieval Oxford. As Martin Camargo (2007), M. Dominica Legge (1939), and H. G. Richardson (1941) have demonstrated, the priorities of these teachers' clients are reflected in the materials that they prepared for them. Among the texts associated with Kingsmill and Sampson there survive treatises on conveyancing and on the writing of letters and bills, as well as model texts written in French and Latin exemplifying these and related genres, a selection of which was reproduced and discussed by Richardson (1942). These texts reflect the important role that French continued to play in a wide variety of written contexts in England well into the fifteenth century. As Rothwell (2001a) points out, these contexts included legal records and the records of various ports, mercantile companies, cities, and religious establishments, as well as the writing of letters internally, between members of the English ruling classes, and externally, to addressees on the Continent.[10]

Spoken French was also apparently in demand among learners in medieval Oxford. A collection of model dialogues dated to 1415 gives a good impression of some of the kinds of oral French that early fifteenth-century learners wanted to use; it includes conversations in which speakers greet each other, exchange pleasantries on the road, organize lodgings, order food, and make provision for the care of their horses. In the form in which it is transmitted in Cambridge, Trinity College MS B. 14. 40, the final conversation in the manual is directly connected to Kingsmill. At the opening of this dialogue, a knight has been asked by a woman to take her twelve-year-old son with him to London and to secure him an apprenticeship there. Calling the boy before him, the knight begins a round of questioning:

> — Moun fiz, avez vous esté a l'escole?
> — Oy, syre, par vostre congé.
> — A quel lieu?
> — Syr, a l'ostelle de Will Kyngesmylle Escriven.
> — Beau fyz, comben de temps avez vous demurrez ovesque luy?
> — Sire, forsque un quart de l'an.
> — Cella n'est que un poi temps, mes qu'avez vous apriz la en ycel terme?
> — Syr, moun maystre m'ad enseigné pur escrire, enditer, acompter et frounceys parler.
> — Et que savez vous en frounceys dire?
> — Sir, je say moun noun et moun corps bien descriere. (Kristol 1995: 76–77)

> [— My son, have you been to school?
> — Yes, sir, by your leave.
> — In what place?
> — Sir, at the hostel of the scrivener, William Kingsmill.
> — Good son, how long have you stayed with him?
> — Sir, only a quarter of a year.

— That's only a little while, but what have you learned there in that time?
— Sir, my master has taught me to write, compose, cast accounts, and speak French.
— And what can you say in French?
— Sir, I can say my name and describe my body in detail.][11]

The boy gives his name as 'Jehan boun enfant' and goes on to specify at some length the French words describing the parts of the body. He also gives briefer lists of the vocabularies of clothing, ecclesiastical and secular rank, and household furniture.

This dialogue provides clear evidence of Kingsmill's teaching; in his edition of the text, Kristol calls this closing conversation a 'publicité *pro domo*', that is, for Kingsmill's own school (1995: 76). It indicates furthermore that a knowledge of spoken French might be desired alongside basic literacy and numeracy by young men hoping to make their careers as craftsmen, an apparently important group among Kingsmill's and Sampson's learners. Elsewhere I have argued that some of the students of the *dictatores* might have harboured the desire to use their French further afield than London, the destination specified in the citation above, in particular in the northern French territories opened up in the wake of Henry V's victory at the Battle of Agincourt in 1415 (Critten 2015). Indeed, explicit reference is made to this event in the second dialogue in Kingsmill's manual. In this extract, a speaker just out of France recounts the latest news from that country to a curious interlocutor:

> Et puis j'ay oye dyre qu'ore tarde, lez seignours de Fraunce ovesque la nombre de .l. ou .lx. mille persones armez ount encontrez le roy par le chymyn, et le roy ovesque la numbre de .x. mille persones ad combatuz ovesque eaux a un lieu apellé Agincourt, a quele bataille i sount pris et tuez .xi. mille personis dez Frounceys et sount tuez forsque .xvi. persones dez Englés, dount le duc d'Everwyk estoit un et le counte de Suffolk un autre. Et le roy avoit le champe et le victorie — loiez soit Dieu — et mist toutz les autrez Frounceys au fewer. Et issint le roy tient soun chymyn ver Calays et soy purpose de retourner en Engleterre par la grace de Dieu. (Kristol 1995: 70)

> [And then I have heard said that before long, the lords of France with the number of fifty or sixty thousand armed men met the King [Henry V] in the road, and the King with the number of ten thousand men fought with them at a place called Agincourt, at which battle eleven thousand men were taken and killed on the French side and only sixteen men were killed among the English, of whom the Duke of York was one and the Count of Suffolk another. And the King had the field and the victory — praise be to God! — and put all the other Frenchmen to flight. And so the King makes his way towards Calais and intends to return to England by the grace of God.][12]

The speaker goes on to recount the names of some of the prisoners taken on the battlefield, stating that they 'serrount anmesniez le jeody prochein aprés le feste de Seint Martyn envers Loundres' [will be brought next Thursday after the feast of Saint Martin to London].

While this is not the most developed of the extant dialogues associated with the *dictatores*, the conversation deploys both voices (active and passive) over a broad range of tenses (present, perfect, imperfect, past simple, future simple); the vocabulary of warfare is likewise mobilized (*encontrer, combatre, bataille, prendre, tuer, mettre au fewer*). These linguistic features are demonstrated in the context of an engaging oral report, indicating one of the situations in which learners at Oxford might have expected to use French either at home or abroad: sharing news of important events with other travellers. Finally, the geopolitical context in which these learners are acquiring the language is brought clearly to their attention: the early fifteenth century saw a sharp upturn in English fortunes in the Hundred Years War that made trade with and travel to northern France attractive and potentially lucrative activities. If the totality of the extant medieval French teaching and reference materials is insufficient to allow a student otherwise ignorant of French to produce language of this sophistication, as Kristol argues, it nevertheless seems reasonable to assume that the learners using the Kingsmill conversation manual could fairly be expected to produce similar dialogues after a little work: what would be the point in providing sample material that was too elaborate to be emulated?

Rather than presupposing the loss of intermediate material, as Kristol and Nissille do, it is worth considering whether explicit treatments of French sentence structure were actually necessary in the classrooms in which Kingsmill's manual and manuals like it were used. In his work on the longevity of French in post-Conquest England, Richard Ingham (2010) demonstrates the vitality of the language as a contact variety of French that could enact influence upon as well as undergo influence from Middle English well into the fourteenth century. The potency of French throughout this period is suggestive of its naturalistic acquisition in middle childhood, either via elementary schools, as Ingham went on to argue (2012: 33–35, 2015), or, as Jocelyn Wogan-Browne has recently proposed (2015), via the more informal modes of education supported by women's involvement in children's learning. These are precisely the conditions under which monolingual teaching in French could flourish at later stages in the curriculum. They also provide a good explanation for the comparatively late appearance of the first grammar of French, the *Donait françois* commissioned or perhaps written by John Barton (c. 1409), and for the composition of that grammar not in English but in French, the target language. Like the Latin grammars in the *Donatus* tradition, the *Donait françois* is framed as a conversation between a teacher and his pupils. It begins with an account of the French alphabet:

> Quantez letters est il? Vint. Quellez? Cinq voielx et quinse consonantez. Quelx sont les voielx et ou seront ils sonnés? Le premier vouyel est *a* et serra sonné en la poetrine. (Colombat 2014: 112)
>
> [How many letters are there? Twenty. Which? Five vowels and fifteen consonants. Which are the vowels and where are they sounded? The first vowel is *a* and is sounded in the chest.]

As was the case with the previously cited dialogues, the most obvious pedagogic application for this text is not translation or even glossing but some kind of oral performance, in this case a drill.[13] In his introduction to this work, Barton claims to want to promote the acquisition of all four of the key language skills, attributing his decision to publish the *Donait* to his recognition that 'les bones gens du roiaume d'Engleterre sont enbrasez a sçavoir lire et escrire, entendre et parler droit françois' [the good people of the kingdom of England are desirous to know how to read and write, listen to and speak correct French] (Colombat 2014: 108). This balanced approach is borne out both in the form of the *Donait*, which facilitates the practice of French pronunciation at the same time as it teaches orthography and morphology, and in the unique manuscript containing the text, Oxford, All Souls College MS 182. This book is an important collection of French teaching and reference texts that treat both the written and spoken language in model letters, petitions, and dialogues and in treatises on vocabulary, pronunciation and conjugation.[14]

Other works among the surviving French teaching and reference materials would appear to target spoken French specifically. Thus Bibbesworth's *Tretiz* proposes to teach 'le dreit ordre en parler e en respundre' [the correct manner of speaking and responding] required in order to manage a rural estate (Rothwell 2009: 1). Originally composed c. 1240–50, the *Tretiz* was continuously copied and used throughout the later medieval period. Part of its popularity doubtless derived from its form: its lessons are couched in rhyme. This is a formal feature that at once aids memorization and defies translation, particularly when homonymy is in focus, as it so often is in this work. The following lines detail the parts of the body and appear designed to draw in the children envisaged as the primary audience of the text:

> Vostre regarde est graciose
> Mes vostre eel est chaciouse.
> Des eus oustés la chacie
> E de nes le rupie.
> Meuz vaut la rubie par .b.
> Ki ne fet le rupie par .p.,
> Car ci bource eut tant des rubies
> Cum le nes ad des rupies,
> Mult serreit riches de pirie
> Qui taunt eut de la rubie.
> (Rothwell 2009: 3)

[Your gaze is gracious | but your eye is full of sleep | You remove sleep from your eyes | and snot from the nose | rubies [la rubie] with a 'b' are worth more | than is snot [le rupie] with a 'p' | For he who had a purse as full with rubies [des rubies] | as the nose is with snot [des rupies] | would be most rich in precious stones | having so many rubies [la rubie].]

The glossing tradition alluded to above suggests that some of the items of vocabulary covered in Bibbesworth's poem posed problems for his readers but the form of the work argues in favour of its consumption and reproduction across oral/aural channels. In his edition of the Kingsmill conversation manual cited above, Kristol (1995: 96–97) notes that Jehan boun enfant lifts entire passages from Bibbesworth in his rendition of the French vocabulary that he knows. The child is of course a fictional construct, but his familiarity with the *Tretiz* suggests that its learning by rote was one of the tasks given by Kingsmill to his younger students. Indeed, rote learning and repetition, drilling, and other modes of oral instruction must perforce have played a large role in medieval language education owing to the difficulty of obtaining books. Outside the universities, the time, cost, and skill required in order to produce even a basic manuscript militated against the common provision and possession of textbooks among learners, especially before the widespread introduction of paper. Texts such as the model letters and petitions whose forms were taught by the *dictatores* would most likely have been delivered to students by dictation in a preliminary phase of instruction before the study of their defining characteristics could begin.

As Rothwell argues (2001c: 7), it would be a mistake to assume that English was entirely absent from the classrooms of the medieval teachers of French, a point that receives reinforcement from John Trevisa's oft-cited comments about the use of English in Latin instruction after 1385 (cf. Baugh and Cable 2013: 145). Certainly, a preference for bilingual learning can be perceived in the 'double' language manuals that appeared from the close of the fifteenth century, among which there survive copies of Caxton's *Cy commence la table* (Westminster, 1480; *ESTC* S109594), de Worde's *Lytell treatyse for to lerne Englysshe and Frensshe* (Westminster, 1497; *ESTC* S100727), and Pinson's reissue of de Worde's manual under the title *Good boke to lerne to speke French* (London, [1500]; *ESTC* S100705). While he ultimately overstates his case, Christopher Cannon (2015) has also recently reminded scholars of the role that Latin must often have played in the instruction of French.[15] Still, many of the extant French teaching and reference materials seem well suited to support monolingual instruction. Even where they focused on the acquisition of writing skills, either by choice or by necessity, the *dictatores* must also have engaged the aural competencies of their learners via the practice of dictation. The medieval French teaching and reference works and the methods that they were apt to engage seem designed to serve the needs of students who approached their studies of French not as beginners but with a view to acquiring specialized forms of the written and spoken language in order to be able to function in a variety of professional and social environments. Looking at the scattering of sources associated with alternative locations of French instruction, such as Chester, the English county with which Barton associates himself, the priorities, methods, and clientele of the *dictatores* would appear to have been paralleled in similar learning situations throughout England.[16]

Shifting Priorities in Early Modern French Education

Rather than marking a continuation of the kinds of instruction offered by the medieval teachers of French, then, the French education supported by Palsgrave's 1530 *Esclarcissement* would seem to have marked a break with the practical concerns and frequently monolingual methods pursued by his predecessors. These changes are best understood as the result of the different conditions in which the medieval teachers and Palsgrave worked. Most obviously, whereas men such as Kingsmill and Sampson had taught pupils of relatively modest means and ambitions, Palsgrave was tutor to, among other nobles, Mary Tudor, the sister of Henry VIII. For men and women of the sixteenth-century court, mastery of French was an accomplishment that might be desired without necessarily having the kinds of direct practical application for which the medieval teachers sought to equip their clients. Second, the political and social status of French in England had changed markedly by the beginning of the sixteenth century. The only continental territory still held by the English in 1530 was Calais, and Edward IV had formally renounced his claim to the French throne when he signed the Treaty of Picquigny with Louis XI in 1475, a date traditionally held to mark the end of the Hundred Years War if this is not predated to the English defeat at the Battle of Castillon in 1453.[17] French had also largely been displaced by Latin or absorbed into English as the language of official record in England by this time (cf. Rothwell 2001a). The conditions that had prompted English clerks and artisans alike to acquire the language thus no longer prevailed to the same degree, and from the end of the fifteenth century the interests of bourgeois learners of the language in particular are imagined to be more narrowly bound up with international trade. Thus Caxton's *Cy commence la table* attempts to engage a student desirous to make his fortune on the world market:

Qui ceste liure vouldra aprendre.	Who this booke shalle wylle lerne
Bien pourra entreprendre	May well entreprise or take on honde
Marchandises dun pays a lautre	Marchandises fro one land to anothir
Et cognoistre maintes denrees	And / to knowe many wares
Que lui seroient bon achetes.	Which to hym shalbe good to be bouȝt.
Ou vendues pour riche deuenir.	Or solde for riche to become.
Aprendes ce liure diligement	Lerne this book diligently.
Grande prouffyt y gyst vrayement.	Grete prouffyt lieth therin truly. (sig. [2]^v)

In this context, Palsgrave's interest in the pedagogic applications of translation is easier to understand: the teaching he offers is designed, firstly, to afford his learners access to the cultural riches of French literature. At the close of his second book, Palsgrave promises his imagined reader that, barring a few difficult constructions not yet covered, he may now with the help of his French word lists 'be sure to vnderstande any authoure that is written in the frenche tong / by his owne studye without any techar' (II: sig. [59]^v). Writing in the era of print and after the widespread adoption of paper as the principal writing support, Palsgrave's teaching is alive to the increased availability of reading matter in England, much of which continued to be in French, as Ardis Butterfield points out (2010: 36). Even Palsgrave's opening section on the pronunciation of French is geared towards the consumption of French literature. It closes with a series of prose and verse samples drawn from popular authoritative texts that are accompanied by a rough phonetic guide. The following lines, for example, are quoted from the opening of Chartier's *Quadrilogue invectif* (1422). The original French is given in a heavier, gothic type than the transliteration; I give it here in bold:

> **A la tres haulte et excellente maieste des princes /**
> Alatreháutoeevssellántomaiestédeprínsos /
> **A la tres honnoree magnificence des nobles /**
> Alatresovnnoréomanifisánsodenóbles .
> (*Esclarcissement*, I: sig. 22^r)

Introducing the third book of the *Esclarcissement*, Palsgrave makes clear that he hopes his learners will proceed from reading French to producing their own utterances in the language (III: sig. 1ʳ) but the gradual plan of his work is manifestly designed to cater to the requirements of users whose needs did not stretch so far. As it turns out, users of any kind of Palsgrave's book do not appear to have been numerous: Gabriele Stein (1997: 37–45) notes that the diffusion of the *Esclarcissement* was narrow and that it was never reprinted in its author's lifetime. Significantly, the most popular French teaching texts of the early sixteenth century were shorter than the *Esclarcissement* and attempted to strike a closer balance between grammatical instruction and language practice. Giles du Wes's *Introductorie for to lerne to rede to pronounce and to speke Frenche trewly*, for example (London, [1533]; ESTC S109850) went through several editions and four printings (cf. ESTC S105412; S109637; S109634). Du Wes mocked Palsgrave's assumption that he, an Englishman, might be able to teach French at the same time as he manifested scepticism regarding the existence of 'rules infallybles' (sig. [A3]ᵛ) that might define the vernacular language, which du Wes spoke as a native. The *Introductorie* is written in French with running interlinear translations into English but, like his peers, who also published fully bilingual texts, du Wes seems little interested in commenting specifically upon the grammatical differences between the two languages that such a layout might make visible.[18] Du Wes provides basic information on pronunciation, conjugation and vocabulary in the first section of his book but differs from Palsgrave in the inclusion of a series of dialogues in his second book, via which spoken French might be more actively practised. The rather highfaluting topics addressed in some of these conversations, which treat the nature of the soul and the mysteries of the mass, distinguish them markedly from the more practically minded conversations used by the medieval teachers of French, but du Wes's understanding of the importance of modelling the spoken language is one area where some continuity between medieval and early modern French didactics might be perceived.

Conclusion

At the same time as it disrupts the narrative of French teaching proposed by Kristol and Nissille, this contrastive analysis of the instruction offered by the medieval teachers of French and by Palsgrave has registered both the sensitivity with which the extant material evidence must be treated and the difficulties inherent in attempting to generalize about the educational methods pursued by teachers and learners of modern languages in the period before organized modern languages teaching became widespread. I have thus sought to underline the pertinence of Howatt and Smith's recent critique of teleological histories of language learning and teaching that present didactic methods as discrete moments in time 'strung together as in a necklace of beads' (2014: 91, cf. Besse 2014: 42). The process of reform so familiar to historians of modern languages education whereby teachers turned away from translation at the opening of the twentieth century towards more communicative modes of instruction in the twenty-first century can be viewed otherwise than as a self-evident amelioration in theory and practice. After all, the extant evidence would seem to suggest some flow in the opposite direction among the developments taking place in early modern language instruction. But the main point to be made here is not that modern teaching practices are unoriginal insofar as they may have been pursued in some form at Oxford or elsewhere in England in the fourteenth and fifteenth centuries. Instead, this study has attempted to demonstrate the necessity of considering a broad range of historical factors when attempting to reconstruct the teaching methods of earlier periods. Even after the introduction of organized language instruction and the advent of modern applied linguistics, language teaching methods would continue to be influenced by the same fundamental pressures: the availability of classroom technologies, the political and social status of the target language, and, above all, the abilities and requirements of learners.

Bibliography

Primary Sources

Manuscripts (by location)

Cambridge, Trinity College MS B. 14. 40
Cambridge, University Library MS Additional 8870
Oxford, All Souls College MS 182
Oxford, Magdalen College MS 188
London, British Library MS Additional 17716

Early Printed Books (by author, where known, or by publisher)

CAXTON, WILLIAM. 1480. *Cy commence la table* (Westminster) [*ESTC* S109594/STC 24865]. EEBO (San Marino: Huntington Library)
DE WORDE, WYNKYN. 1497. *Lytell treatyse for to lerne Englysshe and Frensshe* (Westminster) [*ESTC* S100727/STC 24866]. EEBO (London: British Library)
DU WES, GILES. [1533]. *Introductorie for to lerne to rede, to pronounce, and to speake Frenche trewly* (London) [*ESTC* S109850/STC 7377]. EEBO (Oxford: Bodleian Library)
PALSGRAVE, JOHN. 1530. *Lesclarcissement de la langue francoyse* ([London]) [*ESTC* S104266/STC 19166]. EEBO (Oxford: Bodleian Library)
——. 1540. *Ecphrasis anglica in comoediam Acolasti* (London) [*ESTC* S105662/STC 11470). EEBO (London: British Library)
PINSON, RICHARD. [1500]. *Good Boke to Lerne to Speke French* (London) [*ESTC* S100705/STC 24867]. EEBO (London: British Library)
VALENCE, PIERRE. [1528]. *Introductions in frensshe* ([London]) (Warminster: Longleat House)

Modern Editions and Facsimiles (by editor)

ALSTON, R. C. (ed.). 1967. *Pierre Valence: Introductions in Frensshe* (Menston: Scolar Press)
BRAYER, ÉDITH, and ANNE-FRANÇOISE LEURQUIN-LABIE (eds). 2008. *La Somme le roi* (Paris: Société des anciens textes français)
COLOMBAT, BERNARD (ed.). 2014. *Johan Barton: Donait françois* (Paris: Classiques Garnier)
EEBO = Early English Books Online. Chadwyck-Healey: < http://eebo.chadwyck.com>.
JOHNSTON, R. C. (ed.). 1987. *Orthographia gallica* (London: Anglo-Norman Text Society)
KRISTOL, ANDRES MAX (ed.). 1995. *Manières de langage (1396, 1399, 1415)* (London: Anglo-Norman Text Society)

LEGGE, M. DOMINICA (ed.). 1941. *Anglo-Norman Letters and Petitions from All Souls MS. 182* (Oxford: Blackwell)
MERRILEES, BRIAN, and BEATA SITARZ-FITZPATRICK (eds). 1993. *Liber Donati: A Fifteenth-Century Manual of French* (London: Anglo-Norman Text Society)
ORME, NICHOLAS (ed.). 2013. *English School Exercises, 1420–1530* (Toronto: Pontifical Institute of Mediaeval Studies)
ROTHWELL, WILLIAM (ed.). 2005. *Femina*. The Anglo-Norman Online Hub: <http://www.anglo-norman.net/texts/femina.pdf>
—— (ed.). 2009. *Walter de Bibbesworth: Le Tretiz*. The Anglo-Norman Online Hub: <http://www.anglo-norman.net/texts/bibb-gt.pdf>

Secondary Sources

BAKER, J. H. 1989. 'A French Vocabulary and Conversation-Guide in a Fifteenth-Century Legal Notebook', *Medium Ævum*, 58: 80–102
BAUGH, ALBERT C., and THOMAS CABLE. 2013. *A History of the English Language*, 6th edn (London: Routledge)
BESSE, HENRI. 2014. 'La Société Internationale pour l'Histoire du Français Langue Étrangère ou Seconde (SIHFLES), ou vingt-cinq ans d'investigations historiographiques sur l'enseignement/apprentissage du français langue étrangère ou seconde', *Language & History*, 57: 26–43
BRITNELL, RICHARD. 2009. 'Uses of French Language in Medieval English Towns', in *Language and Culture in Medieval Britain: The French of England, c.1100–c.1500*, ed. by Jocelyn Wogan-Browne et al. (Woodbridge: York Medieval Press), pp. 81–89
BUTTERFIELD, ARDIS. 2010. 'National Histories', in *Cultural Reformations: Medieval and Renaissance in Literary History*, ed. by Brian Cummings and James Simpson (Oxford: Oxford University Press), pp. 33–55
CAMARGO, MARTIN. 2007. 'If You Can't Join Them, Beat Them; or, When Grammar Met Business Writing (in Fifteenth-Century Oxford)', in *Letter-Writing Manuals and Instruction from Antiquity to the Present: Historical and Bibliographic Studies*, ed. by Carol Poster and Linda C. Mitchell (Columbia: University of South Carolina Press), pp. 67–87
CANNON, CHRISTOPHER. 2015. 'Vernacular Latin', *Speculum*, 90: 641–53
CRITTEN, RORY G. 2015. 'Practising French Conversation in Fifteenth-Century England', *Modern Language Review*, 110: 927–45
DEAN, RUTH J., and MAUREEN B. M. BOULTON. 1999. *Anglo-Norman Literature: A Guide to Texts and Manuscripts* (London: Anglo-Norman Text Society)
ESTC = *English Short Title Catalogue* (The British Library) < http://estc.bl.uk>
GILLESPIE, VINCENT. 2008. 'The Haunted Text: Reflections in *The Mirror to Deuout People*', in *Medieval Texts in Context*, ed. by Graham D. Caie and Denis Renevey (London: Routledge), pp. 136–66
HANNA, RALPH. 2005. 'John Dygon, Fifth Recluse of Sheen: His Career, Books, and Acquaintance', in *Imagining the Book*, ed. by Stephen Kelly and John J. Thompson (Turnhout: Brepols), pp. 127–41
HOWATT, A. P. R., and RICHARD SMITH. 2014. 'The History of Teaching English as a Foreign Language, from a British and European Perspective', *Language & History*, 57: 75–95
——, and H. G. WIDDOWSON. 2004 [1984]. *A History of English Language Teaching*, 2nd edn (Oxford: Oxford University Press)
INGHAM, RICHARD. 2010. 'Later Anglo-Norman as a Contact Variety of French?', in *The Anglo-Norman Language and its Contexts*, ed. by Richard Ingham (Woodbridge: York Medieval Press), pp. 8–25

———. 2012. *The Transmission of Anglo-Norman: Language History and Language Acquisition* (Amsterdam: Benjamins)
———. 2015. 'The Maintenance of French in later Medieval England', *Neuphilologische Mitteilungen*, 115: 623–45
KIBBEE, DOUGLAS A. 1991. *For to Speke Frenche Trewely: The French Language in England, 1000–1600* (Amsterdam: Benjamins)
KNOX, PHILIP. 2013. 'The English Glosses in Walter of Bibbesworth's *Tretiz*', *Notes and Queries*, 60: 349–59
KRISTOL, ANDRES MAX.1990. 'L'Enseignement du français en Angleterre (XIIIe–XVe siècles): les sources manuscrites', *Romania*, 111: 289–330
———. 1998. 'Comment on apprenait le français au Moyen Age: ce qu'il nous reste à apprendre', *Acta Romanica Basiliensia*, 8: 177–97
———. 2000. 'L'Intellectuel "anglo-norman" face à la pluralité des langues: le témoignage implicite du MS Oxford, Magdalen Lat. 188', in *Multilingualism in Later Medieval Britain*, ed. by D. A. Trotter (Cambridge: Brewer), pp. 37–52
———. 2001A. 'Le Ms. 188 de Magdalen College Oxford: une "pierre de Rosette" de l'enseignement médiéval du français en Angleterre?', *Vox Romanica*, 60: 149–67
———. 2001B. 'Les Premières Descriptions grammaticales du français', in *History of the Language Sciences: An International Handbook on the Evolution of the Study of Language from the Beginnings to the Present*, ed. by Sylvain Auroux et al. (Berlin: de Gruyter, 2001), pp. 764–70
LEGGE, M. DOMINICA. 1939. 'William of Kingsmill: A Fifteenth-Century Teacher of French in Oxford', in *Studies in French Language and Mediæval Literature*, ed. by Mildred K. Pope (Manchester: Manchester University Press), pp. 241–46
MERRILEES, BRIAN. 1985. 'Le Dialogue dans la méthodologie du français langue seconde au Moyen Age', in *Le Dialogue*, ed. by Pierre Léon and Paul Perron (Ottawa: Didier), pp. 105–15
———. 1990. 'L'Art Mineur français et le curriculum grammatical', *Histoire Épistémologie Langage*, 12: 15–29
MET, MYRIAM. 1998. 'Curriculum Decision-Making in Content-Based Language Teaching', in *Beyond Bilingualism: Multilingualism and Multilingual Education*, ed. by Jasone Cenoz and Fred Genesee (Clevedon: Multilingual Matters), pp. 35–63
NISSILLE, CHRISTEL. 2014.'*Grammaire floue*' *et enseignement du français en Angleterre au XVe siècle: les leçons du manuscrit Oxford Magdalen 188* (Tübingen: Francke)
OLIVA, MARILYN. 2009. 'The French of England in Female Convents: The French Kitcheners' Accounts of Campsey Ash Priory', in *Language and Culture in Medieval Britain: The French of England, c.1100–c.1500*, ed. by Jocelyn Wogan-Browne et al. (Woodbridge: York Medieval Press), pp. 90–102
ORME, NICHOLAS. 2006. *Medieval Schools from Roman Britain to Renaissance England* (New Haven, CT: Yale University Press)
PATTERSON, PAUL J. 2011. 'Preaching with the Hands: Carthusian Book Production and the *Speculum devotorum*', in *Medieval Latin and Middle English Literature: Essays in Honour of Jill Mann*, ed. by Christopher Cannon and Maura Nolan (Woodbridge: Brewer), pp. 134–49
PIZZI, CLEMENTE. 1953. 'La grammatica greca di T. Gaza e Erasmo', *Studi bizantini e neoellenici*, 7: 183–88
POLLNITZ, AYSHA. 2015. *Princely Education in Early Modern Britain* (Cambridge: Cambridge University Press)
RICHARDSON, H. G. 1941. 'Business Training in Medieval Oxford', *American Historical Review*, 46: 259–80
———. 1942. 'Letters of the Oxford *Dictatores*', in *Formularies which Bear on the History of*

Oxford, c. 1204–1420, ed. by H. E. Salter, W. A. Pantin and H. G. Richardson, 2 vols (Oxford: Clarendon), II, 329–450
ROTHWELL, WILLIAM. 1968. 'The Teaching of French in Medieval England', *Modern Language Review*, 63: 37–46
——. 2001A. 'English and French after 1362', *English Studies*, 82: 539–59
——. 2001B. 'Stratford Atte Bowe Re-Visited', *Chaucer Review*, 36: 184–207
——. 2001C. 'The Teaching and Learning French in Later Medieval England', *Zeitschrift für französische Sprache und Literatur*, 111: 1–18
STEIN, GABRIELE. 1997. *John Palsgrave as Renaissance Linguist: A Pioneer in Vernacular Language Description* (Oxford: Oxford University Press)
Short-Title Catalogue of English Books, 1475–1640. 1976–91. Ed. by Alfred W. Pollard and Gilbert R. Redgrave, 2nd edn, rev. by W. A. Jackson, F. S. Ferguson and Katharina F. Pantzer, 3 vols (London: The Bibliographical Society)
WILLIAMS, DEANNE. 2000. 'Mary Tudor's French Tutors: Renaissance Dictionaries and the Language of Love', *Dictionaries*, 21: 37–50
WOGAN-BROWNE, JOCELYN. 2015. '"Invisible Archives?" Later Medieval French in England', *Speculum*, 90: 653–73
——, et al. 2009. *Language and Culture in Medieval Britain: The French of England, c.1100–c.1500* (Woodbridge: York Medieval Press)

Notes to Chapter 2

1. The early printed books discussed in this essay are cited by signature and (where given) section number; any abbreviation marks in the original texts have been silently expanded. The *English Short Title Catalogue* (*ESTC*) citation numbers for these works are given within parentheses. While the *ESTC* makes a wealth of bibliographic information freely available online, the older *Short Title Catalogue* (*STC*) numbers are needed to call up facsimile images at Early English Books Online (EEBO), from where most of the primary texts have been cited. For ease of reference, ESTC numbers are supplemented by STC numbers in the list of works cited.
2. While, as Besse (2014) points out, French language education in the Middle Ages has been largely ignored in the publications of the Société Internationale pour l'Histoire du Français Langue Étrangère ou Seconde (SIHFLES), the bibliography is nonetheless substantial. Beginning researchers can consult two studies by Rothwell (1968, 2001c) as well as the surveys of the extant French teaching and reference materials by Kristol (1990, 2001b) and Dean and Boulton (1999: 157–78). Readers with an interest in the longer *durée* can consult Kibbee's history of early French teaching in England (1991). Most recently, see the revisionist account by Ingham (2015).
3. On Palsgrave's biography, see Stein (1997: 1–36). In her reassessment of princely education in early modern England, Aysha Pollnitz suggests that Palsgrave's proposal of a key to idiomatic French commonplaces in the third book of the *Esclarcissement* is a direct tribute to Erasmus's *Adagia* whereby the Englishman 'extended Erasmus' pedagogical method to the French tongue [...]. Palsgrave's pedagogical compass', Pollnitz concludes, 'pointed straight to Rotterdam' (2015: 95–96).
4. In her monograph on Oxford, Magdalen College MS 188, Nissille provides a detailed description of the book accompanied by several colour images of it (2014: 96–130). Nissille includes a transcription of the trilingual *Somme le roi* as an appendix to her study (2014: 305–492) and it is from this transcription that the text is cited below by folio number. Nissille's expansion of the abbreviation marks in the manuscript has been silently adopted.
5. On the contents, audiences, text, and manuscript tradition of the *Somme le roi*, see Brayer and Leurquin-Labie's Introduction to their edition of the work (2008: 7–89).
6. Kristol went on to develop a more detailed account of the Magdalen translator's handling of *en* (2001a: 156–59). Nissille (2014: 198–210) also provides extensive accounts of the Magdalen translator's treatment of negation and the indefinite pronoun.
7. Compare the recent edition of a group of late-medieval English school notebooks by Nicholas

Orme (2013), which usefully highlights the importance played by the translation of *vulgaria* in the instruction of Latin from the beginning of the fifteenth century.

8. Rothwell has edited both these works (2005, 2009). On the English glosses in the extant copies of the *Tretiz*, see further Knox (2013).
9. On the distinction between content and language driven instruction, see further Met (1998). I am grateful to my colleague at the University of Fribourg, Raphael Berthele, for pointing out this reference to me, and for offering helpful feedback on an early draft of this paper.
10. Britnell moderates Rothwell's claims regarding the prevalence of French among urban records, claiming that the use of the language in such contexts 'peaked around 1350–1415' (2009: 89).
11. All translations into English in this chapter are my own.
12. On the patriotic arithmetic in this passage, see Kristol's note (1995: 93).
13. As Merrilees points out (1985: 109), when the explanations given in the *Donait* become more complex, the dialogue established at the work's opening breaks down. Dictation probably played a part in the reception of the work.
14. Oxford, All Souls College 182 has been described and partially edited by Legge (1941). The manuscript offers an interesting parallel to Magdalen College MS 188 insofar as Legge suggests that it anthologizes French teaching and reference works with a view to facilitating its owner's pursuit of his professional clerical activities (1941: ix–xxi).
15. Cannon's claim (2015: 649) that 'Latin was the language every [English] reader of French could be assumed to know well' is not supported by the reports of medieval French teachers, who complain about their students' imperfect grasp of the classical language. Thus Richardson (1942: 335) cites one of Thomas Sampson's treatises on composition in which the author explains that though the text types he will treat are conventionally written in Latin, he will write his preface in French 'a cause qu je [...] ay conceu qe plousours enfantz sont si tenuement lettrez' [because I have observed that many children have such slight Latin], acting in the belief that his schoolboys 'purront le pluys legerement entendre les reulez en frauncys q'en latyn' [will be more easily able to understand the rules in French than in Latin]. French is the language of approach to Latin in this instance, not vice versa.
16. In the introduction to the *Donait,* Barton calls himself an 'escolier de Paris, nee et nourie toutez voiez d'Engleterre en la conté de Cestre' [scholar of Paris, born and brought up nevertheless in the county of Chester] (Colombat 2014: 110). On the various locations of medieval English business education, which most likely always contained an element of French training, see Orme (2006: 68–73).
17. Deanne Williams (2000) suggests that when he dedicated his work to Henry VIII, Palsgrave was offering the king an opportunity to parallel the military dominance over the French that he hoped to achieve on the battlefield with a symbolic dominance of their language. In the Introduction to the *Esclarcissement*, Palsgrave describes both his attempt to bring the language under 'rules certayn & precepts grammaticall' at the same time as he repeats Geoffroy Tory's lamentation that no Frenchman had achieved the same purpose (sig. [A3]^v).
18. One exception is Pierre Valence, who, in defence of the English translation he includes as part of his *Introductions in frensshe* ([London 1528]) asserts that the English version has been included 'for better / and more euydently [to] shewe the dyuersite of one tongue to the other / & torne worde for worde / and lyne for lyne / for to be to yonge chyldren more easy / and lyght' (sig. [A3]^v). Valence closes his brief text with a nod to the *Esclarcissement*: he suggests that his readers will be able to do without the vocabulary that he would have liked to add to his work since the 'lucubracyons / & werkes of mayster pollygraue' are soon to come to light (sig. [Q3]^v). The *Introductions in frensshe* is not listed in the ESTC or the STC. It is cited here from the facsimile edition by Alston (1967).

CHAPTER 3

❖

Teaching Agreement: A Case Study in the Language Pedagogy of Two Humanist Treatises on Syntax from Early Modern England

Anneli Luhtala

This chapter explores the pedagogical ideas in two sixteenth-century treatises on Latin syntax associated directly or indirectly with the circle of the English Humanist William Lily. In particular, I analyse how these texts — written at a time when grammarians were turning their attention to matters of syntax more than ever before — describe the fundamental syntactical phenomena that they call 'the three concords' (i.e. agreement). The analysis shows both the impact of new Humanist educational ideas on the one hand, and the lasting influence of the medieval 'scholastic' Latin grammars on the other, as well as differentiation in the complexity of explanation depending on the level of instruction.

Introduction

In this article I will discuss two Humanist treatises on Latin syntax, produced in England in the early sixteenth century, both of which are directly or indirectly associated with the circle of the English Humanist William Lily. After briefly introducing these treatises, I will compare how each of them describes what they call 'the three concords', which belong to the core of their syntactical doctrine. The results of this comparison will then be related to the medieval tradition of Latin grammars on the one hand and to Humanist educational ideas on the other. The comparison of these treatises will also permit us to catch glimpses of Latin teaching at different levels of instruction.

Syntactical theory was heavily developed during the Middle Ages and it was then that a section on syntax began to be integrated even into pedagogical grammars for the first time (Luhtala 2013a: 351–53). In Antiquity the study of syntax had belonged to a more advanced level of study, and the late-antique *Donatus minor*, which became the canonical textbook in the Middle Ages, did not have a section on syntax. The medieval Donatuses began to be accompanied by short treatises consisting of syntactical rules and often bearing the title 'Rules' (*Regulae*). Snippets of syntactical doctrine were occasionally integrated even into the discussions on the parts of speech; this is also the case with the English adaptations of Donatus's manual, known as the *Accedence*, of which several versions circulated in the fifteenth century. The present study will show how closely the Humanist treatises follow the inherited medieval works, while simultaneously modifying their doctrine in accordance with Humanist educational ideals.

Two Treatises on Syntax from the Circle of William Lily

The more famous of the two treatises to be scrutinized below is the so-called Lily's grammar, also known as 'Lily & Colet', or 'the King's grammar'; its earliest extant copy bears the title *An Introduction of the Eyght partes of speche*, and I will refer to this work below as the *Introduction*. This grammar, compiled *c.* 1540,[1] was authorized by Henry VIII and dominated the teaching of Latin for more than three centuries as an obligatory textbook in English schools.[2] Its traditional association with William Lily (and John Colet) rests on the erroneous assumption that the authorized grammar was the outcome of a series of revisions made to the grammatical works of these two Humanist scholars, namely Colet's *Aeditio* (1509), a short treatise on Latin accidence in English, and William Lily's *Rudimenta grammatices*, an elementary book on Latin syntax in English, compiled *c.* 1509, which circulated independently and jointly with Colet's *Aeditio*. However, the *Introduction* is in fact the result of the work of a committee commissioned by Henry VIII some twenty years after their death. According to a recent study by Hedwig Gwosdek, the grammatical works of Lily and Colet were important sources for the *Introduction* (Gwosdek 2013: 100, 104), which is more properly regarded as a new compilation, epitomizing the tradition of Latin grammars written in English going back at least to *c.* 1400.[3] In my study I will use Gwosdek's edition of its first extant copy, preserved in the British Library, C.21.b.4., dated 1542.[4]

The same volume also contains a more advanced Latin grammar, entitled *Brevissima institutio seu ratio Grammatices Cognoscendae*.[5] Unlike the *Introduction*, the *Brevissima institutio* has drawn hardly any scholarly attention, nor is there a modern edition of it. Both grammars were granted a royal monopoly by Edward IV and they were normally printed together. I will quote from the first extant copy of this book preserved in the same volume in the British Library, C.21.b.4.

The Structure of the Syntactical Treatises

These treatises are complete grammars, dealing first with the parts of speech followed by a section on syntax. I will now describe the structure of the syntactic sections in these works briefly. In the late Middle Ages and early modern times it was customary to cast syntactical treatises in the form of rules that discuss the construction of each part of speech in turn, starting with the declinable parts of speech. The two treatises to be compared here adhere to this approach, but their order of treatment differs in that the *Introduction* starts from the construction of the verb, whereas the *Brevissima Institutio* starts from the noun.

In these treatises a short account of the 'three concords' precedes the treatment of the construction of the individual parts of speech. According to the *Introduction*, these are the only concords that the Latin language exhibits:

> In order to properly join words in a construction, it must be understood that the Latin language has three concords. The first of them is the agreement between the noun and the adjective, the second that between the noun and the main verb, and the third that between the relative pronoun and its antecedent.[6]

This statement is followed by a pedagogical rule advising the pupil how to proceed when he has to translate an English sentence into Latin: 'Look out for the principal verb [...] and when you have found it, ask the question "Who?" or "What?", and the word that answers this question will be the nominative case of the verb' (Gwosdek 2013: 192). Asking questions like this was a common pedagogical device in early modern grammars; here it is used to single out what the medieval scholars would have called the 'subject' (*suppositum*) and 'predicate' (*appositum*).

In the Middle Ages it was customary to quote a definition of the sentence at the beginning of a syntactical treatise, but none of the syntactical treatises under scrutiny does so,[7] and only the *Brevissima Institutio* defines syntax: 'Syntax is a due composition and combination of the parts of speech, in accordance with the orderly basis of grammar'. The orderly or rational basis (*ratio*) is explained as consisting in the usage of the most respected old authorities both in speech and writing.[8] This is in accordance with the educational ideas of the Humanists, who favoured the use of classical literature as a source of grammatical examples.

The Three Concords

The first concord: the subject/predicate relation

The first of the concords deals with the relationship between a noun and a verb in the nucleus of a simple sentence. In the *Introduction*, the first rule of concord is as follows: 'A verbe personall agreeth with his nomynatyue case, in number and person, e.g. "The master redeth and ye regard not", *Praeceptor legit, uos uero negligitis*' (Gwosdek 2013: 192). English is used as the medium of instruction and the examples are translated into English. The examples are simple, often drawn from the school environment, and some of them have a moral content. The technical terms used in describing the nucleus of a sentence are 'the nominative case' and 'personal verb'. (The term 'principal verb' was used above.) The treatise uses throughout the same term, 'to agree', for concord; the medieval Latin verbs used for concord are *consentire* and *concordare*.

Two further observations follow. The first person is said to be 'worthier' than the second and the second worthier than the third. This idea serves to explain the concord of person when various nominative cases in the singular are associated with a verb in the plural; the verb will agree with the nominative of the most worthy person: for instance, 'I and thou be in sauegarde' ('ego et tu sumus in tuto', where *sumus* is the first person plural 'we are') and 'Thou and thy father are in ieoperdie' ('tu et pater periclitamini', where the verb *periclitamini* is the second person plural) and so on. The other observation concerns the concord of number: when a verb comes between two nominative cases of different numbers, the verb may agree with either of them, for instance, 'The fallings out of lovers is a renewyng of love' ('Amantium irae amoris redintegratio est')[9] and 'For what remayneth savyng [i.e. except for] onely prayers' ('Quid enim nisi vota supersunt?')[10] (Gwosdek 2013: 192).

In the more advanced *Brevissima Institutio* Latin is used as the medium of instruction, and the examples are drawn from classical literature:

> Concordantia nominativi et verbi Verbum personale cohaeret cum nominativo, numero et persona, ut *numquam fera est ad bonos mores via. Fortuna umquam perpetuo est bona.* (Niiv)
>
> [Concord of the nominative and the verb. A personal verb agrees with the nominative in number and person, as in 'The road to good manners is never savage' and 'Fortune is never continuously good'.]

The examples, which have a clear moral content, are not translated into English. The same tools are used for describing the basic sentence as in the more elementary grammar: the nominative case and the personal verb. Here the term *cohaeret* stands for agreement, but the author strives to use different terms for the same concept, probably for stylistic reasons.

Consistent with its nature as a more advanced work, the *Brevissima Institutio* proceeds to offer much more information on special cases than was given in the *Introduction*. The first instance is present in the *Introduction*, namely that the nominatives in the first and second persons are overtly expressed only for the sake of emphasis or in order to distinguish persons. The *Brevissima Institutio* further lists such expressions as *fertur, dicunt, ferunt, aiunt, praedicant, clamitant*,[11] which have a nominative implied in them, and points out that the nominative position can even be occupied by an infinitive, as in 'mentiri non est meum' [It is not my habit to lie].[12] The final two observations concern quite rare and difficult phenomena: the nominative position can be occupied even by a complex clause, as in Ovid's 'Adde quod ingenuas didicisse fideliter artes emollit mores, nec finit esse feros' [Add the fact that to have studied faithfully the liberal arts softens behaviour, not allowing it to be savage];[13] or by an adverb associated with a genitive case, e.g.: 'Partim virorum occiderunt in bello' [Part of the men were killed in war], 'partim signorum sunt combusta' [Part of the standards were burnt].[14]

Two exceptions (as they are labelled) follow, both of which are also discussed in the *Introduction*. The first concerns the embedded construction known as the 'accusative with infinitive', which can be resolved into a subordinate clause, initiated with the explicative conjunctions *quod* or *ut* (that, such that). The examples represent verbs of emotion (*gaudeo*) and will (*volo*): 'Tu rediisse incolumem, gaudeo = Quod tu rediisti incolumis, gaudeo' [I am glad that you have returned safe]. 'Te fabulam agere volo' [I want you to play a part] is turned into 'Ut tu fabulam agas, volo'. This specimen of indirect discourse is discussed in the context of relative pronouns in the *Introduction*. Another observation follows, concerning an instance in which a verb is associated with two nominatives of different numbers — an issue that was discussed in the *Introduction* using the same example ('Amantium irae amoris redintegratio est').

The second exception has to do with the impersonal verbs, which are not preceded by a nominative case, as in 'taedet me vitae' [I am bored with life], where the accusative *me* stands for 'I'. The author promises to touch upon the impersonal verbs again later on. It is further stated that a singular noun indicating a large number (that is, collective nouns, such as 'part') can at times be associated with a verb in the plural: 'Pars abiere' [A part were leaving], where *abiere* = *abierunt* is third person plural; or 'Uterque deluduntur dolis' [Each were deluded by plots], where *delunduntur* is third person plural.

Concord between an Adjective and its Headword

The second concord dealing with the relationship between an adjective and a noun is described in the *Introduction* as follows:

> When ye have an adjective, aske this question, who or what, and that that answereth to the question, shall be the substantive. The nowne adjectyve, *agreeth* with his substantive, in case, gender, number, as 'A sure frende is tried in a doubtfull matter' *Amicus certus in re incerta cernitur*. Lykewyse particyples and pronownes be ioyned with substantyues, as 'A manne armed', *Homo armatus*, 'a fielde to be tylled', *ager colendus*, 'this manne', *hic vir*, 'it is my master' *meus herus est*. (Gwosdek 2013: 192–93)

Questions are asked in order to identify the adjective and its headword. The rule primarily concerns the adjective (exemplified by *certus*), but immediately after it is noted that the position of the adjective can also be occupied by a pronoun or a participle, and examples are given of these different categories respectively: *armatus* is a participle; *colendus* is a gerundive/participle; *hic* and *meus* are pronouns. The examples are translated into English and the same verb, 'to agree', is used consistently for concord.

This rule is accompanied by one further observation only, concerning the concord of gender. According to a hierarchy of genders, the masculine is 'worthier' than the feminine and the feminine worthier than the neuter. When many nouns in the singular are joined to an adjective in the plural, the adjective will agree with the noun of the worthiest gender, the masculine: 'Rex et regina beati' [The king and the queen blessed].

In the *Brevissima institutio* Latin literary examples are used, as usual, and a different term is used for agreement, *consentit*. The rule is first stated as concerning adjectives, but immediately after it is expanded to involve pronouns and participles. As a special case, it is stated that a 'sentence' can replace the noun, as in 'Audito regem Doroborniam proficisci' [Having heard that the king has left for Dorobornia]. This last example is a difficult one. *Audito* is what we understand as an ablative absolute, into which an accusative with an infinitive is integrated. This latter structure is probably what is meant by 'sentence' (*oratio*) here, and it replaces the headword (either a noun or a pronoun) in the ablative absolute construction, which normally consists of two parts (such as *hoc audito* [with this having been heard]):

Concordantia substantivi et adiectivi. Adiectivum cum substantivo genere, numero et casu *consentit*, ut *rara avis in terris, nigroque simillima cygno*. Ad eundem modum participia et pronomina substantivis adnectuntur, ut, *donec eris faelix, multos numerabis amicos. Non hoc primum pectora vulnus mea senserunt, graviora tuli*. Aliquando oratio supplet locum substantivi, ut *Audito regem Doroborniam proficisci*. (Niii[r])

[Concord of substantive and adjective. The adjective agrees with the substantive in gender, number and case, for instance: 'A rare bird in the lands, and very similar to the black swan' (Juvenal). In the same way participles and pronouns are associated with substantives, for instance: 'As long as you are happy, you will have many friends' (Ovid): 'My breast was not conscious of this first wound, for I have endured still greater' (Seneca). Sometimes a sentence can occupy the position of the substantive, for instance, 'Having heard that the king was going to Dorobornia'.][15]

Concord between a Relative Pronoun and its Antecedent

When describing the third concord, concerning the relative pronoun and its antecedent, the *Introduction* again resorts to the method of asking questions, by means of which the antecedent is identified. Then the concept of antecedent is explained:

> The thirde concorde. Whan ye have a relatyve, aske this question, who or what, and that that answereth to this question, shall be the antecedente, whiche is a woorde that goeth before the relative, and is rehearsed again of the relative. The relatyve agreeth with his antecedente, in gender, number, and person, e.g. 'that manne is wyse that speaketh fewe', *vir sapit qui pauca loquitur*. (Gwosdek 2013: 193)

As usual, special cases of concord follow. With reference to the hierarchy of genders, it is stated that when many antecedents in the singular are joined, the relative pronoun will be plural but will agree in gender with the antecedent of the 'worthiest' gender. When inanimate things of neuter and feminine gender are involved, as in 'The rule and dignitie whiche thou haste requyred' (*Imperium* [neuter] *et dignitas* [fem.] *quae* [neuter] *petijsti*), the worthiest gender is neuter. The neuter gender will be preferred even when inanimate objects are involved none of which is of neuter gender: 'The bowe and arowes which thou hast broken' (*Arcus* [m.] *et calami* [m.] *quae* [neuter] *fregisti*).

The *Brevissima institutio* fails to offer any way of identifying or explaining the antecedent. The author may have assumed that the pupil had already learnt the basics of this phenomenon at a more elementary level. Now the medieval verb *concordare* is used for concord:

> Concordantia relativi et antecedentis. Relativum cum antecedente concordat genere, numero, et persona, ut *vir bonus est quis? Qui consulta patrum, qui leges iuraque servat*. (Niii[r-v])

[Concord of the relative (pronoun) and its antecedent. The relative pronoun agrees with its antecedent in gender, number and person, e.g. 'Who is to be called a good man? The one who observes the decrees of the fathers, and who maintains the statutes and laws'.]

The rule is expanded with special cases (which are not organized under any subtitles, such as 'Appendices' or 'Exceptions'). A sentence may replace the antecedent, as in 'In tempore veni, quod omnium rerum est primum' [I came in time, which is the most important thing] (Terence).[16] When the antecedents are of different genders, the relative sometimes agrees with the first mentioned antecedent, for instance, in 'Propius a terra Iovis stella fertur, quae Phaeton dicitur' [Below this and nearer to the earth moves the star of Jupiter, called Phaethon] (Cicero); sometimes with the last-mentioned as in 'Est locus in carcere, quod Tullianum appellatur' [In the prison, there is a place called Tullianum] (Sallust). These examples must probably be understood so that the relative pronoun *quae* (fem.) agrees with *stella* ('star', fem.) rather than *Phaeton* (neuter) in the first sentence and *quod* (neuter) with *Tullianum* rather than *locus* ('place', m.) in the second; but it could also refer to *carcer* ('prison', neuter). Several examples are given of both instances.

Another rule (Niii^v) states that whenever no nominative is inserted between the relative and the verb (in the subordinate clause, *qui potuit*), the relative will be the nominative of the (principal) verb (= the subject of the main clause, *is*), as in 'Faelix [est is] qui potuit boni fontem visere lucidum' [Happy is he who has been able to gaze upon the clear font of goodness] (Boethius). Here the author explains that the relative pronoun may occur as the subject in the subordinate clause, but the analysis becomes awkward for two reasons. Firstly, when the subject function is absent, the 'nominative case' is used instead; and, secondly, because the author fails to draw a clear distinction between the main clause and the subordinate clause. Such a distinction was not part of established grammatical doctrine in early modern times, but the notion of the 'principal verb' was available in the *Introduction* and in the *Compendium totius grammaticae* of John Anwykyll, master of Magdalen College School, Oxford, *c.* 1481–88, who composed the first Humanist grammar in England in 1483 (Orme 1989: 16); Anwykyll also used the term *clausula principalis* for the main clause.[17]

The Medieval Origins of 'Three Concords' in Middle English and Latin Grammatical Manuscripts

I will now compare the above accounts of the three concords with the grammatical treatises composed in England in the fifteenth century before the Humanist reform. The majority of the syntactical treatises composed in England from the early fifteenth century on, such as the *Informacio* (later known as *Parvula*) and *Formula*, differ from the later Humanist treatises in the way they organize their teaching material.[18] Rather than listing rules accompanied by examples, the teaching of Latin took the form of analysing simple sentences by asking questions by which the grammatical rules were illustrated, after which the rule is stated.[19] Some treatises start by quoting a sentence in Latin, which is then analysed step by step, while others proceed from an English sentence, which is translated into Latin after a minute grammatical analysis.

One of the *Formula* texts opens with a discussion of the subject/predicate relation, whereby a Latin sentence 'Ego sum creatura Dei' is first quoted, after which it is explained that the verb *sum* is singular number and the first person just like the nominative case *ego*. Then the rule states that every verb must agree with its nominative in two features: number and person. The rule is then supported by two mnemonic verses, using the Scholastic terminology of subject (*suppositum*):

> *Ego sum creatura Dei*. This verbe *sum* [i]s the syngler nombyr and the fyrst person, for so is his nominatyfe case *ego*; and every verbe schall accord with his nominatyf case in ij, in number and yn person.
> Verbum supposito dic concordare duobus,
> Persona, numero; sic tradit regula nobis. (ed. Thomson 1984: 148)

After analysing four additional examples of the agreement between a nominative and a verb, the treatise moves on to deal with the concord between an adjective and its headword, and the relative pronoun and its antecedent, then instances of government and so forth.

The approach of a fairly advanced anonymous treatise from the first half (probably the second quarter) of the fifteenth century, labelled *EE* in Thomson's edition (1984: 178–85),[20] lends itself better to comparison with the Humanist treatises discussed above because it proceeds by listing rules and giving examples.[21] After introducing a rule of thumb for turning English sentences into Latin similar to the one we found in the *Introduction*, the treatise discusses the 'four concords' using the catechetical method. The four concords include, in addition to the above three, the concord between partitive, distributive and superlative nouns and the genitive. Several other treatises deal with the same rules as 'five concords', regarding the construction of the superlative as a distinct type:[22]

> How many acordys has thou in grammer? Foure. On bytwene the nominatif case and the verbe, the seconde bytwene the adiectyf and the substantyf. The thrydde bytwene the relatyf and the antecedent, the fourthe bytwene the noune partytyf, the noune distributyf, the partytyf, the noune of superlatif degre and the genityf case that folweth.

When discussing examples of concord, the Middle English text first quotes a regular instance, then proceeds to introduce special cases, making heavy use of technical terms. Each special type of concord between the subject and predicate bears a label of its own (evocation, apposition, conception and collection), drawn from the discussions on the figures of speech:[23]

> In how many ways does the nominative agree with the verb? In two, number and person, as 'My comrade reads his books', *Socius meus legit suos libros*. In how many ways can this take place? In four: by evocation, as 'I William am your friend', *Ego Willelmus sum vester amicus*; by apposition, as 'The city of London is full of merchandise', *Civitas Londonie est plena mercibus*; by conception, as 'People are running hurrying to the church', *Populus currunt festinantes ad ecclesiam*; by collection, as 'A large and well equipped company of knights are going from Anglia against the pagans', *Vadunt grandis turma militum bene apparati ab Anglia in paganam*.[24]

Evocation is at issue when the first person pronoun *ego* is associated with *Willelmus*, a noun in the third person, and the verb *sum* [am] agrees with *ego*.

Apposition takes place when the verb *est* joins *civitas* [city, f.] with the adjective *plena* [full, f.], agreeing with it. The figure of conception associates a singular collective noun *populus* [people] with a predicate verb in the plural *currunt* [run], and collection involves agreement of the plural verb *vadunt* [go] not with the subject of the sentence, which is *turma*, a collective noun in the singular, but with *militum*, a partitive genitive in the plural.

The two Middle English texts discussed above employ many medieval technical terms, such as the subject/predicate distinction, which no longer appear in the authorized textbooks as a result of the Humanist reform. The other versions of the *Formula* and *Informacio* texts additionally include such medieval terms as *regimen* [government], *verbum substantivum* [substantival verb], *ex vi transicionis personalis* [by the force of the transition of person], and the division of relative pronouns into *relatio simplex et personalis* [simple and personal relation] (Thomson 1984: 84 and 167–68). However, when we compare these texts with the works composed by John Leylond, the most famous grammar teacher of the early fifteenth century, we notice that the tools of analysis employed by Leylond are even more distinctly Scholastic than those of the mid-fifteenth-century teachers. In his treatise on government (*De regimine casuum*), the subject/predicate distinction is presented as an instance of government (*regimen*) rather than concord, where the verb is said to govern the nominative in seven distinct ways, the first of which is 'by the force of person':[25]

> Quot modis regitur nominativus supponens? Dicendum quod septem modis. Quibus: Uno modo ex vi persone, ut ego lego. Regula est omne verbum personale modi finiti exigit nominativum casum sibi supponentem (Cambridge University Library, MS Hh.i.5., fol. 131^r)
>
> [In how many ways is the nominative governed in the subject position? In seven ways. Which? In one way by the force of person, as *ego lego*. The rule states that every personal verb in the finite mood demands a nominative case as its subject.]

The *Informacio* was, according to Thomson, composed by John Leylond (see n. 18). However, Leylond's treatise on government made much heavier use of medieval technical vocabulary than the popular versions of the *Informacio* and *Formula* texts from the mid- and late-fifteenth century. The complex medieval system in which the verb was said to govern its subject in seven different ways had been criticized by Thomas of Hanney, who compiled a comprehensive Latin grammar (*Memoriale Juniorum*) in 1313; and we know that John Leylond had carried out a reform whose aim was to simplify the tools of grammatical analysis. This simplification, omitting several more theoretical parts of the doctrine, was viewed in the twentieth century as representing 'a debasement' of teaching by Hunt (1964: 181–84). Thomson regarded this reform more positively as being 'more adequate to the needs of schoolboys than the earlier, compendious, grammatical *summae*' and as representing 'a more appropriate and practical approach to teaching' (Thomson 1983: 229).

According to Thomson, 'the five concords' of the pre-Humanist treatises derive from John Leylond's *De concordantiis gramatice* (1984: 236).[26] Leylond devotes twenty-two lines to describing the five concords and two hundred lines to explaining different exceptions to the rules (Thomson 1979: 42). The first rule of concord uses the Scholastic term of *supponens* for the subject in describing the nucleus of a sentence:

> Quot sunt concordancie in grammatica? Dicendum quod sunt 5, quarum prima est hec, scilicet inter nominativum supponentem et verbum cui fit supposicio. Secunda est inter adiectivum et suum substantivum. Tercia est inter relativum et suum antecedens. Quarta est inter nomen partitivum et genitivum sequentem. Quinta est inter superlativum gradum et genitivum sequentem.
>
> [How many concords does grammar have? It must be said that there are five, the first of which is between the nominative subject and the verb in which the supposition takes place. The second is between the adjective and its substantive; the third between the relative and its antecedent; the fourth between the partitive noun and the following genitive; the fifth between the superlative and the following genitive.]

The five concords are copied out at the end of several Middle English *Accedence* texts in the middle of the fifteenth century, accompanied by a short rule of thumb advising how to turn English sentences into Latin. The Scholastic terms of subject and predicate are eliminated from the rules of concord and the treatises ignore Leylond's extensive account of the special cases, the sole exception being the treatise bearing the title *EE*, discussed above.[27] The *Informacio* and *Formula* texts generally use fewer Scholastic terms than Leylond's treatises. These facts suggest to me that there was an ongoing process of simplification of grammatical exposition throughout the fifteenth century rather than one single reform carried out by John Leylond.

The fact that the five rules of concord were integrated into the *Accedence* treatises, which do not otherwise deal with syntax, suggests to me that they were regarded as the most fundamental doctrine for construing Latin sentences and possibly the minimum that any student of Latin grammar ought to know. It is not clear to me who first restricted the number of concord rules to three and eliminated the Scholastic terms from them.[28] It may be significant that 'the three concords' (and no more) occur in the *Regule* of Guarino Veronese, which is generally regarded as the first Humanist grammar. The *Regule*, compiled *c.* 1414–18, is a very simple textbook whose essential characteristic is its brevity. While simplifying the inherited syntactical doctrine, Guarino removed the distinctly Scholastic terminology, including the subject/predicate distinction, from the rules.[29] The three concords subsequently occur in the works of the Italian Humanists Nicolaus Perottus (1429–1480), Sulpitius Verulanus (*c.* 1440–1506) and Aldus Manutius (*c.* 1450–1515), divested of Scholastic terminology (Luhtala 2014: 62).[30] How is it possible that the three concords established themselves as standard doctrine in the English and Italian grammatical traditions, which have otherwise organized their syntactical theories quite differently?

One possible answer lies in a popular grammatical treatise of the Latin tradition, entitled *Regule*, in which the same three concords are listed as the three first rules. I quote from an elementary text, entitled the *Generic Rules of Concord for Children* (*Generales regulae congruitatum puerorum*), consisting of eight rules, of which six are devoted to various kinds of concords. It is contained in a volume consisting of short grammatical treatises that probably represent the entire curriculum of grammatical instruction in the late Middle Ages. This contains Donatus's *Ars minor*; a popular parsing grammar, known as *Remigius* or *Dominus que pars*; and then various treatises containing syntactical and other rules intended for both intermediary and advanced levels of study.[31] Since five of the Middle English grammatical manuscripts also contain treatises from this tradition (Bland 1991: 42; see also Orme 2013: 71 and 148), it may be the ultimate source of the three concords in both English and Italian traditions of syntax.

The concise rules of concord in the *Regule* treatises are very similar to what we find in the three concords of the authorized grammars. I quote only the second rule, dealing with the subject/predicate distinction, in which the Scholastic terms *suppositum* and *appositum* are used.

> Secunda regula congruitatum grammaticalium est ista, quod suppositum et appositum debent convenire in numero persona et rectitudine casus, ut 'Sortes currit', 'Deus regnat'. Unde? Inter appositum et suppositum tria convenientia quero que sunt persona numerus casus habitudo (F 80).

> [The second rule of grammatical concords is that the subject and predicate must agree in number, person and correct case, e.g. 'Socrates is running', 'God reigns'. Why? I look for three features agreeing with the predicate, which are person, number, case and habitude.]

It is not immediately clear by which route the three concords entered the authorized textbooks. It is possible that one of the English Humanists reduced the five concords to three independently, or under the influence of the Italian Humanists whose treatises circulated in England in the late fifteenth century. Perottus's *Rudimenta grammatices* (1473), in which the three concords occupy a central position, was praised in the *Compendium Totius Grammaticae* of John Anwykyll, but none of the concords occurs in Anwykyll's syntactical theory, which is based on the Italian tradition.[32] The authority of Perottus or some other Italian Humanist may have provided a stimulus for reducing the five concords to three. Under the Humanist influence the distinctly Scholastic terms 'subject' and 'predicate', which surface in some versions of the *Formula* and *Informacio* and continued to be used in John Anwykyll's *Compendium*, were finally abolished.

Conclusion

One of the most prominent features of the Humanist reform was a simplification of grammar, and its essence was captured by Battista Guarino, who recommended the use of his father's *Regule*, although there were other works available stating the same rules: 'It is possible to learn rules from many existing works, but the compendium of my excellent father has proved most helpful to me, since there you can find everything relevant — and nothing superfluous — to the composition of correct sentences' (*A Program of Teaching and Learning*, ed. by Kallendorf; my translation). The Humanists criticized the medieval tools of description as too analytical for young pupils, which is why they eliminated the distinctly Scholastic terminology from their manuals. In Antiquity and the Middle Ages, by contrast, no clear distinction had been drawn between the ways in which one would teach a child as opposed to an adult.

The textbooks of the Italian Humanists reached England in the latter half of the fifteenth century, but this reform had not yet been properly carried out in the first Humanist grammar, the *Compendium* of John Anwykyll: his grammar was neither short nor divested of Scholastic terms. According to Thomson (1984: xiv), 'innovation and continental influence only began to take a significant part in the elementary tradition in the next, sixteenth century, wave of development, represented by the work of Colet at St. Paul's School in London'. One of the reasons for the relatively late breakthrough of the Humanist pedagogical ideas in the teaching of Latin grammar in England may be that a simplification of medieval grammar, very similar to that promoted by the Humanist reform, had, as we have seen, already taken place in England earlier in the fifteenth century. (Whether this reform involved influence from Italian Humanism is a question that cannot be addressed here.) However, this earlier reform did not excise all Scholastic terms from grammatical exposition; for instance, the basic distinction between subject and predicate was maintained in several Middle English treatises.

The Humanists criticized not only the terms and concepts introduced by Scholasticism into grammatical analysis but also the use of technical terms in general, even those used by Donatus and Priscian, the favourite grammarians of the Humanists (Luhtala 2014: 60–61). The *Introduction* uses technical terms sparingly, while the more advanced *Brevissima Institutio* constantly seeks variation in their use; this latter tendency is also characteristic of the educational ideals of the Humanists. They abhorred the dry technical exposition of the medieval grammars, preferring stylistic variation, which led the author of the *Institutio brevissima* to choose a different term for concord each time and to introduce twenty-two terms for the government of the verb. This, I think, was hardly very pedagogical. Definitions — one of the cornerstones of ancient and medieval grammar — were another area where the Humanists tended to diverge from medieval practices. They either simplified the inherited definitions or did away with them altogether. To conclude, in spite of the hostility that several Humanists showed towards the medieval heritage, they could not avoid being heavily influenced by it, especially in the field of syntax.

Bibliography

Brevissima Institutio seu ratio grammatices cognoscende (London: Vuolfius, 1569)
BLAND, CYNTHIA RENÉE. 1991. *The Teaching of Grammar in Late Medieval England. An Edition, with Commentary, of Oxford, Lincoln College, MS Lat. 130.* (East Lansing: Colleagues Press)
CUMMINGS, BRIAN. 2002. *The Literary Culture of the Reformation: Grammar and Grace* (Oxford: Oxford University Press)
GUARINO, BATTISTA. 2002 [1459]. *A Program of Teaching and Learning*, in *Humanist Educational Treatises*, ed. and trans. by Craig W. Kallendorf (Cambridge, MA, and London: Harvard University Press, The I Tatti Renaissance Library), 260–309

Gwosdek, Hedwig. 2000. *A Checklist of Middle English Grammatical Manuscripts and Early Printed Grammars, c. 1400–1540*, The Henry Sweet Society Studies in the History of Linguistics, 6 (Münster: Nodus)

—— (ed. and intro). 2013. *Lily's Grammar of Latin in English. An Introduction of the Eyght Partes of Speche, and the Construction of the Same* (Oxford: Oxford University Press)

Hunt, Richard. 1964. 'Oxford Grammar Masters in the Middle Ages', in *Oxford Studies presented to Daniel Callus*, Oxford Historical Society, N.S., 14 (Oxford: Oxford Historical Society), 163–93

Luhtala, Anneli. 2013a. 'Pedagogical Grammars before the Eighteenth Century', in *The Oxford Handbook of the History of Linguistics*, ed. by Keith Allan (Oxford: Oxford University Press), 341–58

——.2013b. Kärnä, Aino, and Anneli Luhtala (eds), *Handbuch frühneuzeitlicher Grammatiken*, Editiones Electronicae Guelferbytanae (Wolfenbüttel: Herzog August Bibliothek) <http://diglib.hab.de/ebooks/ed000171/id/ebooks_ed000171_004/start.htm> [accessed 15 August 2015]

——. 2014. 'Scholastic Influence on Syntactical Theory in Pedagogical Grammars', *Beiträge zur Geschichte der Sprachwissenschaft*, 24: 51–70

Michael, Ian. 1970. *English Grammatical Categories and the Tradition to 1800* (Cambridge: Cambridge University Press)

Orme, Nicholas. 1989. *Education and Society in Medieval and Renaissance England* (London and Ronceverte, WV: Hambledon Press)

——. 2013. *English School Exercises, 1420–1530*, Studies and Texts, 181 (Toronto: Pontifical Institute of Mediaeval Studies)

Pinborg, Jan, and Erik Dal (eds). 1979. *Tre latinske grammatikker. Donatus, Fundamentum, Regulae* (Copenhagen: Det Kongelige Danske Videnskabernes Selskab)

Thomson, David. 1979. *A Descriptive Catalogue of Middle English Grammatical Texts* (New York and London: Garland)

——. 1983. 'The Oxford Grammar Masters Revisited', *Medieval Studies*, 45: 298–310

——. 1984. *An Edition of the Middle English Grammatical Texts* (New York and London: Garland)

Notes to Chapter 3

1. According to Gwosdek (2013: 18) this manual took shape about the year 1540.
2. For the impact of the Reformation on English literary culture, see Cummings (2002: 187–223).
3. In addition to John Colet's *Aeditio* and William Lily's *Rudimenta grammatices*, the following printed treatises exerted an influence on the *Introduction*: the three works attributed to John Stanbridge, the *Parvula, Accidence, Long Parvula*, and *Parvulorum Institutio*, Thomas Linacre's *Progymnasmata grammatices vulgaria* and his *Rudimenta grammatices* (Gwosdek 2013: 105).
4. This copy is a composite volume, consisting of three independent entities which make up the entire curriculum for learning Latin in a Christian context. It fails to mention the authorship of the two grammatical treatises contained in it. The first part of the volume consists of the Latin alphabet, the Lord's Prayer, the Ave Maria, the Creed, and the Ten Commandments in Latin and English. The second part contains *An Introduction of the Eyght partes of speche*, preceded by The Royal Proclamation by Henry VIII, and followed by Lily's and Erasmus's pedagogical texts on Christian education (e.g. *Carmen de moribus, Godly Lessons for Chyldren* and *Christiani hominis Institutum per Erasmum Roterodamum*).
5. 'Under King Edward VI (1547–1553), Henry VIII's son, the title of the English part was changed to *A Shorte Introduction of Grammar* and the Latin part, previously known as *Institutio Compendiaria Totius Grammaticae*, became *Brevissima Institutio seu ratio Grammatices Cognoscendae*' (Gwosdek 2013: 9).

6. I have modernized the English language of the two quotations in this passage.
7. 'Lily had ignored the sentence, presumably regarding it as a rhetorical or logical, not as a grammatical category' (Michael 1970: 479).
8. 'Est igitur syntaxis, debita partium orationis inter se compositio connexioque, iuxta rectam Grammatices rationem. Ea vero est, qua veterum probatissimi, tum in scribendo, tum in loquendo sunt usi' (Nii^v). The references to this book include the fascicule (N), the folio number (ii), r stands for the recto and v for the verso side of the folio.
9. In the Latin sentence *irae* is in the plural, 'the fallings out', and *redintegratio* [a renewing], in the singular, as is also the verb *est*.
10. The verb *supersunt* [remain], agrees with *vota* [prayers], rather than *quid*.
11. These verbs signify saying and are often used impersonally meaning 'it is said that'.
12. This sentence is ascribed to Plautus in the *Introduction*, but similar sentences occur in Lucilius and Seneca.
13. The nominative position (= the subject position) is occupied by the accusative and infinitive construction *ingenuas didicisse fideliter artes*.
14. Instead of the ordinary partitive genitive, in which the headword is a noun (*pars virorum* and *pars signorum*), these examples have an adverb 'partly' as the headword.
15. The first extant copy does not mention the authors of the classical examples, whereas many later editions do so. I have supplied them in my English translation.
16. The relative pronoun *quod* (neuter) refers to the sentence *In tempore veni* [I came in time].
17. The terms *clausula principalis* and *verbum principale* occur on page 93 of the *Compendium totius grammaticae* <http://diglib.hab.de/inkunabeln/p-337-4f-helmst-3s/start.htm>. For Anwykyll's grammar, written in Latin, see Luhtala 2013b <http://diglib.hab.de/ebooks/ed000171/id/ebooks_ed000171_004/start.htm >.
18. The *Informacio* is a syntactical treatise composed by John Leylond, one of the Oxford grammar masters, who taught c. 1401–28; the *Formula* is 'a revision of the *Informacio*, perhaps representing an attempt by John Cobbow or another of Leylond's pupils to produce a collected account of their master's teaching on the elements of syntax' (Thomson 1984: xii; see also Bland 1991: 96–107). Several versions of these treatises have been edited in Thomson (1984: 82–220).
19. Seventeen sentence collections containing school exercises have been edited by Orme (2013).
20. For this treatise, see also Bland 1991: 76–77 and Thomson 1979: 87.
21. According to Thomson, this treatise, preserved in Cambridge, Trinity College, MS O.5.4, fols 4^r and 6^v-7^v, is on a level above the rest of the syntactical treatises (1979: 88).
22. The five concords entitled *Of Concordes of Gramer* can be found in the following *Accedence* texts edited in Thomson 1984, dated in the mid-fifteenth century: A (p. 8), B (p. 15), C (pp. 30–31) and F (pp. 49–50).
23. From the twelfth century onwards, it was customary to draw a distinction between regular and figurative syntax (Luhtala 2014: 54).
24. I have modernized the language of this quotation and the subsequent translations of examples 'In how many maners schall the nominatyf case and the verbe acorde? In tweyne, in noumbre and persone, as "My fellow redyth hys bokes", *Socius meus legit suos libros*. In how many thyngyss may they be lette? By foure. By euocacion, as "I Wylyam am youre frende", *Ego Willelmus sum vester amicus*. By apposicion, as "The cyte of London is ful of merchendyse", *Civitas Londonie est plena mercibus*. By concepcion, as "The folk renneth swythe to churche", *Populus currunt festinantes ad ecclesiam*. By colleccyon, as "Ther gooth a grete company of knyghtes wel aparelled out of Englonde into hethenes", *Vadunt grandis turma militum bene apparati ab Anglia in paganam*'.
25. These terms occur, for instance, in the *Doctrinale* (1199) of Alexander of Villadei and in the *Catholicon* of John of Genoa (d. c. 1298), in which the verb was described as governing both the subject noun (*nominativus supponens*) preceding it and the object noun (*apponens*) after it.
26. It is odd that one and the same author, Leylond, should have described the relationship between the subject and the predicate in one of his treatises as an instance of concord and in another in terms of government.
27. However, it does not follow Leylond's *De concordantiis* very closely (Thomson 1979: 42).
28. A late copy (1534) of the *Parvulorum institutio* of John Stanbridge, the headmaster of Magdalen College School, Oxford, from 1488 to 1494, incorporated the 'three concords' into his

elementary syntax (see 50.25 in Gwosdek 2000: 108); here the pupil is advised to look at Whittington's *Syntaxis* or *Constructione* for further information on the concords; Robert Whittington was Stanbridge's pupil. This copy is in the University Library of Cambridge, Syn. 8.53.74. It is puzzling that the concords are absent from the facsimile edition of the *Parvulorum institutio ex stanbrigiana collectione (1526)* based on the original in the Bodleian library.
29. Guarino's grammar was not the first Italian grammar in which the Scholastic terms had been abandoned; a similar approach can be found in the *Summe* of Goro d'Arezzo a hundred years earlier.
30. The order of the concords is the same (nominative/verb, noun/adjective, relative/antecedent) in the works of Sulpitius and Aldus Manutius, whereas Perottus has followed the order of the medieval *Regule*, placing the concord between the noun and the adjective as the first. Quarino has the order nominative/verb, relative/antecedent, and noun/adjective.
31. This late-medieval book entitled *Tre latinske grammatikker* was printed by Gotfred af Ghemen in Copenhagen in 1493 and published in a facsimile edition in 1979.
32. Anwykyll based his syntactical rules on the *genus verbi*, as was customary in the Italian tradition (see Luhtala 2014: 63).

CHAPTER 4

The Use of Dialogues in Teaching Foreign Languages (Sixteenth Century): Circulations and Adaptations of Berlaimont's *Dictionarium* (1556) in Spain, the Netherlands, and England

Javier Villoria-Prieto and Javier Suso López

This chapter examines the transmission and adaptation, over a period of forty years, of dialogues from a common source, the *Dictionarium quator linguarum* (Leuven, 1556), attributed to Noël de Berlaimont. Such dialogues were a very popular tool in the teaching of vernacular languages from the Renaissance onwards, and were variously recycled and adapted across Europe for different languages and different audiences. By way of example, we discuss adaptations of Berlaimont's 1556 *Dictionarium* by three different authors which circulated in Spain, the Netherlands and England: the *Vocabulario* by Iaques de Liaño/Ledel (1565), the *Family Colloquy* (1568) and *La Guirlande des Jeunes Filles* (1580) by Gabriel Meurier; the *French Schoolemaister* (1573), the *French Littleton* (1576) and *Campo di Fior* (1583) by Claude de Sainliens (also known as Holyband). The case study — of just a small part of the reception of Berlaimont — demonstrates the importance of a pan-European approach to the history of language learning/teaching materials. Second, the comparison reveals cultural specificities and ideological representations that merit analysis if we are to write a socio-cultural history of language learning in Europe. Third, we find that the dialogues examined are best classified as eclectic in method, adapted to a wider variety of audiences wishing to learn modern languages. On the one hand, Sainliens's *Campo di Fior*, aimed at women without any Latin training, eliminates grammar and exemplifies a practical tendency in language learning; at the other extreme, the 'colloquium' model (exemplified by Liaño/Ledel, 1565, and others) catered to a learned and/or aristocratic, bilingual audience, with a focus on morals, good manners, and careful language typical of Latin teaching.

Dialogues in Language Teaching and Learning: A Brief Historical Perspective

Dialogues are part of a long tradition ('la forme dialoguée est sans doute aussi vieille que l'institution scolaire' (Holtz, 1981: 100)) which goes back in its written form to the *Hermeneumata Pseudo-Dositheana* at the beginning of the third century AD. They were copied again and again and were in use for teaching Latin all through the Middle Ages (Riché 1982: 417–26). These texts appeared in numerous versions, such as the *Colloquy* by Aelfric in the tenth century, or the *Liber Donati* by Kingsmill, in the fourteenth century. As Chevalier (1998) points out, this learning tool was also used for teaching French, not only around the linguistic borders of the north of France and Flanders, but also particularly in fourteenth- and fifteenth-century Britain. The reason is to be found in the bilingualism, not to say diglossia, that existed: nobles, jurists, merchants, administrators and *literati* used Latin and Anglo-Norman as H (High) language, while the rest of the population used Anglo-Saxon as L (Low) Language (see Ferguson 1959). French was used until the mid-fourteenth century in administration and justice, and was studied by the nobility as well as Latin (see Bibbesworth's treatise, *Femina, Manière de langage*, letter models, short grammatical treatises, etc., in Kibbee 1991: 74–92).[1]

As an example, the *Manière de langage* (edited in Britain in 1396)[2] is structured in the form of a journey of a young English nobleman and his squire, illustrating how to speak in the different everyday-life situations they will encounter (on waking, while dressing, on the road, at a hostel, courting a lady, dealing with merchants, and talking to children, etc.). This narrative procedure enables the author to gather the different sentence typologies to be used in the form of questions and answers and facilitates the inclusion of lists of thematic vocabulary:

> Et la dame de l'ostel vient avant, disant en ce maniere: 'mon sr, comment avez vous fait anuy?' *vel sic* : 'Coment vous avez vous portee anuyt ?' — Tres bien, dame, vostre mercy, mais je fu un poy malades, car j'avoi trop bu et (e)veillee anuyt. Janyn, baillez ça mon pigne, que m'amie me pourra pigner la teste; et comandez mon garçon qu'il fasse abruver mes chivalx, et puis les donne du fein et des aveines, et ordonnez que nous aions de bon poisson assés, comme des anguilles, lampreous, lampraes, samon fraisse et saleie; et aussi de carpes, bremes, roches, perches, soles plaiz [...]. (Meyer 1870 [1396]: 393)

This book is an example of the 'model conversation book, intended for the use of travellers, merchants, and others desiring a conversational and practical rather than a thorough and grammatical knowledge of French' (Lambley 1920: 35). The *Livre des Mestiers* (edited in Bruges, mid-fourteenth century) has a sentence structure ready to be used in bilingual form, French on the left and Dutch on the right (see Fig. 4.1).

The *Dialogues in French and English* (1480) and the *Book of Travellers* (around 1483) printed by W. Caxton adopt a presentation that imitates the *Livre des mestiers* (with English instead of Dutch) and the *Maniere de langage*. These dialogues adapt the 'conversation' topics to new learner groups.

Two factors influence the transformation of the book of dialogues throughout the sixteenth century. On the one hand, it must not be forgotten that the teaching of

Se vous bargingnies dras,	Of ghi dinghet lakene/
Si demandés : « Que faites vous	So vraegt: "Wat lovedi
L'aune de che drap,	"D'elne van desen lakene/
Le demi aune ou le quartier ? »	"De half elle of tvierendeel?"
[...]	[...]
Et dites en telle manière :	Ende segt in dusghedaner wisen:
— « Dame, que faites-vous	— Vrouwe/ hoe lovedi
L'aune de che drap	"D'elne van desen lakene/
Ou que donres l'aunes » ?	"Of hoe suldi gheven d'elle?"
— « Sire, raison ;	— Heere/ om redene;
Vous l'ares à boin markiet,	"Ghi sultse hebben goeden coep/
Voire pour catel. »	"Ja omme catel."

FIG. 4.1. *Livre des Mestiers*, ed. by Michelant, 1875 [fourteenth century]: 11

Latin was profoundly changed by Humanist pedagogues, who published many Latin conversation manuals, such as those by Erasmus (*Colloquia puerilia* (1516); *Familiarum colloquiorum formulae* (1518)), by L. Vives (*Linguae Latinae exercitation* (1539)), or by M. Cordier (*Colloquia scholastic* (1564)), to name but a few such authors. These books of Latin dialogues also influenced the teaching of vernacular languages, as they were re-published in bilingual versions in most European countries:

> Les sujets sont plus largement empruntés à la vie commune, mais les principes de composition sont très proches des colloques latins. Il se crée alors une vulgate des dialogues quelles qu'en soient la langue et la destination; on retrouve les mêmes thèmes de l'un à l'autre et parfois même des pans entiers de dialogues sont franchement copiés ou décalqués. (Chevalier 1998: 18–19)

A good example of this 'vulgate' version of these dialogues, as Chevalier puts it, is *A Very profitable book to learn English and Spanish* (1554), written to celebrate a historical event, the wedding of Queen Mary and Philip II:

> It contains dialogues, a vocabulary, and some religious material. While there is everyday information in the manual, it also addresses 'the maner of byenge and sellyng [. . .] the ways of callynge upon your debtors' and 'the maner of writing epistles and letters of obligations, solutiõs, and of bargains'. (Corrigan 2005: [n. pag.])

Kibbee, in his study on teaching French in Britain in the sixteenth century, similarly remarks:

> Les œuvres grammaticales de la première moitié du XVI siècle se divisent en deux groupes : (1) les grammaires proprement dites, destinées aux nobles ou aux riches bourgeois [...] (2) les petits manuels destinés aux marchands. [...] Suite à l'arrivée en Angleterre de nombreux réfugiés politiques et religieux, des écoles de français sont fondées [...]. Les professeurs de français [...] composaient des manuels qui combinent la qualité pratique des dialogues destinés aux marchands avec la description grammaticale. (Kibbee 1989: 55)

On the other hand, as Colombo Timelli (1998: 28) notes, dialogues are also present in bilingual and/or multilingual dictionaries. Such works are composed according to a common structure from which authors deviate in various ways: in some cases they add information; elsewhere they make adaptations or omissions (see Sánchez 1992: 18–23). A typical structure is:

— a glossary of usual words, ordered by topic (parts of the body, dress, weapons, food and meals, the weather...), numbers, days of the week, months, seasons, etc.
— dialogues (varying in number and length)
— letters and commercial documents
— prayers (Our Father, Hail Mary, Creed...)

As we shall see below, the *Dictionarium quator linguarum* (1556 and later editions) deserves special attention for the influence it had on later books of dialogues used for teaching languages. The first work of this series (a *Vocabulare*, by the Antwerp language teacher Noël de Berlaimont), contained only two languages (Dutch–French), and was published before 1527 — the title page of the 1527 edition states that it is a 'corrected and ordered' vocabulary (Furno 2013: 11). Redondo Rodríguez did not know of this edition when he affirmed, 'the oldest one that has reached us is a bilingual edition, Dutch–French, published in 1536' (2005: 722). We do not intend to enumerate the different editions and re-editions of the *Dictionarium*. For a more detailed analysis, see Furno's study (2013), which establishes its chronology, though only for the Netherlands. We use the 1556 edition (*Dictionarium quatuor linguarum..., Vocabulaire en quatre langues, Flemengue, Françoise, Latine, Espaignole...*, Leuven, Gravio) as a starting point, as we are interested in later circulations and adaptations.

In the sixteenth century, it was common to present dialogues on a specific topic in a conversational way, mainly in school contexts (cf. the Latin *Colloquia* mentioned above). They were adapted to the necessities of the learners — merchants, travellers and soldiers willing to learn languages, or members of the aristocracy who wanted to stand out in society. A good example are the *Diálogos sobre la lengua* by J. de Valdés (1535), introduced as a work intended to improve the knowledge (elegance and appropriateness) of Spanish among Spaniards on the one hand and foreigners on the other (Italians in this case).

The use of colloquia of both kinds for teaching languages alongside vocabulary lists and dictionaries (*Calepinus* and others) comes from a language conception of the Renaissance, which moves away from the assumption of equivalence between objects, words (terms) and ideas (mental representations) on which the necessity and practice of literal translation had been based in medieval times. This new idea is clearly manifested in the translation of the *New Testament* by Erasmus in 1516. The bilingual (Greek–Latin) text is followed by countless footnotes in which the author interprets or justifies his choice. This was the beginning of the dismantling of literal translation, and of the assumed equation of a word and the concept on which it was based. A new idea of language and the world became established. Humanists such as Estienne Dolet (1540) argued that each language represents external reality in its own particular way and each has a specific vocabulary which does not match that of other languages, or does so only partially; likewise, each has its own disposition of the words in sentences (*constructio*). Literal word-for-word translation was, consequently, a logical nonsense: in order to reproduce faithfully the thinking of the original author, it was now necessary to reorganize his/her discourse (words, syntax) in the target language according to the criteria of the translator (based on his/her linguistic and cultural knowledge).

Circulations and Adaptations of Vocabularies and Colloquia

The publication of vocabularies and multilingual colloquia was a successful editorial publishing practice during the sixteenth and seventeenth centuries. Bourland (1933 and 1938), Gallina (1959), Martín-Gamero (1961), Peeters-Fontainas (1965), Steiner (1970), Niederehe (1994), Lindemann (1994), Corcuera Manso and Gaspar Galán (1999), Núñez (2008 and 2010) and Swiggers (2013) offer a comprehensive catalogue of these works. Moreover, several studies have examined the different editions of the *Dictionarium* by Berlaimont from bibliographical, formal and pedagogical perspectives, including Rossebastiano-Bart (1975), Furno (2008 and 2013), Charlet-Mesdjian and Charlet (2011).

Such studies have not yet completed, in our opinion, the identification of networks of circulation and adaptation referring to the dialogues, interweaving the different editions, countries and authors. During the second half of the sixteenth and beginning of the seventeenth centuries, a number of such dialogue-books, inspired by the *Dictionarium* of 1556, were published by different language masters, including Iacques de Liaño/Ledel (*Vocabulario* (1565)); Gabriel Meurier (*Coloquios familiars* (1568)); Claude de Sainliens/Holyband (*The French Schoolemaister* (1573); *The French Littleton* (1576); *Campo di Fior* (1583)); John Florio (*First Fruits* (1578); *Second Fruits* (1591)); James Bellot (*Familiar Dialogues* (1586)); William Stepney (*The Spanish Schoolemaster* (1591)); John Minsheu (*A Dictionary in Spanish and English* (London, 1599), that includes *Pleasant and delightful dialogues*, already published separately in London in 1623); Cesar Oudin (*Diálogos en Español y Francés* (1604), later republished in his *Grammaire espagnole expliquée en françois* (1606)); Jean Saulnier (*Introduction en la langue Espagnolle* (1608)); Juan de Luna (*Diálogos familiars* (1619)); and Ian Wadsworth (*A Grammar, Spanish and English* (1622)), etc.

The polemic as to whether the *Dictionarium quator linguarum* of 1556 is rather a textbook for learning the spoken language (as claimed by Charlet-Mesdjian and Charlet 2011) or a lexical catalogue (a *vocabulista*, as claimed by Furno 2008) does not seem relevant: both uses were possible depending on the users. Let us briefly say that the composition of the *Dictionarium* (dialogues, lexicon, grammatical rudiments and religious texts) allows for the integration of diverse methodological approaches by combining practice of oral language, learning vocabulary and the grammatical (phonetic, orthographic and morphological) description of language. They thus represent a major tool for an eclectic approach to teaching living languages in the sixteenth century. Scholars like Caravolas (1994: 117; 1995: 275–306) and Howatt (2004: 9–43) establish an opposition between grammaticalized (regular) teaching of languages (see Palsgrave 1530 and Pillot 1550, for the case of French) versus the 'irregular' or 'practical language teaching', represented in the case of French by authors like Du Wes, Caxton, Bellot and Sainliens/Holyband. However, this opposition is not absolute, and Caravolas mentions that there are many proposals for one or the other method, both for Latin (e.g. Ascham, Webbe) and for living languages.

Focusing on the object we have identified, i.e. the circulation and adaptations of Berlaimont's *Dictionarium* in the sixteenth century, we begin with certain external aspects.[3] First, there was a real publishing 'competition' in the Netherlands: the work, first edited in Antwerp (1527, 1536, 1549), was later re-edited in Leuven (1556, 1558, 1561); in Antwerp (1558, 1573, 1576, 1582, 1583, 1586, 1596); and also in Ghent (1568) and in Liege (1589, 1591, 1595). On the other hand, an increasing number of languages and dialogues are progressively incorporated to the primitive *Vocabulaire*, which was initially bilingual — Dutch–French — in 1527, growing to three languages in 1536 (with the addition of Latin), four in 1556 (adding Spanish), and with other languages added later: Italian in 1558; English and German in 1576; Portuguese in 1598 (see Rossebastiano-Bart 1975).

These re-editions not only affected 'external' changes, but also qualitative matters. There was an increase both in the number of dialogues and the overall length of the work: five dialogues in 1579, six in 1583, seven in 1589. Also, the 1558 edition (Antwerp) bore a modified title, incorporating the term *colloquia*: *Dictionarium colloquia*; the 1561 edition of Leuven is entitled *Colloquia familiaria*. Thus the 'dialogue' component was underscored, versus the 'dictionary' or grammatical components. The 1583 edition (Antwerp) illustrates this with its title: *Colloquia cum dictionariolo sex linguarum*. The evolution is therefore very important: a primitive bilingual *Vocabulario* (1527, or trilingual, in 1549) is progressively transformed into a book of dialogues, accompanied by a reduced vocabulary with morphological and spelling notes (not in all languages). Two practical factors influence this transformation: first, the presence of the translation of the dialogues and of the texts in parallel columns made it unnecessary to have a vocabulary list; second, the alphabetical order of presentation of the vocabulary, whatever the language (Latin, Dutch or French), severely limited the text's efficiency with users of other languages. In any case, the multiple editions (more than 150 during the sixteenth and seventeenth centuries, according to the — incomplete — calculation by Verdeyen 1925–35) attest to the success of this tool for language learning (self-instructional) and teaching (at schools, or with the help of a teacher).

The title page of *Dictionarium* (1556) highlights the utilitarian intention of the work, underlining that 'it will be very useful for those who want to learn those languages'. Similarly, the dedication to the reader ('to the very curious reader'), signed by the Spanish Humanist doctor Francisco López de Villalobos, reinforces the idea:

> No ay hombre en toda Francia, ni en Flandes, ni en Alemana, ni en Ingalaterra, ni en todas estas partes de Septentriô que notenga grand necesidad de la cognicion de todas estas quatro lenguas qu'en este libro están escritas, ô sea mercader, ô soldado, ô hôbre de palacio, ô caminante tiene necesidad de una lengua, ô faraute qu'entiende estas lenguas, para que selas declare [...]

[There is no one in all of France, nor in Flanders, Germany or England, not in all these Northern parts who does not recognize the great necessity of knowing all these four languages in which this book is written, whether he be a merchant, or soldier, or gentleman at court, or traveller who needs one language, or a herald who understands these languages, in order to declare himself [...].]

The analysis of such a vast array of materials is far beyond the scope of this chapter. Our objective, therefore, is to examine one specific circulation: how three language masters (Liaño, Meurier, Sainliens) collected the dialogues present in the *Dictionarium* of 1556 and adapted them to the typology of their students and the tastes of each country (Spain, Netherlands, England). We thus intend to complement earlier studies summarizing this issue (Lépinette 1996; Sáez Rivera 2004; Suso López 2015), by contributing a comparative social-cultural approach.

As mentioned above, the *Dictionarium* of 1556 adds a fourth dialogue to the original three — a feast/banquet — and this is the longest and most interesting one for our purposes here (pp. 8–43). In the other dialogues, their functionality is very precise: they refer to business and commercial matters, but the newly added first dialogue, about a banquet, involves ten characters (Hermes, Iuan, Maria, David, Pedro, Francisco, Rogier, Anna, Henrico and Lucas) of different nationalities, ages and professions. It is a source giving clues as to the way of life of that time in Flanders (greetings, habits and customs, types of food, how to say grace, treatment given to visitors, etc.). Radtke (1994) dwells on the analysis of such dialogues for communicative routines such as greetings and farewells; a similar analysis could be done with respect to the features of ways of life and customs. For example, the abundance of special dishes and drinks are common ground for reference. The following socio-cultural practices are modelled: an invitation to have something to eat or drink when someone comes to one's home with a message; speaking French at the table in Dutch middle-class families and the reproach to the young woman Anna for not speaking; making 'toasts'; drinking wine and beer at meals; advice to eat something before drinking and so forth. Also, at the end of the conversation there is reference, among other news, to a battle lost by the King of France against the Spanish monarch (perhaps the Battle of St Quentin, 1557?). The speaker warns listeners against lies about this event, as well as expressing his desire for peace, saying that only God knows what will happen (pp. 40–41).

The *Vocabulario* by Iaques de Liaño/Ledel (1565)

The *Dictionarium* (1556) inspired the first work published in Spain intended for learning French as a foreign language (see Corcuera Manso and Gaspar Galán 1999: xxxvii). It is the *Vocabulario* by Iaques de Liaño/Ledel, printed together with a *Grammar* by Baltasar Sotomayor (1565). The *Vocabulario* has, apart from a bilingual list of words, some comments to facilitate pronunciation and orthography (before the vocabulary), four dialogues, and three letters (pp. 46–63), 'everything presented in two columns: the left one, in italics, for the French text, and the right column for the Spanish text' (Fischer et al. 2004: 62).

The adaptation by Liaño/Ledel (1565) is interesting because the intended readers are members of the aristocracy (the Spanish court of Isabel de Valois), so the practical character of the dialogues has to be combined with an educated (literary) orientation. A number of Liaño's dialogues remain very practical and reproduce the dialogues of *Dictionarium* (reducing their extension): dialogues 1, 2, 5 and 6. The rest — dialogues 3, 4, 7 and 8 — are Liaño's, have a poetic and literary nature, and respond to the Spanish literary tradition (drama and poetry).

The reason to select this type of dialogue lies in the characteristics of the addressees: the French-speaking court comprising gentlemen and ladies who accompanied Elisabeth de Valois to Spain after her wedding with Philip II (1559) and who wished to fit in with the uses and customs of the Spanish court. This text paves the way for the didactic use of literary works in seventeenth-century language learning, not only in the form of *colloquia* but also by including literary, historical and religious texts as well as poetic compositions (normally arranged in anthologies).

The Family Colloquy (1568) and *La Guirlande des Jeunes Filles* (1580) by Gabriel Meurier

Another adaptation including Spanish is the *Family Colloquy* by Gabriel Meurier (Antwerp, 1568),[4] which includes thirty bilingual Spanish–French dialogues in 128 double pages. The work continues with a bilingual grammatical treatise (*Coniugaciones, arte, y reglas muy proprias, y necesarias para los que quisieren deprender, Español y Frances*) in sixty-eight pages (pp. 299–367), followed by examples of commercial letters in Spanish: bills, bonds, loan checks, and letters by merchants with their answers (pp. 368–75).

The dialogues are mainly practical and functional, following the *Dictionarium* (1556) model: a journey; at the tavern; buying and selling; dealing with craftsmen (tailors, shoemakers) and retailers (butchers, fruit sellers, cheesemakers, fishmongers, spice sellers, sugar sellers); solving health problems; or quarrels between servants and masters, etc. The last dialogue, which represents a 'very funny philosophical feast' (pp. 118–28), will be analysed below.

In contrast to the *Dictionarium* (1556), in Meurier's *Colloquy* cultural references are present in all dialogues, mostly through proverbs that establish values and regulate social behaviours. Hernán Núñez had published *Refranes o proverbios en romance* (Salamanca, 1555), opening an interesting paremiological tradition.[5] These proverbs and sayings were later published in a Spanish–French bilingual version (Oudin 1605), with great success in France (twelve editions between 1605 and 1702), creating an image of the inclination of Spaniards for proverbs, one reinforced by the reading of *Don Quixote*. Meurier marks with an asterisk the presence of proverbs and sayings in *Don Quixote*, such as: 'amor haze mucho, y el dinero todo || Amour fait mout, mais argent fait tout' [Love does much, but money does everything] (p. 79).

There are also references to 'classical' and Christian cultural knowledge (Venus, Bacchus; Justice is represented with an image of an armless, blindfolded woman; and Saint Peter is represented 'very angry and annoyed to know the vices that are committed every day in the world' (p. 62)); reference to the value of moral aspects, such as knowledge and virtue ('Des lettres provient la vertu, & la vertu est un fruit sans comparaison, plus presieux que tout argent, gemme ny or' (p. 64)). Of course, there is room to talk about the laziness and mischief of the servants ('Les serviteurs à esprit picaresque, faignéants et rusés' (Chap. XVIII)), who are always trying to cheat the master 'quien no se fia, no se halla engañado / qui ne se fie n'est pas deceu' [He who does not trust, is not disappointed].

Dialogue 30 presents the servant Diogenes, the chatterbox Platon, and Papagayo, who all talk in burlesque and parody answers (the servant is doing nothing, just sitting under the sun), sprinkled with common sense reflections ('he who talks a lot errs a lot'), some sayings that are by today's standards misogynist ('la mujer y la gallina por mucho andarse pierden ayna' [women and hens are lost by hurrying about]). As for food, Spanish dishes are prominent (olive oil, cold meat, smoked meat, etc.), and the abundance of food is a common topic at the table:

Mandadnos traer	*Ask for*
la ensalada	*the salad*
bien lavada	*well washed*
con un poquito	*marinated with a drop*
de vinagre	*of vinegar*
mucho aceite	*much olive oil*
y bien salada	*and well salted*
la cecina	*smoked meat*
y carne fiambre	*and cold meat*
la grulla encecinada	*smoked crane meat*
la gallina salpimeriada	*seasoned poultry*
y luego la capilotada	*and later a sauce made with*
con la olla podrida	*oil and cheese with hotpot*

Meurier (1568: 122)[6]

Meurier's *La Guirlande des Jeunes Filles* (1580) is a relatively early example of a language manual dedicated to a female audience, comprising bilingual French–Dutch dialogues (eighteen dialogues, sixty-eight pages), presenting female characters (for example, in the first dialogue: Marthe, Anne, Rose, Marie, Jeanne, Magdelon) who converse about various situations in daily life (getting up, greetings, on the way to school, the lesson, games, meals, writing, going to bed, etc.). All dialogues end with a prayer. *La Guirlande* also includes two odes praising G. Meurier (at the beginning), and the Ten Commandments in rhyme (at the end).

The *French Schoolemaister* (1573), the *French Littleton* (1576) and *Campo di Fior* (1583) by Claude de Sainliens (also known as Holyband)

We turn now to three sixteenth-century French–English adaptations. *The French Schoolemaister* (1573) and *The French Littleton* (1576) by Claude de Sainliens were written specifically for schoolboys ('escholiers') who were tutored at home, or for any other person interested in self-study of the French language. The number of editions (twenty-one in the case of *Schoolemaister*, up to 1668 (cf. Berec 2013: 102); fifteenth re-editions of the *French Littleton* up to 1630 (cf. Berec 2013: 166)) shows the success of the format that Sainliens chose. While the *French Schoolemaister* starts with phonetic and grammar guidelines, the *French Littleton* follows the reverse order, first offering the dialogues (pp. 10–75) with bilingual English–French presentation, changing, therefore, the usual order: it is no longer a matter of first learning grammar in order to understand a text, but of first directly facing a text and then turning to a grammatical or lexical tool when in doubt. In these dialogues, Sainliens brings together, as noted by Berec (2012: 168), both the tradition of the 'manieres de langage' and the dialogues for adults (merchants, travellers, or more advanced learners), including the tradition of the *colloquia* intended for scholars, such as those by Erasmus, Vives or Cordier mentioned above.

In the *The French Schoolemaister* (1573), Sainliens offers two bilingual English–French dialogues, which follow a brief orthographic-phonetic and grammatical overview (pp. 1–24). The first dialogue (pp. 26–62) is titled: 'Devis familiers pour parler en tous lieux et places' [Familiar talke to use in all places] (pp. 25–62). Berec considers this dialogue to be 'dans la veine des *colloquia* latins d'Erasme, Mathurin Cordier et Juan Luis Vives, tous très en vogue dans les collèges européens du XVI siècle' (Berec 2012: 105). The conversation is built around everyday 'sentences' that anyone can use in similar situations, as they were used in the *Manieres de langage*.

The 'familiar talke' is divided into two scenes. The first one is articulated around Francis, a teenager who gets up, gets dressed, has breakfast and says goodbye to his father. The second one deals with two friends who are going to attend a wedding ceremony at Saint Paul's Cathedral; one of them has not slept at all, because he is returning from an all-night party. They attend the wedding ceremony and later listen to a Bachelor of Theology preaching near the Cathedral; then they go to the banquet, which is followed by a dance (with music). They finish with a prayer and a thanksgiving.

The second dialogue (pp. 62–84) is titled 'Pour demander le chemein, acheter et vendre avec autres familiares communications' [to ask the way, buy and sell: with other familiar communications]; later Sainliens includes some proverbs (in bilingual presentation (pp. 85–86)), the Commandments and the Catechism (only in French, with a question–answer presentation (pp. 87–95)); and it concludes with a list of bilingual words ordered by topic (pp. 96–139). The 'familiar communications' (1573: 62–84) are built around two persons from the provinces who meet on their way to St Bartholomew's Fair (24 August) in London; they join a group of merchants; rest at an inn; have dinner; one of the fellows falls ill and a servant takes care of him; the following day, the dialogues start again: they make a fire; dress; wash; have breakfast; arrive at the fair and sell their goods (clothing); after a day's work they return to the inn, pay and say goodbye to each other.

A careful reading of both texts allows us to conclude that Sainliens integrates in an original and brilliant way both dialogue traditions: more literary/educated dialogues and familiar dialogues. The last dialogue, built around the family life of a teenager, includes complaints about the laziness and bad attitude of servants, a common topic in the dialogues of adults; the second scene and dialogue are specifically for adults. Furthermore, the description of the way of life of those times includes episodes that are more typical of a carnival than the rigid Protestant morality that might be thought to dominate the training of students. The wedding banquet ends with a Morris dance (inherited from pagan festivities, celebrated at the beginning of May). The banquet is a veritable feast, with all types of meat, and very well supplied with wine. It could be expected that the talk of the Bachelor in Theology would include moral or religious advice, but, on the contrary, the dialogue is thoroughly secular, indeed worldly. The sons of the attendants fulfil the religious requirements without any sign of enthusiasm; on many occasions one of the diners praises the food and wine. The dialogues include frequent sharp answers with double meaning and innuendo, such as the dialogue between the sick merchant who requests the female servant to raise up his pillow and asks for a kiss for a good night's sleep (1573: 71–72).

The details of daily life given in such dialogues offer a potential source for reconstructing the way of life and social behaviours of the time. The two merchants at the end of their day's work buy dolls for their daughters and tip the servants at the inn. Their farewell from each other is very warm and full of good wishes. The price-bargaining is witty; and the two protagonists reveal details of the current social ideology about women, family values, the respect children should show their parents, children's punishments in case of disobedience, but also father–son care and love. The following is their opinion about women's beauty and marriage, which reveals not only the role of women as dependents on their husbands but also the fact that most marriages were arranged like a commercial transaction:

> Yea gossip. Truly it is a faire girl.
> She will cost you nothing toward her
> marriage: she will be married for her
> beautie and good grace (1573: 38)

> Ouy compere Certes c'est une belle fille
> elle vous couscera rien à la
> marier : elle se mariera pour sa
> beauté & bonne grace (1573: 38)

As for the *French Littelton* (1576), four dialogues are intended for adults or teenagers (travelling around France) and only one takes place at school. The dialogues are followed by a list of proverbs, a lexicon, and religious texts (only in French, pp. 114–22), as well as a *Traicté des danses* (in French (pp. 123–49)), in which the author condemns both dancing (which takes place at popular fairs) and gambling (for further socio-cultural aspects in these publications, see Berec 2012: 165–89; 2013: 50, 107–10).

We must also briefly mention a last work by Sainliens, edited in 1583, *Campo di Fior or else the flourie field of four languages*. Apart from a sonnet by J. Bellot on the first page, this publication, in four languages (Latin, French, English and Italian), dedicated to Mistress Harington, a female addressee, is entirely (387 pages) comprised of a collection of dialogues reproducing the conversation young girls hold in different situations of daily life (getting up, on the way to school, the lesson, meals, games, writing etc., as in *la Guirlande des Jeunes Filles* by G. Meurier).

The dialogues by Sainliens/Holyband thus contain two essential components marking the history of language teaching in Europe. On the one hand, they serve as tools ('language material') and as a model to follow in modern-language learning (in this case, French) from the perspective of oral language, in dialogue format. On the other hand, they transmit cultural ethnographic features (social behaviour, socio-cultural practices, values, ideological representations). Let it also be said that these dialogues are interesting from the perspective of European cultural history and offer a basis for the comparative study of the model of life, social behaviours, ideological representations about women (their family and social function, marriage, beauty, etc.), hygiene habits, family values, parent–children relations, the type of education transmitted to boys and girls, and so forth.

This study would be incomplete without at least some mention of two works published in England in the 1590s: *The Spanish Schoolemaster containing seven Dialogues* by William Stepney (1591); and the *Pleasant and Delightful Dialogues in Spanish and English* by John Minsheu (1599), which served as a basis for numerous adaptations throughout the seventeenth century (see Cid n.d.). We also note the *First Fruits* (1578) and *Second Fruits* (1591) by John Florio (see Arcangeli, who highlights between the former and the latter a 'passage from the moralizing tone of Protestant ethics to the more relaxed one of polite conversation' (2005: 11). These few references must suffice as indications of the vast field offered for research.

Conclusion

This chapter has presented only a few examples of the circulation and adaptation of dialogues as learning tools in the sixteenth century through a number of works published in Spain, the Netherlands and England (Liaño/Ledel, Meurier, Sainliens/Holyband). They have served to highlight three points. First, it is necessary to build a history of language learning/teaching materials from a pan-European perspective, as these resources circulated among different European countries, being adapted and contextualized to different learning contexts. Further research along these lines could help to understand these contexts. Second, these adaptations reflect cultural practices and ideological representations that merit analysis if we are to write a socio-cultural history of language learning in Europe, thus opening before us a field that we consider of great interest. The brief commentaries that we have offered above are intended only to illustrate such an analytical approach, which must be undertaken in collaboration with social historians. Third, from a methodological perspective, we believe that the books of dialogues examined in this article are best classified as exhibiting teaching methodology of an eclectic tendency, for both pedagogical and social reasons. The diversity of audiences wishing to learn modern languages (school students, untrained adults, adults with Latin training, aristocrats, bourgeoisie etc.) entailed the need for an adaptation of tools and teaching practice, but this adaptation could lead to two opposite results: the *Campo di Fior*, intended for women, usually without Latin training, eliminates grammar and exemplifies a practical tendency in language learning. On the other hand, the 'colloquium' model, of learned inspiration, addressed a learned and/or aristocratic, bilingual audience, prepared for language learning (Liaño/Ledel, 1565; Florio, *First Fruits*

(1578); *Second Fruits* (1591)), whose members relate to the conversation textbooks that speak about morals, good manners and a careful language typical of Latin teaching (Erasmus, Vives) or teaching vernacular languages (Valdés).

Bibliography

Primary sources

A Very Profitable Book to Learn English and Spanish. 1971 [1554]. Ed. by R. C. Alston (Menston: Scolar Press)
BELLOT, JAMES. 1969 [1586]. *Familiar Dialogues*, ed. by R. C. Alston (Menston: Scolar Press)
Biblioteca Virtual Miguel de Cervantes. 1999–2007. [Online catalogue] (Madrid: Fundación Biblioteca Virtual Miguel de Cervantes) <http://www.cervantesvirtual.com/catalogo/index.jsp>
CAXTON, WILLIAM. 1900 [1480]. *Dialogues in French and English*, ed. by Henry Bradley (London: Kegan Paul, Trench and Trübner)
CORDIER, MATHURIN. 1568. *Colloquia Scholastica: libri IV* (Paris: Gabrielis Buonis)
DOLET, ESTIENNE. 1540. *Manière de bien traduire d'une langue à une autre* (Lyon: Dolet)
DU WES, G. c. 1532. *An introductorie for to lerne to rede, to pronounce and to speke French trewly [...]* (London: Thomas Godfray)
Early English Books, 1475–1640. 1940 (Ann Arbor, MI: University Microfilms International)
Early English Books Online (EEBO). 1999 (Ann Arbor, MI: ProQuest Information and Learning Company) < https://eebo.chadwyck.com/home>
ERASMUS, DESIDERIUS. 1518. *Familiarum colloquiorum formulae* (Basle: Jean Froben)
FLORIO, JOHN. 1578. *First Fruits, which yield Familiar Speech, Merry Proverbs, Witty Sentences, and Golden Sayings* (London)
——. 1591. *Second Fruits* (London: Thomas Woodcock)
Le Livre des Mestiers: Dialogues français-flamands composés au XIVe siècle par un maître d'école de la ville de Bruges.1875 [14th century]. Ed. by H. Michelant (Paris: Librairie Tross)
Le Livre des métiers de Bruges et ses Dérivés: Quatre anciens Manuels de Conversation. 1931. Ed. by Jean Gessler (Bruges: Imprimerie Sainte Catherine)
LIAÑO, IAQUES DE. 1565. *Vocabulario de los vocablos* (Alcalá de Henares: Francisco Cormellas y Pedro de Robles)
Manieres de langage (1396, 1399, 1415). 1995. Ed. by Andres M. Kristol, Anglo-Norman Text Society, 53 (London: Anglo-Norman Text Society)
MEURIER, GABRIEL. 1568. *Coloquios familiares muy convenientes y mas prouechosos de quantos salieron fasta agora para qualquicra qualidad de personas desseosas de saber hablar y escribir Espanol y Frances* (Anvers: Ian van Waesberge)
——. 1580. *La guirlande des Jeunes Filles* (Anvers: Ian van Waesberge)
MEYER, PAUL (ed.). 1870. 'La Maniere de Langage: qui enseigne a parler et a écrire le Français', *Revue Critique d'Histoire et Litterature*, 27: 373–408
SAINLIENS, CLAUDE DE (Holyband). 1573. *The French Schoolemaister* (London: Abraham Veale)
——. 1576. *The French Littleton* (London: Thomas Vautrollier)
——. 1583. *Campo di Fior, or else The Flourie Field od foure Languages* (London: Thomas Vautroullier)
SOTOMAYOR, BALTASAR DE. 1565. *Grammatica con reglas muy prouechosas y necessarias para aprender a leer y escriuir la lengua Francesa conferida con la Castellana, con vn vocabulario copioso de las mesmas lenguas [...]* (Alcala de Henares: Pedro de Robles y Francisco de Cormellas)
VALDÉS, JUAN DE. [1535] 1940. *Diálogo de la lengua* (Buenos Aires: Sopena)
VIVES, JUAN LUIS. 1539. *Linguae Latinae exercitatio* (Basle: Robert Winter)

Secondary sources

ARCANGELI, A. 2005. 'Les Second fruits de John Florio ou la vie comme un jeu', *Actes des congrès de la Société française Shakespeare*, 23 <http://shakespeare.revues.org/651> [accessed 9 December 2013]

BENNETT, H. S. 1969. *English Books & Readers, 1475 to 1557: Being a Study in the History of the Book Trade from Caxton to the Incorporation of the Stationers' Company*, I (Cambridge: Cambridge University Press)

BEREC, L. 2012. *Claude de Sainliens, un huguenot bourbonnais au temps de Shakespeare* (Paris: Orizons)

BEREC, L. 2013. 'Claude de Sainliens, un huguenot bourbonnais au temps de Shakespeare [...]', *Documents pour l'Histoire du français langue étrangère et seconde*, 50: 101–15

BOURLAND, C. B. 1933. 'The Spanish School-Masters and the Polyglot Derivatives of Noel de Berlaimont's Vocabulare', *Revue Hispanique*, 81: 283–318

——. 1938. 'Algo sobre Gabriel Meurier maestro de español de Amberes (1521–1597?)', *Hispanic Review*, 6: 139–52

CARAVOLAS, J. 1994. *La Didactique des langues: précis d'histoire I (1450–1700)* (Montréal: Presses de l'Université de Montréal; Tübingen: Narr)

——. 1995. 'Apprendre une langue étrangère à la Renaissance', *Historiographia linguistica*, 22: 275–307

CHARLET-MESDJIAN, B., and J.-L. CHARLET. 2011. 'Une méthode Assimil pour apprendre le latin à l'époque humaniste: les *Colloquia* dérivés du Vocabulare de Noël de Berlaimont', *Rursus, Poiétique, réception et réécriture des textes antiques*, 6 <http://rursus.revues.org/495> [accessed 22 May 2015]

CHEVALIER, J.-CL. 1998. 'Les Dialogues médiévaux: origines, filiations, méthodes. Quelques pistes', *Documents pour l'Histoire du français langue étrangère et seconde*, 22: 17–26

CID, J. A. [N.D.]. 'Leve introducción a unos diálogos hispano-ingleses' <http://cvc.cervantes.es/literatura/clasicos/dialogos_minsheu/introduccion/default.htm> [accessed 12 February 2014]

COLOMBO TIMELLI, M. 1998. 'Dialogues et phraséologie dans quelques dictionnaires plurilingues du XV siècle (Berlaimont et *Solenissimo Vocabulista*)', *Documents pour l'Histoire du français langue étrangère et seconde*, 22: 27–63

CORCUERA MANSO, F., and A. GASPAR GALÁN. 1999. *La lengua francesa en el siglo XVI: estudio y edición del 'Vocabulario de los vocablos' de Jacques de Liaño (Alcalá de Henares, 1565)* (Saragossa: Prensas Universitarias de Zaragoza)

CORRIGAN, A. J. 2005. *Manuals for Teaching English as a Foreign Language in the 15th and 16th Centuries* <http://homes.chass.utoronto.ca/~cpercy/courses/6361corrigan.htm> [accessed 24 May 2015]

DE CLERQ, J., J. LIOCE, and P. SWIGGERS (eds). 2000. *Grammaire et enseignement du français, 1500–1700* (Leuven: Peeters)

ESPARZA TORRES, M. A., ET AL. 2008. *Bibliografía temática de historiografía lingüística española: fuentes secundarias*, 2 vols (Hamburg: Buske)

FERGUSON, CHARLES A. 1959. 'Diglossia', *Word*, 15: 325–40

FISCHER, D. ET AL. 2004. *Repertorio de gramáticas y manuales de francés para la enseñanza del francés, 1565–1940* (Barcelona: PPU)

FURNO, M. 2008. 'Du commerce et des langues: latin et vernaculaires dans les lexiques et dictionnaires plurilingues du XVI siècle', *Histoire et civilisation du livre*, 4: 93–116

——. 2013. 'La Défense de la langue vernaculaire en Espagne (XV-XVII siècles): paratextes et textes', in *Modus legendi atque scribendi linguæ hispanicæ*, Corpus Eve (Emergence du vernaculaire en Europe) <http://eve.revues.org/198> [accessed 18 April 2014]

GALLINA, A. 1959. *Contributi alla storia della lessicografia italo-spagnola dei secoli XVI e XVII* (Florence: Olschki)
HOLTZ, L. 1981. *Donat et la tradition de l'enseignement grammatical: étude et édition critique* (Paris: CNRS)
HOWATT, A. P. R. 2004. *A History of English Language Teaching* (Oxford: Oxford University Press)
KIBBEE, D. A. 1989. 'L'Enseignement du français en Angleterre au XVI siècle', in *La Langue française au XVI siècle: usage, enseignement et approches descriptives*, ed. by P. Swiggers and W. Van Hoecke (Leuven: Leuven University Press; Peeters), 54–77
——. 1991. *For to Speke Frenche Trevely: The French Language in England, 1000–1600: Its Status, Description and Instruction* (Amsterdam: Benjamins)
KOERNER, E. F. K., H.-J. NIEDEREHE, and A. QUILIS. 2001. *History of Linguistics in Spain: Historia de la lingüística en España (II)* (Amsterdam: Benjamins)
KUKENHEIM, L. 1974. *Contributions à l'histoire de la grammaire italienne, espagnole et française à l'époque de la Renaissance* (Utrecht: H&S)
LAMBLEY, K. 1920. *The Teaching and Cultivation of the French Language in England during Tudor and Stuart Times* (Manchester: Manchester University Press)
LÉPINETTE, B. 1996. 'Les Premières Grammaires du français (1565–1799) publiées en Espagne: modèles, sources et rôle de l'espagnol', *Histoire, Épistémologie, Langage* 18.2: 149–77
LINDEMANN, M. 1994. *Die französischen Wörterbücher von den Anfangen bis 1600: Entstehung und typologische Beschreibung* (Tübingen: Niemeyer)
MARTÍN-GAMERO, S. 1961. *La enseñanza del inglés: desde la edad media hasta el siglo XIX* (Madrid: Gredos)
MEYER, NIEDEREHE, H. J. 1994. *Bibliografía cronológica de la lingüística, la gramática y la lexicografía del español (BICRES I): desde los comienzos hasta el año 1600* (Amsterdam: Benjamins)
NIETO, L. 1988. 'Estudio introductorio', in Antonio del Corro, *Reglas gramaticales para aprender la lengua española y francesa* (Madrid: Arco), pp. 5–75
NÚÑEZ, L.P. 2008. *Lexicografía hispano-francesa de los siglos XVI y XVII: catálogo y estudio de los repertorios* (Madrid: Universidad Complutense de Madrid)
——. 2010. *El arte de las palabras: diccionarios e imprenta en el siglo de oro* (Mérida: Editora Regional de Extremadura)
PEETERS-FONTAINAS, J. 1965. *Bibliographie des impressions espagnoles des Pays-Bas méridionaux* (Nieuwkoop: B. De Graaf)
RADTKE, E. 1994. *Gesprochenes Französisch und Sprachgeschichte: zur Rekonstruktion der Gesprächskonstitution in Dialogen französischer Sprachlehrbücher des 17.Jahrhunderts unter besonderer Berücksichtigung der italienischen Adaptionen* (Tübingen: Niemeyer)
RICHÉ, P. 1982. 'La Vie quotidienne dans les écoles monastiques d'après les colloques scolaires', in *Colloque sous la règle de saint Benoît : structures monastiques et société en France du Moyen Age à l'époque moderne (1980)* (Geneva: Droz), pp. 417–26
REDONDO RODRÍGUEZ, M. J. 2005. 'Manuales para la enseñanza de lenguas en la Europa del s. XVI: el embrión de la lingüística aplicada', *XV Congreso Internacional de la ASELE. Las Gramáticas y los Diccionarios en la Enseñanza del Español como Segunda Lengua: Deseo y Realidad (2004)* (Seville: Universidad de Sevilla), pp. 719-26
ROSSEBASTIANO-BART, A. 1975. 'I 'Colloquia' di Noel de Berlaimont nella versione contenente il portoghese', *Annali dell'Istituto Universitario Orientale, Sezione Romanza*, 17: 31–85
SÁEZ RIVERA, D. M. 2004. 'La explotación pedagógica del diálogo escolar en la didáctica del español (ss. XVI–XIX)', *ESELE. Actas XV*: 792–97
SÁNCHEZ, A. 1992. *Historia de la enseñanza del español como lengua extranjera* (Madrid: SGEL)

STEINER, R. J. 1970. *Two Centuries of Spanish and English Bilingual Lexicography (1590–1800)* (The Hague: Mouton)
SUSO LÓPEZ, J. 2015. 'Los "útiles" para enseñar/aprender Lenguas en el Renacimiento y la Ianua Linguarum de W. Bathe (1611)', *Porta Linguarum*, 23: 233–46
SWIGGERS, P. 2013. 'Regards sur l'enseignement du français aux Pays-Bas', *Documents pour l'Histoire du français langue étrangère et seconde*, 50: 49–80
——, W. VAN HOECKE, and C. DEMAZIÈRE (eds). 1989. *La Langue française au XVI siècle: usage, enseignement et approches descriptives* (Leuven and Paris: Leuven University Press; Peeters)
VERDEYEN, W. R. R. 1925–35. *Colloquia et Dictionariolum septem linguarum* [reprint of the edition of Amberes of 1616], 3 vols (Antwerp: Uitgave van de Vereeniging der Antwerpsche Bibliophilen)

Notes to Chapter 4

1. 'The loss of [...] French territories in the 1430s and 1440s [Normandy, 1450; Aquitaine, 1453] correspondingly led to a progressive decline in the use and study of French towards the end of this period [fifteenth century]' (Kibbee 1991: 62).
2. Different manuscripts are preserved with important variances (1396, 1399, 1415). We have used Meyer's 1870 edition.
3. We limit our observations to sixteenth-century editions.
4. 1563. Gabriel Meurier also edited, in 1563, *Communications familieres non Moins Propres Que tres Utiles à la nation angloise desireuse et diseteuse du langage françois. Communications Familiare Verrie proffytable à la nation Inglishe désireux et nedinge la langue Frenche*. (Amberes, Pierre Keerberghe). Unfortunately we have been unable to consult this publication.
5. The Romance languages represented were Catalan, Valencian, Asturian/Leonese, Galician, Italian, French, and Portuguese.
6. The English translation is the authors' own.

CHAPTER 5

Histoire de quelques règles de prononciation pour savoir lire le français: de Berlaimont (1527) à Reixac i Carbó (1749)

Marc Viémon

In this article, we recount the history of some rules for a proper reading/pronunciation of French and, particularly, of their various adaptations intended for a Spanish audience. The history of these rules is traced from their arrival in 1527 in the oldest edition known to date of the Berlaimont vocabulary, to their last version in a pedagogical work of the Catalan Reixac i Carbó in 1749. Surveying this two-century-old historical process we offer an inventory and demonstration of the different copies, transformations and translations, which start from an initial set of nine rules, written in Dutch in their original version. They were first developed, then successively reduced and, eventually, they entirely disappeared in the middle of the eighteenth century. They were translated into many different languages; here, although we also highlight the Latin, Italian and French versions, we are especially interested in the Spanish and Catalan one, because of its uncommon longevity.

La dissymétrie existant en français entre langue écrite et langue parlée ne date pas d'hier. Elle a traditionnellement été — et continue d'être — l'un des principaux écueils auxquels se heurtent les apprenants étrangers de cette langue, surtout en ce qui concerne la lecture/prononciation correcte d'un texte écrit. À propos des œuvres d'apprentissage du français adressées aux Espagnols et publiées entre le XVIe et le XVIIIe siècle, Bruña Cuevas (1996: 85) affirme que 'depuis le XVIe siècle [...], une même vision a été présente avec une force variable selon les périodes: celle d'une langue française dont la principale difficulté [...] était de ne pas s'écrire comme elle se prononçait'. La préoccupation principale en matière de prononciation au sein des œuvres d'apprentissage du français n'était donc pas tant d'enseigner comment se prononçait tel ou tel son, mais bien de fournir des règles qui permettraient au lecteur de savoir interpréter une graphie.[1] C'est ce genre de règles que nous trouvons au sein du vocabulaire de Berlaimont en 1527.

Première version des règles de prononciation

L'Edition de 1527

Cette année-là, alors qu'il est maître d'école à Anvers, Noël de Berlaimont (mort en 1531) fait publier par Jacob van Liesuelt le *Vocabulaire de nouveau ordonne et de rechief recorrige pour apprendre legierement a bien lirre escripre et parler francois et flameng lequel est mis tout la plus part par personnaiges*. Le titre suggère qu'il existerait une édition antérieure, mais la plus ancienne connue à ce jour est celle de 1527. Jouissant d'un succès sans pareil, cette production de la renaissance a été rééditée plus de cent quatre-vingts fois.[2] Ces rééditions ont évolué, subissant parfois quelques remaniements, réductions ou ajouts, mais aussi et surtout augmentant progressivement le nombre de langues en jeu.[3]

Il est bien connu que le *vocabulaire* de Noël de Berlaimont n'est pas uniquement une liste de mots. Dans la publication de Liesuelt, avant le vocabulaire proprement dit, l'auteur propose trois dialogues et des modèles de lettres, contrats et quittances aux usagers de l'époque. À cela il faut ajouter les règles pour lire correctement le français, qui sont placées à la toute fin de l'ouvrage. Alors que celui-ci est entièrement bilingue, tout le contenu étant rédigé en deux versions, l'une néerlandaise et l'autre française disposées toutes deux en colonnes parallèles, les règles n'apparaissent qu'en néerlandais; bien entendu, les exemples fournis, eux, sont en français. Il paraît logique que des règles destinées à l'apprentissage de la lecture correcte du français ne soient pas rédigées dans cette même langue, du moins si l'on considère qu'elles s'adressaient à un public non francophone. Signalons de toute façon que le titre promettait à l'usager d'apprendre à 'bien lirre escripre et parler francois et flameng'; or l'absence d'indications similaires à l'usage de francophones désirant perfectionner leur néerlandais démontre, selon nous, que cette œuvre a été plutôt publiée pour répondre aux besoins d'un public flamand.

Au sein de l'édition la plus ancienne que nous connaissons actuellement des vocabulaires de Noël de Berlaimont, la section de prononciation s'intitulait 'Dan ontallike letteren diemen niet heel oft gheensins pronuncieren ofte nit spreken en mach in fransoys int lesen oft spreken'. Une possible traduction de ce titre serait: 'Ensuite, une innumérable quantité de lettres que l'on ne peut prononcer ou proférer en français partiellement ou complètement en lisant ou en parlant'. Dans la table des matières, la version française annonçait la section de prononciation par l'intitulé suivant: 'Item en la fin est lart de parfaictement lire et parler franchois a scavoir de innumerable quantité de lettres quil fault pler [*sic*] et point profferer en lisant ou en parlant le franchois'. À la lueur de ces titres, l'usager savait ce qu'il trouverait dans les règles de prononciation: des indications sur les lettres — nous nous situons toujours dans une démarche graphophonétique — qui sont visibles à l'écrit mais que l'on ne doit pas prononcer à l'oral. Voyons avec plus de détail le contenu de ces règles.

Le Contenu des règles

En 1527, les règles étaient au nombre de neuf. La brève introduction qui les précède se contente d'énumérer les voyelles (*a, e, i, o, u*) et les consonnes (*b, c, d, f, g, k, l, m, n, o* [*sic*], *p, q, r, s, t, x, z*), en donnant une explication classique aux lecteurs de cette séparation: les voyelles peuvent être prononcées seules, elles 'font voix' (*voys maker*); les consonnes, en revanche, sont dépendantes des voyelles. Quelques nuances cependant sont apportées à cette classification: *u* et *i* peuvent être aussi bien voyelles que consonnes; *l* et *r* sont appelées liquides, dénomination habituelle qui s'utilise encore de nos jours; enfin, il est fait une différence entre consones muettes (*stommen*), *b, c, d, f, g, k, p, q, t*, et demi-voyelles (*half vocalen*) *l, m, n, r, s*.

   La première règle donne à l'utilisateur un précepte qui semble évident: si l'on veut bien parler français, il faut savoir prononcer les voyelles 'als die fransoysen doen' (comme le font les Français), mais aussi les consonnes qui les accompagnent et syllabes qui se forment autour d'elles. Comme l'ont déjà signalé Corcuera Manso et Gaspar Galán (1999: xl) à propos de l'adaptation de Ledel en 1565, aucune explication n'est fournie au lecteur pour l'aider à appliquer ce conseil: pas de description articulatoire ni auditive; pas de confrontation avec les sons du néerlandais; pas même de renvoi à la vive voix du maître ou du locuteur natif. Mais, en réalité, ceci n'a pas dû étonner le lecteur. S'il avait lu attentivement les intitulés que nous avons commentés plus haut, il devait s'attendre à ce qu'on lui indique uniquement les lettres ou groupe de lettres qu'il devait ou ne devait pas prononcer, et non pas à ce qu'on lui donne des explications sur la prononciation des sons du français, le but étant de maîtriser la lecture à haute voix. Le titre de l'édition suivante, celle de 1536, ne fera que confirmer cette idée, nous le verrons.

   Mis à part, donc, la première règle, qui est une sorte d'avertissement qui relève du bon sens, le reste d'entre elles fait exclusivement référence à des lettres écrites en français, mais muettes à l'oral dans certains contextes ou dans certains mots. Les lettres concernées sont les consonnes finales (deuxième règle),[4] le *s* intérieur implosif (règles trois à huit)[5] et l'ancien *l* implosif (neuvième règle).[6] C'est le *s*, nous le voyons, qui accapare la plupart du contenu: cinq règles sur neuf, et une partie des explications de la deuxième. La raison de ce choix peut résider dans le fait que cette lettre se trouvait dans de nombreux mots et possédait une grande diversité de valeurs. Voyons plutôt ce que nous dit Catach (2001: 142) au sujet de cette lettre muette au XVIe siècle:

> Il nous faut en effet particulièrement insister sur le *s*, phonème très fréquent dans les étymons latins, qui s'était amuï très tôt devant toute autre consonne ou à la pause. Dix mille mots écrits du vocabulaire de l'époque, selon un témoignage du temps, comprenaient un ou plusieurs *s* muets, qui étaient loin d'être tous étymologiques.

Quoi qu'il en soit, parmi toutes les valeurs possibles, l'auteur des indications se borne à évoquer la prononciation du *s* qui marque le pluriel au sein de la deuxième règle, et donne de courtes listes de mots au sein desquels le *s* peut être muet, comme par exemple dans les règles trois à sept où tous les mots comportent un digramme *st* intérieur, précédé dans chacune des règles, respectivement, par l'une des cinq voyelles dénombrées dans l'introduction: *a, e, i, o, u*. La règle générale, dans les cas de *est* (estranger / honneste / feste / cest / est) et *ost* (nostre / hoste / sera / tantost / apostre), c'est que le *s* ne se prononce pas sauf dans certaines exceptions; dans les cas de *ast* (Astrologue / pasteur / chaste), *ist* (distance / histoire / cisterne) et *ust* (iuste /

iustice), c'est l'inverse. L'auteur aurait pu organiser ses explications sur le *s* muet suivi de *t* en deux groupes, mais il a préféré une démarche énumérative, chère par ailleurs à la grammaire des observations représentée en Espagne par quelques grammairiens du français, surtout au XVIIIe siècle (Lépinette 1996: 159-64). Le premier groupe, composé de mots dont le *s* intérieur était le plus souvent muet, aurait même pu être intégré dans la huitième règle, qui ne présentait que des combinaisons où le *s* ne se prononçait pas : *sc* (eschever / eschevin / escumer / escouter), *sl* (masle / pasle / mesler / eslire / ysle / brusler), *sm* (pasmer / blasme / mesme / tesmoig [sic] / abisme), *sn* (chesne / asne / fresne / iosne / mesnaige), *sp* (aspre / espaule / esprit / esprouuer).

Évolution au sein de la série des Berlaimont

1536: premier changement substantiel

Dès l'édition de 1536, publiée par Vorsterman à Anvers, nos règles s'annoncent dans la table des matières uniquement par 'Item en la fin est lart de parfaitement lirre et parler francoys'. L'intitulé de 1527 a donc été tronqué, perdant par là une information sur le contenu de la section correspondante. Cela ne changera plus dans les éditions successives du vocabulaire. Pas plus d'ailleurs que le titre de la section proprement dite, qui, dès 1536 également, prendra sa forme (néerlandaise) définitive: 'Om perfectelick Francoys te leeren lesen', 'ce qui signifie Pour apprendre parfaitement à lire le français'. Il sera ensuite traduit à quatre langues.

En ce qui concerne le contenu, la réédition de Vorsterman présente surtout un ajout important: trois nouvelles règles. Cette structure sera définitive dans les Berlaimont postérieurs incluant la section, hormis pour ceux de la Péninsule Ibérique. Les règles dix, onze et douze maintiennent une cohérence interne. En effet, il s'agit à nouveau de signaler les lettres muettes qui peuvent apparaître dans un mot écrit. Les lettres en question sont respectivement *e* final (prononcé parfois [e], parfois non prononcé, c'est-à-dire quand c'est un *e* muet), *u* dans le trigramme *qu* + voyelle (*a*, *e*, *ou y*) et enfin *u* dans le trigramme *gue*. La dixième règle, de manière secondaire, mentionne également le phénomène de l'enchaînement.[7]

L'introduction, quant à elle, est pratiquement la même. Deux modifications apparaissent néanmoins: d'une part, le commentaire précisant la différence entre muettes et demi-voyelles a disparu; d'autre part, deux exemples illustrent la double condition des lettres *i* et *u*, *japrins* et *vivant*. Ce qui ne change pas en 1536, c'est la langue dans laquelle sont rédigées les indications qui nous intéressent: comme en 1527, malgré un titre qui promettait aussi bien l'apprentissage du néerlandais que du français et la présence continuelle d'une version française parallèle au néerlandais, la prononciation n'est pas traduite. C'est probablement pour la même raison que neuf ans plus tôt.

Les Traductions chez Grave

Le premier vocabulaire à proposer une traduction des règles de lecture/prononciation voit le jour en 1551 sous les presses de l'imprimeur juré de Louvain Bartholomy de Grave. La traduction se fait en latin. Mais le titre proposé pour cette section était

'De perfecta linguae Gallicae locutione', ce qui changeait un tant soit peu le sens, faisant plutôt référence à la parole (*locutione*) qu'à la lecture (*lectione*). Cette dernière était pourtant textuellement mentionnée dans son titre original en néerlandais. Cinq ans plus tard, cette étourderie fut rectifiée. En effet, en 1556, le nouveau titre sera bien 'De perfecta linguae Gallicae lectione'. Puis en 1558, fait exceptionnel dans les vocabulaires de Berlaimont incluant les règles qui nous occupent, la version néerlandaise va disparaître au profit de l'italien. Mais ce ne sera que de courte durée: au sein des éditions de 1560 et 1561, le néerlandais reprend sa place et la version en italien disparaît. Par rapport à 1536, le contenu des règles ne varie pas, à part quelques exemples isolés. Par contre, c'est bien à ce continuateur de Berlaimont que revient l'honneur d'être le premier à proposer une traduction, d'abord en latin, puis en italien, des règles de lecture du français. La version latine est sans doute due à Cornille Valere d'Utrecht, l'italienne à Antonio Maria Calabria.[8]

En fait, Bartholomy de Grave, qui a donc cinq éditions différentes du vocabulaire de Berlaimont à son actif, publie une version quadrilingue du vocabulaire bilingue d'origine dès 1551. C'est d'abord le néerlandais, le français, le latin et l'espagnol qui sont présents, tout comme en 1556. Puis deux ans plus tard l'italien remplace le néerlandais, comme nous l'avons vu. En 1560 et 1561, les langues sont de nouveau celles de 1551. Mais ce qui est réellement curieux dans ces éditions, c'est que toutes les parties sont en quatre langues, sauf celles qui portent sur la prononciation. Nous avons vu, par exemple, que 'De perfecta' apparaît toujours chez Grave au maximum en deux langues, l'une d'elle étant toujours le latin. Si ces règles s'adressaient à des étrangers voulant savoir parler le français, il semble logique qu'elles n'apparaissent pas en français. Mais il est plus difficile de déterminer la raison pour laquelle nous ne trouvons pas de traduction en espagnol, qui était l'une des quatre langues mises en jeu dans le premier vocabulaire de Grave. D'autant plus qu'en 1558, une version italienne voit le jour.

Alors qu'en 1551, les seules explications de lecture/prononciation présentes dans le vocabulaire étaient les règles auxquelles nous nous intéressons dans cet article, dès 1556, en revanche, Grave inclut définitivement dans ses éditions du vocabulaire deux sections supplémentaires sur la prononciation. La première, d'origine obscure, se dénomme 'La maniere d'orthographier en langue françoyse' et, contrairement à ce que l'on pourrait croire, elle contient de nombreuses indications portant sur la prononciation et non pas seulement sur la graphie, comme cette indication sur la lettre *a*: 'A veult estre prononcé, à bouche ouuerte, auec esperit congru, & prend sa resonance droict au cœur'. Ces explications, exclusivement rédigées en français, pourraient, à la limite, justifier l'absence d'une version française de 'De perfecta', malgré l'incongruité d'un tel procédé, comme nous l'avons signalé auparavant. Présente chez Grave dès 1556, 'La manière d'orthographier' n'est reprise, à notre connaissance, par aucun autre continuateur de Berlaimont.

La deuxième section sur la prononciation ne concerne pas la langue française, mais espagnole. Elle est rédigée en deux langues: le latin et le français. Le 'Modus legendi atque scribendi linguae Hispanicae' (en français, 'La manière d'escripre et de prononcer la langue Espaignole') trouve son origine dans l'*Vtil y breve institution para aprender los principios y fundamentos de la lengua hespañola*, publiée par le propre Grave à

Louvain en 1555 (Lépinette 2001: 104). Somme toute, ce qui choque principalement chez Grave, c'est l'absence d'une version en espagnol de 'De perfecta'. Celle-ci verra le jour dans les presses d'un autre imprimeur: Jean Verwithagen.

Les Editions quadrilingues (1565–1647)

La première édition que nous avons pu consulter au sein de laquelle apparaît 'De perfecta' en quatre langues est celle de Jean Verwithagen publiée en 1565 à Anvers. Nous avons déjà signalé le fait que, dans la série des Berlaimont, le contenu des règles n'a pas subi de changement substantiel. Ici aussi, ce qui est important c'est la présence de nouvelles traductions des règles, surtout la version espagnole et accessoirement la version française. En espagnol, le titre des règles était 'Para aprender perfetamente [sic] a leer Frances'. Le responsable de ces versions nous est inconnu.

Dès la table des matières, cette nouveauté est annoncée par la formule suivante: 'L'art de parfaitement apprendre à lire & parler François, traduite en quatre langues à l'utilité & proufit des nations estranges'. Toute une famille de Berlaimont reprendra cette formulation au sein de sa table des matières pour faire référence à nos règles de lecture/prononciation en quatre versions. Au sein de celle-ci se trouvent les éditions de Verwithagen (1558, 1562, 1571, 1584, 1586), Jean Bellère (1569), Hans Coesmans (1582), Hierosme Verdussen (1608), Jean Mommaert (1624, 1647). Remarquons que le latin est souvent absent de ces éditions quadrilingues au profit d'une langue vernaculaire. Cela pourrait être un signe du changement de statut progressif de cette langue historiquement véhiculaire en Europe.

Signalons au passage que toutes les éditions appartenant à cette famille, hormis celles de Verwithagen, comportent également les conjugaisons et la prononciation de Gabriel Meurier (1558).[9] Cependant, d'autres continuateurs ont préféré ne conserver que ces dernières parties au détriment des douze règles, celles-ci étant donc absentes d'un grand nombre de vocabulaires de la série de Berlaimont. C'est ce que nous abordons dans le paragraphe suivant.

La Prononciation de Meurier face à De perfecta

Il semblerait que, dans la famille des Berlaimont, le premier à abandonner les règles de prononciation d'origine soit l'imprimeur Girard de Salenson, dans son édition de 1568 publiée à Gand (Bourland 1933: 295). Il supprime la section intitulée en latin 'De perfecta linguae Gallicae lectione', mais aussi le 'Modus legendi atque scribendi linguae Hispanicae', et insère par contre d'autre indications de prononciation puisées dans un ouvrage de 1558: *Conjugaisons, regles, et instructions, mout propres et necessairement requises, pour ceux qui desirent apprendre François, Italien, Espagnol, & Flamen* publiées conjointement avec la *Breue instruction contenante la maniere de bien prononcer & lire le François, Italien, Espagnol, & Flamen* à Anvers par Jean Waesberghe.

De ce que nous avons pu consulter,[10] une grande proportion des continuateurs de Berlaimont poursuivent le modèle de Salenson, en d'autres termes, la section 'De perfecta' disparaît pratiquement de la circulation au XVIIe siècle, si l'on omet les éditions que nous avons signalées de Verdussen et Mommaert. Pourtant, la disparition des règles n'est pas totale. Une traduction espagnole de notre section présente dans le *Vocabulario de los vocablos* de Jacques Ledel publiée à Alcalá de Henares en 1565 va être à l'origine d'une résurgence au XVIIe puis au XVIIIe siècle.

Traductions et adaptations dans la Péninsule Ibérique

Jacques Ledel: 1565

En 1559, Isabelle de Valois devient reine consort d'Espagne par son mariage avec Philippe II. Celle-ci arrive à la cour espagnole accompagnée de sa suite, dont fait partie Jacques Ledel.[11] Ce dernier est l'auteur du *Vocabulario de los vocablos*, sorti six ans plus tard des presses d'Alcalá de Henares et souvent publié conjointement avec la première grammaire de français publiée en Espagne, œuvre de Baltasar de Sotomayor.[12]

L'ouvrage présente, précédant une liste de mots et quelques dialogues, deux parties de prononciation: d'une part les règles dont nous retraçons l'histoire, et d'autre part la prononciation de l'espagnol connue sous le nom latin de 'Modus legendi atque scribendi linguae Hispanicae'. Il est prouvé que la publication de Ledel est, en partie, le remaniement d'un des vocabulaires de Berlaimont, mais il est difficile de déterminer lequel. Les diverses opinions à ce sujet se résument à deux positions. La première serait que Ledel prend comme source le vocabulaire de Grave de 1558 (Lépinette 2001: 104; Suárez Gómez 2008: 60), ce qui revient aussi à dire que l''Estilo para bien leer y hablar la lengua Francesa', c'est-à-dire la version en espagnol de 'De perfecta' présente chez Ledel, serait le fruit de la traduction de celui-ci à partir de la version latine (Bruña Cuevas 2000: 64-65). La deuxième désigne plutôt l'une des éditions de Verwithaghen (1558 ou 1562) comme source possible (Pablo Núñez 2010: I, 373), et dans ce cas, la version en espagnol de Ledel serait une simple adaptation d'une première version déjà existante dans cette langue.

Toujours est-il que nos règles de prononciation du français apparaissent pour la première fois dans la Péninsule Ibérique et elles présentent quelques différences notables en comparaison avec les règles originales. Nous ne nous arrêterons pas sur les différences mineures telles que les changements d'exemples ou d'ordre de présentation de ceux-ci, mais nous signalerons les modifications les plus substantielles.

Avant toute chose, il faut savoir que Ledel a eu tendance à réduire toutes les parties du vocabulaire de Berlaimont dans lesquelles il a puisé. Les règles de prononciation n'ont pas échappé à cet élagage général. En effet, la différence la plus notable réside dans l'élimination des deux dernières règles et dans la troncation de la dixième. Rappelons que les deux dernières règles portaient sur la non prononciation de *u* précédé de *q* ou de *g*.

La raison de cette élimination pourrait se trouver dans la correspondance partielle entre le système de lecture français et espagnol sur les deux dernières règles: en espagnol patrimonial, le *u* ne se prononce pas dans les trigrammes *que* et *qui*, pas plus que dans *gue*, tant que *u* ne porte pas de tréma bien entendu. L'auteur aurait donc adapté les explications à son public, des hispanophones. En ce qui concerne la dixième règle, si l'on admet que Ledel a traduit en s'appuyant sur la version latine, il se pourrait qu'il n'ait pas saisi l'idée transmise dans le texte original et l'ait adaptée tant bien que mal. Il tente de maintenir la différence entre [e] et [ə] en fin de mot, mais omet la mention à l'enchaînement.

L'autre différence majeure se trouve dans la deuxième règle. Ledel change l'exemple qui est censé illustrer les indications portant sur la prononciation des consonnes finales, mais conserve les mêmes explications, ce qui donne lieu à plusieurs erreurs: deux indications fausses et un renvoi à une remarque non fournie, qui en revanche existait bel et bien dans l'original.

Mis à part ces erreurs, la version de Ledel a pu être utile dans une certaine mesure à son public. En effet, nous avons dit que la majorité des explications portaient sur la non prononciation du *s* implosif; or, ce n'est qu'en 1740 que l'académie française adopte la réforme de l'orthographe en ce qui concerne les accents aigu et circonflexe remplaçant un *s* implosif non prononcé, comme dans les mots *étranger*, *blâme* ou *chêne*, pour ne citer que trois exemples apparaissant chez Berlaimont (1527). Il en ira donc de même dans les reprises postérieures, comme celle de 1647 arrangée et publiée par l'imprimeur catalan Antoni Lacavalleria.

Antoni Lacavalleria: 1647

Antoni Lacavalleria était le fils d'un autre imprimeur, Pere Lacavalleria, natif de Guyenne mais qui avait passé vingt-trois ans à Barcelone. Quand celui-ci meurt en 1645 ou 1646, Antoni s'occupe du négoce familial. Il ne tarde pas à publier, en 1647, une œuvre intitulée *Grammatica con reglas muy provechosas, y necesarias para aprender a leer, y escrivir la lengua Francesa, conferida con la Castellana*. Avec, en toile de fond, la *Guerra dels Segadors* (1640-59) opposant la couronne espagnole et la couronne française en Catalogne, cet ouvrage s'adressait sans doute aux Catalans hispanophones qui devaient se confronter, entre autres, à l'administration française; les Français résidant en Catalogne, pour leur part, ont également pu utiliser la *Grammatica* pour apprendre l'espagnol.

Cette 'grammaire' présente une courte licence après la page de titre, puis immédiatement après, l'«Estilo para bien leer, y hablar la lengua Francesa»: cent vingt ans après leur première publication, les règles de Berlaimont réapparaissent. Lacavalleria copie presque littéralement Ledel (1565): le nombre de règles est le même, la dixième est tronquée également et la deuxième présente les mêmes erreurs que dans la version du courtisan du XVIe siècle. Il effectue tout de même une correction mineure au sein de la deuxième règle, ce qui prouve qu'il avait ne serait-ce que survolé les règles avant de les copier. Antoni Lacavalleria sera lui-même l'une des sources dans lesquelles puisera Baldiri Reixac i Carbó pour rédiger une partie de ses règles sur la prononciation du français.

Baldiri Reixac Carbó: 1749

Baldiri Reixac Carbó était un maître d'école, en plus d'être le curé de Sant Martí d'Ollers. C'était aussi un pédagogue actuellement reconnu (Marqués 1993) qui fit publier en 1749, à Gérone, une œuvre singulière rédigée en catalan et regroupant ses idées sur l'éducation des enfants intitulée *Instruccions per a l'ensenyança de minyons*. Il y préconise, entre autres, l'apprentissage du catalan, du latin, de l'espagnol, du français et de l'italien et insère à ce dessein une petite grammaire de chacune de ces langues. La visée de Reixac est donc celle de donner une formation générale aux enfants et de permettre l'accès aux ouvrages rédigés en français, en ce qui nous concerne.

Pour le français, il propose, au long de trente-deux pages et selon une structure classique, une partie de prononciation et une autre de morphologie. Dans la première partie, après une présentation des lettres/sons dans l'ordre alphabétique suivi d'explications sur les diphtongues et les triphtongues, l'auteur inclut une section qu'il nomme 'Apendix' [*sic*]. Les neuf premières lignes sont un commentaire sur certaines combinaisons vocaliques, mais dès la page 357, une liste de règles et d'exemples bien connus refait surface. Notre Catalan reprend certaines des règles de l''Estilo' d'Antoni Lacavalleria sans le nommer. Après comparaison des deux versions, il ne fait aucun doute que la source de Reixac est la *Grammatica* de 1647.

Dans la longue histoire de ces règles, le maître d'école de Gérone a apporté son grain de sel. Par rapport à son modèle, il effectue deux modifications principales. Tout d'abord il supprime tout bonnement plusieurs parties: l'introduction aux règles et la première règle elle-même, qui n'avait pas vraiment de raison d'être, même dans sa toute première version. Il a donc le mérite d'être le premier adaptateur qui décide d'omettre ce commentaire si évident sur la nécessité d'apprendre à prononcer les voyelles et les consonnes, un conseil qui ne pouvait que faire sourire le lecteur puisqu'aucun moyen ne lui était fourni pour parvenir à cette fin; les règles neuf et dix sont également retranchées de l'*Apendix*. La deuxième modification réside dans la correction de la deuxième règle, fausse en partie chez Ledel et Lacavalleria, et qui récupère, finalement, une certaine cohérence.

Conclusions

Le recyclage, et autres emprunts et récupérations diverses étaient une pratique répandue à l'époque où nous situons notre étude. Signalons tout de même que l'histoire des règles de lecture/prononciation que nous avons exposée dans cet article s'est étalée sur plus de deux siècles, une longévité peu commune pour des œuvres d'apprentissage des langues vulgaires, du moins en ce qui concerne ce type d'explications.[13] Bien que le propre vocabulaire dont sont issues lesdites règles a joui lui-même d'un nombre considérable de rééditions, nous avons vu que ce n'est pas au sein de cette série que se sont perpétuées le plus longtemps nos indications sur les lettres/sons du français. Dès le milieu du XVIe siècle, en effet, et jusqu'au milieu du XVIIe, elles disparaissaient graduellement des rééditions de Berlaimont au profit de la prononciation d'un autre maître de français anversois, Gabriel Meurier.

Au sein de cette exposition, nous avons montré que c'est aux trois récupérations successives des XVIe, XVIIe et finalement XVIIIe siècles de la Péninsule Ibérique que nous devons la réapparition — plus de deux cents ans après sa première publication — d'un matériel didactique sans doute adressé, au départ, aux marchands néerlandophones désireux d'apprendre le français, et destiné, en fin de course, à former les enfants catalanophones. Entre-temps, Ledel et A. Lacavalleria les avaient récupérées, l'un pour des courtisans hispanophones et l'autre, certainement pour des Catalans, hispanophones également. Nous voyons que les publics qui ont été confrontés à ces règles ont sensiblement varié tout au long de leur histoire.

Mais pourquoi, dans le cas de Lacavalleria, publier de nouveau en 1647 des règles orientées à la lecture correcte du français datant du milieu du XVIe siècle (1565),[14] puis, en ce qui concerne Reixac, reprendre, en 1749, ces mêmes règles anciennes d'un siècle pour l'auteur ? Plusieurs raisons s'offrent à nous.

En premier lieu, il faut signaler le fait qu'entre les œuvres de Ledel et de Sotomayor, publiées en 1565 et la première réapparition des règles en 1647, seuls deux ouvrages d'apprentissage du français voient le jour en Espagne: la réédition à Madrid en 1635 de la partie française de la grammaire de Diego de Cisneros et le *Dictionnaire* de Pere Lacavalleria publiée en 1642. Cela ne laissait pas beaucoup de choix à Lacavalleria fils: voulant publier une grammaire de français sans se compliquer la tâche, il élude l'ouvrage de Cisneros, trop complexe, et profite de deux œuvres certainement oubliées à son époque pour effectuer une refonte dont nos règles de lecture font partie. En ce qui concerne Reixac, il était catalan, tout comme notre imprimeur barcelonais. La grammaire de ce dernier bénéficiait peut-être d'une certaine notoriété en territoire catalan; dans tous les cas, Reixac la connaissait et il en réutilise une partie, sans le nommer. La longévité des règles de lecture a donc pu être favorisée par certaines circonstances éditoriales et territoriales.

En second lieu, aucun des deux auteurs ou imprimeur/auteur ayant repris ces règles n'était spécialiste du français, de l'enseignement du français ni même des langues étrangères en général: ceux-ci se seraient alors contenté de les reproduire sans se poser la question de leur utilité vis-à-vis de leur adaptation aux normes de lecture/prononciation de chaque époque et de leur conformité aux habitudes de lecture d'un public particulier. Nous avons vu que Ledel, avant, avait déjà supprimé les deux dernières règles, peut-être dans un souci d'adapter les informations à un public espagnol. Ce n'est pas si surprenant, puisqu'il était français. Mais Lacavalleria pouvait également posséder des rudiments de français: son père était originaire de Guyenne et s'il avait effectivement corrigé certaines des erreurs commises par Ledel, c'est qu'il était à même d'apprécier la validité des indications données. Quant à Reixac, il effectue également quelques corrections, ce qui prouve qu'il n'avait pas copié les règles telles quelles, sans les comprendre et sans évaluer un tant soit peu leur validité. Il ne semblerait donc pas que ce soit la négligence ou l'ignorance qui aient été le motif de la longévité de nos indications de prononciation.

Il faut alors peut-être chercher dans le contenu des règles elles-mêmes la raison de leur résurgence en Espagne à deux siècles d'intervalle. Nous avons déjà commenté le fait que la plupart d'entre elles portaient sur le *s* implosif intérieur. Or, à ce sujet, Thurot (1883: II, 319-20) affirme, en se situant à son époque, que 'depuis Palsgrave l'usage n'[a] pas varié sensiblement dans la prononciation de l'*s*. Elle était, dès le XVIe siècle, sonore ou muette dans les mêmes conditions qu'aujourd'hui, à un petit nombre d'exceptions près'. Cela signifie que les règles générales et les exceptions possédaient la même validité au XVIe siècle, qu'aux XVIIe et XVIIIe. Les successives rééditions de nos règles ont donc pu être utiles aux étrangers de ces différentes époques mais également nécessaires, puisque 'l'embarras pour les étrangers était très grand de savoir quand l's devait être prononcée ou muette' (Thurot 1883: II, 319). Cela pourrait nous amener à penser que ce n'est peut-être pas uniquement le fruit du hasard si une courte liste d'indications de lecture a réussi à traverser l'histoire de l'apprentissage du français pendant plus de deux cents ans, d'Anvers à Gérone.

Bibliography

Primary sources

BERLAIMONT, NOËL DE. 1527. *Vocabulare van nieus ge-ordineert. Vocabulaire de nouveau ordonne et derechief recorrige* (Antwerp: Jacob van Liesuelt)

———. 1536. *Vocabulare van nyeus gheordineert. Vocabulaire de nouveau ordonne pour aprendre legierement a bien lire, escripre et parler francois et flameng* (Antwerp: Willem Vorsterman)

———. 1551. *Vocabulaer in vier spraken Duytsch, Francois, Latijn, ende Spaensch. Vocabulaire en quatre langues, Flamengue, Francoise, Latine, Espagnole. Dictionarium Quadrilingue, Teutonicum, Gallicum, Latinum, atq; Hispanicum. Vocabulario de quatro lenguas, Tudesco, Frances, Latino, y Español* (Leuven: Bartholomy de Grave)

———. 1565. *Dictionnaire, Colloques, ou Dialogues en Quatre Langues, Flamen, François, Espaignol, & Italien. Vocabulaer, Colloquien oft Tsamencoutinghen van vier Spraken, Duyts, Fransoys, Spaens, ende Italiens* (Antwerp: Jan Verwithagen)

———. 1568. *Dictionnaire, Colloques, ou Dialogues en Quatre Langues, Flamen, François, Español, & Italien. Vocabulaer, Colloquien oft Tsamensprekinghen, in vier vier Spraken, Vlaemsch, Françoysch, Spaensch, ende Italiaensch* (Ghent: Girard de Salenson)

CISNEROS, DIEGO DE. 1635. *De Grammatica Francesa en Español* (Madrid: Imprenta del Reino)

LACAVALLERIA, ANTONI. 1647. *Grammatica con reglas muy prouechosas y necessarias para aprender a leer, y escriuir la lengua Francesa, conferida con la Castellana* (Barcelona: Antoni Lacavalleria)

LACAVALLERIA, PERE. 1642. *Dictionario Castellano – Dictionaire François – Dictionari Catala* (Barcelona: Pere Lacavalleria)

LEDEL, JACQUES. 1565. *Vocabulario de los vocablos que mas comunmente se suelen vsar* (Alcalá de Henares: Pedro de Robles & Francisco de Cormellas)

MEURIER, GABRIEL. 1558. *Conivgaisons, regles, et instrvctions, movt propres et necessairement reqvises, pour ceux qui desirent apprendre François, Italien, Espagnol, & Flamen* (Antwerp: Jean van Waesberge)

REIXAC I CARBÓ, BALDIRI. 1749. *Instruccions per la ensenyança de minyons* (Girona: Antón Oliva)

SOTOMAYOR, BALATASAR DE. 1565. *Gramatica con reglas mvy prouechosas y necessarias para aprender a leer y escriuir la lengua Francesa, conferida con la Castellana* (Alcalá de Henares: Pedro de Robles & Francisco de Cormellas)

THUROT, CHARLES, 1881 (vol. 1)-1883 (vol. 2). *De la prononciation française depuis le commencement du XVIe siècle, d'après les témoignages des grammairiens* (Paris: Imprimerie nationale)

———. 1555. *Vtil y breve institution para aprender los principios y fundamentos de la lengua española* (Leuven: Bartholomy de Grave)

Secondary sources

AUROUX, SYLVAIN, ET LOUIS-JEAN CALVET. 1973. 'De la phonétique à l'apprentissage de la lecture : la théorie des sons du langage au XVIIIe siècle', *La Linguistique*, 9: 71-88

BOURLAND, CAROLINE. 1933. '*The Spanish School-Master* and the Polyglot Derivatives of Noel de Berlaimont's *Vocabulare*', *Revue Hispanique*, 81: 283-318

BRUÑA CUEVAS, MANUEL. 1996. 'Le Problème de l'orthographe française dans les grammaires de français à l'usage des Espagnols et dans les dictionnaires bilingues français-espagnol et espagnol-français (XVIe-XVIIIe siècles)', in *La lingüística francesa: gramática, historia y epistemología*, ed. by Emilia Alonso Montilla, Manuel Bruña Cuevas and María Muñoz Romero, 2 vols (Séville: Grupo Andaluz de Pragmática), I, 85-101

——. 2000. 'L'Enseignement de la prononciation française aux Espagnols (XVIe et XVIIe siècles)', in *Grammaire et enseignement du français, 1500–1700*, ed. by Jan De Clercq, Nico Lioce and Pierre Swiggers (Louvain and Paris: Peeters), pp. 61-96

CATACH, NINA. 2001. *Histoire de l'orthographe française* (Paris: Champion)

CORCUERA MANSO, JUAN FIDEL, and ANTONIO GASPAR GALÁN. 1999. *La lengua francesa en España en el siglo XVI: estudio y edición del* Vocabulario de los vocablos *de Jacques de Liaño* (Saragossa: Prensas Universitarias de Zaragoza)

LÉPINETTE, BRIGITTE. 1996. 'Les Premières Grammaires du français (1565-1799) publiées en Espagne : modèles, sources et rôle de l'espagnol', *Histoire, Épistémologie, Langage*, 18: 149-77

——. 2001. *El francés y el español en contraste y en contacto (siglos XV–XVII): estudios de historiografía lingüística. Lexicografía. Gramática. Traducción* (Valencia: Universitat de València)

LINDEMANN, MARGARETE. 1994. *Die französischen Wörterbücher von den Anfängen bis 1600: Entstehung und typologische Beschreibung* (Tübingen: Niemeyer)

MARQUÉS, SALOMÓN. 1993. 'Baldiri Reixac', in *Historia de la educación en España y América*, ed. by Buenaventura Delgado Criado (Madrid: Fundación Santa María / Ediciones SM), pp. 761-64

NIEDEREHE, HANS-JOSEF. 1994. *Bibliografía cronológica de la lingüística, la gramática y la lexicografía del español (BICRES I). Desde los comienzos hasta 1600* (Amsterdam/ Philadelphia: Benjamins)

——. 1999. *Bibliografía cronológica de la lingüística, la gramática y la lexicografía del español (BICRES II). Desde el año 1601 hasta el año 1700* (Amsterdam/Philadelphia: Benjamins)

PABLO NÚÑEZ, LUIS. 2010. *El Arte de las Palabras: diccionarios e imprenta en el Siglo de Oro*, 2 vols (Mérida: Editora Regional de Extremadura)

PEETERS-FONTAINAS, JEAN. 1965. *Bibliographie des impressions espagnoles des Pays-Bas méridionaux* (Nieuwkoop: de Graaf)

SUÁREZ GÓMEZ, GONZALO. 2008. *La enseñanza del francés en España hasta 1850. ¿Con qué libros aprendían francés los españoles?*, ed. by Juan Francisco García Bascuñana and Esther Juan Oliva (Barcelona: Promociones y Publicaciones Universitarias)

VIÉMON, MARC. 2014. 'Phonétique syntactique et resyllabation dans les grammaires de français pour Espagnols (XVI–XVIII siècles)', *Thélème*, 29: 199-222

Notes to Chapter 5

1. Les explications de type graphophonétique, c'est-à-dire prendre l'écrit comme point de départ pour en expliquer la réalisation orale, vont se poursuivre sur plusieurs siècles, pour la simple et bonne raison que le cheminement inverse, dénombrer les sons pour en donner ensuite les diverses graphies, ne sera complètement adopté que bien plus tard, au terme de nombreux progrès effectués dans le domaine de la phonétique surtout à partir du XVIIIe siècle. Auroux et Calvet (1973: 72) sont formels à ce sujet: 'Aucun siècle cependant, excepté le nôtre, n'a fait de tels progrès dans l'étude du matériau phonique du langage humain'.

2. Faute d'espace, nous ne pouvons consigner dans nos références bibliographiques la totalité des sources primaires que nous avons consultées. Pour plus d'informations sur les différentes rééditions du vocabulaire de Berlaimont, voir Niederehe (1994: 441-42; 1999: 445-46), Peeters-Fontainas (1965: 166-87), Lindemann (1994: 604-06, 608-11, 615-19), Pablo Núñez (2010, II, 202-311). Ces deux derniers chercheurs proposent également une filiation des œuvres étudiées.
3. Au XVIe siècle, les petits ouvrages permettant l'apprentissage de plusieurs langues foisonnent. Ils sont souvent destinés aux marchands et aux voyageurs en général et servent de 'guides' de conversation que l'on peut emporter avec soi du fait de leur petite taille. Cependant, les manuels de langues vernaculaires à orientation pratique sont plus anciens: dès le milieu du XIVe, le *Livre des mestiers* fait son apparition à Bruges et, à la fin du siècle sont rédigées les *Manières de Langage*. En 1483, William Caxton publie les *Dialogues in French and English*, qui font également partie de ce groupe d'œuvres visant une communication orale et qui dérivent directement du *Livre des mestiers*, tout comme le *Gesprächbüchlein*, publié par Hoffmann von Fallersleben c. 1420, ou le *Vocabulair romain et flameng* imprimé avant 1501 à Anvers, par Roland Van Dorpe. Nous le voyons, le manuel de Berlaimont, lorsqu'il est publié, perpétue une histoire déjà vieille de presque deux cents ans.
4. Cette deuxième règle, recommandant de ne pas prononcer une consonne finale suivie d'une autre consonne, est illustrée par l'exemple suivant: 'vous mauez faict grand tort / quant vous mauez prins mes liures'.
5. Nous donnons des exemples de ces règles lorsque nous l'étudions plus en détail.
6. Les mots concernés sont 'aultre / aultrement / hault / moult / ceulx / eulx'.
7. L'enchaînement est la jonction qui se produit dans la chaîne parlée entre une consonne finale toujours prononcée et la voyelle initiale du mot suivant, créant ainsi une nouvelle distribution syllabique des mots en question. Pour plus de renseignements sur le traitement des phénomènes de phonétique syntactique au sein des œuvres d'apprentissage du français pour les Espagnols aux XVIe, XVIIe et XVIIIe siècles, voir Viémon (2014).
8. Dans l'avis au lecteur de 1551, l'imprimeur Grave explique qu'il a 'prins l'inuention de Noel de Barlemont, lequel a tourné de Flameng en Latin treselegament, et le plus proprement que faire se pouait, le tresçauant home en diuerses langues et arts M. Cornille Valere d'Vtrecht'. En 1558, nous pouvons lire cette fois-ci au sein de l'avis au lecteur également 'Apres nous auons au lieu du Flamen mis l'Italien, diligement reueu et corrigé par Maistre Antoin Maria Calabria'.
9. Chez Meurier (1558), la prononciation apparaît au sein d'un traité intitulé *La Breue instruction contenante la maniere de bien prononcer & lire le François, Italien, Espagnol, & Flamen*. Pour ce qui est du français, les explications — rédigées elles-mêmes en français — commencent par un rapide exposé des diphtongues suivi de la prononciation de chaque lettre ou combinaison graphique selon un ordre non strictement alphabétique et terminent par la *Breue instruction pour sçavoir lire le François*. Ces règles de lecture concernent les consonnes finales et l'élision.
10. Voir note 2.
11. Pour plus d'informations sur ce personnage et son œuvre, nous renvoyons à Corcuera Manso et Gaspar Galán (1999).
12. Ces deux ouvrages étaient principalement destinés aux courtisans espagnols désireux d'apprendre la langue française, même si la grammaire de Sotomayor pouvait également être utile aux Français pour apprendre l'espagnol.
13. Certains dialogues et conjugaisons, pour leur part, ont été réutilisés et réédités bien des fois également.
14. En effet, A. Lacavalleria prend comme source le vocabulaire de Ledel. Il ne connaissait probablement pas l'existence de la toute première version en néerlandais de 1527.

CHAPTER 6

❖

Latin Schoolbooks in Late Seventeenth-Century Finland

Suvi Randén

This chapter discusses Latin schoolbooks in late seventeenth-century Finland. Bishop Johannes Gezelius the Elder's (1615-1690) printing house published approximately thirty different schoolbooks for Latin studies during Gezelius's episcopacy (1664–90) in Turku, the capital of the Finnish region in the Kingdom of Sweden. Many of the books have prefaces and epilogues expounding their pedagogical thought and recommending appropriate teaching methods for Latin teachers. The prefaces highlight the importance of learning vocabulary, reading text before studying grammar, and taking into account the pupils' learning capacity. Some of the prefaces emphasize the moral aspects of language studies, while others discuss the benefits of also knowing languages other than the classical ones. The texts bear influences from a number of pedagogical thinkers, both from Sweden and from the European Continent. Therefore, the books enabled Latin teachers in Finland to become acquainted with recent ideas relating to teaching methods. The schoolbooks published by Gezelius's printing house represent a significant attempt to improve teaching and learning of Latin in seventeenth-century Finland. Publishing these schoolbooks coincided with a major reform in educational curriculum and pedagogical ideas.

The educational system in the Kingdom of Sweden — which then included Finland — underwent extensive changes during the seventeenth century. New schools were founded, a new school level, the *gymnasium*, was introduced, and the School Law was repeatedly under revision. Improvements were required both by the Church and the state as more priests and civil servants were needed in the Swedish Kingdom, which was one of the major powers in Europe and intellectually characterized by Lutheran Orthodoxy. Although the need for improvements and for the unification of the school system was widely accepted, there was also disagreement among the Swedish bishops, professors and leading politicians about the content of the reforms. The educational discussion was inspired by an increasing interest in new pedagogical theories, and thoughts of educational reformers on the European Continent, including Petrus Ramus (1515–1572), Wolfgang Ratke (1571–1635) and Johannes Amos Comenius (1592–1670).[1]

Throughout this time, Latin dominated language teaching at all school levels in Sweden — the university, the *gymnasium* and the elementary level consisting of children's schools (*scholae triviales inferiores* or *paedagogia*) and upper trivial schools (*scholae triviales superiores*).[2] In addition to Lutheran Orthodoxy, the cultural life of seventeenth-century Sweden was characterized by classical Humanism with its emphasis on Latin literature and rhetoric.[3] According to the School Law of 1649, *Ratio Informandi in Scholis Trivialibus*, fluency in Latin was required because of 'its most frequent use in studies and in all fields of life' (*propter uberrimum ejus usum, in studijs et omni vita*). The purpose was to be able to write and speak Latin 'not only congruently but also purely' (*non congruenter tantum, sed et pure*).[4]

Until the latter half of the seventeenth century, schoolbooks for Latin and other subjects were mainly imported to Finland from Sweden proper or from Germany.[5] The first printing house in Finland was the Academy Press in Turku (Åbo), the capital of the Finnish region in the Kingdom of Sweden. It was founded in 1642, two years after the Academy.[6] Still, all kinds of books were expensive and difficult to obtain. Wishing to improve both university studies and popular education in his diocese, Swedish-born Bishop Johannes Gezelius the Elder (1615–1690) founded his own printing house in Turku in the late 1660s. Gezelius appointed Swedish printer Johan Winter (d. 1705) to operate the press and not only hired a binder but also acquired his own paper mill.[7]

During the next quarter of a century, Gezelius's printing house issued a variety of books for different school subjects and levels.[8] The majority of the books were in Latin, as other school subjects such as religion and Greek were also taught by means of Latin books. For teaching and learning the Latin language itself, Gezelius published approximately thirty different books including grammars, textbooks and dictionaries.[9] According to the title pages, most of these books were meant for children's schools and upper trivial schools[10] or — meaning practically the same — 'for boy age' (*in usum aetatis puerilis*),[11] i.e. approximately from age seven onwards. According to the School Law of 1649, this age was suited for learning languages.[12]

Gezelius's printing house continued to produce schoolbooks during the episcopacy (1690–1718) of the Bishop's son, Johannes Gezelius the Younger (1647–1718). From 1689 onwards, schoolbooks for Latin studies began to be printed also in Vyborg (Viipuri), in the eastern part of Finland.[13] As the Latin books published in Turku by Gezelius the Elder form the first major body of books printed for teaching and learning Latin in schools in Finland, this article concentrates on them. The books are discussed from the perspective of pedagogical thought, as it appears in the prefaces and on the title pages of the books.

The Authors

The approximately thirty books published by Gezelius for Latin studies include textbooks by both classical authors and Early Modern writers. Works of Cicero, for example, were commonly used as textbooks and models for writing and speaking in schools.[14] Newly composed works include plays by Dutch playwright and teacher Cornelius Schonaeus (1540–1611), who was called the Terentius Christianus,

'Christian Terence'; and dialogues written or collected by German professors Johannes Posselius the Younger (1565–1623) and Christophorus Helvicus (1581–1617) and Danish professor Stephanus Johannis Stephanius (1599–1650).[15] In addition, no fewer than four editions of the elementary encyclopaedia *Orbis sensualium pictus* by the Czech pedagogue Johannes Amos Comenius were printed by Gezelius during the 1680s.[16] Desiderius Erasmus's (1466–1536) *Libellus aureus* and some other textbooks were printed twice, and an elementary grammar named *Donatus* three times.[17]

In addition to these books, more or less commonly used in schools in Sweden and elsewhere in Europe, Gezelius's printing house issued schoolbooks written by authors based in Finland, including the Bishop himself. Firstly, Gezelius himself compiled a pedagogical Latin–Swedish dictionary *Vocum Latinarum Sylloge* (printed in 1672 and 1688) with an extensive preface. He composed a preface also for *Aureae sententiae*, a collection of proverbs from both the Bible and profane authors of different eras, which was printed four times during the 1670s and 1680s. The preface deals elaborately with the method that Latin teachers should use. In the preface, Gezelius discusses the importance of learning vocabulary and recommends the method of using root words: by examining the roots and words stemming from them, the pupils can familiarize themselves with a large number of words effectively. He also emphasizes that the teacher must adjust his teaching to the capacity of the pupils (*Aureae sententiae* 1671: preface). Gezelius's elaborate preface to Comenius's *Orbis sensualium pictus* is also notable: among other things, Gezelius discusses common deficiencies in teaching.[18] Three of the Latin books published by Gezelius have unsigned prefaces, but these resemble the other prefaces of the publishing house in content, including the ones written by the Bishop himself.[19]

The Finnish authors Barthollus Thomae Rajalenius (d. *c.* 1703) and Henricus Matthiae Florinus (1633–1705) also wrote prefaces for their own works, expounding their pedagogical thought. Rajalenius, Vicar of Rauma, composed a Latin grammar, *Breviarium grammaticae Latinae* (1683), which contains not only a preface and an epilogue, but also ten pages of pedagogical discussion (*Informandi modus*) in the style of academic dissertations. The grammar includes exercises for the 'future student of Latin' (*cum exercitiis, futuro Latinitatis studioso*, according to the title page). Florinus, Schoolmaster of Hämeenlinna trivial school and later Vicar of Paimio, compiled an elementary Latin–Swedish–Finnish dictionary, *Nomenclatura Rerum brevissima, Latino–Sveco–Finnonica* (1678), with a preface for the teacher. The words in this elementary dictionary are not organized by root words, as in Gezelius's *Vocum Latinarum Sylloge*, nor in strict alphabetical order, but are divided according to subject under twenty-two different headings.[20]

Each of the three authors based in Finland mentions the shortage of proper schoolbooks as the reason for composing and publishing their works. Gezelius says this explicitly in one of his prefaces: his aim was to improve the availability of schoolbooks and to lower their price.[21] The books also share other kinds of aims with respect to their publication. For example, Gezelius hopes his dictionary will help pupils learn Latin 'without weariness' (*sine taedio*).[22] *Bellum grammaticale,* a textbook about 'a grammar war', is meant to generate both utility and pleasure (*Ob usum & Jucunditatem*),[23] as is Comenius's illustrated *Orbis sensualium pictus*, which is meant to be 'given to the hands of the pupils for their delight' (*dandum pueris in manus hunc libellum, ad oblectandum*).[24] Also Florinus and Rajalenius hope their books will render learning easier.[25] In reality, according to the authors, teachers did not use proper methods and therefore made learning tedious and difficult.[26] The authors' clear aim is to improve the situation.

Advice on Teaching Latin

Some of the Latin textbooks published by Gezelius's printing house include little or no advice regarding their use. Works of Cicero, for example, were to be read all through trivial school and in *gymnasium* according to the School Law of 1649,[27] but the editions published by Gezelius contain no further information on using them, apart from mentioning the most suitable school level for the book.[28] The works on elementary grammar, *Donatus* and *Paradigmata declinationum & conjugationum Latina*, have no prefaces, but the title pages advise that easy texts should be read, and writing and speaking in Latin be practised while studying the paradigms (*Donatus. Seu grammaticae Latinae rudimenta* 1684: title page; *Paradigmata declinationum & conjugationum Latina* 1670: title page).

Those books which have extensive prefaces, however, do share several pedagogical ideas and advice for the teachers. Firstly, the importance of learning vocabulary is emphasized in all types of the books. For example, Henricus Florinus recommends in the preface for his elementary dictionary that one should begin language studies by learning vocabulary: 'without (a) vocabulary, the pupils can hardly proceed with studies of Latin or the Liberal Arts' (*Pueros in Latinae linguae, artiumq(ue) liberalium studio, sine rerum Nomenclatura parum aut nihil progredi posse*, in *Nomenclatura Rerum brevissima, Latino–Sveco–Finnonica* 1678: preface). According to Gezelius's preface in *Aureae sententiae*, 'language consists of words; if you know the words, you know the language' (*Lingua vero vocabulis constat, quae si quis didicerit, utiq(ue) lingvam novit*). Grammatical rules should be dealt with only after learning the language, i.e. the words (*Ergo lingua prius discenda, quam regulae Grammaticae*). Even Barthollus Rajalenius — in his grammar — advises that pupils 'should not be vexed with long grammatical rules from the beginning: the language should be learned first, and then grammar will teach to use the language correctly' (*non mox prolixis Grammaticis praeceptis vexandus: Lingva prius discatur quam illa ars postea correcte docebit*, in *Breviarum grammaticae Latinae* 1683: *Informandi modus*). However, Florinus stresses that elementary grammar should not be omitted, 'as often happens due to the teachers' preposterous haste causing much harm to the pupils' (*ut vulgo fieri solet praepostera paedagogorum festinatione, maximo cum damno puerorum*, in *Nomenclatura Rerum brevissima, Latino–Sveco–Finnonica* 1678: preface). In addition, it is emphasized in several of the prefaces that Latin text should be read already during elementary studies, and that reading text should be connected with studying grammar: 'grammatical rules should be demonstrated from the text itself' (*praecepta Grammatices, &c. ex ipso textu demonstrentur*).[29]

In accordance with the emphasis on vocabulary and reading text, some of the textbooks have vocabulary lists attached. These *indices* were originally compiled by notable German scholars: the works by ancient authors Cornelius Nepos, Curtius Rufus and Annaeus Florus include vocabulary lists abridged from editions by Johannes Boeclerus (1611–1672) and Johannes Freinshemius (1608–1660), German professors invited to Uppsala University during the reign of Queen Christina (r. 1632–1654) (Lindroth 1975: 186 and passim). The vocabulary lists consist mostly of synonyms or explanations in Latin for words appearing in the text. Occasionally only the location of the headword in the text is indicated, but for some words there are explanations or related words even in modern languages.[30] On the title pages of these works, there is no mention of the target readership of the books, as was usual. Instead, the authors of the original vocabulary lists are mentioned, highlighting their work.[31] Via the schoolbooks published by Gezelius in Turku, the philological work of these important scholars of the era came to be known in schools in Finland.

Besides emphasizing vocabulary in general, the method of using root words and word families is praised and utilized in the books. For example, in Gezelius's Latin–Swedish dictionary *Vocum Latinarum Sylloge*, the words are not in strict alphabetical order, but arranged as families deriving from the same root.[32] The concepts of root word (*primitivum*), derived word (*derivatum*) and compound word (*compositum*) are discussed extensively in prefaces of different kinds of books.[33] According to Gezelius, the teacher should begin with words familiar to the pupils and then advance to related words and synonyms, using word families such as *anima* [breath], *animus* [soul], *animal* [animal, living creature]; *caput* [head], *capillus* [hair], *capitium* [covering for the head]; *manus* [hand], *manica* [sleeve], *mantile* [napkin]. With this method, the pupils are said to learn several words at one time: as they look up a word in the dictionary, seeing the root and related words, they learn them all easily.[34] Rajalenius says the same eloquently: words are suspended from their roots like precious stones from a golden chain.[35]

In addition, the use of proverbs is especially advised in elementary studies, as proverbs provide excellent material for learning conjugation and word formation.[36] According to Gezelius, the teacher may use only one proverb a day, for example *Pietas ad omnia utilis* [Piety is profitable for all things]. After the pupil can read the sentence fluently, he translates it first word by word, then idiomatically. Next, the pupil writes the sentence down 'with his own interpretation' (*cum genuina interpretatione*) and memorizes it. Then all the words of the proverb are discussed separately, including not only roots, derived and compound words (*pius, piissimus, magis pius, pie, piissime, impietas, impius, impiissimus, impie*) but also alternative words and expressions (e.g. *universus* and *totus* for the word *omnis*). By means of one sentence, the teacher can discuss a multitude of words compared to the original sentence. However, if the teacher wishes to deal with more sentences than one in a day, he is free to do so, according to Gezelius: the advice given in the prefaces is not to be considered compulsory and the teacher should always use his own judgement. Furthermore, it is said to be essential to pay attention to the ability and capacity of the pupils (*captus discentium*, in *Aureae sententiae* 1671: preface). The teacher must have diligence, carefulness and endurance, it is stressed, but above all, he should adjust his teaching to the understanding of the pupils.[37] Rajalenius uses the same phrase, *pro captu*, and the importance of the understanding of the pupils and the diligence of the teachers are highlighted also in Florinus's preface and in the unsigned ones.[38]

Moral Education and Other Languages

Although the Latin books of Gezelius's printing house share some basic pedagogical ideas, differences can be perceived in the views expressed on moral and Christian education. Florinus and Gezelius stress the importance of teaching Christian values and mentality.[39] According to Gezelius's preface in *Aureae sententiae*, after the philological analysis, the teacher should discuss the moral meaning of the sentence by asking questions, such as 'what is piety?' (*Quid est pietas?*) Besides classical literature, Gezelius recommends biblical texts and Christian authors to be read by the pupils.[40] In accordance with the emphasis on religion, Martin Luther's *Small Catechism* was bound together with the elementary grammar *Donatus* (*Donatus. Seu grammaticae Latinae rudimenta 1684*). On the other hand, most proverbs in *Aureae sententiae* recommended for use are from classical authors, including Cicero, Horace, Ovid, Seneca and many others.[41]

In contrast, Rajalenius does not seem to combine religious or moralistic objectives with teaching Latin. After Comenius's *Orbis sensualium pictus* at the elementary level, he recommends ancient authors, including the Roman poets: Terence, Phaedrus, Cicero, Caesar and Ovid. Later he mentions Cornelius Nepos, Curtius Rufus, Suetonius, Valerius Maximus, Velleius Paterculus, Florus and Virgil. Furthermore, Rajalenius emphasizes the pragmatic benefits of knowing different languages — not only Latin, but also modern languages — and he even mentions the importance of correct pronunciation. Rajalenius discusses ten different languages, stating, however, that Latin is the most important one, as it 'contains all the erudition and all the sciences' (*omnem eruditionem omnesq(ue) scientias continet*). According to Rajalenius, there is 'nothing more noble, necessary, pleasant and honourable than knowing languages' (*Notitia lingvarum nihil nobilius, nihil magis necessarium, nihil jucundius, nihil illustrius*); and people who have travelled abroad and had discussions without interpreters know this well. In addition to the benefits for the individuals, he stresses the benefits of knowing languages for the state. Furthermore, the grammarian advises that the teacher should guide his pupils towards certain fields of study and professions, such as medicine, jurisprudence and theology.[42]

Rajalenius's thoughts are in accordance with the political and economic context of the time, as more and more civil servants and different kinds of professionals were needed for governing the enlarged Swedish Kingdom and for supervising commerce and manufacturing. However, Latin was still the language of the universities and science. In contrast to Rajalenius's thoughts, Gezelius and Florinus represent a more clerical standpoint. The manner in which they combined Christian and moral education with Latin studies — as was natural for a bishop and a vicar — reflects the Lutheran Orthodoxy of the era.

However, if Rajalenius's emphasis on classical authors is interpreted as reflecting the other intellectual characteristic of the era, classical Humanism, even Gezelius's work as a publisher has traces of Humanist ideas relating to biblical studies: Gezelius promoted the knowledge of the Biblical languages of Hebrew and Greek. He had published books for teaching and learning Greek as early as the 1640s in Tartu (Dorpat), where he was Professor of Biblical Languages and Theology before becoming Bishop of Turku.[43] In Turku he put most effort into enhancing the knowledge of Latin, which he thought needed improvement when he arrived (Laasonen 1977: 299). Still, some of the books published by him in Turku were meant for teaching and learning both Greek and Latin, such as the bilingual collections of the Gospels and Aesop's Fables.[44]

At the same time, schoolbooks and grammars for modern languages were being printed in Sweden and elsewhere on an increasing scale, and modern languages were taught in the universities (Hovdhaugen et al. 2000: 27–29, 66–98). Although Gezelius published books mainly relating to classical languages, notable exceptions are Erasmus's *Libellus aureus* (1670), which contains translations from Latin to Swedish, German and Finnish, and an early German grammar *Grammaticae Germanicae synopsis* (1667).[45] Furthermore, Gezelius's dictionary *Vocum Latinarum Sylloge* has translations for the Latin entries in Swedish and Florinus's *Nomenclatura* in both Swedish and in Finnish. In his prefaces, Gezelius regards the use of these mother tongues as important during elementary studies.[46] Still, in all the works considered, the mother tongues or differences between languages are barely discussed in the books meant for Latin studies. The only exceptions worth mentioning are Gezelius's preface in *Vocum Latinarum Sylloge* (1672) explaining the entries in the dictionary; and Rajalenius's discussion of exercises. Rajalenius recommends exercises such as changing words and phrases, translation etc. He also recommends books about modern languages (*Breviarium grammaticae Latinae* 1683: *Informandi modus*).

Influences from Sweden and the European Continent

Influence from German philologists based in Sweden has already been noticed. Taking a closer look, a variety of influences appear in the pedagogical thought of the books published by Gezelius. To begin with Swedish predecessors, Bishop of Västerås Johannes Rudbeckius (1581–1646) had founded not only the first *gymnasium* of Sweden in 1623, but also a printing house in order to publish schoolbooks for his diocese. Gezelius had himself been Rudbeckius's pupil in Västerås, and he followed his teacher by becoming both Bishop and a publisher (Leinonen 1998: 29–32). As is known from the curriculum of the Västerås school, different parts of Latin grammar were studied there later than the School Laws of 1571 and 1611 recommend.[47] Also, Gezelius advises against teaching grammar too soon.[48]

Additionally, the Chancellor of Uppsala University, Johan Skytte (1577–1645), and the Bishop of Strängnäs, Johannes Matthiae Gothus (1592–1670), both teachers of future Swedish monarchs, share ideas with the books published by Gezelius. Skytte, following the Ramist method, was a pioneer in Sweden in recommending practice and learning by example — reading Latin authors and writing — instead of studying grammar and its rules.⁴⁹ Like Rudbeckius in Västerås and Gezelius in Turku, Bishop Johannes Matthiae published schoolbooks with elaborate prefaces in Strängnäs. Among other things, Matthiae discusses in the prefaces the benefits of being able to have conversations with foreigners — in a similar manner to Rajalenius later.⁵⁰ According to Matthiae, 'grammatical rules are needed more for strengthening than for learning the language' (*Praecepta igitur non tam ad perceptionem quam confirmationem linguae sunt necessaria*),⁵¹ which again is an idea shared with the books published by Gezelius.

The last School Law (1649), the composition of which was led by Professor Laurentius Stigzelius (1598–1676), also includes many ideas notably similar to those in the prefaces of the books published in Turku. For example, grammar should be taught only after the pupils have been reading texts and once they can understand grammatical rules. Also, the teacher should adjust his lessons and the materials he uses to the age and understanding of the pupils.⁵² The pedagogy in the prefaces of Gezelius's publishing house seems to reflect very precisely current ideas in Sweden proper.

In addition, Gezelius mentions having adopted the idea of word families from German Professor Johannes Scapula (*c.* 1540–1600). Following Scapula's method, Gezelius states that pupils learn words most easily as they see the words 'swarm forth almost emulously from their roots' (*quasi certatim ex suis pullulare Primitivis*).⁵³ While compiling the dictionary *Vocum Latinarum Sylloge*, Gezelius used also the *Lexicon Lincopense* by the Bishop of Linköping, Jonas Petri Gothus (1587–1644).⁵⁴ Furthermore, Gezelius mentions German lexicographers Johannes Conradus Merckius (1583–1659) and Andreas Corvinus (1589–1648) as his sources in *his Vocum Latinarum Sylloge* (1672: preface). Methodologically close to Gezelius is German School master Ezechiel Vogel (fl. 1620), whose *Ephemerides totius linguae Latinae* is mentioned as the source for three proverbs in *Aureae sententiae*. Vogel discusses a method fairly similar to that of Gezelius: both recommend discussing one proverb a day. According to Vogel in his *Ephemerides totius linguae Latinae* (1631: title page), an extensive philological analysis of only one sentence a day is so effective that a pupil can learn the basics of Latin in one year.

To these German and Swedish sources of influence, works published by the press of the local Academy of Turku must be added. For example, the collection of dissertations *Gymnasium Capiendae Rationis humanae* (1662) by Professor Enevaldus Svenonius (1617–1688) is a major work on education to which Rajalenius refers.⁵⁵ In addition to stressing the importance of the understanding and the capacity of the pupils, Svenonius and Rajalenius share ideas on the importance of knowing foreign languages, not only Latin but also modern languages.⁵⁶ There are similarities with others as well, as many of the ideas included in the prefaces of the books published in Turku were common pedagogical wisdom of the era. The ideas of Johannes Amos Comenius, Wolfgang Ratke, Juan Luis Vives (1493–1540) and others were known and even translated in Sweden.⁵⁷ In previous research, the impact of Comenius on Gezelius's pedagogy has been noted,⁵⁸ but we have seen above that Comenius was certainly not the only source of inspiration.

Since it was customary in the era to use works by other authors with or without referring to them, it is difficult to know for certain what the exact sources used by the authors of Gezelius's publishing house were. Their pedagogy seems to be combined and modified from several different sources both from within Sweden and from the European Continent. Even though the ideas are not original, it is remarkable that the method of teaching is discussed and emphasized, often already on the title pages.[59] The pedagogical characteristics of the books themselves, such as the vocabulary lists and the use of root words, are also often highlighted on the title pages.[60] The schoolbooks published by Gezelius indicate that current European pedagogical thinking was known even 'in these remote lands' (*in remotis his terris*), as Gezelius called them (*Sulpiti Severi Historia sacra* 1669: preface).

Conclusion

The books published by Gezelius's printing house represent a major attempt to improve the teaching and learning of Latin and the availability of schoolbooks in seventeenth-century Finland. The prefaces and the title pages highlight the importance of learning vocabulary, reading text before studying grammar, and taking into account the pupils' learning capacity. Some of the prefaces emphasize the moral aspects of the studies, while others discuss the benefits of also knowing languages other than the classical ones.

The pedagogy of the Finnish schoolbooks is pragmatic, albeit neither methodologically nor philologically original. Wider pedagogical or theoretical questions are not discussed in these books, printed during a time of religious and philosophical confrontations. Still, the books enabled Latin teachers in Finland to become acquainted with recent ideas relating to teaching methods. Printing schoolbooks with prefaces by writers based in Finland was unprecedented on this scale and set an example for the future. The books published by Gezelius embody a time when Latin still dominated the schools, but pedagogical thought had advanced.

Bibliography

Sources printed by Gezelius's printing house in Turku (=Aboae)

Aureae sententiae. 1671. (Aboae; later editions in 1680, 1682 and 1686) (Unsigned preface written by Gezelius)
Bellum grammaticale. 1669. (Aboae; 2nd edition in 1687)
Breviarium grammaticae Latinae. 1683. Per B. Rajalen. (Aboae) (Preface, *Informandi modus* and *Epilogus* by Rajalenius)
Caspari Seidelii Portula lingvae Latinae. 1671. (Aboae)
Cornelii Nepotis, Vulgo Aemilii Probi Excellentium imperatorum vitae. 1685 [1674]. (Aboae)
Disticha moralia, sive Cato. 1669. (Aboae; 2nd edition in 1685)
Dominicalia & festivalia evangelia, Graeco–Latina. 1687 [1679]. (Aboae) (Preface by Gezelius)
Donatus. Seu grammaticae Latinae rudimenta. 1684. (Aboae; other editions in 1669 and 1688, but no copies of them are known)
Fabulae Aesopi selectae Graece & Latine. 1669. (Aboae; 2nd edition in 1688)
Familiaria colloquia. Opera Christophori Helvici Ex Erasmo Roterodamo, Ludovico Vive, &

Schottenio Hasso selecta. 1668. (Aboae; printed by the Academy Press, but financed by Gezelius)
Familiarium colloquiorum libellus Graece & Latine. 1690. Autore Johannes Posselio (Aboae)
Index librorum & tractatuum. 1689 [1684]. (Aboae)
Johannis Amos Comenii Orbis sensualium pictus. 1684. (Aboae; other editions in 1680, 1682 and 1689) (No copies of the first two editions are known) (Preface by Gezelius)
L. Caecilii Firmiani Lactantii, De mortibus persecutorum. 1684. (Aboae)
Libellus aureus, de civilitate morum pueriiium. Olim a Des. Erasmo Roterodamo Conscriptus. 1670. (Aboae; 1st edition printed by the Academy Press in 1665) (Unsigned preface)
Lucii Annaei Flori Rerum Romanarum, Editio Nova. 1675. (Aboae) (Unsigned preface for the Index)
Methodus informandi. In Paedagogiis tam ruralibus quam urbicis. Nec non Scholis Trivialibus. 1683. (Aboae)
M. T. Ciceronis Consolatio. 1670. (Aboae)
M. T. Ciceronis Epistolae selectae ac perbreves. 1670. (Aboae)
M. T. Ciceronis Scipionis somnium. Item Ejusdem Ciceronis Paradoxa sex. 1670. (Aboae)
M. Tullii Ciceronis Orationum selectarum liber. 1669. (Aboae; 2nd edition in 1686)
Nomenclatura Rerum brevissima, Latino–Sveco–Finnonica. Studio & sumptibus Henrici M. Florini. 1678. (Aboae) (Preface by Florinus.)
Paradigmata declinationum & conjugationum Latina. 1670. (Aboae)
Phaedri fabularum Aesopiarum Libri Quinque. 1694. (Aboae) (Printed during Gezelius the Younger's time, but an earlier, now lost version was published already in 1670) (Unsigned preface)
Q. Curtii Rufi De rebus gestis Alexandri Magni editio nova. 1675. (Aboae; 2nd edition in 1686)
Stephani Johannis Stephanij Colloquia minora. 1687. (Aboae)
Sulpiti Severi Historia sacra. 1669. (Aboae) (Preface by Gezelius)
[Terentii Christiani] Comoedia Dyscoli. 1670. A Cornelio Schonaeo. (Aboae)
Terentii Christiani Daniel. 1670. A Cornelio Schonaeo. (Aboae)
Terentii Christiani Josephus. 1670. A Cornelio Schonaeo. (Aboae)
Terentii Christiani Pentecoste. 1670. A Cornelio Schonaeo. (Aboae)
Terentii Christiani Triumphus Christi. 1670. A Cornelio Schonaeo. (Aboae)
Vocum Latinarum Sylloge. 1672. (Aboae; 2nd edition in 1688) (Preface by Gezelius)

Other sources

Ephemerides totius linguae Latinae. 1631. A M. Ezechiele Vogelio (Leipzig)
Gymnasium Capiendae Rationis humanae. Cum cura Professionis Eloquentiae Romanae incubabat authori Enevaldo Svenonio. 1662. (Aboae)
Lexicon Graeco–Latinvm novvm. 1628. Joannis Scapulae opera & studio. (Basle)
Lexicon Graeco–Latinvm. 1649. Opera & Vigiliis M. Johannis Georgii Gezelii. (Tartu)
Libellus puerilis, In quo continentur, Quinque primaria Capita doctrinae Christianae. 1626. (Stockholm)
Ratio Discendi linguam Latinam Pro Christina, Suecorum &c. Regina designata. 1635. (Stockholm)
Ratio Informandi in Scholis Trivialibus and *De Gymnasijs* (1649) (These have been printed in Hall (1921); see below)

Secondary sources

BRANDELL, GEORG. 1931. *Svenska undervisningsväsendets och uppfostrans historia. Andra delen. Ortodoxiens tidevarv* (Lund: Gleerups)

HALL, B. RUD. 1921. *Sveriges allmänna läroverksstadgar 1561–1905. I–III. 1561, 1611 och 1649 års skolordningar i avtryck och, de båda senare, i översättning.* Årsböcker i svensk undervisningshistoria, IV (Jena: Neuenhahn)

HANHO, J. T. 1947. *Suomen oppikoululaitoksen historia I. Ruotsin vallan aika* (Porvoo: Söderström Osakeyhtiö)

HOVDHAUGEN, EVEN, ET AL. 2000. *The History of Linguistics in the Nordic Countries* (Jyväskylä: Societas Scientiarum Fennica)

INGEMARSDOTTER, JENNY. 2011. *Ramism, Rhetoric and Reform: An Intellectual Biography of Johan Skytte (1577–1645)* (Västerås: Uppsala Universitet)

JOUTSIVUO, TIMO. 2010. *Papeiksi ja virkamiehiksi* in *Huoneentaulun maailma. Kasvatus ja koulutus Suomessa keskiajalta 1860-luvulle* (Hämeenlinna: Suomalaisen Kirjallisuuden Seura)

KAJANTO, IIRO. 1989. *Humanism in a Christian Society, I: The Attitude to Classical Mythology and Religion in Finland, 1640–1713* (Tammisaari: Suomalainen Tiedeakatemia)

KEINÄSTÖ, KARI. 1991. *Grammaticae Germanicae synopsis von Johannes Gezelius dem Älteren (Turku 1667) und ihre Vorlage: Ein Beitrag zur Lehrbuchgeschichte des Deutschunterrichts in Finnland* (Göppingen: Kümmerle)

LAASONEN, PENTTI. 1977. *Johannes Gezelius vanhempi ja suomalainen täysortodoksia* (Loimaa: Suomen Kirkkohistoriallinen Seura)

LAINE, TUIJA. 2006. *Kolportöörejä ja kirjakauppiaita. Kirjojen hankinta ja levitys Suomessa vuoteen 1800* (Tampere: Suomalaisen Kirjallisuuden Seura)

LEINONEN, MARKKU. 1998. *Johannes Gezelius vanhempi luonnonmukaisen pedagogiikan soveltajana. Comeniuslainen tulkinta* (Jyväskylä: Jyväskylän yliopisto)

LINDROTH, STEN. 1975. *Svensk lärdomshistoria. Stormaktstiden* (Stockholm: Norstedt & Söners)

Notes to Chapter 6

1. Hanho (1947: 23–43); Ingemarsdotter (2011: 260–61 and passim); Joutsivuo (2010: 112–22); Laasonen (1977: 345–69); Leinonen (1998: 22–28); Lindroth (1975: 65–69 and passim).
2. *Ratio Informandi in Scholis Trivialibus* (1649: 46), reprinted in Hall (1921).
3. E.g. Kajanto (1989: 11–12 and passim); Lindroth (1975: 179–234).
4. *Ratio Informandi in Scholis Trivialibus* (1649: 60).
5. Laine (2006: 55–56, 63).
6. The Royal Academy of Turku was founded in 1640 by Queen Christina of Sweden at the proposal of Count Per Brahe (1602–1680), Governor General of Finland. The Academy was the third university in the Kingdom of Sweden following the universities in Uppsala and Tartu (Dorpat).
7. Laasonen (1977: 412–17); Laine (2006: 85–87).
8. In addition to schoolbooks, Gezelius published in 1683 *Methodus informandi*, a collection of regulations for children's schools and trivial schools in the diocese of Turku. Within these regulations, Gezelius recommends books — many of which were published by himself — and a schedule for reading them in schools. Gezelius published schoolbooks also in Swedish and in Finnish, e.g. a Catechism *Ett Rätt Barna-Klenodium* or *Yxi paras lasten tawara* (*A Best Thing for Children*).
9. Books dealing with religion and/or Greek but containing pedagogical vocabularies in Latin are included: e.g. *Dominicalia & festivalia evangelia, Graeco–Latina* (1687). See list of sources.
10. *Caspari Seidelii Portula linguae Latinae* (1671); *Disticha moralia, sive Cato* (1669); *Dominicalia & festivalia evangelia, Graeco–Latina* (1687); *Donatus. Seu grammaticae Latinae rudimenta* (1684); *Fabulae Aesopi selectae Graece & Latine* (1669); *Familiaria colloquia* (1668); *Familiarium colloquiorum libellus Graece & Latine* (1690); *Libellus aureus, de civilitate morum puerilium* (1670); *M. T. Ciceronis Epistolae selectae ac perbreves* (1670); *M. T. Ciceronis Scipionis somnium. Item Ejusdem Ciceronis Paradoxa sex* (1670); *M. Tullii Ciceronis Orationum selectarum liber* (1669); *Paradigmata declinationum & conjugationum Latina* (1670); *Phaedri fabularum Aesopiarum Libri Quinque* (1694); *Stephani Johannis Stephanij Colloquia minora* (1687); *[Terentii Christiani] Comoedia Dyscoli* (1670).

11. *Aureae sententiae* (1671); *Vocum Latinarum Sylloge* (1672). The following books were published for the 'studying youth' (*pro Studiosa Juventute*): *Bellum grammaticale* (1669); *Nomenclatura Rerum brevissima, Latino–Sveco–Finnonica* (1678); *Sulpiti Severi Historia sacra* (1669); *Terentii Christiani Daniel* (1670); *Terentii Christiani Josephus* (1670); *Terentii Christiani Pentecoste* (1670); *Terentii Christiani Triumphus Christi* (1670). Barthollus Rajalenius's grammar was meant for the 'future student of Latin' (*futuro Latinitatis studioso*) (*Breviarium grammaticae Latinae* 1683: title page).
12. *Ratio Informandi in Scholis Trivialibus* (1649: 60).
13. For example, *Lives* by Cornelius Nepos, *Ars Poetica* by Horace, Nathanael Chytraeus's (1543–1598) Latin grammar and books on rhetoric were printed in Vyborg in the 1690s (See Laine 2006: 113–17).
14. *M. T. Ciceronis Consolatio* (1670, considered a forgery); *M. T. Ciceronis Epistolae selectae ac perbreves* (1670); *M. T. Ciceronis Scipionis somnium. Item Ejusdem Ciceronis Paradoxa sex* (1670); *M. Tullii Ciceronis Orationum selectarum liber* (1669).
15. *Familiaria colloquia* (1668); *Familiarium colloquiorum libellus Graece & Latine* (1690); *Stephani Johannis Stephanij Colloquia minora* (1687); *[Terentii Christiani] Comoedia Dyscoli* (1670); *Terentii Christiani Daniel* (1670); *Terentii Christiani Josephus* (1670); *Terentii Christiani Pentecoste* (1670); *Terentii Christiani Triumphus Christi* (1670).
16. *Johannis Amos Comenii Orbis sensualium pictus* (1680, 1682, 1684 and 1689).
17. The 1665 edition of Erasmus's *Libellus aureus, de civilitate morum puerilium* was printed by the Academy Press, but financed by Gezelius: *Index librorum & tractatuum* (1689). There are no known copies of the 1669 and 1688 editions of *Donatus*, which is named after the most popular elementary grammar of Antiquity and the Middle Ages. However, most of the grammars named *Donatus* during this period have little to do with the real *Ars minor* of Aelius Donatus (fourth century AD) (Hovdhaugen et al. 2000: 33). See list of sources for works printed twice.
18. *Johannis Amos Comenii Orbis sensualium pictus* (1684: preface).
19. *Libellus aureus, de civilitate morum puerilium* (1670), the *Index* in *Lucii Annaei Flori Rerum Romanarum Editio Nova* (1675) and *Phaedri fabularum Aesopiarum Libri Quinque* (1694) have unsigned prefaces. In these prefaces, as in the ones published with the name of Gezelius, the importance of adjusting the teaching to the understanding of the pupils is stressed. Also the preface in *Aureae sententiae* is printed without the name of the writer. However, elsewhere Gezelius mentions having written it: *Vocum Latinarum Sylloge* (1672: preface).
20. *Nomenclatura Rerum brevissima, Latino–Sveco–Finnonica* (1678).
21. *Sulpiti Severi Historia sacra* (1669: preface). Cf. *Breviarium grammaticae Latinae* (1683: *Epilogus*); *Nomenclatura Rerum brevissima, Latino–Sveco–Finnonica* (1678: preface).
22. *Vocum Latinarum Sylloge* (1672: title page and preface). See also *Aureae sententiae* (1671: preface); *Dominicalia & festivalia evangelia, Graeco–Latina* (1687: preface).
23. *Bellum grammaticale* (1669: title page). The idea for this textbook was originally launched by the Italian Humanist Andrea Guarna (fl. 1511). A German adaptation of the book was composed by Johannes Spangenberg (1484–1550). The ideal of combining utility and pleasure (*prodesse et delectare*), mentioned already by Horace, was popular in the Early Modern period.
24. *Johannis Amos Comenii Orbis sensualium pictus* (1684: preface).
25. *Breviarium grammaticae Latinae* (1683: preface); *Nomenclatura Rerum brevissima, Latino–Sveco–Finnonica* (1678: preface).
26. E.g. *Aureae sententiae* (1671: preface); *Breviarium grammaticae Latinae* (1683: preface); *Johannis Amos Comenii Orbis sensualium pictus* (1684: preface).
27. *Ratio Informandi in Scholis Trivialibus* (1649: 46–50); *De Gymnasijs* (1649: 97–99).
28. Interestingly, the 1669 edition of the selected speeches by Cicero is said to be meant for students of the academy and the trivial schools but the 1686 edition for students of the academy and the *gymnasium*: *M. Tullii Ciceronis Orationum selectarum liber* (1669 and 1686: title pages).
29. *Libellus aureus, de civilitate morum puerilium* (1670: preface). See also *Dominicalia & festivalia evangelia, Graeco–Latina* (1687: preface); *Paradigmata declinationum & conjugationum Latina* (1670: title page). Cf. *Methodus informandi* (1683).
30. For example, *Ab tenui initio* [from a small beginning] in the *Index* to Cornelius Nepos is explained to mean *occasione & ope rei tam parvae: Cornelii Nepotis, Vulgo Aemilii Probi Excellentium*

imperatorum vitae (1685: *Index*). In the *Index* to Florus, the phrase *ad arma* is followed by related words in Italian, French and Swedish: *Ad arma, Itali a L'arme, unde Gallorum vox alarme, & nostra Allarm/ 2.15.14: Lucii Annaei Flori Rerum Romanarum Editio Nova* (1675: *Index*).

31. *Cornelii Nepotis, Vulgo Aemilii Probi Excellentium imperatorum vitae* (1685: title page); *Lucii Annaei Flori Rerum Romanarum, Editio Nova* (1675: title page); *Q. Curtii Rufi De rebus gestis Alexandri Magni editio nova* (1675: title page).
32. For example, under the word *Aeger, a, um* [sick], there are words *Aegre, Aegrimonia, Aegritudo, Aegrotus, Aegroto, Aegrotatio: Vocum Latinarum Sylloge* (1672).
33. *Aureae sententiae* (1671: preface); *Dominicalia & festivalia evangelia, Graeco–Latina* (1687: title page and preface); *Johannis Amos Comenii Orbis sensualium pictus* (1684: preface); *Vocum Latinarum Sylloge* (1672: preface).
34. *Aureae sententiae* (1671: preface); *Dominicalia & festivalia evangelia, Graeco–Latina* (1687: preface); *Vocum Latinarum Sylloge* (1672: preface).
35. See *Breviarium grammaticae Latinae* (1683: *Informandi modus*).
36. The proverbs are regarded as good learning material because textbooks can be too difficult and dialogues have deficiencies: *Aureae sententiae* (1671: preface). See also *Caspari Seidelii Portula lingvae Latinae* (1671); *Disticha moralia, sive Cato* (1669).
37. *Aureae sententiae* (1671: preface); *Breviarium grammaticae Latinae* (1683: *Informandi modus*); *Disticha moralia, sive Cato* (1669: title page); *Johannis Amos Comenii Orbis sensualium pictus* (1684: preface); *Nomenclatura Rerum brevissima, Latino–Sveco–Finnonica* (1678: preface); *Paradigmata declinationum & conjugationum Latina* (1670: title page); *Phaedri fabularum Aesopiarum Libri Quinque* (1694: preface); *Vocum Latinarum Sylloge* (1672: preface). Cf. *Methodus informandi* (1683).
38. E.g. *Breviarium grammaticae Latinae* (1683: *Informandi modus*); *Nomenclatura Rerum brevissima, Latino–Sveco–Finnonica* (1678: preface); *Phaedri fabularum Aesopiarum Libri Quinque* (1694: preface).
39. E.g. *Aureae sententiae* (1671: preface); *Dominicalia & festivalia evangelia, Graeco–Latina* (1687: preface); *Nomenclatura Rerum brevissima, Latino–Sveco–Finnonica* (1678: preface and first chapter). See also *Phaedri fabularum Aesopiarum Libri Quinque* (1694: preface).
40. According to Gezelius, books to be read by trivial school pupils included an Alphabet book, a Catechism, the Psalms, the Gospels, Comenius's *Orbis sensualium pictus, Aureae sententiae, Disticha Catonis, Donatus*, dialogues collected by Helvicus, and Cicero's, Terence's and Cornelius Nepos's works: *Methodus informandi* (1683). In addition to Christian author Sulpicius Severus, Gezelius published in 1684 an edition of Lactantius's *De mortibus persecutorum*. This edition was printed notably soon after the manuscript containing the text was found in 1678: *L. Caecilii Firmiani Lactantii, De mortibus persecutorum* (1684).
41. After the proverbs for each day of the year, there are 'moral sentences' from classical authors Laberius, Publilius Syrus, Plautus, Terence, Seneca and Virgil (*Aureae sententiae* 1671).
42. *Breviarium grammaticae Latinae* (1683: preface and *Informandi modus*). In addition to Latin, Rajalenius discusses Finnish, Swedish, German, Polish, Russian, Estonian, Latvian, French, Hebrew and Greek. Also, he recommends books by contemporary authors for studying history, philosophy and other subjects.
43. In Tartu Gezelius published a Greek grammar (1647), a Greek–Latin dictionary (1649) and Comenius's *Janua lingvarum reserata aurea* (1648): Hovdhaugen et al. (2000: 36–37); Laasonen (1977: 346); Leinonen (1998: 37).
44. *Dominicalia & festivalia evangelia, Graeco–Latina* (1687); *Fabulae Aesopi selectae Graece & Latine* (1669). See also *Familiarium colloquiorum libellus Graece & Latine* (1690).
45. Keinästö (1991). The 1665 version of *Libellus aureus, de civilitate morum puerilium* contains translations to Swedish and Finnish, but not German.
46. E.g. *Aureae sententiae* (1671: preface); *Johannis Amos Comenii Orbis sensualium pictus* (1684: preface).
47. Brandell (1931: 84–85, 147–48); Hall (1921: 14, 28); Hanho (1947: 215–16). The School Law of 1611 was never implemented (Hanho 1947: 26–27; Joutsivuo 2010: 115).
48. E.g. *Aureae sententiae* (1671: preface).
49. Ingemarsdotter (2011: 261–62). Skytte's book recommendations include several authors published

later by Gezelius, e.g. Aesop, Cato, Cicero, Cornelius Nepos, Comenius, Sulpicius Severus and Terentius Christianus (Brandell 1931: 232–33).
50. *Libellus puerilis, In quo continentur, Quinque primaria Capita doctrinae Christianae* (1626: preface).
51. *Ratio Discendi linguam Latinam Pro Christina, Suecorum &c. Regina designata* (1935: Documenta).
52. See *Ratio Informandi in Scholis Trivialibus* (1649: 61–65 and passim).
53. *Lexicon Graeco–Latinvm* (1649: preface). Cf. *Lexicon Graeco–Latinvm novvm* (1628: preface).
54. *Vocum Latinarum Sylloge* (1672: title page). Rajalenius also mentions this pioneering Latin–Swedish–German dictionary (*Breviarium grammaticae Latinae* 1683: Informandi modus).
55. *Breviarium grammaticae Latinae* (1683: Informandi modus).
56. *Gymnasium Capiendae Rationis humanae* (1662: De Lingvae Latinae Usu & Praestantia).
57. Brandell (1931: 267–68); Ingemarsdotter (2011: 260–61). Rajalenius mentions Vives: *Breviarium grammaticae Latinae* (1683: Informandi modus). Vives is also mentioned in the School Law (*Ratio Informandi in Scholis Trivialibus* 1649: 66 and passim).
58. Leinonen (1998). It is possible that Gezelius and Comenius even met in Thorn in 1645 (Laasonen 1977: 346; Leinonen 1998: 37).
59. E.g. *Vocum Latinarum Sylloge* (1672: title page). Also, Gezelius mentions the prefaces in his collection of regulations for schools (*Methodus informandi* 1683).
60. E.g. *Cornelii Nepotis, Vulgo Aemilii Probi Excellentium imperatorum vitae* (1685); *Dominicalia & festivalia evangelia, Graeco–Latina* (1687); *Stephani Johannis Stephanij Colloquia minora* (1687).

CHAPTER 7

Teaching Czech in a Plurilingual Community in the Age of Enlightenment: The Case of František Jan Tomsa

Alena A. Fidlerová

The chapter deals with the complicated situation in the field of first- and second-language teaching in Bohemia at the turn of the eighteenth to the nineteenth century.[1] First, it sketches briefly the mutual relations of the Czech and German languages in Bohemia, the educational reforms carried out by Empress Maria Theresa and her sons, and their influence on the language situation in primary and secondary schools. Subsequently, it uses the example of Czech educator and philologist František Jan Tomsa (1751–1814), the economic director of the Normal School Printing House in Prague, translator of primary school textbooks from German into Czech and author of numerous grammatical, orthographical and lexicographical works written both in Czech and German, to demonstrate the polyfunctionality of linguistic works and language textbooks, the uncertainty about their anticipated and real readership, and the multiple functions they fulfilled in the cultural life of the period. It shows that Tomsa not only articulated the outcomes of his linguistic research and his concept of modern cultivated Czech in his grammatical and orthographical works, intended for Czech, German and Slavic elites, but that he also sought to incorporate them into his translations of school textbooks.

Introduction

In the pre-modern era, the demand for grammars, language textbooks and dictionaries of a minor language like Czech was rarely large enough to enable strictly specialized editions. In fact, it is often difficult to distinguish between books intended for native speakers and for pupils learning Czech as a second or foreign language. As almost half of the population of the Czech Lands did not use Czech as their mother tongue,[2] at least some of them wanted or needed to learn Czech, both as children and as adults. On the other hand, many Czechs received insufficient education in their mother tongue or lost full command of it thanks to long periods spent among the speakers of other languages, e.g. during their military service or professional engagement in a German-speaking milieu. Thus, they often did not achieve proficiency in Czech written discourse, or even lost fluency in speech. As a result, the educational needs of these two groups of potential users, though far from identical, were less different than we would assume today. For these, and of course also for financial reasons, the authors of grammars, dictionaries etc. often sought to address both groups at the same time, using Latin or German as the language of instruction. Additionally, language textbooks may also have fulfilled other functions at this time, serving codification, polemic, scientific or representational purposes as well.

The aim of this chapter is to follow these intricate and complicated relationships between first- and second-language instruction and other functions of textbooks in Bohemia at the turn of the eighteenth to the nineteenth century, taking the example of an interesting figure of the time, František Jan Tomsa. Although his achievements cannot rival those of his contemporary, the outstanding Slavist Josef Dobrovský, he was an important educational and typographic reformer, and a prolific author and translator of diverse sorts of books, most of them dealing with practical or theoretical instruction in the Czech language. Thus, his work can provide an interesting insight not only into the complicated linguistic situation of Bohemia during this period, but also into pedagogical goals and methods in language instruction of the time.

The Czech Language Situation at the Turn of the Eighteenth to the Nineteenth Century

In the mid-eighteenth century, the situation of Czech was not easy. More than one hundred years previously, the unhappy uprising of the non-Catholic Estates against the ruling Habsburg dynasty resulted in a catastrophic defeat in the Battle at White Mountain in 1620, leading to the forced emigration of non-Catholic wealthy and educated elites. Thus, the country almost completely lost its upper classes capable of financing and enjoying literature, theatre or scholarship in Czech. The exiled aristocracy was replaced mostly by noble families coming from Spanish, Italian or German speaking areas who did not show any inclination to support Czech-language culture. Also, the imperial court resided outside the Czech Lands and did not use Czech in its internal communications. As a consequence, despite the fact that the majority of the population still spoke Czech, the social and functional basis of the Czech language narrowed gradually and the language lost its social prestige.

This asymmetry of Czech-language culture (to use Alexandr Stich's term)[3] can be seen both with respect to its German-language counterpart and to its inner structure, relying heavily on translations and adaptations from other languages, lacking ambitious works and prestigious genres, and consisting predominantly of texts of religious content, practical manuals or undemanding fiction intended for a popular readership. Such texts, although preserving and developing the lower prose style of the preceding periods quite well, seemed deeply disappointing and insufficient to the educated Czech elite of the second half of the eighteenth century, influenced by the ideals of Enlightenment, by the budding national revival movements and by the ongoing German language reform. Having received their higher education in German or Latin schools, many of these young men dreamed of devoting their lives to the reform of their mother tongue, elevating its literature to the level that they had experienced during their studies. In this, they sought support from the Bohemian aristocracy and international scholarly community, but in their educational efforts they focused mostly on the popular classes as the core of the Czech-language-speaking community. In fact, most of them knew the situation of the people only too well, because they themselves had been born in a tiny cottage in a Czech village or small town. One of these men was František Jan Tomsa.

The Austrian Educational System in Tomsa's Lifetime

School reforms of Maria Theresa and Josef II

The Enlightenment reached the Habsburg Empire in the second half of the eighteenth century and flourished there under Empress Maria Theresa and Emperor Joseph II.[4] It comprised a huge amount of reform, not least in the sphere of education. One of the best known and most quoted phrases of the Empress asserts that education is and always has been a 'politicum' (Gant 2008: 99). The school reform, launched soon after her ascent to the throne, was designed to improve the economic situation of the state, to supply qualified officials for a new and effective state administration and, most importantly, to prevent the monarchy from falling apart, to strengthen it and to transform this complex of economically, politically and culturally heterogeneous parts into a modern unitary state.[5]

For Maria Theresa, and even more for her successor Joseph II, primary education was of extreme importance, more important than the higher levels. In 1774, Johann Ignaz Felbiger created for her the *Allgemeine Schulordnung für die deutschen Normal-, Haupt- und Trivialschulen in den sämtlichen kayserl. königl. Erbländer*, the first general regulations obligatory for all primary schools in the Empire, establishing the network of trivial schools (in villages with a parish office), main schools (in towns) and normal schools (in the capital of each land). In the last group, the use of German as the language of instruction was presumed.

Simultaneously, Latin, the traditional (and nationally neutral) language of higher education, was gradually giving way to German. This affected Czech rather severely because it lost its position as one of the vernacular counterparts to Latin in the formal educational process at the secondary level and was essentially driven out of it. This process was completed by the replacement of Latin by German at Prague University in 1784. Thus, a good command of German became a prerequisite for admission already to a secondary school; and language instruction in German, including poetics and rhetoric, went on also at the first level at university, the Faculty of Philosophy.

Czech as a Language of Instruction and as a School Subject

Though originally not directed explicitly against the multiplicity of vernaculars in education, after 1765 Austrian language policy started to focus systematically on the promotion of German as the intended common means of communication in all spheres of public life (Eder 2006: 34). As a consequence, even at the primary level pupils were to familiarize themselves with German as the language of higher social status (Eder 2006: 40); and at secondary schools Czech was not even taught as a subject in the Czech Lands. Not until the 1810s was it allowed as an optional subject at gymnasia in the regions with Czech or mixed population. Prague University had to wait till 1793 to be granted a Chair of Czech Language and Literature. Thus, the possibilities of formal instruction in Czech were rather limited at the turn of the century, both for native speakers and for other learners. Czech native speakers usually ceased to be educated systematically in their mother tongue at an early age and later in their lives were often more proficient in German than in Czech, especially in written discourse.[6]

The only places where Czech was taught at secondary and higher level at this time were selected elite schools for future civil servants and officers in Vienna and Wiener Neustadt. At the elite Theresianum gymnasium in Vienna, educating mostly the sons of Catholic aristocratic families, Czech had been among the subjects offered since its establishment in 1746 and was first taught by Jan Václav Pohl. From 1755, he also taught Czech at the Aristocratic Military Academy (Adelige Militärakademie) in Vienna.[7] For these purposes, Pohl assembled an oft re-edited and re-worked German grammar,[8] which was severely criticized by some of his contemporaries for its purist tendencies. From 1752, Czech was also on the curriculum of the Theresian Military Academy (Theresianische Militärakademie) in Wiener Neustadt, where the first professors were Václav Michal Wiedemann and Antonín Prokop Klobás, succeeded by Maximilián Václav Šimek[9] and Josef Valentin Zlobický.[10]

When, in 1775, Czech language and literature were added to the curriculum of the University of Vienna, Zlobický became their first professor there. Though he was very popular among his pupils, due to his insufficient income as a university professor he also had to accept other engagements and consequently never wrote his anticipated grammar of Czech and other linguistic works. However, some of his materials were included in the works of his collaborators: the *Handbuch für einen Lehrer der böhmischen Literatur* (1785, *Knihopis* K15912) by Maximilián Václav Šimek (without Zlobický's consent); and *Knjha k Čtenj a Překládanj* by Aleš Jan Spurný (1785, *Knihopis* K04011, K15639), later published in a re-worked version as *České Cwičenj pro Schowance Cys. Kral. Kadetnjho Domu* (1786, 1793, *Knihopis* K15640, K15640a). All these works were explicitly designed for non-native speakers and, especially in the case of Spurný's work, were also thematically adjusted to the needs of a specific group (i.e. future army officers). However, since Vienna was the only place where Czech was taught at higher than primary level, these schools also represented the only possibility for other textbooks to be used in the formal education of non-native speakers.

The Normal School in Prague and its Press

The first normal school was opened in 1771 in Vienna. In 1772, it was granted the right to print school textbooks for all the lands of the Habsburg Empire. Without delay, its publishing house, the *Verlag der deutschen Schulanstalt*, was created, predominantly publishing textbooks in German (Polák 1968: 9, 13). As it soon became clear that one press was not able to supply all the schools of the Empire and that the transportation expenses were unnecessarily high, the Empress decided to grant the *privilegium impressorium* to all normal schools, provided that they produce unaltered copies of Vienna exemplars (Polák 1968: 11).[11]

The Prague Normal School opened on 15 November 1775. Its publishing house had already been established earlier in that year, with the right to print primary school textbooks (ABC tables, primers, elementary readers, catechisms etc.).[12] Originally, its editions were printed by the printing office of Johann Ferdinand Schönfeld (Polák 1968: 12), but because it was too busy to supply all the necessary textbooks in time, the Prague Normal School Printing Office (*Normalschulbuchdruckerei*) was founded in 1776 to produce cheap school books of higher quality than the Schönfeld printing house did (Helfert 1860: 498–500). Initially, it was only allowed to produce reprints of Vienna editions, but in 1777 it acquired the *privilegium impressorium privativum*, i.e. the exclusive right to supply the Czech Lands with its own (approved) versions of trivial school textbooks in Czech, too (Polák 1968: 13).

František Jan Tomsa — a Biographical Sketch

About the life and work of František Jan Tomsa (1751–1814), we are informed primarily by his two manuscript autobiographical sketches, one written in Czech[13] and one in German.[14] They are both autographs almost identical in content, comprising a brief biographical narrative mostly concerned with Tomsa's youth, accompanied by a long, but not exhaustive, list of his works up to the year 1812 (in the German version a later entry concerning 1813 is added). As they are in many aspects far too concise and not always exact, I also consulted other archival sources and the existing (rather scarce) secondary literature.[15]

František Jan Tomsa was born at dawn on 4 October 1751, in a secluded dwelling called Hamry in the vicinity of the town of Turnov in the Czech-speaking region of north-eastern Bohemia. In the afternoon, he and his mother were transported to the village of Morký, where his parents lived, and in the evening he was christened in the church of the nearby village of Všeň. His father was a farmer, probably relatively well-off, but the details of his social status are not known. Tomsa proved a bright boy and so was allowed to study at the Piarist gymnasium in Kosmonosy. When in the fourth class there, he first took interest in the study of Czech and its development thanks to the efforts of his teacher, Father Ildefons Bierfeind,[16] and started to dream of becoming a Czech writer.[17] In 1772, he began his studies at the Prague Faculty of Philosophy, having very probably attended higher gymnasium classes also in Prague. During this time, he studied (mostly privately) both classical and modern languages (Czech, German, Polish, Russian). He was in touch with many leading figures of Czech culture of the time, including Josef Dobrovský, František Faustin Procházka and Václav Matěj Kramerius (Schamschula 1973: 239). On the other hand, he was known to have a close relationship with Ferdinand Kindermann, a German native speaker and a leading school reformer in Bohemia,[18] whose personal secretary he became in 1782 (Winter 1926: 128). Thereafter he was always counted among the Czech Josephinists, which brought him a certain dislike from some representatives of the nationalist movement, such as František Martin Pelc and Josef Jungmann, who suspected him of insufficient resistance to Germanization (Winter 1945: 193).

In 1777, Tomsa was appointed the corrector and translator of Czech books published by the Normal School Printing Office in Prague. From 1785 almost until his death he worked as its economic director, the so called 'factor of economy', responsible for the operation not only of the printing house, but also of the printing office and the repository of books. He received an annual salary of six hundred guilders (with occasional supplements), which meant that he had a stable income but had to devote much of his time and energy to the administration of the institution, especially to the translating, editing and printing of Czech versions of primary school textbooks. However, this highly exhausting occupation did not prevent him from having higher ambitions in the field of Czech language teaching and study: in 1792, and again in 1801, he applied (unsuccessfully) for the position of Professor of Czech Language and Literature at Prague University.

Like a great many of his contemporaries, Tomsa sought the support of diverse Czech aristocratic families. According to the literature, he attended regular meetings in the house of the Knight Jan František z Neuberka (Johann Franz Ritter von Neuberg), where the Czech patriotic elite met.[19] In the Literary Archive of the Museum of Czech Literature two letters to Count František Kašpar Šternberk are preserved, apparently written to accompany some of Tomsa's works, which had been sent to him, and asking for financial support.[20] Moreover, Tomsa composed and had printed several congratulatory poems praising aristocrats, especially those who showed some inclination to learn Czech or to encourage popular education in Czech. Thanks to them we are informed that he had at least some practical experience in teaching Czech to young adults. For an unknown period of time towards the turn of the century, he worked as a private teacher to the daughters of Count Christian Philipp Clam-Gallas and his wife Karolina:[21] Johanna, who later married to become Baroness Kocová z Dobrše (Kotz von Dobrz, 1778–1810), and Maria Aloisia, who later married to become Princess von Auesperg (1774–1831).[22] He was also in touch with the Fürstenberg family: in one of his congratulatory poems he praised the widowed Princess Elisabeth zu Fürstenberg, *née* von Thurn und Taxis, who at the age of thirty-six started to learn Czech and also made her children Karl Egon (1796–1854) and Maria Leopoldine (1791–1844) do so (Tomsa 1804a). To the last-mentioned young lady, another poem was dedicated when she was just seven years old, exalting her for her diligent study of Czech (Tomsa 1798b).[23] From its tone it seems quite probable that Tomsa may have taught Czech also in this aristocratic family.[24] In 1813, Tomsa was pensioned off because of serious health problems and he died in Prague on 1 November 1814. He was buried at the so-called Lesser Town Cemetery (Kalinová, Hnojil et al. 2016: 389-390), but the location of his grave is now unknown.

František Jan Tomsa — Works Devoted to Language Teaching

The list of works known to be written or translated by Tomsa is quite long, but even so it is probably far from complete.[25] The reason for this is not only the lack of a modern monograph devoted to him, but also the fact that he published many of his works anonymously and at his own expense, often in the form of tiny booklets that may easily have been lost over the centuries. Moreover, the primary school textbooks that he translated into Czech went through many editions and not all of them may be extant today, as they are often inconspicuous little books, in many cases bound together in compendia , and may still escape the attention of librarians. Thus, the editions mentioned below constitute only a preliminary list, almost certainly far from complete.

It is neither possible nor useful to discuss here the whole of Tomsa's work. It comprises translations of primary school textbooks (mostly primers, readers and catechisms); dictionaries; grammatical and linguistic treatises, including orthographical manuals; editions of older Czech literature; congratulatory poems; translations of collections of short stories for children and of Enlightenment religious literature; journal articles concerning themes from the natural sciences; journals and educational books for farmers; and works on issues concerning health and social care. Of all these, only the first three groups will be touched on here.

Lexicographical Works

Only the first and smallest of Tomsa's dictionaries, the German-Czech dictionary entitled *Malý německý a český Slownjk* (1789), is endowed with a short Czech preface. Here, the author unequivocally destines it for Czechs learning German; members of other nations learning or using Czech are not even mentioned.[26] The slightly later and more comprehensive *Vollständiges Wörterbuch der böhmisch- deutsch- und lateinischen Sprache* (1791) represents that part of Tomsa's work in which he still partly followed the linguistic approach of Josef Dobrovský, who, inspired among others by Adelung, advocated the concept of modern literary Czech based more on the best literary tradition of the past than on contemporary usage and free from dialect and regional expressions.[27] Consequently, the dictionary, intended among other things as a tool of codification, does not include dialect terms, though it does not exclude colloquial expressions (e.g. *pentljkář – Bandmacher*; *počurati – bepissen*, or *podawky – Gabel, zum Heu oder Getreide*). It features a preface sketching the history of Czech lexicography and a lengthy treatise entitled *Ueber den Ursprung und die Bildung der slawischen und insbesondere der böhmischen Sprache*, both written by Dobrovský.

According to Dobrovský, the tasks of the dictionary are 'to serve towards a more correct judgement of the riches of a language, and especially as an aid both in learning it and in understanding it better and more thoroughly' ('überhaupt zur richtigern Verurtheilung des Reichthums einer Sprache und besonders zu einem Hülfsmittel dienen, dieselbe theils zu erlernen, theils besser und gründlicher zu verstehen' (Dobrovský 1791: 3)). That is, it should serve a twofold readership: those who want to learn Czech and those who already know it, but want to broaden their knowledge. Whether the second group should comprise native speakers only or also the more advanced members of other nations is not clear. However, among the learners of Czech Dobrovský does not anticipate Germans only, but also members of other, presumably Slavic, nations, whom the Latin equivalents in the dictionary should serve:

> Die Erklärungen der böhmischen Wörter durch angemessene lateinische Ausdrücke, die hier beigefügt sind, haben auch ihren vielfachen Nutzen, besonders für die böhmische Jugend in den lateinischen Schulen, wie auch für diejenigen, die nicht deutsch verstehen, und doch ein böhmisches Wort nachschlagen wollen. (Dobrovský 1791: 10)

Also the choice of alphabetical rather than etymological order (deemed more 'scientific' at that time) was aimed at users not well versed in Czech word formation (Dobrovský 1791: 8). In summary, it is clear that both Czech and non-Czech users belonged to the anticipated audience of the dictionary and were probably equally important for its author.

However, the absence of dialect expressions was not appreciated by all users, as can be seen from the dispute between the Vienna University professor Josef Valentin Zlobický and Josef Dobrovský. From their correspondence we learn that Zlobický considered the dictionary generally good, especially because it comprised colloquial expressions, but that he was not fully satisfied with it because it did not cover the entire vocabulary of Czech, Moravian and Slovak dialects (Schamschula 1973: 157–58). Consequently, he entered numerous manuscript additions in his own copy,[28] not only archaic words and phrases that he found in old Czech documents, but also popular names of plants and animals, words from Moravian dialects, diminutives, phraseology, etc. (Reichel 2004: 32, 125; Vojtová 2004: 73, 75, 174, 178). Evidently the aim of serving several purposes at once was not always easy to fulfil. However, the irreconcilable disagreement lay rather between different concepts of modern literary language or different functions of the book (codification v. enlarging one's vocabulary) than between different groups of users.

Grammatical and Linguistic Works

From the rich list of Tomsa's grammatical works, only two will be discussed here in detail: one of his best-known works, his grammar of Czech, and a little handbook of Czech, German and Latin phraseology. The first of these represents Tomsa's older, more conservative and more conventional views on literary language, similar to Dobrovský's, the second his own specific approach, namely the effort to give priority to contemporary usage over ancient literary style.

Tomsa's *Böhmische Sprachlehre* (1782) begins with a statement that it is intended for Germans to learn Czech, especially those who need it because of their profession or social status.[29] To this end, but also in accordance with its possible model, *Verbesserte*

Anleitung zur deutschen Sprachlehre, supposedly by Johann Ignaz Felbiger (see Keipert 1991), the book begins with a chapter describing the pronunciation of individual Czech letters, the basis for comparison being German, before going on to deal with orthography, word-formation, grammatical gender, declension of nouns, adjectives, pronouns and numerals, verb conjugation and elementary syntax. At the end, an interesting appendix is added, 'Vom Uibersetzen', in which Tomsa articulates his attitude towards translation: 'through translation a language can be refined, but also butchered' ('Durch das Uibersetzen kann eine Sprache verfeinert, und auch verhunzt warden' (Tomsa 1782: 425)). He also criticizes Pohl's tendency to create unnecessary neologisms, points out differences between Czech and German, and concludes that before a writer thinks of creating a new word, he should first search in old books and dictionaries or ask ordinary people. This part seems to be written with a view to influencing the situation in both Vienna and Prague, since Pohl's grammar was prescribed as a textbook in Vienna, and in Prague, though the danger of accepting Pohl's neologisms was quite low, the tendency to create new words was generally quite strong, as was the contempt of some philologists for popular usage.

However, at the very beginning of the book the author expresses also his doubt about its suitability for German native speakers: 'Aber wird den Deutschen damit wirklich geholfen werden? — Das muß die Erfahrung lehren'. Was this doubt pessimistic, or simply realistic? First, we can presume that Tomsa used his grammar (possibly together with his other works) when teaching Czech to aristocratic young ladies of the Clam-Gallas family, whose mother tongue was almost certainly not Czech.[30] We do not know how successful these efforts were, but very probably they did not use the language actively during their adult lives.

What we do know is that Tomsa's grammar was in use, from its first publication, by German-speakers at the University of Vienna (Vintr 2004: 18, 107; Reichel 2004: 31, 124). Here, it competed indirectly with Pohl's grammar, used by its author at the Theresianum. And it seems that it emerged as the winner: in his letter written to Dobrovský, Zlobický claims that when the students at the Theresianum were permitted to attend his lessons instead of Pohl's, they often chose this option, and thus also Tomsa's grammar (Reichel 2004: 32, 124; Newerkla 2004: 44–45; 140). According to the findings of Pleskalová (2004), Zlobický kept, in his translations, more or less to the phonetic and morphological forms recommended by Tomsa's grammar. Its influence is also clearly visible in the grammatical treatise written by Zlobický and published by Spurný within his *České Cwičenj* (see Pleskalová 2004: 61, 159). On the other hand, Maximilián Šimek claims in his *Handbuch für einen Lehrer der böhmischen Literatur* (partly based on Zlobický's material, but published without his permission) that it is too detailed and complicated, and consequently more suited to the teacher than the pupil. Moreover, it lacks model dialogues and examples of translations, which, according to Šimek, were particularly valued in Austria (Šimek 1785: 40, 72; see also Pleskalová 2004: 62, 160; Schamschula 1973: 156). However, this may simply mean that Zlobický actually used and valued Tomsa, because Šimek, in his effort to justify his unauthorized use of Zlobický's materials, repeatedly accused his work and anything connected to him of being of low quality (Reichel 2004: 35, 128).

On the other hand, we know little about the employment of this grammar in the instruction of Czech-speaking students and adults. When Czech started to be taught at Prague University in 1793 by František Martin Pelcl, one of his official tasks was to publish a grammar of Czech, which he fulfilled in 1795 with his *Grundsätze der Böhmischen Grammatik*.[31] His successor to this chair, Jan Nejedlý, also composed his own grammar and used it in his lectures.[32] Moreover, in 1809 Dobrovský's long-awaited *Ausführliches Lehrgebäude der Böhmischen Sprache* (*Knihopis* K01982) was finally published, which to a certain extent side-lined other grammatical works. Thus, it seems probable that only interested individuals, not whole classes of Czech students, used Tomsa's grammar to improve their knowledge of Czech, and that its main use in formal education may have been in teaching non-native speakers after all.

Among the works Tomsa probably did not value much, because he did not mention it in his autobiography, is an interesting little booklet combining teaching Czech, German and Latin: *Elementarwerk der boehmisch- deutsch- und lateinischen Sprache* (Tomsa 1784b). According to its preface, its aim was not only to educate Czech and German children in Latin, but also to help both these groups to learn the language of their neighbours. Although the author seemingly preserves symmetry between the languages, dividing the book into three parts with German, Czech and Latin source languages respectively, the very argumentation in the preface betrays a deep asymmetry among the languages. While German is declared universally important for all Czech children and indispensable for a great many of them, in putting the case for German speakers to learn Czech the argumentation is quite different:

> Aber auch jene deutschen Kinder oder Jünglinge, welche dazu gebildet werden, um einst sowohl ihre böhmischen als deutschen Nebenchristen zu belehren und zu bessern, oder ihren böhmischen Unterthanen, und Untergeordneten in allen Fällen, so viel möglich, Gerechtigkeit wiederfahren zu lassen, müssen, wenn sie sonst ihr Amt mit gutem Gewissen vertreten wollen, mit der Kenntniß der böhmischen Sprache — so lange sie lebt — ausgerüstet werden. (Tomsa 1784b: *2–*3)

> [But also those German children or youths who are being educated to teach and improve their Bohemian and German fellow-Christians, or to obtain, as far as possible, justice for their Bohemian subjects and subordinates in their cases, must — if they want to represent their office with a good conscience — be equipped with a knowledge of the Bohemian language — as long as it lives.]

Here, Tomsa describes the real relationship between the two languages, Czech being the language of lower classes and German that of wealthy people and of the government. The feeling of asymmetry is further strengthened by the fact that the Czech phrases are taken from colloquial speech (to judge from their content, probably mostly overheard from domestic servants, e.g. *Wede gi do služby. – Er führt sie in Dienst; Dáwag pozor na ni (na slepicy)! – Geben Sie Acht auf sie (auf die Henne)!* (Tomsa 1784b: 7, 21)), while the German (and, of course, Latin) phrases are taken mostly from books of other authors, the translations into both other languages being in any case Tomsa's own. On the other hand, the part where Czech is the source language is much longer than the other two (forty pages v. eight and eleven pages respectively), providing a rather comprehensive glossary, including not only explanations of words used in the text together with information about their grammatical gender and declension, but also lists of words that are linguistically and thematically related. As the book does not provide such detailed information about the vocabulary of the other two languages, it is clear that it is not German but Czech that is its primary focus. Thus, this book, too, may have been intended to serve several purposes. Besides teaching Czech children German and/or Latin it could, at least hypothetically, teach contemporary colloquial Czech to German children, German-speaking adults (both native and non-native speakers, e.g. members of other Slavic nations), and even educated Czech adults who had lost contact with their mother tongue.

Orthographical Works

Besides his grammar and other linguistic works, Tomsa also published, often anonymously and at his own expense, several tiny booklets concerning Czech orthography and orthoepy. They were initially written in Czech, but towards the end of his life he also published German versions. The Czech versions usually declare in their title that they are intended for school use (Tomsa 1784a, 1793, 1800a), while the German versions lack any information about their anticipated readership (Tomsa 1801, 1802, 1812).

These works are of interest because of a reform of one aspect of Czech orthography that they suggest, namely the spelling of /j/ and /i:/. The details of this proposed reform may not bother us here; it will suffice to note that traditionally these phonemes were spelled <g> (<y>) and <j> respectively: *gežek, deg/dey, pegcha/ peycha, gjsti*. Tomsa suggests that syllable-initial [j] be spelled <j>, syllable-final [j] <i> or <y>, and /i:/ <í>: *ježek, dei, peycha, jíst* (Tomsa 1800a: 5, 9, 11; Tomsa 1801: 9, 14-15). He also discloses that the goal of the reform is the convergence of writing systems of the Slavic languages in the Habsburg Empire, which he considers the first, and easiest, move towards the convergence of these languages themselves:

> Fast jede Provinz hat ihren besondern Dialekt, der Sache ist nicht so leicht abzuhelfen; aber in der Orthographie könnte mehr Uibereinstimmung sein, und dies würde den Provinzen, und folglich dem State nicht wenig Nutzen bringen. (Tomsa 1802: 3)
>
> [Almost every province has its particular dialect, a situation which is not so easily resolved; but in the orthography there can be more agreement, and this would be of no little use to the provinces, and consequently to the State.]

In the next edition of 1812, he summons some new arguments for his proposal and even suggests some orthographic reforms for other Slavic languages using Czech graphemes with diacritics, e.g. *čas, řepa* instead of *czas, rzepa* in Polish; *člowěk, žiwad* instead of *chlowěk, siwad* in Croatian; and even the use of the Latin alphabet with diacritics like *čitať, dožď* in Russian (Tomsa 1812a: 17-19, 41-48).

At the turn of the century, Tomsa used his reformed orthography in those of his works that were not subject to the direct supervision of his superiors: his congratulatory poems and an edition of a prayer book (Tomsa 1803). However, his proposals were approved of neither by Josef Dobrovský, who articulated his unfavourable opinion in a review of the prayer book and expressed his satisfaction that so far Tomsa had not found any imitators,[33] nor by the authorities, as we learn from the pamphlet by Jan Nejedlý, aimed against a later orthographical reform and published approximately thirty years later, where the author claims that Tomsa's reforms were prohibited by the authorities (Nejedlý 1828: 12).[34]

The switch from Czech to German in the newer versions, together with the nature of argumentation and the proposals for other Slavic languages, suggests that, unlike the older ones, these versions were not primarily intended for schools, but for other philologists or writers, Czech, German and Slavic. This is confirmed by the fact that, even after the unfavourable assessment by Dobrovský, Tomsa continued to use his orthography in his linguistic works published in German and intended for a learned public (Tomsa 1804b, 1805, 1812b). Among this public, his efforts were not completely unsuccessful, as some of the authors used his orthography during the 1830s, for example Jan K. Dvořáček, the learned Moravian lawyer living in Vienna (Čenský 1875: 251). Finally, a slightly modified version of the reform was generally accepted in 1842.

Translations of Primers

Although it may seem incredible to the modern reader, the school reforms of Maria Theresa and her sons required that even the primary school textbooks be unified throughout the Habsburg Empire. Thus, German textbooks issued by the Normal School Printing House in Vienna were sent to Prague and translated there into Czech. This set of textbooks included not only catechisms or elementary arithmetic books, but also readers and, most curiously, primers. Consequently, Czech children were taught how to read and write from ABC books originally designed for another language.

It was Tomsa's task to translate most of these books, and not just once but any time Vienna issued a new edition of the German version. He did not regard this work as unimportant or inferior,[35] as we can see from his manuscript biographies; although the list of his works is far from complete there, it includes these translations right at the beginning.[36] Of them, only the primer, published under the title *Slabikář, pro sskoly w cýsařských králowských zemjch W Praze, nákladem cýs. král. normálnj sskoly*, will be treated as an example here.[37] According to Tomsa's autobiography, it represented a revision of an older translation of 1775, a revision he considered so substantial that he did not hesitate to call it a new translation.[38] The older version was probably *Slabikář, obsahugjcý w sobě Způsob, gak se Djtky magj včiti Pjsmeny znáti, slabikowati, a čjsti*.[39] A cursory comparison of the 1775 edition with the revised one of 1793 shows that Tomsa made linguistic revisions on several levels. He changed most of the linguistic terminology (here, surprisingly, he was more dependent on tradition and foreign models than his predecessor: he introduced, for example, *litery* instead of *pjsmeny* [letters]; *hlasyté* instead of *samohlásky* [vowels]; and *syllaba* instead of *slabika* [syllable]), and simplified the theoretical passages (e.g. he does not treat long vowels as 'hidden diphthongs' or divide consonants into 'natural' and 'softened'), omitting all unnecessary details (e.g. about the pronunciation of foreign proper names). Most importantly, he reformulated many texts (except the most set ones, e.g. the Lord's Prayer etc.), using morphologically and stylistically more modern language, while still avoiding phonetic innovations typical of the Baroque period and perceived as uncultivated.[40] He clearly endeavoured to avoid speech 'overcrowded with superfluous words in the manner of monastic preachers' (Kabát 1926: 53–54). As a whole, except for its rather conservative linguistic terminology, his revision rejects the language common for Baroque religious literature in all its aspects and replaces it with language that is morphologically, syntactically and stylistically closer to contemporary colloquial speech, but phonetically closer to the classical usage of the 'Golden Age' of the late sixteenth century. In the second aspect, Tomsa is completely in line with the language ideals and efforts of his contemporaries; in the first, he is considerably ahead of time. However, as seen in the polemic about his translation of the catechism, he was not always free to make all the corrections he desired.[41]

Conclusion

This chapter has touched on selected aspects of Czech-language teaching in Bohemia in the formative period at the turn of the eighteenth to the nineteenth century. Using the example of an inconspicuous, but prolific and innovative philologist and educator, František Jan Tomsa, it has sought to show how difficult (and even impossible) it is to distinguish between first- and second-language teaching materials and scholarly works in the plurilingual milieu of the Habsburg Empire at the time of budding nationalist movements.

We have seen that Tomsa's works are functionally indeterminate, aiming at a heterogeneous audience including both native speakers (children and adults) and non-native speakers. Among the latter, two groups can be distinguished: first, German-speaking children and adults who need the language because of their contacts with Czechs; and, second, speakers of other (especially Slavic) languages who want to study it because of their scholarly interests. Both groups are explicitly mentioned in the dictionary; the former is mentioned as a target group also in the grammar. The needs of the latter group are also taken into account in the reformed orthography that Tomsa proposes and uses in his linguistic works. In addressing both these groups, Tomsa may have been rather successful, at least temporarily, as can be seen from the evidence of his grammar and dictionary being in use in Vienna and of his educational activities in aristocratic families.

The trivial school textbooks translated by Tomsa from German were not monofunctional either. Although they were mainly aimed at Czech children, they were also subject to philological disputes, because in them Tomsa materialized his concept of modern literary Czech, differing from the concepts of his contemporaries. Thus, it is vital to analyse all these works together; only then does the picture of multi-purpose books functioning in a milieu of complicated inter-national and interlingual relations emerge in all its complexity.

Bibliography

AIGNER, JOSEF. 1867. *Der Volks- und Industrieschulen-Reformator Bischof Ferdinand Kindermann* (Vienna: Mayer)

ČENSKÝ, FERDINAND. 1875. *Z dob našeho probuzení* (Prague: Fr. A. Urbánek)

DOBROVSKÝ, JOSEF. 1787. 'Den 31 Oktober desselben J. starb Hr. Johann Ritter von Neuberg', *Litterarisches Magazin von Böhmen und Mähren. Drittes Stück* (Prague: von Schönfeldische Handlung), 179–80

——. 1791. 'Vorrede', in František Jan Tomsa, *Vollständiges Wörterbuch der böhmisch- deutsch- und lateinischen Sprache. Mit einer Vorrede begleitet von Herrn Rektor Joseph Dobrowsky* (Prague: von Schönfeld-Meißnerische Handlung), pp. 3–10

——. 1803. [REVIEW] 'Modlitby pro Krestany Katolické; prací a nákladem Frantisska Tomsy, d. i. Gebethe für katholische Christen; verfasst und verlegt von Franz Tomsa. 8. Prag, 1803 mit Schriften der k. k. Normalschule. 112 S. 21. kr.', *Annalen der Literatur und Kunst in den österreichischen Staaten*, 2, 1, Januar bis Junius (Vienna: Degen), No. 85, VII. Stück, October 1803, 693-95

DOUCHA, FRANTIŠEK. 1865. *Knihopisný slovník česko-slovenský, aneb seznam kněh, drobných spisův, map a hudebných věcí, vyšlých v jazyku národa česko-slovenského od roku 1774 až do nejnovější doby* (Prague: Kober)

EDER, ULRIKE. 2006. *'Auf die mehrere Ausbreitung der teutschen Sprache soll fürgedacht werden'. Deutsch als Fremd- und Zweitsprache im Unterrichtssystem der Donaumonarchie zur Regierungszeit Maria Theresias und Josephs II* (Innsbruck, Vienna and Bolzano: StudienVerlag)

FIŠER, ZDENĚK (ed.). 2003. *Korespondence Aloise Vojtěcha Šembery. Svazek 3: Listy Klácelovi* (Vysoké Mýto: Regionální muzeum Vysoké Mýto)

GANT, BARBARA. 2008. '"National-Erziehung": Überwachung als Prinzip. Österreichische Bildungspolitik im Zeichen von Absolutismus und Aufklärung', in *Josephinismus als Aufgeklärter Absolutismus*, ed. by Helmut Reinalter (Vienna etc.: Böhlau), pp. 97–124

GLÜCK, HELMUT, ET AL. 2002. *Deutsche Sprachbücher in Böhmen und Mähren vom 15. Jahrhundert bis 1918* (Berlin and New York: de Gruyter)

HAMMER, WENZEL. 1904. *Geschichte der Volksschule Böhmens von der ältesten Zeit bis zum Jahre 1870* (Warnsdorf: Opitz)

HANUŠ, JOSEF. 1921-23. *Národní museum a naše obrození*, 2 vols (Prague: Národní museum)

HANZAL, JOSEF. 1998. *Ferdinand Kindermann (1740–1801): školský reformátor a osvícenský duchovní* (Kostelní Vydří: Karmelitánské nakladatelství)

HELFERT, JOSEPH ALEXANDER VON. 1860. *Die österreichische Volksschule. Geschichte, System, Statistik*, I, *Die Gründung der österreichischen Volksschule durch Maria Theresia* (Prague: Tempsky)

JUNGMANN, JOSEF. 1849. *Historie literatury české*, 2nd edn (Prague: Řiwnáč)

JUNGMANN, JOSEF. 1998. *Zápisky* (Prague: Budka)

[KABÁT, KAREL.] 1926. *Prvých padesát roků trvání Knihtiskárny Státního nakladatelství. Ke stopadesátému výročí* ([Praha: Státní nakladatelství])

KALINOVÁ, GABRIELA, ET AL. 2016. *Malostranský hřbitov, historie a současnost* (Prague: ARSCI)

KEIPERT, HELMUT. 1991. 'Die "Wiener Anleitung" in der slavischen Grammatikographie des ausgehenden 18. Jahrhunderts', *Zeitschrift für slavische Philologie*, 51: 23-59

KLUETING, HARM (ed.). 1995. *Der Josephinismus. Ausgewählte Quellen zur Geschichte der theresianisch-josephinischen Reformen* (Darmstadt: Wissenschaftliche Buchgesellschaft)

KPS – Databáze Knihopis <http://www.knihopis.cz/>

KRUMMHOLZ, MARTIN. 2007. *Clam-Gallasův palác. Johann Bernhard Fischer von Erlach. Architektura — výzdoba — život rezidence. Clam-Gallasův palác 30/11 2007 — 27/1 2008* (Prague: Archiv hlavního města Prahy)

KUSÁKOVÁ, LENKA 2008. 'Tomsa, František Jan', in *Lexikon české literatury. Osobnosti, díla, instituce*, IV, S–Ž. Dodatky k LČL 1–3. A–Ř (Prague: Academia), pp. 971–73

NEJEDLÝ, JAN. 1828. *Widerlegung der sogenannten analogisch-orthographischen Neuerungen in der böhmischen Sprache* (Prague: Sommersche Buchdruckerey, in Skt. Anna-Kloster) (*Knihopis* K06116)

NEWERKLA, STEFAN MICHAEL. 1999. 'Johann Wenzel Pohl — Sprachpurismus zwischen Spätbarock und tschechischer Erneuerung', in *Tschechisches Barock: Sprache, Literatur, Kultur = České baroko: Jazyk, literatura, kultura*, ed. by Gertraude Zand and Jiří Holý (Frankfurt am Main etc.: Lang), pp. 49–67

——. 2004. 'Josef Valentin Zlobický v kruhu svých předchůdců a současníků. Josef Valentin Zlobický im Kreise seiner Vorgänger und Zeitgenossen', in *Vídeňský podíl na počátcích českého národního obrození — J. V. Zlobický (1743–1810) a současníci: život, dílo, korespondence. Wiener Anteil an den Anfängen der tschechischen nationalen Erneuerung — J. V. Zlobický (1743–1810) und Zeitgenossen: Leben, Werk, Korrespondenz*, ed. by Josef Vintr and Jana Pleskalová (Prague: Academia), pp. 42–60

NEWERKLA, STEFAN MICHAEL, VÁCLAV PETRBOK and TAŤÁNA VYKYPĚLOVÁ (eds). 2014. *Maximilian Schimek: Vorläufer der wissenschaftlichen Slawistik: Leben, Werk, Editionen* (Vienna: Holzhausen)

Ottův slovník naučný. Illustrovaná encyklopaedie obecných vědomostí, v, C–Čechůvky. 1892. (Prague: Otto)

PLESKALOVÁ, JANA. 2004. 'Jazykovědné zájmy Josefa Valentina Zlobického. Die sprachwissenschaftlichen Interessen Josef Valentin Zlobický's', in *Vídeňský podíl na počátcích českého národního obrození — J. V. Zlobický (1743–1810) a současníci: život, dílo, korespondence. Wiener Anteil an den Anfängen der tschechischen nationalen Erneuerung — J. V. Zlobický (1743–1810) und Zeitgenossen: Leben, Werk, Korrespondenz*, ed. by Josef Vintr and Jana Pleskalová (Prague: Academia), pp. 61–69, 159–70

POLÁK, KAREL. 1968. *Třemi stoletími. Stručné dějiny Státního pedagogického nakladatelství* (Prague: SPN)

REICHEL, WALTER. 'Josef Valentin Zlobický — první profesor českého jazyka a literatury: život, působení a zásluhy na pozadí osvícenství. Josef Valentin Zlobický — erster Professor für böhmische Sprache und Literatur: Leben, Wirken und Verdienste vor dem Hintergrund der Aufklärung', in *Vídeňský podíl na počátcích českého národního obrození — J. V. Zlobický (1743–1810) a současníci: život, dílo, korespondence. Wiener Anteil an den Anfängen der tschechischen nationalen Erneuerung — J. V. Zlobický (1743–1810) und Zeitgenossen: Leben, Werk, Korrespondenz*, ed. by Josef Vintr and Jana Pleskalová (Prague: Academia), pp. 24–41, 115–36

REINALTER, HELMUT (ed.). 2008. *Josephinismus als Aufgeklärter Absolutismus* (Vienna etc.: Böhlau)

RITTER VON RITTERSBERG, JOHANN. 1838. *Christian Christoph Graf v. Clam-Gallas [...] Biographischer Umriss* (Prague: Haas)

RYBIČKA, ANTONÍN. 1883. *Přední křisitelé národa českého* (Prague: Šimáček)

ŠAFRÁNEK, JAN. 1913. *Školy české. Obraz z jejich vývoje a osudů. I. svazek. R. 862–1848* (Prague: Matice českiá)

SCHAMSCHULA, WALTER. 1973. *Die Anfänge der tschechischen Erneuerung und das deutsche Geistesleben (1740–1800)* (Munich: Fink)

ŠIMEK, MAXIMILIÁN VÁCLAV. 1785. *Handbuch für einen Lehrer der böhmischen Literatur* (Vienna: Christian Friedrich Wappler) (*Knihopis* K15912)

Slovník naučný. Díl devátý. Š — Vzývání svatých. 1872. Ed. by František Ladislav Rieger (Prague: Kober)

STICH, ALEXANDR. 2009. 'Asymétries du baroque tchèque et "culture de la langue" (du début du XVIIe siècle à la Grammatica linguae boëmicae de Václav Jandyt — 1715)', in *Baroque en Bohême*, ed. by Marie-Elisabeth Ducreux, Xavier Galmiche, Martin Petráš and Vít Vlnas (Lille: Université Charles-de-Gaulle — Lille 3), pp. 29–47

TIMOFEJEV, DMITRIJ. 2008. '"...čeština ve většině okresů země je stále ještě nezbytná...". Existoval jazykový program v nařízeních Josefa II. pro země Koruny české?', *Cornova* 3: 63–82

TOMSA, FRANTIŠEK JAN. 1782. *Böhmische Sprachlehre* (Prague: Verlag der k. k. Normalschule) (*Knihopis* K16252)

———. 1784a. *Vwedenj k České Dobropjsebnosti, k vžjwánj Českých sskol w cýs. král. Zemjch* (Prague: cýs. král. normálnj Sskola) (*Knihopis* K16259)

———. 1784b. *Elementarwerk der boehmisch- deutsch- und lateinischen Sprache, entworfen von Franz Johann Tomsa. Erstes Baendchen* (Prague: k. k. Normalschulbuchdruckerei) (*Knihopis* K16236)

———. 1789. *Malý německý a český Slownjk* (Prague: at the author's expense) (*Knihopis* K16251)

———. 1791. *Vollständiges Wörterbuch der böhmisch- deutsch- und lateinischen Sprache. Mit einer Vorrede begleitet von Herrn Rektor Joseph Dobrowsky* (Prague: von Schönfeld-Meißnerische Handlung) (*Knihopis* K16261)

[———]. 1793. *Naučenj, gak se má dobře česky psát. Pro české sskoly* (Prague: cýs. král. normálnj sskola) (*Knihopis* K16247)

———. 1798a. *Karoline Klamowé Galasowé hrabence 28. den mesyce Ledna, léta 1798* (*Knihopis* K16240)

———. 1798b. *Leopoldine, knezne z Firstenberku. 10. dne mesyce Dubna, léta 1798* (*Knihopis* K16242)

———. 1798c. *Aloyzyi, dceri hrabecy Krystyana Klama Galase a Karoliny manzelky jeho. 21. dne mesyce Cerwna, léta 1798* (*Knihopis* K16235)

[———]. 1800a. *Naučenj, gak se má dobře česky psát. Pro české sskoly* (Prague: cýs. král. normálnj sskola) (*Knihopis* K16248)

———. 1800b. *Na památku Karla Iozefa knížete z Firštenberku, rozeného Čecha a generála českého w cýsařském královském woiště, který byl 25. den měsýce Března, léta 1799. w bitwě u Štokachu w Švábích zabit* (*Knihopis* K16246)

———. 1801. *Über die Aussprache der čechischen Buchstaben, Sylben und Wörter nebst Leseübungen* (Prague: at the author's expense) (*Knihopis* K16254)

———. 1802. *Über die čechische Rechtschreibung mit einem Anhange, welcher dreizehn čechische Gedichte enthält* (Prague: at the author's expense) (*Knihopis* K16256)

———. 1803. *Modlitby pro Křesťany katolické* (Prague: at the author's expense) (*Knihopis* K16244)

———. 1804a. *Knížecý Oswícenosti, Alzbete, owdowělé kněžně w Firstenberku, rozené kněžně z Turn a Taxis, 13. den mesyce Unora, léta 1804* (*Knihopis* K16241)

———. 1804b. *Über die Bedeutung, Abwandlung und Gebrauch der čechischen Zeitwörter* (Prague: at the author's expense) (*Knihopis* K16255)

———. 1805. *Über die Veränderungen der čechischen Sprache, nebst einer čechischen Chrestomathie seit dem dreizehntem Jahrhunderte biß jetzt* (Prague: at the author's expense) (*Knihopis* K16257)

———. 1812a. *Grössere čechische Orthographie, gemeiniglich böhmische Orthographie genannt* (Prague: at the author's expense) (*Knihopis* K16249)

———. 1812b. *Von den Vorzügen der čechischen Sprache, oder über die Billigkeit und den Nutzen, die čechische Sprache zu erhalten, empor zu bringen, und über die Mittel dazu* (Prague: at the author's expense) (*Knihopis* K16260)

Vídeňský podíl na počátcích českého národního obrození — J. V. Zlobický (1743–1810) a současníci: život, dílo, korespondence. Wiener Anteil an den Anfängen der tschechischen nationalen Erneuerung — J. V. Zlobický (1743–1810) und Zeitgenossen: Leben, Werk, Korrespondenz. 2004. Ed. by Josef Vintr and Jana Pleskalová (Prague: Academia)

VINTR, JOSEF. 2004. 'Josef Valentin Zlobický — zapomenutý český vlastenec z osvícenské Vídně. Josef Valentin Zlobický — ein vergessener tschechischer Patriot aus dem Wien der Aufklärung', in *Vídeňský podíl na počátcích českého národního obrození — J. V.*

Zlobický (1743–1810) a současníci: život, dílo, korespondence. Wiener Anteil an den Anfängen der tschechischen nationalen Erneuerung — J. V. Zlobický (1743–1810) und Zeitgenossen: Leben, Werk, Korrespondenz, ed. by Josef Vintr and Jana Pleskalová (Prague: Academia), pp. 13–23, 101–14

VOJTOVÁ, JARMILA. 2004. 'Lexikografické zájmy Josefa Valentina Zlobického. Die Lexicographischen Interessen Josef Valentin', in *Vídeňský podíl na počátcích českého národního obrození — J. V. Zlobický (1743–1810) a současníci: život, dílo, korespondence. Wiener Anteil an den Anfängen der tschechischen nationalen Erneuerung — J. V. Zlobický (1743–1810) und Zeitgenossen: Leben, Werk, Korrespondenz*, ed. by Josef Vintr and Jana Pleskalová (Prague: Academia), pp. 70–79, 171–82

WEISS, ANTON. 1906. *Geschichte der Theresianischen Schulreform in Böhmen. Zusammengestellt aus den halbjährigen Berichten der Schulen-Oberdirektion 17. September 1777 — 14. März 1792*, 1 (Vienna and Leipzig: Fromme)

WINTER, EDUARD. 1926. *Ferdinand Kindermann, Ritter von Schulstein (1740/1801), der Organisator der Volksschule und Volkswohlfahrt Böhmens: ein Lebensbild nach archivalischen Quellen* (Augsburg: Stauda)

——. 1945. *Josefinismus a jeho dějiny. Příspěvky k duchovním dějinám Čech a Moravy 1740–1848* (Prague: Jelínek)

WOTKE, KARL. 1905. *Das österreichische Gymnasium im Zeitalter Maria Theresias* (Berlin: Hofmann)

Notes to Chapter 7

1. The chapter was prepared with the support of the Charles University project Progres 4, 'Language in the shiftings of time, space, and culture'.
2. According to the estimates, at the end of the eighteenth century approximately 40% of the population spoke German (Timofeev 2008: 68).
3. See Stich 2009.
4. Because of his rather distinct approach, the late and most specific phase of this process was called 'Josephinism'. See, for example, Winter 1945, Klueting 1995 and Reinalter 2008.
5. About the details of these reforms, see, for example, Helfert 1860, Hammer 1904, Wotke 1905, Weiss 1906 or Šafránek 1913; and recently, for example, Eder 2006.
6. As evidence, two leading Czech scholars of the first half of the nineteenth century can be cited: Josef Jungmann recalls in his autobiographical notes (1998: 21) an embarrassing moment from his youth when he, a student at Prague University, was humiliated by his 'stammering' during a dinner at his uncle's, i.e. by his inability to find adequate Czech expressions. Similarly, his contemporary František Matouš Klácel confessed in one of his letters to his friend Alois Vojtěch Šembera that it was easier for him to write in German than in Czech (Fišer 2003: 7).
7. For Pohl's life and work and also for the description of the structure of his grammar, see Newerkla 1999.
8. 1756 (*Knihopis* K14094), 1764 (*Knihopis* K14095), 1773 (*Knihopis* K14096), 1776 (*Knihopis* K14100), 1783 (*Knihopis* K14097).
9. See Newerkla, Petrbok and Vykypělová 2014.
10. See Vintr and Pleskalová 2004.
11. For this purpose, five copies of each edition were to be sent to Vienna.
12. About its earliest history see Kabát 1926 or Polák 1968.
13. Strahov Monastery Library, Prague, DC IV 11.
14. Literary Archive of the Museum of Czech Literature (LA PNP), Collection Dobrovský Josef, item Tomsa, František Jan => Dobrovský Josef, 2 dopisy z let 1793–1801, příloha *Kurze Lebensbeschreibung des Franz Tomsa*.
15. Besides the most recent entry in the *Lexikon české literatury* (Kusáková 2008) and the literature quoted there, see also the respective entry in the ninth volume of the so-called *Riegrův slovník naučný* (Rieger 1872: 506–07) and the archive material quoted below.

16. Born in Slavkov in Moravia (*Bio- bibliografická databáze řeholníků v českých zemích v raném novověku*, entry: Ildefonsus a S. Maria, Bierfeind Joannes OPi, 1742–? <http://reholnici.hiu.cas.cz/katalog/lat/l.dll?hal~1000119546> [accessed 20 April 2015].
17. In both versions of his autobiography Tomsa mentions a story about his classmates, who complained that there were not enough good books written in Czech. Father Bierfeind replied to them: 'Tomsa will write them for you'.
18. About him, see, for example, Aigner 1867, Winter 1926, or Hanzal 1998.
19. See, for example, Hanuš (1921: 156–57), Schamschula (1973: 239), or Rybička (1883: 11).
20. LA PNP, collection Šternberk Kašpar, item 2 dopisy z let 1804-1812, připojeny opisy obou dopisů.
21. See the contemporary manuscript note on a copy of the poem dedicated to Countess Marie Karolina (Tomsa 1798a), identifying Tomsa as its author and calling him 'the Czech teacher of her daughters' ('Složil Fr. Tomsa včitel dcer gegjch wgazyku českém'), LA PNP, collection Varia — Tomsa František Jan, item Tomsa František Jan => Klamová-Galašová Karolina, 1 tisk z r. 1798). In this poem, Tomsa praises the Countess for her interest in the Czech language and for making her children study it. To Aloisia, another poem is dedicated (Tomsa 1798c).
22. See Ritter von Rittersberg (1838: 9) and Krummholz (2007: 36).
23. To please the little girl, Tomsa did something unusual and had the poem printed in two colours, black and red, the latter being used for the title, small floral ornaments and two expressions in the text: 'wlast' [homeland] and 'česká řeč' [Czech language].
24. He also published a poem commemorating the heroic death of the father of these children, Karl Aloys zu Fürstenberg (1760–1799) (Tomsa 1800b).
25. See the most recent version in Kusáková 2008.
26. See Tomsa 1789, 'Předmluwa' (unpag.)
27. See Schamschula 1973: 156.
28. The copy is preserved in the National Museum Library in Prague (63 D 13) (Vojtová 2004: 72, 173; Hanuš 1923: 254).
29. 'Alles klagte darüber, es wäre keine böhmische Sprachlehre da, woraus sich der Deutsche mit der böhmischen Sprache leicht bekannt machen könnte. Denn es gibt immer einige, die diese Sprache lernen müssen, weil es von ihnen entweder die Berufs- oder doch die gesellschaftliche Pflicht fordert' (Tomsa 1782: 'Vorrede', unpag.).
30. Both because of the origin of the family (Austrian nobles coming from Carinthia, the first generation to live in Bohemia being their grandparents ('Clam', in *Ottův slovník naučný* 1892: 426), and because of the fact that even Czech aristocratic families mostly ceased to use Czech as their mother tongue during the late-seventeenth and early eighteenth centuries.
31. *Knihopis* K06969. A second, enlarged edition appeared in 1798 (*Knihopis* K06970).
32. 1804 (*Knihopis* K06109), 1809 (*Knihopis* K06110), 1821 (*Knihopis* K06111).
33. 'Zum Glück findet zwar derselbe in dieser nach den Schriftstellern der ältesten Zeiten gemodelten, und nun von ihm wieder aufgewärmten Schreibart, die er seinen Landesleuten so gern aufdringen wollte, bisher noch keine Nachahmer' (Dobrovský 1803: 695).
34. 'So hat Fr. Tomsa etwa vor 30 Jahren ähnliche orthographische Neuerungen jedoch ohne Erfolg, in der böhmischen Sprache vornehmen wollen; es ward ihm sogar von der hohen Lander regierung eingestellt!'. Some correspondence summarized in Kabát 1926: 47–48, 69 seems to confirm this claim.
35. Unlike modern secondary literature, which only rarely mentions them.
36. Tomsa's list gives only short titles and the place of print. If possible, I have identified the title in the bibliographies and/or in the catalogues of public libraries and supplied the dates of editions I was able to trace.
37. 1793 (*Knihopis* K15459), 1798 (*Knihopis* K15460), 1800a, 1801, 1805, 1807, 1810 (Jungmann 1849: 367 (VI/9c); Doucha 1865: 231).
38. 'Zwar war das Namenbüchlein schon Im Jahr 1775 von einem andern ins Böhmische übersetzt und gedruckt, aber Tomsa hat es hernach so stark verbessert, daß es kann für seine Übersetzung gehalten werden' (LA PNP, collection Dobrovský Josef, item Tomsa, František Jan => Dobrovský Josef, 2 dopisy z let 1793–1801, příloha *Kurze Lebensbeschreibung des Franz Tomsa*).

39. *W PRAZE, W Nákladu sskolnjho Včenj 1775*, reprinted also in 1778 and 1781 (*Knihopis* K15466, K15467, K15469) (Doucha 1865: 231).
40. As an example, I quote the beginning of the morning prayer: 'Má prwnj mysslenj pozdwjhugi k tobě, ó Bože! přigmi to dětinské djků činěnj za ono weliké dobrodinj, že sy mne nechal čerstwýho a zdrawýho opět proceytnauti; z čehož poznáwám, že Dnem y Nocy práwě Otcowsky o mne pečugess, že tobě gedině patřjm, že gsy Pán Žiwota y Smrti' (1775: 18-19); and 'K tobě, Bože, neyprw mysljm; přigmi, když ti vpřjmně děkugi za to weliké dobrodinj, žes mi dal čerstwému a zdrawému opět procýtit; z čehož poznáwám, že we dne y w nocy dobrotiwě o mne pečugeš, že w twé mocy sem, že sy Pán žiwota y smrti' (1793: 12-13).
41. See the controversy with Aleš Vincenc Pařízek summarized in Kabát (1926: 53–56); or the letter from his superior criticizing the on-going linguistic changes in his textbooks quoted in Polák (1968: 44).

CHAPTER 8

Native Tongues and Foreign Languages in the Education of the Russian Nobility: The Case of the Noble Cadet Corps (1730s-1760s)

Vladislav Rjéoutski

This chapter deals mainly with one question: the choice of languages to learn in the major Russian educational institution for the nobility, the Noble Infantry Cadet Corps in St Petersburg, in the first period of its existence (1731-62). A combination of various sources gives us some idea of the evolution of language learning at the Corps over the period and the reasons why a given language was learned to a greater or lesser extent. The choice of languages to learn depended, indeed, on various factors, such as: the educational model followed by the Corps; the national origins and cultural outlook of the pupils and teachers; the organization of non-linguistic teaching; and, more broadly, considerations about the cultural and social value of given languages in the Russian Empire in general and, more specifically, for the two major ethnic groups (Russian and Baltic German) of nobility present at the Corps.[1]

    Eighteenth-century Russia was characterized by an increasing interest in foreign languages. The situation upended Russian society as far as the knowledge of foreign languages was concerned because, before Peter the Great (1696-1725), only a few people knew the rudiments of foreign languages. This lack of knowledge of foreign languages affected the development of general knowledge and scientific studies, the transfer of technological knowledge, diplomacy, printing etc. Whenever, before Peter the Great, Russia had somehow been able to cope with these needs, it had often been with the help of foreigners. With the acceleration of exchanges with Western countries under Peter the Great, it now became vital for at least some social and professional groups of people in Russia to have a command of foreign languages.

    Language learning and usage have deeply affected some social groups like the nobility. The choice of one language rather than another, as I will argue, not only shows the nobility's cultural orientation: it is also an indicator of changes in the social and cultural identity of this estate or, at least, of a new perception of its identity and desire to refashion itself according to new ideas about the nobility's education, outlook and sociability.

In Russia, the hubs for the acquisition of foreign languages included state schools for noble boys and, later, from the time of Catherine the Great (r. 1762-96) onwards, the Smolny Institute for noble girls in St Petersburg. The most important school of this sort was the Noble Infantry Cadet Corps, founded in St Petersburg in 1731. Foreign languages were of great importance in the professional education of a nobleman because many key works — for example, books on fortification — were not yet available in Russian. In addition, foreign languages were useful for the social life of a nobleman or noblewoman. French was becoming essential for life at the court. At the same time, command of the mother tongue was gaining in importance.

In this chapter, I focus my attention on one point in particular: the choice of languages to learn and the variety of factors that explain it. I do not discuss the books used in language classes but very briefly discuss the teachers' methods. I intend to show the links between the imagined value of a given language and the rating of that language at the Corps, the social and cultural outlook of the pupils and the teachers, and their national origin. For a long period, cadets could choose the languages they wanted to learn, not because these subjects were thought to be unimportant, but because the 'founding fathers' of the institution shared the idea that learning had to correspond to the personal tastes and talents or *génie* of each pupil (Fedyukin 2014). I begin by briefly presenting the position reserved for language teaching at the Corps and discussing the possible reasons for the proposal to teach certain languages there. I then present the social and cultural outlook of the main ethnic and linguistic group at the Corps, i.e. the Russian cadets. Finally, I discuss the relationships between the popularity of given languages and the cultural outlook(s) of the pupils and teachers.

Choosing Languages to Learn: Planning Language Learning at the Corps at the Time of its Foundation

The Cadet Corps was what we would today call a 'secondary school' for the nobility of the Russian Empire, including the German-speaking nobility of the Baltic provinces which Russia had invaded under Peter the Great. The acquisition of foreign languages was, from the start of the school, considered to be of utmost importance for the Russian nobility. Incidentally, among the main reasons given for the fact that the Cadet Corps was opened in St Petersburg and not in Moscow was the presence of numerous foreigners in St Petersburg, the Russian capital of the time, which could be beneficial to language learning at the Corps (Luzanov 1907: 16).

The first list of the staff of the Corps (published on 18 November 1731) included one Russian-teaching position, three German-teaching positions, two French-teaching positions, and one Latin-teaching position. There were four positions for instructors of writing: two for Russian and one each for German and Latin (*PSZ* 1830, 43: 185). From this first list of positions, published before the Corps came into being (in 1732), it is apparent that German was already considered to have the potential to become the most important language at the Corps, at least in terms of the number of classes offered. The staff regulation published on 6 July 1732 provides a modified list of language-teaching positions: two for Russian, three for German, two for French, one for each of the other languages: Latin, Italian and English. For each language there was also an apprentice teacher. Moreover, there were positions for teachers in writing: three for Russian and three for both German and Latin (RGADA, f. 248, op. 1, d. 396 (1732-42), fol. 16^{r-v}).[2] The small increase in the number of positions is probably attributable to an increase in the number of cadets and, probably, the need to cope with the problem of illiteracy among a minority of Russian cadets. New on the list were positions for Italian and English. This certainly reflects a broad view of the education of nobility and the prioritization of access to a variety of languages of professional, social, or cultural relevance. There would also have been a position for a professor of Russian (with a salary of six hundred rubles per year; cf. two hundred rubles for language teachers and one hundred rubles for writing teachers). The role of the professor of Russian would have been to teach Russian not only to the cadets but also to the teachers and officers working at the Corps, thus enabling them to communicate with the Russian cadets in Russian.

In reality, the composition of the language-teaching staff varied somewhat from these staff regulations. In 1737, there were classes in Latin (two), French (four), Russian (one) and German (three); there were writing classes in Russian (one) and German (four); there were also classes in basic German and orthography (two); and, finally, there were classes in Russian style (two) and German style (five). Italian was not taught before the 1760s and English was not taught at the Corps at all during the eighteenth century. The number of classes did not correspond to the number of pupils. The latter varied between thirteen and eighty-six per class (RGADA, f. 248, op. 1, d. 396, fols 65-67). Obviously, pupils were progressing from the fundamentals to writing and finished with 'style', the highest level of language study, though this was not available for French at the time.

Various factors could explain the choice of German. Some were specific to the Corps, namely, the presence of many German or German-speaking teachers among the staff. It was difficult to find enough teachers who could teach various subjects in Russian and therefore pupils had to learn German and French in order to understand their teachers (*PSZ* 1830, 8: 558-59, n°5881; see more on this below). Other reasons were extrinsic to the Corps and could have played a role in securing the exceptional position for German. Among these, it is necessary to mention the new geopolitical situation of the Russian Empire. The Empire's Baltic provinces had a German-speaking nobility who needed to be culturally and linguistically integrated into the Russian nobility and bureaucracy. Furthermore, German held international prestige as one of the major European languages and the language of some countries with which Russia had historically been in contact, such as the Hanseatic cities (Lübeck, Danzig, Hamburg), Brandenburg-Prussia etc. The choice of French was even more understandable as French was the *lingua franca* of Europe, the 'universal language', and the sign of a good education (Rjéoutski, Offord and Argent 2014). Whether French was also considered a social marker of nobility at the Corps is not clear.

If we compare the situation at the Cadet Corps in St Petersburg with the situation at its German model, the Corps des Cadets in Berlin (Fedyukin and Lavrinovich 2014), some similarities as well as some striking differences are evident. On the one hand, in Berlin French does not seem to have been described as a social marker of nobility, at least not in the initial period of its existence (1717-70 (cf. Crousaz 1857)). However, the cadets needed French for their future professional lives (e.g. literature on fortification was often available in French). On the other hand, Latin was not taught in Berlin (while it was taught at the Cadet Corps in St Petersburg). Latin was probably first introduced into the curriculum of the Corps des Cadets in Berlin in 1771. The initial exclusion of the language from the curriculum at the foundation of the Corps in Berlin can be attributed to the personal antipathy of the Soldier-King, Frederick William I, to Latin. He forbade his son, the future Frederick the Great, from learning Latin (see, for example, Boehm 2013).[3] Like the St Petersburg school, Berlin's Cadet Corps was conceived as a school for nobility (in Berlin, French, dance, and fencing, together with military training, were among the most important subjects). However, the Cadet Corps in St Petersburg seems to have been conceived with a broader scope. Indeed, not only was its curriculum targeted at nobles preparing for careers as army officers, but also at those seeking to become civil servants. The inclusion of Latin on the curriculum was an indicator of this orientation: Latin was the key to accessing knowledge in some subjects, such as civil law, that were not taught in Berlin. Indeed, books in Latin were used for this subject (*Materialy* 1886: 445). This broad definition of the curriculum of the Russian school for the nobility and the inclusion of Latin in particular were probably the result of the influence of the Academy of Sciences. In the 1730s, relations between the Academy of Sciences and the Cadet Corps were very close: the administration of the Corps reported to the Academy on the subjects taught at the Corps and the books used in classes; some teachers from the Academy came to the Corps and the Academy was generally expected to become a source of qualified teachers for the new institution; the Academy actively participated in discussing the organization of exams at the Corps; and several academicians attended the exams (see, for example, RGADA, f. 248, op. 1, d. 396, fols 17^v, 71-76, 543-45^v; *Materialy* 1886: 462-66).

The Cultural Outlook of Young Russian Nobles before their Entrance into the Cadet Corps

It is not clear how many nobles learned foreign languages at home (which was then the most frequent form of education in Russia) prior to their entrance into the Corps. However, some idea of foreign language learning through private education in Russia at the time can be grasped from the following figures (Fedyukin 2015). Out of 714 young Russian nobles who were present at the 1736 general inspection (a public examination for nobles), 164 (23%) were illiterate, and most of the latter were poor (they possessed no more than twenty serfs); only seventeen (2.5%) out of 714 said that they had learned German, one French, and one Latin. However, it is not clear whether they had been asked to indicate the languages they had learned or whether they volunteered the information on their own initiative. On the basis of these figures, one could think that the vast majority of the Russian nobility probably neglected foreign languages. According to the *ukaz* of 9 February 1737, all young nobles had to learn arithmetic, geometry, reading and writing (in their native tongue), and foreign languages (which their parents could choose). Education at home was the responsibility of parents. However, it was proposed that those who were not wealthy (i.e. who possessed fewer than one hundred serfs) should put their boys into state schools (e.g. the Noble Infantry Cadet Corps) (*PSZ* 1830, 10 (no. 7171): 43-45). It seems that the situation did not change considerably in the years after this *ukaz*. In 1745, at a new general inspection of the nobility, the state of play was quite similar to that in 1736. If we compare these figures with the level achieved by the boys who entered the Cadet Corps in the years 1732-62, it turns out that their level was higher than the general level achieved by the young nobles present at the 1736 inspection. Among some 1760 cadets who studied at the Corps over the period, 239 (or about 13.5%) stated, when entering the Corps, that they had learned more than reading and writing in Russian. Among them, 101 had studied German (6.25%), fifty-nine French (2.5%), and twenty-eight Latin (1.5%). The difference between the figures of the general inspection of the Russian nobility in 1736 and the figures for the Cadet Corps of 1732-62 can be explained less by the progress in education among Russian nobles over three decades than by differences in wealth among these groups of nobility. Indeed, while the poorest nobles (with fewer than twenty serfs) never constituted more than 17.6% of all the cadets before the reign of Catherine II (this was to change in her reign), they made up between 51% and 60% of all the Russian nobles over the same period (Fedyukin 2015).

The fact that an average Russian cadet was more cultivated than an average Russian nobleman does not mean that he was well prepared for the curriculum of the Corps. Concerning language learning, there were a number of difficulties. The first was the ethnic origins of the pupils, which were far from uniform. In 1732 the Director of the Corps, Baron Johann Lüdwig Luberas von Pott, reported to the Empress that, among the pupils registered at the Corps, 237 were Russian, thirty-two belonged to the Livonian nobility, and thirty-nine to the Estonian nobility (RGADA, f. 248, op. 1, d. 396, fol. 2). In other words, seventy-one out of 308 pupils (or about 23%) came from Baltic noble families whose mother tongue was typically German. In April 1734 there were 265 Russian pupils, thirty-eight pupils from Livonia, twenty-eight pupils from Estonia (Estland), and twenty-nine pupils from the families of foreigners, giving an overall number of 360 pupils (Tatarnikov and Yurkevich 2009: 57). Thus, Baltic Germans made up 18.3% of all the pupils, and foreign pupils constituted 8% of the total. Clearly, then, as far as language learning was concerned, the goals of these groups varied. Another major difficulty was the absence of uniformity in age and knowledge among the pupils during the first years of the existence of the Corps. The first cadets were of various ages; some were aged about twenty. Many of them were ignorant (they 'had no notions in any science' (RGADA, f. 248, op. 1, d. 396, fol. 61)) and some illiterate. Indeed, the director of the Corps, Abel Friedrich von Tettau, specified clearly in his report of August 1737 to the Empress, Anna Ivanovna, that some Russian cadets could neither read nor write in their 'natural' language. He was of the opinion that there was no possibility of teaching Latin to these pupils, their age being an obstacle. According to the director, even German pupils (who spoke German and thus could more easily follow what was taught at the Corps) could not have an easy grasp of Latin (which was generally considered to be a difficult language at the time). As for other languages, the situation was similar. Some of the Russian cadets, who had hardly any training in their native tongue, had some knowledge of German or French or Latin, but rarely all three. Some had only oral command of one of the living foreign languages; others could read and write. The Baltic Germans' abilities were hardly better: some could barely write their names in their mother tongue, although they were nearly adults (RGADA, f. 248, op. 1, d. 396, fol. 61).

Language Learning and the National Origins of the Cadets (1730s–1760s)

What languages did the pupils learn and what levels could they achieve over the long period of their studies at the Corps (which could last twelve years)? Below, I provide data based on various documents, including summary tables produced by the administration of the Corps and examination records.

Language/Origin	*Russian cadets*	*Other cadets*	*Total*
Number of pupils	117 (69.5%)	51 (30.5%)	168 (100%)
Russian	0	48 (94%)	48 (31%)
German	104 (89%)	51 (100%)	155 (92.5%)
French	65 (62.5%)	40 (78.5%)	105 (67.5%)
Latin	1 (1%)	3 (6%)	4 (2.5%)
Not studying any language	13 (11%)	0	13 (8.5%)

TABLE 1. Languages studied at the Corps in 1732. Based on a list of pupils which probably represented only half of the cadets. Russian State Archive for the History of the Armed Forces (RGVIA — Rossiiskii gosudarstvennyi voenno-istoritcheskii arkhiv), f. 314, op. 1, d. 1654, fols 1–176. (In this and the following tables, the percentages have been rounded up or down to the nearest half.)

Language/Origin	Russian cadets	Baltic cadets	Foreign cadets	Total
Russian	24 (9%)	49 (74%)	23 (79.5%)	96 (26.5%)
German	215 (81%)	15 (22.5%)	15 (51.5%)	245 (68%)
French	85 (32%)	51 (77%)	28 (97%)	164 (45.5%)
Latin	4 (1.5%)	15 (22.5%)	19 (65.5%)	38 (10.5%)
Total	265 (73.5%)	66 (18.5%)	29 (8%)	360 (100%)

TABLE 2. Languages studied at the Corps in 1734. Based on a summary table (April 1734) published in: Tatarnikov and Yurkevich 2009: 57

Subject	Number of pupils learning the subject
Basic German style	30 (8%)
German	215 (58%)
German writing	313 (84.5%)
German style	117 (31.5%)
French	251 (67.5%)
Latin[4]	24 (German cadets) /16 (Russian cadets) (11%)
Russian	56 (15%)
Russian writing	41 (11%)
Total number of cadets	371 (100%)

TABLE 3. Number of pupils per language subject in 1737. Based on: *Materialy* 1886: 446-50

Language/Origin	Russian	Other	Total
Russian	60 (23.5%)	44 (70%)	104 (32.5%)
German	249 (97%)	59 (93.5%)	308 (96.25%)
French	98 (38%)	53 (84%)	152 (47.5%)
Latin	13 (5%)	1 (2%)	14 (4.5%)
Total	257 (80.5%)	63 (19.5)	320 (100%)

TABLE 4. Languages studied at the Corps in 1748. Based on examination records (RGVIA, f. 314, op. 1, d. 2178).

Language/Origin	Russian cadets	Other cadets	Total
Number of pupils	120 (69.5%)	53 (30.5%)	173 (100%)
Russian	58 (48.5%)	47 (88.5%)	105 (60.5%)
German	120 (100%)	44 (83%)	164 (95%)
French	65 (54%)	48 (90.5%)	113 (65.5%)
Latin	8 (6.5%)	10 (19%)	18 (10.5%)
Italian	8 (6.5%)	5 (9.5%)	13 (7.5%)
History in French	7 (6%)	2 (4%)	9 (5%)
Geography in French	1 (1%)	0	1 (0.5%)

TABLE 5. Languages and subjects studied in foreign languages at the Corps in 1764. Based on the examination records of the pupils finishing their studies at the Corps (RGVIA, f. 314, op. 1, d. 3213 (1764))

Language/Origin		Russian	Other
No. of students		120 (69.5%)	53 (30.5%)
Courses in Translation	Russian → German	Nearly all	7 (13%)
	German → French	6 (5%)	17 (32%)
	Russian → French	27 (22.5%)	4 (7.5%)
Courses in German	Basics	60 (50%)	3 (5.5%)
	Orthography	89 (74%)	4 (2%)
	Style	24 (20%)	44 (83%)
Courses in French	Basics	29 (24%)	26 (49%)
	Orthography	10 (8.5%)	6 (11.5%)
	Style	8 (6.5%)	11 (21%)

TABLE 6. Languages studied at the Corps in 1764. Based on the examination records of the pupils finishing their studies at the Corps (RGVIA, f. 314, op. 1, d. 3213 (1764))

Table 1 is based on a list of cadets aged between seventeen and twenty-two, representing the oldest pupils at the institution. This age group was of particular concern to the Director of the Corps because of its disparate levels of knowledge. In 1732 it seems that German was mandatory for the Russian pupils,[5] and Russian was quasi-mandatory for Baltic Germans. In 1737, the new Director, von Tettau, thought that German was necessary for all the pupils, including Baltic Germans. The insistence on this mutual linguistic training of the two major ethnic and linguistic groups within the nobility of the Russian Empire denotes the desire for their cultural rapprochement. This rapprochement was probably considered to be a factor for stability in the Empire. Many years later, in 1773, the Senate sent a decree to Moscow University, the Noble Infantry and Noble Navy Corps, and the Academy of Sciences (RGA VMF, f. 432, op. 1, d. 70, fol. 2^{r-v}). The Senate regretted that the Russian nobility had little knowledge of German and saw the acquisition of the language as one of the state's priorities. The main reason that the decree invoked for strengthening training in German was the integration of the Baltic provinces into the Empire. The Senate ordered that German be given priority over other languages in the aforementioned institutions.

In the 1730s, however, German was absolutely not an 'endangered language' at the Corps. Training in German was rather intensive: in 1737, there were twenty-two hours a week available in German; twenty-two in German writing (or four hours in a different group); four in German style; and four in 'orthography', probably spelling. Out of a total of 371 students 217 took training in German, 150 in German writing for 22 hours a week and 163 for four hours a week, 97 took German style and 30 took German orthography (RGADA, f. 248, op. 1, d. 348, fols 65-67). In fact, even training in French and in Latin was based on German: texts were translated from German into French or Latin and vice versa. However, in 1734 (Table 2) not all Russian pupils studied German and even fewer Baltic Germans studied it. Pupils had been divided into levels and those at the higher levels of mastery were obviously exempted from attending German class. The Baltic pupils who studied the language did so probably because they did not have a good command of written German.

At the time German (and not French) was the main language of teaching at the Corps, irrespective of the pupils' ethnic origins and native tongues. In April 1734, roughly two years after the opening of the Corps, there was only one Russian teacher of a non-language subject and one German teacher of mathematics who knew some Russian (RGADA, f. 248, op. 1, d. 396, fol. 29). In 1737 the books used for teaching non-language subjects were still nearly all in German or, rarely, in Latin. Only in the geometry class was a Russian compendium, translated from a German one which one of the teachers had authored, used to teach Russian pupils (*Materialy* 1886: 464-65). As shown by Kristine Dahmen (Koch), this was by no means an exceptional situation in Russian educational institutions in the first half of the century. Thus, somewhat paradoxically, German became more than a foreign language. It became a language of teaching that played a role in Russia similar to that played by Latin in Jesuit colleges or universities in Europe. This was a source of continuous outrage because many pupils did not understand the teachers, and the benefits of such teaching could be rather poor (Koch 2002: 155-68). As shown by a letter written by two Italian teachers teaching French at the Corps in 1781 (Rjéoutski and Offord 2013), even in the second half of the century such resentment was evident. In 1747 a decision was taken to ban the use of German or French in non-language classes at the academic institutions and to leave in place only two teaching languages, namely, Russian and Latin. However, nothing changed much because of the lack of teachers capable of teaching in Russian (Koch 2002: 160). In the Cadet Corps in 1734 language classes in German, Russian and Latin were organized separately for Russian and Baltic German pupils (Koch 2002: 158). However, it is not clear whether that improved the situation: in 1737 the teachers teaching German to the Russian pupils were still all German-speaking and presumably had insufficient knowledge of Russian (RGADA, f. 248, op. 1, d. 348, fols 65-67). This was to change progressively but it would take considerable time. Judging by the following case, the shortage of Russian-speaking teachers seems to have been dramatic in the first years of the existence of the Corps: a German-speaking teacher, Ebel, was recruited in 1738 with the hope that, having already studied Polish, he could learn some Russian quickly and teach Russian cadets history and geography in Russian (Koch 2002: 158).

In the beginning French was not studied by all the cadets and the number of Russian cadets who studied French varied between one third and two thirds.[6] Among the Baltic and foreign pupils, the proportion of pupils studying this language was much higher. The first impression is that Baltic and foreign nobles were more exposed to modern European trends and had chosen French because of its role in the sociability of nobility and, more generally, its role as a *lingua franca* in Europe (Rjéoutski, Offord and Argent 2014); and that the Russian nobility, who followed traditional ways, lagged behind. Whether all the families of the Russian cadets were aware of the role of French in Europe and, particularly, its role as a social marker for nobility is not obvious. However, there was a different reason for the small number of Russian pupils who opted to study French. In his report to the Empress in 1739, the Director, von Tettau, explained:

> before they [some Russian cadets] entered the Cadet Corps they did not know any German; and the teachers who teach them are all foreigners and do not know any Russian. Therefore the cadets (because they like French more than German) have to be taught German first so that the teachers could then teach [other subjects] to them and they would understand the teachers better. (RGADA, f. 177 (1739), d. 70, fol. 5^v)[7]

Among the four teachers of French working at the Corps in 1737, at least three (including a father and son Feray; and Ruynat, who was also teaching French at the Academy school) were of Huguenot origin; the fourth (Gay) taught German as well as French, so he was probably of Huguenot origin too (RGADA, f. 248, op. 1, d. 396, fols 65-67). These teachers could use German as a 'supporting' language in their French classes: that is, they could translate from German into French and vice versa, but they did not use Russian (see Rjéoutski and Offord 2013). It is striking to note the degree to which all the major Russian institutions in which vernacular foreign languages were taught encountered similar difficulties: one of the professors of the Academy of Sciences, Pierre Louis Le Roy, complained in 1745 that the use of German in French classes at the Academy's school put off Russian pupils (Koch 2002: 160). This system resulted in rather poor knowledge of French among the Russian cadets, at least during the first thirty or forty years from the foundation of the Corps. Some works produced by the best cadets were shown to the Empress in 1739. Not only did these extant French texts have spelling errors, but they also frequently included non-colloquial constructions (RGADA, f. 177, op. 1, 1739, d. 70, fols 29-30).[8] Thus, the problem involved human resources as well as the choice of teaching methods.[9] In 1733 Gottlieb Siegfried Bayer, a member of the St Petersburg Academy of Sciences, proposed adopting in the Academy's school the 'direct method' of teaching languages that was used to teach Latin in Kiev. This would facilitate access to Latin for those pupils who were not fluent in German (Koch 2002: 159). The use of the direct method, as we would call it today, explains the successful learning of French in private education, particularly at the highest levels of nobility. Indeed, teachers in private education mostly taught their pupils languages by emphasizing speaking, dictation, and copying, probably because many of these teachers knew no languages apart from their own (Rjéoutski 2013).

The number of Russian students studying French at the Corps increased over the period (from 38% in 1748 to 54% in 1764), but a closer investigation seems to indicate that French was still rather neglected at the Corps in 1764. A small number of Russian pupils (see Table 6; 27.5% of this group) tried their hand at translating into French; and only eight of them (6.5%) studied French style, which was the highest level at which the language was taught. In other words, only a small proportion of Russian pupils left the Corps with a fairly good knowledge of French sufficient for a fluent conversation or for correspondence in the language. In this regard, the situation does not seem to have changed substantially between the 1730s and 1760s. It was different, though not markedly so, among the non-Russian students. Nearly

21% of them had studied French style by the time they graduated and about 40% had studied translation into French.

In 1748 (Table 4), as in previous years, the majority of Baltic German and foreign pupils studied Russian. The documents I have seen do not comment on the absence of Russian as a subject for Russian pupils in 1732. In 1748, fewer than a quarter of Russian students studied Russian. Does this mean that only one quarter of all Russian students (or families) considered Russian (a subject) of use to them? The proportion of those who chose Russian continued to grow. In 1764 (Table 5), approximately 50% of the students from Russian families were studying Russian. This figure may show a growing awareness of the necessity to study Russian among the Russian nobility. Interestingly, this trend went along with a debate about the role of various languages, including Russian, in the education of the nobility (Betskoy 1766). However we shall not deal with this subject here because this discussion took place essentially in the following period.

The first charter of the Corps specified that only those who were willing to study Latin should do so (*PSZ* 1830, 8: 558-59, n°5881). The number of pupils studying Latin was small, and the Russian pupils were the least enthusiastic about Latin. The situation was more or less the same in other institutions where noble children were studying: at the school attached to the Academy of Sciences and later in the school depending on Moscow University. Unlike noble students, the students of other social origins (children of priests, soldiers, low court officials etc.) often studied Latin, which was becoming for some of them a language of social and professional distinction, as French was for the nobility. Latin was thoroughly studied in Church schools in the time after Peter the Great's death, when it was introduced into Church education thanks to Ukrainian bishops close to the Tsar. Therefore, in this respect there was a considerable contrast between the nobility and other classes who learned languages. There was also a considerable gap between Western European nobles, many of whom were still learning Latin, and the Russian nobility.

This confirms Max J. Okenfuss's conclusion about the unwillingness of the Russian nobility to learn the language (Okenfuss 1995). The proportion of foreign pupils studying Latin in 1734 (Table 2: the only year for which it is easy to distinguish between Baltic and foreign pupils) is extremely high (65.5%) compared to that of Baltic nobles (22.5%) and to that of Russian pupils (1.5%). In the case of foreign pupils (and certainly partly in the case of Baltic pupils) we are very probably dealing with a population which was in contact with the tradition of studying Latin. The low figures for Latin among Russian pupils in the first years of the existence of the Corps can be explained by the advanced age of the first pupils and their general level of knowledge, which seems to have been rather poor, with a proportion of illiterates. However, other factors certainly played a more important role: there was hardly any tradition of learning Latin in Russia among the nobles, and the language was progressively associated with the clerical Estate or the medical profession. Interestingly, despite the obvious failure of Latin at the Corps, it was included in official ceremonies during the exams. In October 1738, in front of selected guests, cadets made speeches in Latin, French and German (but not Russian).

Latin speeches were probably included as an indication of the thoroughness of the education provided at the Corps and as a courtesy to the professors of the Academy of Sciences present in the audience (RGADA, f. 248, op. 1, d. 396, fols 543-57). One can observe a slight progression in the proportion of Russian pupils taking Latin over the period between 1732 and 1764. However, it is not significant enough to change our opinion about the Russian nobility's lack of interest in Latin.

This situation was not completely at odds with what was going on in other European countries. In the eighteenth century, in France, as in many other parts of Europe, Latin was progressively losing its hegemonic place at the institutions we would consider institutions of 'secondary education' today. According to André Chervel, Latin ceased to be spoken in university colleges at the end of the seventeenth century and persisted in Jesuit colleges only until the 1730s (Chervel 2006: 36). Françoise Waquet asserts that Latin maintained its role as the language of teaching in France until the middle of the eighteenth century and in Jesuit colleges until the expulsion of the Jesuits from France in 1764 (Waquet 2002: 9). Institutions for the nobility also progressively replaced Latin with vernacular languages, inspired by the idea that teaching should be quick, practical and more focused on professional skills. Latin authors were not excluded from studies, but they were progressively read in the native languages of pupils or in other vernacular languages, often French (all the main authors of antiquity were translated into French). Vernaculars also facilitated noble boys' access to the 'sciences' because Latin was considered to be a difficult language (see, for example, the programme of the proposed Academy of Richelieu in France (Gras 1642: 23-30)).

Conclusion

In this chapter I show that the choice of languages to study at the first major educational institution for the nobility in Russia, the Noble Infantry Cadet Corps, depended on a multitude of factors. Among these, the most decisive were probably the educational model followed by the institution, the national origins and cultural outlook of the pupils and teachers, and the organization of non-language teaching. More broadly, other decisive factors included considerations about the cultural and social value of given languages in the Russian Empire in general and, more specifically, for the two major ethnic groups (Russian and Baltic German) of nobility present at the Corps. However, making distinctions between the most important reasons is no easy task, especially as the official documents which have been preserved rarely give any direct explanations of language choice. In the case of personal language use, particularly in a linguistic situation characterized by some stability (e.g. in the second half of the eighteenth century or in the early nineteenth century), testimonies which could give us insight into the reasons for the preference for one language over another are rare (with the exception of satirical comedy and the press, which indirectly reflect the linguistic situation (see, for example, Offord 2015)). However, a combination of sources gives us some idea of the evolution of language learning at the Corps over the period and the reasons why a given language was studied to a greater or lesser extent.

As we have seen, during the entire period under consideration German was the major foreign language at the Corps and *de facto* the first teaching language in general. Notwithstanding its role as the European *lingua franca* and the major prestige language, French did not have such a brilliant position. Without a doubt, this was partly due to the slow progress of Russian *francophonie* in general before the reign of Catherine the Great and partly because of the primarily German-speaking staff and the teaching methods used at the Corps. By the end of the century, though, French would play the leading role at the Corps, corresponding to the huge social success of the French language in Russia at the time. Russian was studied by Baltic nobles: it was a means to integrate the group linguistically into the Russian nobility. Moreover, it was progressively studied to a greater extent by Russian cadets, probably a sign of growing national consciousness on the part of this group. The latter process could also be linked to the (slow) development of Russian as the language of teaching at the Corps. Under Catherine II, Russian would become one of the three 'official' languages of the Corps (Offord, Argent and Rjéoutski 2015). The rise of Russian was obviously caused by the development of national consciousness in Russia, which affected the elites. There was one loser in this story: Latin. Efforts to promote the language at the Corps at the beginning of its existence did not give rise to any substantial results.

The data presented in this chapter allow us to question one of the best-established ideas in the historiography of Russian eighteenth-century education. Starting from the nineteenth century up to the present day, the advance of education in Russia over this period has been regarded as the direct result of the reforms carried out by the government. Where language learning is concerned, this point of view has been formulated by Max J. Okenfuss. In his well-known article with the provocative title 'The Jesuit Origins of Petrine Education' (1973), Okenfuss presents Latin education in Russian schools as a direct result of Petrine reforms. In the same way, in his book on Latin in Russia (Okenfuss 1995) he considered that the failure of Latin among the Russian nobility should be attributed not only to the latter's backwardness but also to a voluntary action of the authorities of the post-Petrine period.

The story of language learning at the Noble Cadet Corps in Saint Petersburg helps to correct this picture and relativize the scope and the results of the action of the authorities. Latin was hardly studied at the Corps, but not because there was any unwillingness of the authorities to promote it among the pupils. On the contrary, before the time of Ivan Betskoy (1760s) there seem to have been combined efforts on behalf of the administration of the Corps and the Academy of Sciences to further Latin training at the Corps. However, Russian pupils were reluctant to study the language. It would also be simple, but in my view incorrect, to attribute the rejection of Latin to the traditional character of the culture of Russian nobility stressed by Okenfuss.

An important clue is given by the Director of the Corps, von Tettau, who points out in 1739 that young Russian nobles were very eager to learn French. If they followed traditional ways and were reluctant to embrace cultural innovations, why did they reject Latin and not French or German? I think that as early as the

1730s parts of Russian nobility associated French with their estate and with noble sociability. Just a couple of years after von Tettau's report, a French theatre troupe was hired for the Court of Saint Petersburg, thus symbolically indicating the place of French in Russian Court culture. Latin on the contrary, as mentioned before, was more and more associated with the clerical estate (because training in Latin developed in ecclesiastical seminaries in the period after Peter the Great), academic research and the medical profession. Unlike Jesuit colleges in Europe or colleges in Ukraine, Russian ecclesiastical schools accepted hardly any noble pupils. Therefore, the social contrast between ecclesiastical and civil educational establishments was very pronounced in Russia and led to social connotations of the languages learned in these institutions.

When Ivan Betskoy became *de facto* Russia's Minister of Education, Latin was already a defeated language in Russian noble education, so it would be an exaggeration to say that Betskoy's position on Latin, as formulated in his writing (Betskoy 1766), had any serious consequences in this situation. Betskoy was himself a product of this time; and his views reflected what in the eighteenth century many Russian nobles thought about languages, their usefulness and suitability for their estate.

Bibliography

BETSKOY, IVAN. 1766. *Ustav imperatorskogo shliahetnogo suhoputnogo kadetskogo korpusa uchrezhdennago v Sankt-Peterburge dlia vospitaniia i obucheniia blagorodnogo rossiiskogo iunoshestva* (St Petersburg: Tip. Suhoputnogo shliahetnogo kadetskogo korpusa)

BOEHM, MANUELA. 2013. 'Huguenots précepteurs du Prince Frédéric: Frédéric II, Praeceptor Germaeniae', in *Le Précepteur francophone en Europe: XVIIe–XIXe*, ed. by Vladislav Rjéoutski (Paris: L'Harmattan), pp. 241–57

CHERVEL, ANDRÉ. 2006. *Histoire de l'enseignement du français du XVIIe au XXe siècle* (Paris: Retz)

CROUSAZ, ADOLF VON. 1857. *Geschichte des Königlich Preußischen Kadetten-Corps* (Berlin: Schindler)

FEDYUKIN, IGOR. 2014. '"Chest' k delu um i ohotu razhdaet": reforma dvorianskoi sluzhby i teoreticheskie osnovy soslovnoi politiki v 1730-e gg', in *Gishtorii rossiiskie*, ed. by Elena Smilianskaia (Moscow: Drevlekhranilishche), pp. 83-143

——. 2015. 'Literacy and Learning among Noble "Minors" in the Late 1730s-1740s'. Paper presented at the conference 'Literacy and Learning in 18th-Century Russia' at the Higher School of Economics, Moscow, 25 April 2015

——, and MAYA LAVRINOVICH. 2014. 'Suhoputnyi kadetskii korpus v Sankt-Peterburge i ego berlinskii proobraz', in *'Reguliarnaia akademiia uchrezhdena budet...' Obrazovatel'nye proiekty v Rossii v pervoi polovine XVIII veka*, ed. by Igor Fedyukin and Maya Lavrinovich (Moscow: Novoe izdatel'stvo), pp. 264-316

GLÜCK, HELMUT, 2013. *Die Fremdsprache Deutsch im Zeitalter der Aufklärung, der Klassik und der Romantik. Grundzüge der deutschen Sprachgeschichte in Europa* (Wiesbaden: Harrassowitz)

GRAS, NICOLAS LE. 1642. 'L'Académie Royale de Richelieu, a son Eminence' (Bibliothèque nationale de France, Arsenal 4-H-8289). I am grateful to Andrea Bruschi for pointing out this source.

HÄBERLEIN, MARK, and CHRISTIAN KUHN (eds). 2010. *Fremde Sprachen in frühneuzeitlichen Städten: Lernende, Lehrende und Lehrwerke* (Wiesbaden: Harrassowitz)

KOCH, KRISTINE. 2002. *Deutsch als Fremdsprache im Russland des 18. Jahrhunderts: Ein Beitrag zur Geschichte des Fremdsprachenlernens in Europa und zu den deutsch-russischen Beziehungen* (Berlin; New York: de Gruyter)

LUZANOV, P. F. 1907. *Suhoputnyi shliakhetnyi kadetskii korpus (nyne 1-i kadetskii korpus) pri grafe Minikhe (s 1732 po 1741)* (St Petersburg: Schmidt)

OFFORD, DEREK. 2015. 'Linguistic Gallophobia in Russian Comedy', in *French and Russian in Imperial Russia*, ed. by Derek Offord et al., 2 vols, II: *Language Attitudes and Identity* (Edinburgh: Edinburgh University Press), pp. 79-99

——, GESINE ARGENT and VLADISLAV RJÉOUTSKI. 2015. 'French and Russian in Catherine's Russia', in *French and Russian in Imperial Russia*, I: *Language Use among the Russian Elite*, ed. by Derek Offord et al. (Edinburgh: Edinburgh University Press), pp. 25-44

OFFORD, DEREK, ET AL. (eds). 2015. *French and Russian in Imperial Russia*, 2 vols, I: *Language Use among the Russian Elite*, II: *Language Attitudes and Identity* (Edinburgh: Edinburgh University Press)

OKENFUSS, MAX J. 1973. 'The Jesuit Origins of Petrine Education', in *The Eighteenth Century in Russia*, ed. by J. G. Garrard (Oxford: Oxford University Press), pp. 106-30

——. 1995. *The Rise and Fall of Latin Humanism in Early Modern Russia: Pagan Authors, Ukrainians and the Resiliency of Muscovy* (Leiden etc.: Brill)

Polnoe Sobranie Zakonov Rossiiskoi Imperii [PSZ]. 1830. (St Petersburg)

RJÉOUTSKI, VLADISLAV. 2012. 'Le Précepteur français comme ennemi: la construction de son image en Russie (deuxième moitié du XVIIIe — première moitié du XIXe siècle)', in *L'Ennemi en regard(s): images, usages et interprétations dans l'histoire et la littérature*, ed. by Brigitte Krulic (Paris: Lang), pp. 31-45

——. 2013. 'Le Français et d'autres langues dans l'éducation en Russie au XVIIIe siècle', in *Apprendre la langue de l'Europe: le français parmi d'autres langues dans l'éducation en Russie au XVIIIe siècle*, ed. by Vladislav Rjéoutski, Derek Offord and Gesine Argent, *Vivliofika*, I (2013): 20-47

——, and DEREK OFFORD. 2013. 'French in Public Education in Eighteenth-Century Russia: The Case of the Cadet Corps', *Online corpus of documents* (Bristol University) <https://frinru.ilrt.bris.ac.uk/introduction/french-public-education-eighteenth-century-russia-case-cadet-corps> [accessed 12 April 2015]

——, DEREK OFFORD and GESINE ARGENT (eds). 2014. *European Francophonie: The Social, Political and Cultural History of an International Prestige Language* (Oxford: Lang)

Materialy dlia istorii Imperatorskoi Akademii nauk, III: *1732–38*. 1886. Ed. by M. I. Suhomlinov (St Petersburg: Imp. Akademia nauk)

TATARNIKOV, K. V., and E. I. YURKEVICH. 2009. *Suhoputnyi shliahetnyi kadetskii korpus. 1732–1762. Obmundirovanie i snariazhenie* (Moscow: Kniga)

WAQUET, FRANÇOISE. 2002. *Latin, or the Empire of a Sign* (London and New York: Verso)

Notes to Chapter 8

1. I am grateful to Sandra Dahlke, Kristine Dahmen, Igor Fedyukin, Gary Marker, Denis Sdvižkov and two anonymous reviewers for their valuable comments on this paper.
2. RGADA = Rossiiskii gosudarstvennyi arkhov drevnikh aktov [Russian State Archives of Ancient Documents].
3. His antipathy to Latin was by no means a whim and should be explained as reflecting a wider hostility to Latin education which was developing in Europe at that time.
4. Presumably taught in separate groups for German Baltic and Russian pupils.
5. However, some of them did not learn any language, probably because they were considered to be 'too old'. The figures published by P. Luzanov are quite different from these data. According to him, in July 1732 of 282 cadets only 163 (58%) learned German (Luzanov 1907: 31).

6. These data roughly correspond to those published by P. Luzanov, according to whom ninety-one out of 282 cadets (32.5%) learned French in July 1732.
7. Translation from Russian by the author. I am grateful to Igor Fedyukin for drawing my attention to this document.
8. I am grateful to Igor Fedyukin for drawing my attention to this document. For more detail, see Rjéoutski and Offord 2013.
9. On the question of the qualification of teachers of languages, see Häberlein and Kuhn (2010) and Glück (2013).

CHAPTER 9

Veneroni en Espagne:
l'*Explicación de la gramática francesa* (Madrid, 1728) d'Antoine Courville

Manuel Bruña Cuevas

Many researchers have highlighted the great influence of Le Maître italien (Paris, 1678) by Giovanni Veneroni (pseudonym of Jean Vigneron, 1642-1708) on other manuals for the teaching of modern languages. In the eighteenth and nineteenth centuries this book was often translated, revised and adapted in various European countries for the teaching of Italian as well as for the teaching of other languages. However, despite the attention given to works derived from Le Maître italien, researchers do not mention any edition or adaptation of this book in Spain in the first half of the eighteenth century. We find comments on the influence of Veneroni on authors of Italian grammars for Spanish speakers published in the second half of the eighteenth century or the first half of the nineteenth; but it has thus far been overlooked that a part of Le Maître italien was translated and published in Spain by Antoine Courville as early as 1728, and this not for the teaching of Italian, as one might have expected, but for the teaching of French. This chapter thus aims to reveal and prove the presence of Veneroni in Spain, to expose the factors which explain it and to analyse Courville's grammar (the *Explicación de la gramática francesa* (Madrid, 1728)).

Giovanni Veneroni est l'un des auteurs les plus connus dans l'histoire de l'enseignement des langues vernaculaires européennes. Né à Verdun en 1642, il s'appelait en réalité Jean Vigneron; mais il acquiert une telle maîtrise de la langue italienne que, dès son arrivée à Paris en 1672, il italianise son nom et se fait passer pour florentin.[1] Mis à part quelques traductions du français en italien et de l'italien en français,[2] ce sont surtout deux publications — un dictionnaire bilingue franco-italien[3] et une grammaire pour l'apprentissage de l'italien par les Français — qui le rendent célèbre et lui valent d'être nommé interprète du roi en 1680, un poste où il succède à d'autres grammairiens réputés, tels que César Oudin (?-1625), Lorenzo Ferretti ou Antoine Oudin (1595-1653).

Malgré l'importance du dictionnaire de Veneroni dans l'histoire de la lexicographie italo-française[4] et son influence sur les dictionnaires bilingues ou multilingues postérieurs concernant l'italien et le français, mais également l'allemand, le néerlandais ou le russe,[5] nous allons centrer ici notre attention sur sa grammaire italienne pour les Français.

Celle-ci, *Le Maître italien ou Nouvelle Méthode pour apprendre facilement la langue italienne*, paraît premièrement à Paris en 1678. Il est vrai que Veneroni a également composé une autre grammaire italienne différemment structurée: sa *Nouvelle metode* [sic] *pour apprendre la langue italienne avec grande facilité et en tres peu de tems* (Paris: Étienne Loyson, 1688). Mais cette dernière n'a jamais été rééditée, alors que *Le Maître italien* connaîtra, avant la mort de son auteur en 1708, plusieurs rééditions à Paris et à Lyon, révisées et augmentées par lui-même.[6] L'ouvrage aura un tel succès (Mormile 1989: 97-101, 145) que bientôt, dès 1689, il commencera à être édité aussi à Amsterdam; et, assez vite également, il paraît en Italie, en version italienne revue par Louis de Lépine. Celui-ci avait publié en 1681 un *Maestro Francese* (Mormile 1989: 56-57 et 1991), c'est-à-dire une grammaire de français pour Italiens, dont le titre, comme on le voit, rappelle celui de la grammaire italienne de Veneroni; en 1690, il publie à nouveau son *Maestro,* mais cette fois-ci précédé du *Maître italien* de Veneroni. C'est justement sous la forme revue et augmentée ainsi initiée par Lépine que ce dernier ouvrage s'est figé dans les nombreuses rééditions lancées en Italie jusqu'à la fin du XVIIIe siècle (Minerva, 1989: 99; 1996: 39-40), époque à laquelle il subit dans ce pays quelques remaniements qui assurent sa survie pendant une partie du XIXe siècle.

En dehors de l'Italie, l'histoire du *Maître italien* sera bien plus mouvementée du fait qu'il sera revu, dès 1729, par de nombreux auteurs (Minazio, Stanglini, Castelli, Placardi, Barrère, Gattel, Dupont et Pujoulx, Lauri, Zotti, Vergani, Bottarelli, Lates, Peretti, Rota, etc.); de même que dans le cas des éditions en italien, il aura aussi en version française une longue vie éditoriale qui arrivera au moins jusqu'en 1844. Comme déjà dit, Paris, Lyon et Amsterdam seront les villes où la plupart de ces remaniements de la version française verront le jour, mais il y en a qui paraissent à Bâle ou à Avignon.

Or, l'influence du *Maître italien* de Veneroni s'étend au-delà de l'Italie et des pays francophones. Dès les années 1690 (2e édition en 1694) paraît en Allemagne et en allemand une première adaptation de l'ouvrage pour l'enseignement de l'italien et du français aux germanophones, dont de nouvelles versions prolongeront le parcours de la méthode de Veneroni en allemand tout au long du XVIIIe siècle.

Quelque chose de pareil arrivera en Angleterre, où le nom de Veneroni finira par être associé à toute grammaire pour l'apprentissage de l'italien. Dès 1701, Arrigo Pleunus avait incorporé dans sa grammaire italienne pour anglophones quelques dialogues provenant de l'ouvrage de Veneroni, et un emprunt similaire a été fait en 1709 par L. Casotti dans la sienne (Pizzoli 2004: 71-72). Deux années après, en 1711, paraît à Londres la première version intégrale en anglais de la grammaire italienne de Veneroni; il s'agit de *The new Italian grammar* d'Uvedale. En 1728, l'ouvrage, revu par Edward Martin, paraît sous le titre de *The Italian Master* (Mormile et Matteucci 1997), et c'est avec ce titre que son parcours éditorial en Angleterre s'étend jusqu'au milieu du XIXe siècle, évidemment avec des remaniements par divers auteurs.

La grammaire de Veneroni a exercé également son influence sur les grammaires d'italien composées pour d'autres communautés linguistiques européennes et même sur des grammaires d'autres langues que l'italien: Étienne de Blégny, par exemple, s'inspire largement de Veneroni dans l'édition de 1707 de ses *Élémens ou premières instructions de la jeunesse* (Paris: Guillaume Cavelier);[7] Jean de Vayrac fait déjà référence à notre auteur dans sa grammaire de l'espagnol pour francophones (1714: 224), ainsi que dans sa grammaire du français pour hispanophones (1714: préface, 133); et son influence peut être également perçue — soit directement, soit par l'intermédiaire de Blégny — dans un certain nombre d'exemples donnés par Grégoire de Rostrenen dans sa *Grammaire françoise-celtique, ou françoise-bretonne* (Rennes: Julien Vatar, 1738).

En ce qui concerne l'Espagne, diverses études (notamment Silvestri 2001: 34, 119, 207) ont également mis en relief l'influence tardive de Veneroni sur les grammaires d'italien destinées aux hispanophones, telles que celle d'Esteban Rosterre (pseudonyme d'Esteban de Terreros; 1771), Luis Bordas (1824), José López de Morelle (1851), Eduardo Benot (1852), etc. Mais il est passé inaperçu jusqu'à présent qu'une partie de la grammaire de Veneroni a été traduite pratiquement au pied de la lettre en espagnol et a été publiée à Madrid à une date aussi précoce que 1728. L'auteur de cette adaptation a été Antoine Courville, qui a donné à son ouvrage le titre d'*Explicacion de la Gramatica Francesa, con el mas facil, y breve modo de entender, y comprehender la Lengua Francesa*. Ce titre révèle par lui-même la raison pour laquelle cette présence de Veneroni en Espagne n'a pas été remarquée jusqu'à présent. L'ouvrage de Courville se présente comme une grammaire du français adressée aux Espagnols; de ce fait, les historiens des grammaires italiennes pour hispanophones ne s'y sont pas intéressés. De leur part, les historiens des grammaires françaises pour Espagnols, tout en ayant remarqué le caractère particulier de l'ouvrage de Courville, n'ont pas eu l'idée d'aller chercher ses sources dans la série grammaticographique constituée par les ouvrages destinés à l'apprentissage de l'italien, l'analysant, de ce fait, comme un ouvrage original né de la vision personnelle qu'aurait eue Courville de l'enseignement du français (Lépinette 2000; 2001: 150-55).

Il est probable qu'Antoine Courville est arrivé à Madrid en 1721, peut-être comme maître de français du duc d'Osuna, dont il a dû faire la connaissance à Paris cette même année, lorsque ce noble négociait le mariage de la princesse française Louise Isabelle d'Orléans avec l'héritier du trône espagnol, le futur Louis I. C'est en fait au duc d'Osuna qu'il adresse la dédicace de son *Explicación de la gramática francesa*. Au moment de sa parution en 1728, Courville devait gagner sa vie comme maître de français à Madrid. Étant donné l'importante communauté française qui y résidait après l'intronisation de la dynastie des Bourbons en Espagne et après l'arrivée d'une princesse française comme future reine, il n'a peut-être pas manqué de clients, ce qui pourrait justifier la publication de son ouvrage, mais il est vrai aussi qu'il devait faire face à la concurrence d'autres maîtres de français. En cette même année 1728, il paraît à Madrid deux autres grammaires du français pour les Espagnols: celle de Francisco de la Torre y Ocón (1660-1725) et celle de José Núñez de Prado (1666-1743), bien plus complètes que la sienne. L'ouvrage de Courville, en effet, donne l'impression d'avoir été composé à la hâte et par un simple praticien de l'enseignement de sa langue maternelle, pas spécialement instruit, peut-être à cause de son passé comme militaire en France.[8] De fait, lui-même proclame, avec une humilité qui va au-delà des conventions, le caractère modeste de l'ouvrage qu'il offre à sa clientèle. Dans sa dédicace au duc d'Osuna, on perçoit déjà comment il a besoin d'un haut personnage pour arriver à placer son ouvrage sur le marché, et, dans sa préface, il déclare ouvertement: 'No enseño en este Arte, recojo en menos volumen lo que otros han enseñado' [Je n'enseigne pas dans cet ouvrage: j'y recueille plus brièvement ce que d'autres ont enseigné]. En fait, il justifie par là la brièveté de son ouvrage, tout en passant sous silence que non seulement il y enseigne ce que d'autres ont déjà enseigné, mais qu'il s'y limite en réalité à plagier l'œuvre d'autrui: celle de Veneroni.

Le Maître italien de Veneroni s'ouvrait par une 'Introduction à la Langue Italienne, pour les Dames et pour ceux qui ne sçavent pas le Latin'. Convaincu que l'apprentissage des langues vivantes devait être premièrement fondé sur des bases grammaticales, c'est-à-dire convaincu que les langues modernes devaient s'apprendre selon la méthode grammaticale appliquée dans l'enseignement du latin, Veneroni commence sa grammaire de l'italien par une explication des concepts grammaticaux essentiels (voyelle, consonne, syllabe, phrase, discours), par les définitions des parties du discours (nom, pronom, verbe, etc.) et par une exposition des fonctions des cas et de la déclinaison en général; il s'agit là d'une sorte d'introduction aux principes grammaticaux destinée à ceux qui ne les possédaient pas encore du fait de ne pas avoir fait d'études de latin, ce qui était particulièrement le cas des femmes.[9] Voici, en fait, la phrase qui clôt cette 'Introduction': 'Il est impossible que ceux qui ne sçavent point de Latin, puissent jamais parler bien Italien, à moins de sçavoir cette Introduction, qui leur facilitera le moyen de l'apprendre, & les avancera de la moitié du temps' (*Le Maître italien* 1681, 2e édition). De façon cohérente, toute la terminologie grammaticale présentée dans cette introduction et tous les exemples (sauf les premiers) sont en français. Ce n'est qu'après les quinze pages consacrées à l'introduction que Veneroni commence son enseignement de l'italien proprement dit. Or, c'est justement cette introduction rédigée par Veneroni qui constitue la partie essentielle de l'ouvrage de Courville.

L'*Explicación de la gramática francesa* de Courville se présente à sa page de titre comme composée de trois parties: la première sur les lettres et leurs correspondances phoniques, la deuxième sur la grammaire et la troisième sur les adverbes. Des trois, seule la deuxième nous apparaît aujourd'hui comme bien structurée. Mais ce n'est pas un mérite propre à notre auteur: cette deuxième partie n'est que l'Introduction du *Maître italien* de Veneroni, traduite en espagnol de façon pratiquement littérale, ce qui n'exclut pas quelques variations et quelques ajouts ou retranchements. Comme nous l'avons dit, les exemples de l'introduction de Veneroni étaient presque tous donnés en français, ce qui a permis à Courville de les garder tels quels.

Quant aux deux autres parties, la troisième n'est en réalité qu'une liste bilingue français-espagnol de phrases, chacune d'entre elles comportant une préposition, un adverbe ou une locution prépositionnelle ou adverbiale. Cette liste est également extraite de la section consacrée aux adverbes dans la grammaire italienne de Veneroni, avec une substitution des équivalences espagnoles aux équivalences italiennes de l'original. Deux traits distinguent donc la liste de Veneroni de celle de Courville. Veneroni ne proposait qu'une liste d'adverbes (plus quelques prépositions) ou de locutions adverbiales, alors que Courville insère chacun de ces éléments dans une phrase complète, ce qui n'arrive qu'exceptionnellement chez Veneroni. De ce fait, Veneroni n'a pas eu de difficulté à ordonner alphabétiquement ses entrées françaises en base à la première lettre de chaque adverbe ou préposition; Courville, par contre, finit par s'embrouiller et par établir un ordre alphabétique partant de la première lettre de la phrase dont fait partie l'adverbe. C'est pourquoi, lorsque l'adverbe ouvre la phrase correspondante, il se trouve correctement rangé à la lettre par laquelle il commence ('Heureusement, je l'attrapay par le manteau', par exemple, rangé à la lettre H). Mais il en va autrement dans les cas où l'adverbe apparaît à l'intérieur de la phrase; la locution à *l'écart*, par exemple, n'est pas rangée chez Courville à la lettre A,[10] mais à la lettre N, du fait que la phrase qui sert à montrer son emploi commence par *nous*: 'Nous nous metrons à l'ecart pour mieux voir la fête'.

La première partie de l'œuvre de Courville, concernant les lettres et leur valeur phonique, s'éloigne un peu plus de l'original de Veneroni. Dans l'Introduction de celui-ci, cette partie était très sommaire. Certainement à cause du fait que les grammaires de l'époque commençaient généralement par de longs développements grapho-phonétiques, Courville a dû éprouver le besoin d'élargir quelque peu l'original. C'est pourquoi, tout en commençant par copier littéralement le texte de Veneroni, il ajoute à ses explications quelques pages sur les 'diphtongues' et les 'triphtongues' françaises. Toutefois, ces explications ne sont pas non plus originales; elles suivent de près la partie correspondante de la *Gramática francesa* de Billet, l'auteur qui, au moment de l'arrivé de Courville en Espagne, y jouissait encore du plus grand prestige comme maître de français.[11]

Malgré ce double plagiat — ou à cause de cela — , cette première partie grapho-phonétique de l'*Explicación* de Courville est la moins réussie des trois qui la composent. Il n'y parvient ni à proposer des commentaires contrastifs sur la prononciation française comparée à l'espagnole, ni à proposer un exposé cohérent sur les lettres et les sons du français construit dès la perspective du seul français. Sur les lettres *e* et *u*, par exemple, Courville se limite à dire qu'elles gardent leur son naturel (p. 2); si cette affirmation, du moins en ce qui concerne la lettre *e*, est déjà largement insuffisante considérée d'une perspective interne au français, considérée du point de vue contrastif français-espagnol elle est tout simplement inappropriée; alors que la plupart des grammaires de français pour Espagnols antérieures et postérieures à celle de Courville insistent largement sur les diverses valeurs phoniques correspondant à la lettre *e* en français et sur la difficulté pour les hispanophones de reproduire l'articulation correspondant à la lettre *u*, Courville n'y fait pas la moindre référence.

Quant à la seconde partie de l'ouvrage de Courville, c'est-à-dire celle qui suit de plus près l'original de Veneroni, elle commence, malgré ce qu'annonce la page de titre,[12] sans un avis préalable. Courville entame ses explications grammaticales tout simplement à la ligne suivante de la dernière correspondant à ses explications grapho-phonétiques. Si, sans compter les pages préliminaires ni la table des matières, l'ouvrage se compose de quatre-vingt-deux pages, la seconde partie s'étend de la page 10 à la page 50, la troisième partie (clairement délimitée par le titre 'Frases, o adverbios, compuestos por alfabeto') occupant le reste. Cette distribution montre déjà le peu de travail personnel apporté par Courville, mis à part le fait d'avoir traduit le *Maître* de Veneroni. Une traduction, d'autre part, et comme nous l'avons dit, qui est plus loin de l'adaptation que du simple plagiat, étant donné son haut degré de littéralité. À preuve:

Veneroni, 1696 [n. p.]	Courville, 1728, pp. 21–22
Il y a sept Pronoms conjonctifs, qui sont, *me, te, se, lui, nous, vous, leur*. Les Pronoms Conjonctifs ont beaucoup de rapport avec les Pronoms Personnels, en ce qu'ils sont toûjours devant les Verbes; mais avec la difference, que les Pronoms Personnels font l'action du Verbe devant lesquels [sic] ils sont, & les Pronoms Conjonctifs la reçoivent, Exemple: *Ie chante, nous chantons, vous parlez;* c'est *je, nous, vous,* qui font l'action des Verbes *chante, chantons, parlez,* devant lesquels ils sont; & par consequent ce sont des Pronoms Personnels. Mais quand on dit, *Dieu me regarde, le maître te prie, le peuple se plaint, le Soleil nous éclaire, mon frere vous prie, le Capitaine leur payera;* dans la premiere phrase *Dieu me regarde*, c'est *Dieu* qui fait l'action du Verbe *regarde;* & ainsi, *me*, qui ne la fait point, est un Pronom Conjonctif, qui est auprés du Verbe, & qui ne fait pas l'action de *regarder*.	Ay siete pronombres conjuntivos, que son *me, te, se, luy, nous, vous, leur,* estos pronombres conjuntivos tienen mucha afinidad con las [sic] personales, en quanto ellos siempre rigen à los verbos; pero con la diferencia, que los pronombres personales hazen la accion del verbo, que se les sigue, y los conjuntivos la reciben de èl: V.g. *Je chante, nous chantons, vous parlès*; este *je, nous, vous,* que hazen la accion de los verbos *chante, chantons, parlès,* delante los quales estàn puestos, son pronombres personales; pero quando se dize: *Dieu me regarde,* Dios me mira; *le Maitre te prie,* el Maestro te ruega, *le peuple se plaint,* el pueblo se quexa; *le Soleil nous eclaire,* el Sol nos alumbra; *mon frere vous prie,* mi hermano os ruega; *le Capitaine leur payera,* el Capitan los pagarà; *mon pere luy parla,* mi padre le hablò: en la primera frasse *Dieu me regarde,* es Dios quien haze la accion del verbo *regarde;* y assi, el pronombre *me*, que no la haze, es pronombre conjuntivo...

Comme conséquence du fait que le gros de l'*Explicación* de Courville n'est que l'Introduction de Veneroni, on est devant un ouvrage avec lequel on ne pouvait pas vraiment apprendre les particularités morphosyntaxiques du français, mais devant une introduction aux concepts grammaticaux usuels dans l'enseignement de la langue latine, présentés comme également essentiels pour aborder l'étude de la langue française. Courville, en effet, garde la phrase (citée ci-dessus) qui fermait l'introduction de Veneroni: 'Es impossible, que aquellos que no son Latinos, pudiessen jamàs hablar bien la Lengua Francesa, à menos de hazerse capaces de esta introducion, ò explicacion, que les facilitarà el medio de saberla, como se desea'.

Il se peut que Courville, dans ses cours particuliers, ait réussi non seulement à renforcer cette formation grammaticale de base que son livre propose déjà, mais à élargir considérablement ce que ce livre n'abordait que d'une façon succincte; certainement, dans ses cours, il enseignait d'une façon plus approfondie les caractéristiques des paradigmes morphologiques du français et leur fonctionnement en syntaxe. Mais, en tout cas, il est évident que la perspective habituelle se trouve inversée dans son ouvrage: celui-ci ne permet réellement pas l'apprentissage de la langue française en partant de l'acquisition des concepts fondamentaux de la science grammaticale; le français y est un simple moyen avec lequel pouvoir exemplifier la formation en grammaire, ce qui aurait pu être également fait à l'aide de l'espagnol ou du latin. L'ouvrage de Courville n'est ainsi ni une grammaire du français expliquée à partir du français ni une grammaire du français expliquée contrastivement à l'aide de l'espagnol.[13]

Ce caractère peu pratique de sa grammaire, ainsi que la concurrence des autres grammaires françaises publiées en Espagne la même année que la sienne (voir ci-dessus), pourraient expliquer que l'ouvrage de Courville n'ait jamais été réédité. Courville a bien continué à enseigner sa langue à Madrid[14] au moins jusqu'au milieu du siècle, puisque c'est par 'Antonio Courville, m[aestro] de lengua franzesa' qu'il signe une lettre datée à cette ville le 28 juillet 1745 et adressée au professeur de l'Université de Salamanque Ignacio Osorio; mais les ressources qu'il tirait de son activité ne devait pas être suffisantes: dans cette lettre, il prie le jésuite Osorio de continuer à pratiquer la charité envers sa femme et sa fille jusqu'au moment où il pourrait leur venir en aide.[15]

Puisque, comme déjà dit, *Le Maître italien* a connu beaucoup de rééditions — ainsi que quelques révisions par son auteur — avant la parution de l'*Explicación* de Courville, il est pertinent de se demander laquelle d'entre elles a été consultée par notre auteur. Nous écartons d'emblée les versions parues en Italie, pour la simple raison qu'elles suivent le remaniement effectué en 1690 par Lépine (Minerva 1989: 99; 1996: 40-41), qui n'y a pas inclus l'Introduction de Veneroni dont il est question ici. Et nous écartons également les éditions faites en anglais ou en allemand; mis à part le fait qu'il serait surprenant que Courville ait choisi des modèles rédigés en d'autres langues que le français, celle parue à Londres en 1724, par exemple, réduit trop l'Introduction de l'original, s'écartant ainsi du texte espagnol de Courville. Celui-ci a dû donc partir de l'une des éditions en français parues à Paris, à Lyon ou à Amsterdam.

Nous excluons comme modèle les premières éditions révisées par l'auteur: celles de Paris 1681 (2e) et 1687 (5e) et celle d'Amsterdam 1690 n'incorporent pas encore quelques ajouts présents dans l'Introduction des éditions postérieures et recueillis dans la version de Courville.[16]

Parmi ces éditions postérieures, le texte de notre auteur ne coïncide ni avec la lignée constituée par les éditions parisiennes de 1709 (9e), 1720 et 1726, ni avec celle constituée par les éditions d'Amsterdam 1709, Lyon 1711 et Lyon 1722. Ces deux traditions textuelles divergent sur un bon nombre de points, la version de Courville coïncidant tantôt avec les contenus de l'une, tantôt avec ceux de l'autre. Cela est dû au fait que Courville est en réalité parti d'une lignée antérieure: celle des éditions parisiennes de 1696 (7e) et 1700 (8e).

En effet, si l'on excepte quelques suppressions mineures, quelques interventions personnelles de Courville et l'augmentation des explications grapho-phonétiques inspirée de la *Gramática* de Billet, la version espagnole traduit au pied de la lettre le texte en français des éditions parisiennes de 1696 et 1700. Celles-ci sont pratiquement coïncidentes en tout, du moins en ce qui concerne les parties qui nous intéressent ici, c'est-à-dire l'Introduction pour ceux qui ne connaissent pas le latin et la liste bilingue des adverbes incluse dans la grammaire italienne proprement dite. Mais il y a deux ou trois détails secondaires où elles divergent et, lorsque cela se produit, le texte de Courville répond plutôt à celui de l'édition de 1696.[17] Il est donc fort probable que Courville a eu cette dernière sous les yeux lors de la rédaction de son ouvrage,[18] ce qui revient à dire que Courville ne s'est pas servi d'une édition du *Maître* proche de l'année de parution de son ouvrage et qu'il n'est même pas parti de la dernière édition révisée par Veneroni.

Voici nos conclusions. Nous pensons avoir démontré que le *Maître italien* de Veneroni a eu aussi, comme dans le cas d'autres pays européens, une présence relativement précoce en Espagne. La première section de cette grammaire est arrivée aux Espagnols dès 1728, grâce à l'*Explicación* de Courville. Malheureusement, et contrairement à ce qui s'est passé dans d'autre pays, Courville n'a pas avoué la source de son plagiat. C'est cette occultation qui rend compte du fait que la première manifestation de l'introduction du *Maître italien* de Veneroni en Espagne soit passée inaperçue jusqu'à présent. Toutefois, même si son ouvrage n'a jamais été publié au complet en Espagne; même si la partie qui en a été traduite se trouve cachée, non pas dans une grammaire de l'italien, mais dans une grammaire du français adressée à des débutants en cette langue; même si son influence en Espagne a été moins importante dans la première partie du XVIIIe siècle que celle que le *Maître italien* a exercée ailleurs, l'ouvrage de Veneroni a bien eu assez tôt, avant qu'on ne le pensait, une présence en Espagne. Il nous semble que, dorénavant, il faudrait en tenir compte.

Bibliography

BARTOCCIONI, STEFANIA. 2005. 'Les Français en Russie et les Russes en France au XVIIIe siècle: note sur la lexicographie français-russe et le *Dictionaire manuel en quatre langues* de Veneroni (Moscou, 1771)', *Quaderni del CIRSIL*, 4: 89-118

BECK-BUSSE, GABRIELE. 1994. 'Les "femmes" et les "illitterati"; ou la question du latin et de la langue vulgaire', *Histoire, Épistémologie, Langage*, 16: 77-94

——. 2012. 'À propos d'une histoire des "Grammaires des Dames": réflexions théoriques et approches empiriques', *Documents pour l'histoire du français langue étrangère ou seconde*, 47-48: 13-43

BINGEN, NICOLE and ANNE-MARIE VAN PASSEN. 1991. 'La Lexicographie bilingue français-italien, italien-français', in *Wörterbücher / Dictionaries / Dictionnaires. Ein internationales Handbuch zur Lexikographie / An International Encyclopedia of Lexicography / Encyclopédie internationale de lexicographie*, ed. by Franz Josef Hausmann, Oskar Reichmann, Herbert Ernst Wiegand and Ladislao Zgusta, 3 vols (Berlin; New York: de Gruyter), III, 3007-13

BLÉGNY, ÉTIENNE DE. 1707. *Les Élémens ou premières instructions de la jeunesse* (Paris: Guillaume Cavelier)

BRUÑA CUEVAS, MANUEL. 2010. 'Dos maestros de francés en el Madrid de finales del siglo XVII: Pierre-Paul Billet y Jean-Pierre Jaron', in *Enseigner les langues modernes en Europe, XVe-XVIIe siècles*, ed. by Marie-Hélène Maux-Piovano (Strasbourg: Université de Strasbourg), pp. 219-60

CARAVOLAS, JEAN-ANTOINE. 2000. *Histoire de la didactique des langues au Siècle des Lumières: précis et anthologie thématique* (Montreal: Presses de l'Université de Montréal; Tübingen: Narr)

DUREY DE NOINVILLE, JACQUES-BERNARD. 1758. *Table alphabétique des dictionnaires, en* toutes sortes de Langues & sur toutes sortes de Sciences & d'Arts (Paris: Hugues Chaubert & Hérissant)

LÉPINETTE, BRIGITTE. 2000. L'Enseignement du français en Espagne au XVIIIe siècle dans ses grammaires: contexte historique, concepts linguistiques et pédagogie (Münster: Nodus)

——. 2001. 'La Grammaire contrastive franco-espagnole de la première moitié du XVIIIe siècle: analyse de six ouvrages édités en Espagne', in History of Linguistics in Spain II / Historia de la Lingüística en España II, ed. by E. F. Konrad Koerner and Hans-Josef Niederehe (Amsterdam; Philadelphia: Benjamins), pp. 137-79

LILAO FRANCA, ÓSCAR, and CARMEN CASTRILLO GONZÁLEZ (eds). 1997. Catálogo de manuscritos de la Biblioteca Universitaria de Salamanca, 2 vols (Salamanca: Ediciones Universidad de Salamanca)

LILLO, JACQUELINE. 2002. 'Bilan et pistes de recherche en histoire de la lexicographie bilingue français-italien', Quaderni del CIRSIL, 1: 47-58

MINERVA, NADIA. 1989. 'Storie di manuali: la didattica delle lingue straniere in Italia nell'Arte d'insegnare la lingua francese e nel Maître italien', in Grammatiche, grammatici, grammatisti: per una storia dell'insegnamento delle lingue in Italia dal Cinquecento al Settecento, ed. by Carla Pellandra (Pisa: Libreria Goliardica), pp. 55-117

——. 1996. 'Histoire de manuels: l'Arte di insegnare la lingua francese, Le Maître Italien et Il Maestro francese in Italia de Berti-Veneroni-Lépine (1677-1752)', in Nadia Minerva, Manuels, maîtres, méthodes: repères pour l'histoire de l'enseignement du français en Italie (Bologna: CLUEB), pp. 17-78

——. 2012. 'Les Toponymes dans la tradition des Recherches italiennes et françoises... velléités encyclopédiques dans les dictionnaires bilingues des XVIIe et XVIIIe siècles', in Lexiques. Identités. Cultures, ed. by Pierluigi Ligas et Paolo Frassi (Verona: QuiEdit), pp. 257-80

——. 2013. 'Un siècle de lexicographie bilingue: le Dictionnaire de Giovanni Veneroni et ses adaptations', in Les best-sellers de la lexicographie franco-italienne. XVIe–XXIe siècle, ed. by Jacqueline Lillo (Rome: Carocci), pp. 33-51

MORMILE, MARIO. 1989. L'italiano in Francia, il francese in Italia: storia critica delle opere grammaticali francesi in Italia ed italiane in Francia dal Rinascimento al Primo Ottocento. In Appendice: Repertorio cronologico delle opere grammaticali e lessicografiche italo-francesi dalle origini al Primo Ottocento (Turin: Meynier)

——. 1991. 'Louis Lépine, le Maestro Francese à Venise (fin XVIIe siècle)', Documents pour l'histoire du français langue étrangère ou seconde, 8: 27-34

——. 1993. Storia dei dizionari bilingui italo-francesi: la lessicografia italo-francese dalle origini al 1900 (Fasano: Schena)

——, and RICCARDA MATTEUCCI. 1997. Le grammatiche italiane in Gran Bretagna. Profilo storico: secoli XVI, XVII, XVIII (Lecce: Argo)

PIZZOLI, LUCILLA. 2004. Le grammatiche d'italiano per inglesi (1565–1776): un'analisi linguistica (Florence: Accademia della Crusca)

SANSON, HELENA. 2014. '"Simplicité, clarté et précision": Grammars of Italian "pour les dames" and Other Learners in Eighteenth- and Early Nineteenth-Century France', The Modern Language Review, 109: 593-616

SILVESTRI, PAOLO. 2001. Le grammatiche italiane per ispanofoni (secoli XVI–XIX) (Alessandria: Edizioni dell'Orso)

SUÁREZ GÓMEZ, GONZALO. 2008 [1956]. La enseñanza del francés en España hasta 1850. ¿Con qué libros aprendían francés los españoles?, ed. by Juan F. García Bascuñana and Esther Juan Oliva (Barcelona: Promociones Publicaciones Universitarias)

VAN PASSEN, ANNE-MARIE. 1981. 'Appunti sui dizionari italo-francesi apparsi prima della fine del Settecento', Studi di lessicografia italiana, 3: 29-65

VAYRAC, JEAN DE. 1714. Nouvelle Grammaire Espagnole (Paris: Pierre Witte)

Notes to Chapter 9

1. Pour un résumé de la vie et de l'œuvre de Veneroni, voir Minerva (1996: 63-68).
2. Veneroni traduit du français en italien les *Pensées chrétiennes pour tous les jours du mois* (1670) de Dominique Bouhours (*Pensieri cristiani per tutti i giorni del mese* (Paris: S. Mabre-Cramoisy, 1685)) et les *Considérations chrestiennes pour tous les jours de l'année* (1683) de Jean Crasset (*Considerationi cristiane per tutt'i giorni della settimana* (Paris: S. Loyson, 1691)); il traduit de l'italien en français les *Lettres du cardinal Bentivoglio* (Paris: E. Loyson, 1680), les *Lettres de Loredano* (Paris: veuve Mabre-Cramoisi, 1695) et la *Scielta di favole italiane e francesi* (Paris: veuve Mabre-Cramoisy, 1695), tous trois édités en version bilingue.
3. Il s'agit d'une révision par Veneroni du *Dictionnaire Italien et François* (1662) de Lorenzo Ferretti, lequel n'est à son tour qu'un remaniement des *Recherches italiennes et françoises* d'Antoine Oudin, dont la première édition date de 1640-42; de fait, il faut attendre l'édition de 1695 (Paris: Étienne Loyson) pour que les noms d'Oudin et de Ferretti ne figurent plus sur la page de titre du dictionnaire de Veneroni (Van Passen 1981: 43; Minerva 2012: 260). La première édition actuellement connue du remaniement dû à Veneroni est celle de 1681-80 (Paris, plusieurs tirages, chacune avec un imprimeur différent), mais plusieurs chercheurs (Caravolas 2000: 191; Lillo 2002: 50) signalent sa participation à une édition antérieure, faite à Amsterdam en 1677. L'idée que cette édition ait pu exister a été répandue par Van Passen (1981: 43, 56); or, certainement du fait qu'elle n'a pu la consulter ni la situer à une bibliothèque précise, elle remet en doute son existence dans un travail postérieur (Bingen and Van Passen 1991: 3009). Nous ne savons pas quelle a été la source ayant inspiré à Van Passen (1981) sa référence à cette édition de 1677, mais la conviction qu'elle a été faite vient de loin: au XVIIIe siècle, elle est déjà mentionnée par Durey de Noinville (1758: 64) avec Veneroni comme auteur. Récemment, Minerva (2013: 38) a énuméré plusieurs raisons pour croire à son existence.
4. Vers la fin du XVIIe siècle et le début du XVIIIe, le dictionnaire de Veneroni était le bilingue italien-français le plus vendu. Au cours du XVIIIe siècle, il sera concurrencé par d'autres dictionnaires, notamment par celui d'Annibale Antonini (1735), mais ses rééditions, parues à Paris, Venise, Amsterdam ou Bâle et remaniées par divers auteurs (Louis de Lépine, Filippo Neretti, Pierre Meunier, Carlo Placardi, Antonio Polaccho, etc.), se succèdent jusqu'en 1800 (58 rééditions en tout d'après Lillo 2002: 50). Pour le détail de ces rééditions, voir Van Passen 1981: 56-61; Mormile 1993: 110-126; ou Minerva 2013: 48-51.
5. Le dictionnaire bilingue de Veneroni paraît en 1700 (Francfort-sur-le-Main: Johann David Zunner) en version quadrilingue (italien, français, allemand, latin); il s'agit du célèbre *Dictionnaire impérial*, revu par Nicolò di Castelli, puis par Carlo Placardi, et plusieurs fois réédité (1714, 1743, 1766, 1804). Pour ces versions avec l'allemand, ainsi que pour des versions avec le néerlandais, voir Van Passen 1981: 51-53. L'ouvrage paraîtra également à Moscou en 1771 avec le russe (*Dictionaire* [sic] *manuel en quatre langues, savoir la Françoise, l'Italienne, l'Allemande & la Russe, par Mr. Veneroni*). Sur ce dernier, voir Bartoccioni 2005: 98-107.
6. Il s'agit des éditions faites à Paris par Étienne Loyson (2e en 1681, 4e en 1685, 5e en 1687, 6e en 1690), Edme Couterot (7e en 1696, avec une tirade par E. Loyson) et Michel David (8e en 1700, 9e en 1709). Les premières éditions à Lyon datent de 1695, 1701, 1709, etc.
7. Les *Élémens* de Blégny commencent en 1707 par la section 'Les elemens de la jeunesse. Premiere partie. La grammaire, ou l'art de bien parler', inspirée du *Maître* de Veneroni et absente dans la première édition (Paris: Charles Cabri, 1691). Voir également la section de Blégny intitulée 'Explication des Cas' (1707: 20-24).
8. Courville nous le révèle dans sa dédicace: 'haviendo sido militar algunos años'.
9. Les références aux dames comme destinataires de cette 'Introduction' se maintiendront dans le corps de celle-ci au cours des diverses éditions. Par contre, dès les dernières éditions du XVIIe siècle, l'allusion aux dames disparaît du titre de l'Introduction. Celui de l'édition de 1696, par exemple, est le suivant: 'Introduction à la Langue Italiene, pour ceux qui ne savent pas le Latin'. Sur la mise en parallèle des femmes et de ceux qui ne connaissent pas le latin, voir Beck-Busse (1994, 2012) et Sanson (2014).
10. Veneroni, par contre, donne 'À l'écart, *in disparte*' à la lettre A.

11. La dernière édition de la *Gramática francesa* de Pierre-Paul Billet date de 1708, cet auteur étant sans doute décédé peu de temps après. Sur l'œuvre et le prestige de Billet, voir Bruña Cuevas (2010).
12. *Explicacion de la Gramatica Francesa* [...]. *Dividida en tres partes. La primera, trata de las Letras* [...]. *La segunda, contiene toda la explicacion de la Gramatica. La tercera, comprehende los Adverbios, compuestos en Frases por Alfabeto.*
13. Comme dans le cas de la partie consacrée aux lettres, dans cette seconde partie Courville passe le plus souvent sous silence ces divergences essentielles entre le français et l'espagnol. Il est vrai que, parfois, s'écartant de Veneroni, il adopte un point de vue contrastif (pour les possessifs, par exemple), mais sa fidélité à l'original fait que ce ne soit généralement pas le cas (en parlant de l'accusatif, il ne dit rien, par exemple, sur la façon différente de construire le complément d'objet direct de personne dans une langue et dans l'autre).
14. Il se pourrait qu'il ait également enseigné le français à Salamanque, car c'est à cette ville qu'a été publiée une autre œuvre de Courville, un opuscule imprimé par Eugenio García de Honorato et intitulé *Papel nuevo tocante a la mayor perfección de hablar la Lengua Francesa*. Cet ouvrage n'est pas accessible aujourd'hui aux chercheurs, mais, d'après la seule description disponible (celle qu'en fait Suárez Gómez 2008: 122), il ne porte pas de date. Ce sont là des circonstances qui nous empêchent de savoir si ce *Papel* est antérieur ou postérieur à l'*Explicación* et de connaître si ses contenus, quoique sommaires, étaient originaux ou empruntés.
15. Si la lettre de Courville nous est parvenue, ce n'est que parce qu'elle a été employée comme support pour la rédaction manuscrite d'un texte religieux. Elle constitue les feuillets 29-30 du tome XIII, *Sermones varios* (MS 1600), de la bibliothèque de l'Université de Salamanque (Lilao Franca et Castrillo González 1997: I, 674).
16. Voir, par exemple, les paragraphes de l'Introduction consacrés aux adverbes, aux prépositions ou aux conjonctions. Nous exclions également les éditions faites à Lyon en 1695 et à Amsterdam en 1697 parce que leur liste d'adverbes ne suit pas l'ordre alphabétique adopté aussi bien dans la troisième partie de l'*Explicación* de Courville que dans la plupart des éditions du *Maître italien* antérieures à la parution de celle-ci (1728).
17. Voici, à titre d'exemple, un de ces cas de petite divergence entre les éditions parisiennes de 1696 et 1700. En parlant de l'ablatif, on lit dans celle de 1696 (f. B iij^v) la phrase suivante: 'C'est de même comme si l'on disoit (pour ainsi dire) qu'on a ôté ou enlevé du Prince, *l'amour, cent écus, & la Princesse*'. En 1700, le dernier terme, 'la Princesse', n'apparaît pas: 'qu'on a ôté ou enlevé du Prince, *l'amour & cent écus*' ([n. p.]). Courville, comme l'édition de 1696, n'oublie pas cette référence à la princesse. Coïncident avec la version de Paris 1696 l'édition d'Amsterdam 1709 y les éditions lyonnaises de 1711 et 1722, mais suivent la leçon de Paris 1700 les éditions, également parisiennes, de 1709, 1720 et 1726.
18. Étant donné qu'il y a quelques éditions que nous n'avons pu nous procurer, nous ne sommes pas à même d'exclure radicalement la possibilité que Courville soit parti d'une réédition du *Maître italien* différente de celle de 1696 (Paris: E. Couterot); mais nous pouvons assurer que, dans ce cas, cette autre édition devrait être pratiquement coïncidente en tout avec celle de 1696 en ce qui concerne les parties ici analysées.

CHAPTER 10

Giuseppe Baretti's Multifarious Approach to Learning Italian in Eighteenth-Century Britain

Vilma De Gasperin

Unpoetical people ought never to assume the right of teaching
GIUSEPPE BARETTI

This chapter offers a comprehensive analysis of the eclectic and original approach to Italian language learning in eighteenth-century Britain by the Turinese man of letters Giuseppe Baretti (1719–1789). It examines some linguistic aspects and pedagogical ideas that emerge from six widely different texts united in the common aim of passing on to English learners knowledge of the Italian language. Baretti's texts for learning Italian engage with a variety of approaches dealing with different skills. They comprise a pamphlet on recommendations as to what authors to read to perfect one's language; an Italian-English dictionary; a grammar of the Italian language; an anthology of Italian literary texts with grammatical annotations and a literal translation for self-study; a collection of dialogues written for a young pupil; and a selection of his own writings as a model for written Italian. Many of his pedagogical works were informed by his experience as a learner and as a teacher of foreign languages.

Baretti lived in England for many years, at a time when the Italian language enjoyed a revival of interest after the Renaissance period. His interest in the Italian language, as well as his need for employment, led him to become a private tutor of Italian, as well as being involved in a variety of other cultural and intellectual endeavours. Through one of his pupils, the writer Charlotte Lennox, he was introduced to the literary circle of Samuel Johnson, who was to have a major influence on his *A Dictionary of the English and Italian Languages* and *An Italian and English Grammar* (printed together in 1760), while his employment as a tutor to the children of Henry Thrale led to the composition of bilingual dialogues. By viewing this corpus together for the first time, the chapter aims at giving a more coherent, albeit rich, multifaceted and variegated picture of Baretti as a linguistic thinker and pedagogue, as a lexicographer and grammarian, as a teacher and writer.

In the second half of the eighteenth century Britain witnessed the combination of, on the one hand, a growing interest in the Italian language and, on the other, the pedagogical engagement of the Piedmontese man of letters Giuseppe Baretti, who lived and worked in England from 1751 to 1760, and again from 1766 to 1770, when he briefly returned to Italy. He lived in England again from 1771 until his death in 1789.[1] During this quarter of a century as an intellectual expatriate, Baretti, who knew English, French and Spanish, published several pedagogical works aimed at assisting learners in acquiring a mastery of literary Italian: *Remarks on the Italian Language and Writers from Mr Joseph Baretti to an English Gentleman at Turin, Written in the year 1751* (1753); *An Introduction to the Italian Language. Containing Specimens both of Prose and Verse [...] With a literal Translation and Grammatical Notes, for the Use of those who being already acquainted with Grammar, attempt to learn it without a Master* (1755); *A Dictionary of the English and Italian Languages [...] To which is added, An Italian and English Grammar* (1760); *Easy Phraseology for the Use of Young Ladies, Who Intend to Learn the Colloquial Part of the Italian Language* (1775); *Scelta di lettere familiari. Fatta per uso degli studiosi di lingua Italiana* (1779). These texts testify to the breadth of Baretti's engagement with several aspects of Italian language learning: from reading and using literature as a tool to achieve linguistic accuracy to lexicography; from grammar to speaking; and addressing learners of different ages and degrees of familiarity with the Italian language. They reveal a multifarious and innovative pedagogical approach, coupled with a pragmatic and tolerant attitude towards the difficulties encountered by learners of Italian as a foreign language, which contrasts sharply with the scathing criticism of the linguistic and stylistic use of Italian by his fellow countrymen that he would unleash from the pages of *La Frusta letteraria* in 1763–64.

In eighteenth-century Britain, Italian was learnt by members of the upper and middle classes of both sexes for literary, cultural and practical reasons, linked principally to commerce and travel. As the lexicographer Ferdinando Altieri wrote in the Preface to his Dictionary of 1726:

> The Italian language [...] is deservedly esteem'd on account of those excellent Authors that have written in it; and it is also useful to be understood by nobility, gentry and merchants; there being few, if any, Courts in *Europe* where it is not used, and but few ports in *Italy* where the merchants of *Great-Britain* do not carry on an advantagious traffick. (Altieri 1726)

The Grand Tour to Italy for young aristocrats was very popular in the first half of the eighteenth century; it declined but did not die out in the second half, while travelling to Italy appealed and became possible to a broader social spectrum: 'By 1760, young men from the landed elite were still being sent to Italy for the final polish to their education', as well as 'older men, professional writers, wealthier members of the middle classes, wives and family groups', the sons of merchants, booksellers, artists and architects, up to the outbreak of the French Revolution in 1793, which made travel in the continent more difficult (Sweet 2012: 7–10). In 1754 Giuseppe Baretti wrote to his friend Agudio in Milan that the Italian language was also gaining ground in Britain thanks to the ever-increasing popularity of opera

(Lubbers-Van Der Brugge 1951: 54). Baretti's work is a major contribution to the corpus of textual tools for learning and refining the Italian language, for which there was a growing thirst.

Reading Models

Baretti's earliest approach to language learning is rooted in reading Italian literature as a means of language acquisition. In 1753 he published his first short text on issues relating to language learning, *Remarks on the Italian Language and Writers from Mr Joseph Baretti to an English Gentleman at Turin, written in the year 1751*. This twenty-four-page pamphlet is addressed to an unnamed upper-class male and offers recommendations about which Italian authors to read and, conversely, which to avoid, in order to 'attain the purity of the Italian tongue' (Baretti 1753: 9). Before reviewing literary models, Baretti traces an unflattering picture of the development of Italian up to his day. He gives a brief account of the fall of the language from the 'perfection' that had been achieved between the fourteenth and the start of the sixteenth century, through seventeenth-century linguistic corruption, to the point, in his view, of being on the brink of 'extinction' in his own times.[2] In his catastrophic representation, Baretti asserts that 'there are not, at this day, twenty persons in all *Italy* who understand [the Italian tongue] thoroughly, and can write it correctly' (Baretti 1753: 3–4). In 'A History of the Italian Tongue', which prefaced *The Italian Library* in 1757, Baretti was less drastic and was content to claim that '[t]he present state of our language in Italy is neither very good nor very bad' (Baretti 1933: 143). Italian was indeed not a unified language in the states of the Italian peninsula. In the education system Italian was competing with Latin; French and the local vernacular were spoken in Piedmont; everywhere dialects were spoken by the vast majority of the population; and in writing, for those in possession of some degree of literacy, a mixture of dialect and Italian was employed.[3] Italian was the language of the cultivated elites alone, who could master it only by means of long dedicated study, and Baretti is aiming his criticism squarely at writers, those among the learned elites whose language he fiercely accused in *La Frusta letteraria* of lacking elegance, purity and clarity or displaying unpardonable traits of affectation, cumbersome syntax and foreign words.[4]

In his *Remarks* Baretti gives an overview of Italian literary works through lively, albeit somewhat impressionistic, linguistic scrutiny, recommending their virtues or warning against their vices. The first model hailed by Baretti as being exemplary of fourteenth-century linguistic excellence is Giovanni Boccaccio (1313–1375), who 'carried the *Italian* [language] to a height which [...] can scarce be surpassed': 'This Writer I would recommend before all others, notwithstanding the criticism of some ignorant moderns, who think his phrases too far-fetched, and tell us it is no longer customary to place the verb at the end of the sentence' (Baretti 1753: 4). Baretti is referring to the syntactical order of Boccaccio's prose, but while in *Remarks* he described it as a model for writing, in virtue of his 'beautiful, lively, and natural expressions', and the 'admirable disposition of his periods' (Baretti 1753: 4), he later came to reject the model of Boccaccio's syntax, which consisted of a complex construction of clauses, with the verb frequently placed at the end of a clause, which did not reflect the order of subject, verb and object in which, in Baretti's view, ideas occur to the mind (Baretti 1932b: 60; 1932a: 88). Baretti does not exemplify his observations on Boccaccio's style, but among the stylistic features of Boccaccio the critic Mengaldo identifies the relative pronoun at the beginning of a sentence, the verb at the end of the clause, long sentences abounding in subordinate clauses, and what he broadly calls 'stylistic and syntactic sumptuousness' (Mengaldo 2012: 37). What Baretti criticized, however, was not so much Boccaccio's style in itself, but the imitation of its complexity and convolution by later writers. At the same time Baretti alerts the foreign learner to the presence of archaisms in Boccaccio — as he does with another icon of linguistic and poetic purity, Petrarch — and advises that they can only be avoided by acquiring familiarity through practice:

> I own that some of [Boccaccio's] terms are not now to be used: but they are so few, that when you have made a little progress in our language, you will readily avoid them in writing without being told of them. (Baretti 1753: 4)

As may already be glimpsed from these examples, Baretti's stylistic description is characterized by a degree of vagueness which makes it difficult to pin down exactly what he is praising or condemning, and hence what a foreign reader should avoid. For example, of Giovanni Della Casa's *Il Galateo*, Baretti claims that it is written with 'wonderful perspicuity and elegance' (Baretti 1753: 5); in Firenzuola 'there is much sweetness and grace' and 'agreeable and beautiful manner'; Cellini wrote with 'inimitable grace' (Baretti 1753: 5). Dante's language is 'lofty, sublime, and haughty' (Baretti 1753: 6), though he is 'sometimes very clownish, and even unintelligible' (Baretti 1753: 7). More bluntly, Baretti decries the style of Pulci, whose phrases are 'often coarse and obscure' (Baretti 1753: 7) and singles out Aretino for being 'as ignorant of his own tongue, as of good manners' (Baretti 1753: 6).

Dealing with issues of style rather than of grammar, *Remarks* clearly presupposes a learner who is already well acquainted with Italian and who seeks to refine his own grasp of written, literary language. At the same time, the text confers an objective value on the author's own views on language and style and lends authority to his pedagogical advice, verging on a sort of intellectual censorship, particularly as far as poetry is concerned. Regarding the minor poets Cyr of Pers, Achillini, Ciampeli, Testi, Maggi and others, Baretti claims: 'Never, Sir, entertain a thought of reading any of these miserable butchers of poetry' (Baretti 1753: 21). Again, he does not give any reason for being so disparaging other than his own scathing judgement.

Remarks deals specifically with attaining competence through reading. The issue of pronunciation, however, is touched upon briefly. Baretti has in mind a foreigner who can already speak and understand Italian well and who may only be debating whether he ought to adopt the accent of one geographical area or another. Baretti recalls the proverb 'Lingua Toscana in bocca romana' [Tuscan tongue in a Roman mouth], which advocates Tuscan language with the accent of a native of Rome. However, Baretti claims that Italians themselves cannot agree on the best accent due to the diverse linguistic situation that has always characterized the peninsula. As

Baretti says, some Italians favour the pronunciation of Siena, others that of Florence, others that of Rome. Baretti does not feel an allegiance to any of these varieties and claims that 'I, for my part, who am neither of *Florence*, *Sienna*, nor *Romagna*, but of a province of *Italy* whose accent differs greatly from all three, think this article of the pronunciation, is a thing not worth contending about'. Thus, for him, born and bred outside Tuscany, the debate on which Tuscan variety to adopt is a matter of little importance and the choice of one variety over the other is subject to individual taste. For a foreign learner, '[t]he point of greatest importance is to attain to write the language well; and afterwards to learn to speak it with that accent which is most agreeable to the ear of the person who studies it' (Baretti 1753: 23). Thus, while declaring he personally favours the Florentine accent, Baretti is not excessively prescriptive. On the contrary, he appears to be aware of the variation in pronunciation of Italian (i.e. Tuscan) on the Italian peninsula even within Tuscany itself, and allows for some personal choices: '[a]fter all [...] every one has his peculiar ear, which he ought to consult more than the opinion of others' (Baretti 1953: 23).[5]

Having provided learners with guidelines as to which authors to study and emulate (or avoid) in order to produce good written Italian, Baretti proceeded to publish, in 1755, an anthology of literary texts, *An Introduction to the Italian language. Containing Specimens both of Prose and Verse. [...] With a literal Translation and Grammatical Notes, for the Use of those who, being already acquainted with Grammar, attempt to learn it without a Master*. The book is a collection of twenty-seven excerpts of Italian literary texts, mostly from Petrarch, Boccaccio and sixteenth-century authors, as well as one sonnet in Italian by 'Giovanni' Milton. John Milton had learnt Italian both at school and at home with private tutors at the insistence of his father during the 1620s and 1630s; he spent some time in Florence in September 1638 and in his first collection of English poetry in 1645 he included five sonnets and one *canzone* in Italian which attest to his mastery of the language (Lawrence 2011: 179–81). Baretti's anthology presents itself not merely as a collection of writings, but rather as a helpful tool for learning the Italian language by drawing on several pedagogical techniques set out in the Preface. First, it consists of 'as large a quantity of our language' as he found possible (Baretti 1755: vi), which seems to me to point to his awareness, though he does not say so explicitly, of a basic requirement of a corpus if it is to be sufficiently representative of the language. Secondly, Baretti follows qualitative as well as quantitative criteria and says he has selected 'the best [Authors] that Italy has produced [...] unknown to nobody that knows books' (Baretti 1755: vi). Baretti accounts for the absence in his anthology of an introduction to the authors themselves and to their literary merits by emphasizing the pedagogical nature of his collection as a tool for language learning:

> I do not give an account of them, because I did not make my collection to satisfy curiosity, but to assist instruction and facilitate study. Scholars know who those Authors are; and the unlearned, who study our language for other purposes, will not value such information. (Baretti 1755: vi–vii)

This collection of literary texts can be used, if one so wishes, 'only as a simple vocabulary, as indeed it is nothing else' (Baretti 1755: viii). Baretti thus conceives that reading literature may be entertained purely for the sake of linguistic knowledge without necessarily having knowledge of literary values and authors; and he therefore suggests that his collection of literary excerpts be taken as a mere collection of words and phrases in context, which in turn justifies both the lack of information he provides on authors and the literal, rather than faithful, translation of texts.

Baretti warns his learner of a further difficulty inherent in studying Italian, a language that is not unified, either in speaking or in writing, which subsequently displays lexical, spelling and morphological variation:

> The student will often wonder at finding both in my text and notes that the Italians spell and pronounce the same word different ways; [...] He will be astonished at the endless variety of terminations in some of our tenses; as for instance, the third person plural of the preterimperfect of the conjunctive mood of the verb *avere*, which is written by different writers ten different ways: *avrèbbero, arèbbero, avrèbbono, arèbbono, avrèbbeno, arèbbeno, avrìano, arìano, avrièno, arièno*. The reason of this is, that our Language at first was written by many persons of different parts of Italy [...]. Every one writ in his own dialect. (Baretti 1755: ix–x)

In his own 1760 grammar, Baretti gives the variant *avrébbero*, and in a footnote he adds 'Or, with as much elegance, *avrébbono*, and in poetry *avriéno*' (Baretti 1760: xix). Altieri gives three forms (*averebbero, avrebbero, avriano*) (Altieri 1756: 106) and later three further variants 'which are used only in Poetry' (*Hariano, havriano*, or *haverebbero*) (Altieri 1756: 118). While making the reader aware of the non-standardized nature and lack of uniformity of the Italian language, Baretti shows that he is aware of the pedagogical need to balance explanatory thoroughness with practicality, and suggests that overloading the learner with an excessive amount of explanation might deter the student and impede his progress. This explains why in his own grammar he gives one set form and two variants, while Altieri gives twice as many variants of this particular verb. This is the pedagogical ground for his keeping explanatory notes to a minimum while at the same time making allowances for what critics might consider a lack of thoroughness: 'Many of these differences and variations I have pointed out in my notes; though not always, because the notes would have filled too great a part of my book, and bewildered perhaps, rather than helped my readers' (Baretti 1755: xi). In spite of the difficulties awaiting the readers, Baretti concludes his Preface with a tone of encouragement and praise for his own literary language:

> But let none of them be frightened away from studying Italian by this, in appearance, unconquerable difficulty. A little practice will soon clear such obstructions, and make the path easy before them, to the most harmonious of all living Languages. (Baretti 1755: xi)

In order to assist the reader with linguistic comprehension, Baretti provides his own translation of each literary text, which 'I have made as literal as possible': 'A free translation was not intended, because it would not have served my end, which is to teach Italian, not English' (Baretti 1755: vii). Hence, the pedagogical use of literary texts in this collection requires that the aesthetic rendering of the translation be secondary to an understanding of the source language. The translation need not reproduce excellent English, rather it must clarify the source text entirely, and this entails the occasional addition of a word or phrase. Such additions are highlighted in the translated text in italics, so that the learner is wise to the fact that she or he will not find the equivalent signifier in the original. For example, 'onde spero la prossima settimana poter mandare essa lettera costì in Parigi' is rendered as 'so I hope next week I shall *have an opportunity* to send that letter to Paris' (Baretti 1755: 5); similarly 'ebbi dal nostro Zanotti' is rendered with the addition of 'friend' in 'I had, from our *friend* Zanotti (Baretti 1755: 13).

The most innovative feature of this collection is the apparatus of footnotes, which offers a glimpse of Baretti's range of different methods for explaining obscure linguistic points. First, grammatical problems are clarified by drawing on examples rather than using grammatical terminology. For instance, Baretti explains the verb combined with the clitic pronouns *mandarglielo* 'send it to him' as follows: '*Mandarglielo* is a coalition of words, for *mandare* [send] *lo* [it] and *gli* [to him]. The *e* inserted between *gli* and *lo* is only to assist the flow of the syllables' (Baretti 1755: 3). Vocabulary is explained through reference to different languages, from English to Latin, French and Spanish: '*Solcare il mare*, answers to the English expression *to plow the sea*' (Baretti 1755: 34); *Anteporre* 'to place before', from the Latin *anteponere*' (Baretti 1755: 9); '*Se non* answers to the Spanish, *se no, except*' (Baretti 1755: 4); *andarsene* 'to go away', 'that is *se ne andare*, in French, *s'en aller*' (Baretti 1755: 11). Clearly Baretti assumes that most of his learners are already familiar with another Romance language and possibly Latin.

An alternative way of explaining vocabulary is through recourse to etymology as well as translation into English. Baretti explains *Arrotino* as 'a *knife-grinder*, from *rota*, a *wheel*, with which he turns the engine' (Baretti 1755: 7). In so doing, Baretti seems to me to help the reader to think about the word in a broader sense and to visualize its meaning, which is useful in aiding memorization of vocabulary.

Idiomatic expressions may call forth more subjective considerations on the language: *comparire in petto ed in persona*, is explained as '[l]iterally *in breast and in person*. A ludicrous expression for *showing a man compleatly*. We say, *un uomo pare in petto ed in persona*, and [it] answers the English phrase, *from head to foot*' (Baretti 1755: 7). While the Italian expression is thus explained, in the translation it is simply rendered as 'appear' and Baretti's subjective appreciation of the Italian phrase as 'ludicrous' is not given any further explanation; and we may only guess that he either disliked it stylistically or he found it redundant.

Idioms add further methodological interest. The English translation of a letter from Anton Maria Salvini included in the collection begins: 'Sir, To propose to me to write about certain matters, is just, as is said, to scratch the grasshopper's belly' (Baretti 1755: 29). This is the literal translation of an Italian expression which means 'to get somebody to talk, to loosen somebody's tongue for them'. The idiom *grattare il corpo alla cicala* had been recorded in the *Vocabolario della Crusca*[6] since its second edition of 1623, where it is explained as *Dire per far dire*, that is, to say something in order to prompt someone else to speak. Baretti's footnote reads:

> *Grattare il corpo alla Cicala*, to scratch the body of the Cicada, an insect, which though often translated by the English *grasshopper*, is of a very different kind. It sits in the trees in the summer, and is very troublesome by continual chirping. As scratching her body is supposed to make her chirp more, this is a proverb used when any man is excited to do that, which he is too fond of doing already. (Baretti 1755: 28)

Thus, Baretti does not offer a mere explanation of the phrase, but a colourful vignette which helps the reader visualize its meaning and therefore memorize it more effectively.

Baretti's 1779 volume *Scelta delle lettere familiari* brings the skill of reading for language purposes to another level, where the linguistic model consists no longer of selected Italian literature from previous ages, as in *Remarks* and *An Introduction*, but of a collection of familiar letters written by the author. This in itself was not new. In 1671 and 1676 the French language teacher and author of French grammars Claude Mauger published his own collection of bilingual letters, *Mauger's Letters. Written upon Several Subjects*. But Baretti's endeavour was remarkably different. In explaining the genesis of this book, Baretti wrote to his Milanese friend Francesco Carcano in 1777 that a bookseller had offered him fifty guineas for a collection of letters by various authors. The sum was tantalizing, but Baretti was at a loss as to where he could find enough *good* letter writers, with the exception of Annibal Caro. Therefore, he decided to make up for the lack of good epistolary writers in Italy with his own letters and other writings of his and attribute some of them to his friends and acquaintances. While the letters purport to be by the best Italian authors, of the eighty-six collected letters, only the first one is actually by Annibale Caro (1507–1566), as it claims to be. The others are Baretti's own writings, presented as being the work of some fictional characters. Luigi Piccioni's examination of the corpus reveals that the letters can be grouped into three categories: first, the letters written by Baretti for this occasion; second, letters written by Baretti to his friends and family of which he had either made or asked for a copy: these two categories make up seventy out of eighty-six; third, letters drawn from his own previously published work, such as *La Frusta letteraria* (1763–64) and *Lettere familiari a' suoi tre fratelli* (1762–63), which amount to fifteen letters in all (Piccioni 1912: 425–30). For example, Letter XXXI in Part I 'Di Pietro Molini ad una dama inglese' [By Pietro Molini to an English Lady] (Baretti 1912: 132–35) reproduced what he had published as 'Lettera di Onesto Lovanglia' [A Letter from Honest Lovanglia] in *La Frusta letteraria*, N. X, 15 February 1764; and Letter XII in Part I 'Di Gianfrancesco Arcasio al Padre Paolo Pacciaudi' [From Gianfrancesco Arcasio to Father Paolo Pacciaudi] (Baretti 1912: 52–57) reproduced a letter Baretti had written to his brothers on his journey back to Italy (Baretti 1941: 171–76). Texts in this third group were revised from their previous published version to fit the new context.

The collection is aimed at 'i miei signori inglesi, studiosi della lingua italiana' [my Englishmen, learners of the Italian tongue] (Baretti 1912: 7) and 'damine che studiano l'italiano' [English young ladies learning Italian], that is, cultivated readers already familiar with the Italian language. As Baretti says in the Preface, in order to help the foreign learner with pronunciation, Baretti shows where the stress falls in most words, as in, for example, *fúria, faccénde, Signór*. But there are no grammatical or lexical notes to aid the foreign reader, except for foreign words, e.g. '"*Posada*", vocabolo spagnuolo che significa "osteria"' ['*Posada*', Spanish word meaning 'inn'] (Baretti 1912: 62); dialect terms; names of people, places and so forth: in other words, contextual references rather than grammar or Italian lexis, as was the case with *An Introduction to the Italian Language*. In addition, the Preface discusses the three different modes of writing according to the social standing of correspondents, which we might now call register, and its sociological impact as it emerges in three different forms of address: the non-egalitarian and semantically 'absurd', as he calls it, third person feminine *Lei*, used when addressing an interlocutor of higher social standing; the friendlier plural *voi* between persons of the same social class; and the more affectionate and familiar *tu* (Baretti 1933: 3-7).

The Role and Purpose of Grammar

Shortly after *An Introduction to the Italian Language*, Baretti began work on a revision of the bilingual dictionary compiled by Ferdinando Altieri in 1726, and he published his own *A Dictionary of the English and Italian Languages* in 1760. His revision was influenced by Samuel Johnson's *Dictionary of English*, which had come out in 1755. Following the example of Johnson, with whom he had struck up an acquaintance, Baretti opened his dictionary with a *Grammatica della Lingua Inglese* for Italian learners of English, and *A Grammar of the Italian Tongue* for English speakers,[7] which was republished independently shortly afterwards (Baretti 1762).[8] Compared to other eighteenth-century grammars, Baretti's is less comprehensive and provides far less information. From the point of view of learning Italian, however, Baretti's grammar is remarkable in trying to achieve a balance between a prescriptive and a descriptive attitude to linguistic norms, particularly in terms of pronunciation, and the need to take grammar rules with a pinch of salt to avoid becoming overwhelmed by a large number of rules that might be dispiriting to learners: 'That I may not frighten my young readers with a multiplicity of puzzling rules' (Baretti 1760: xiii). Thus Baretti's approach to aspects likely to cause special difficulties to learners tends towards synthesis, simplification and the notion of an independent learner relying on her/his own ears as much as on the grammarian's word. For example, on the pronunciation of open versus closed *e* and *o*, he comments:

> I have no infallible rule to give how to find out these differences. A Foreigner must find them out by practice, by asking the natives, or by consulting the Crusca and those other Italian books, in which such distinctions are marked. (Baretti 1760: ii)

Similarly, Baretti criticizes authors of Italian grammars in England — possibly another reference to Veneroni, Altieri and Palermo — for laying down strict rules on the pronunciation of voiced versus unvoiced *s*, which he knew varied considerably from one province of Italy to another and thus did not deem essential to be too particular about:

> Their confidence went even so far, that their rules leave no perplexity behind, and every word in the Italian language may be pronounced by an Englishman, French, Turk, Chinese, or Californian as well as by the Presidents of the Florentine Academies. Yet, those English that will be pleased to follow my advice [...] must fling those magisterial rules into the fire; for it is better not to go on a journey than miss one's way for ever. (Baretti 1760: iv)

In his characteristically exuberant tone, Baretti makes the innovative assertion that one should not have unreasonable expectations of the language learning process, and that rules, unless they are reasonably recognizable and applicable, can and should be disregarded.

On morphological aspects Baretti has a similarly flexible take, and he recommends learners, and indeed teachers, not to spend too long on articles, which would be discouraging and, consequently, fruitless. He derives this experience not so much from linguistic study, but from observation of his pupils' performance and progress:

> I might add a great many more things to this chapter of the articles, but what I have already said I think sufficient for the instruction of an Englishman. I am even afraid of having bewildered him by saying too much; for I have observed that in general the right way to keep a learner backward in his Italian is to keep him long upon these puzzling minutenesses. [...] Let me give this caution to all English beginners, to skim over the most difficult parts of Italian Grammar, especially the articles: to treasure up words and sentences; and to enable themselves to read Italian tolerably. When this is done, let them come back to grammar, and carefully read the whole affair of articles. [...] and I give you my word that they will be pleased at their progress. I could name half a dozen young ladies that in a few months read Metastasio and Tasso by following this method. (Baretti 1760: vii)

Baretti thus advocates a learning method that privileges first the acquisition of basic grammatical knowledge without going into too much detail or focusing on irregularities, followed by learning vocabulary and phrases (presumably through lists included in most language manuals, including Baretti's), which in turn allows the learner to read and enjoy texts. Once a reading ability has been established, though reading 'tolerably' is what is required at this stage, the learner may focus, if she or he so wishes, on more difficult or irregular grammatical problems. Furthermore, we infer that this method has a major advantage, encapsulated in phrases from the above citation: learners 'will be *pleased* at their progress', rather than being 'bewildered' and kept 'backward', thus suggesting the importance of motivation, progress and pleasure in language learning, which are now acknowledged as important factors in language acquisition.[9] Such a method may be regarded as unscientific and not sufficiently rigorous, or, on the other hand, as anticipating modern learner-centred approaches; and it shows how Baretti also accords importance to psychological factors deriving from encouragement, discouragement and steadiness as opposed to swifter progress. Such an approach naturally attracted criticism, as the following excerpt from *The Monthly Review* shows:

> If Mr Baretti's Italian grammar has anything to recommend it [...] it is the brevity with which the principal rules are laid down: But by consulting this brevity too much, he has sometimes left the learner in the dark. In point of pronunciation, particularly, we can by no means recommend this work; nor can we approve of the Author's determination to say nothing on points where he could not lay down any unexceptional rule. [...] Mr Baretti may suppose the students [sic] previous knowledge of grammar; but that is seldom the case, even with adults, and hardly ever with younger pupils; who, for the most part, begin to apply themselves to the study of French or Italian, without any foundation in grammar. (*The Monthly Review* 1762: 74–75)

The reviewer accuses Baretti's grammar of brevity and incompleteness compared to others available at the time which Baretti had explicitly belittled in his Preface to *A Dictionary of the English and Italian Languages*: 'One by *Messieurs* of Port Royal, translated from the French, a second by Altieri, and a third by Veneroni' (Baretti 1760a). It can be assumed that Baretti is here referring to the three most important grammars in eighteenth-century Britain: *A new method of learning the Italian tongue. Translated from the French of Messieurs de Port Royal* (London 1750), a translation of *Nouvelle methode de Messieurs de Port Royal, pour apprendre facilement et en peu de temps la langue italienne* (1696); *A New Italian Grammar* by Ferdinando Altieri (1736, 1753, 1756); and the *Maitre Italien* by the French translator and lexicographer Giovanni Veneroni [Italianized form of Jean Vigneron] (1678), translated into English by Uvedale in 1711 and by Edward Martin in 1729. Baretti does not brush aside grammar at all, but neither does he presuppose previous grammatical knowledge. On the contrary: since foreign language teaching in eighteenth-century England was also aimed at girls, for whom it was not customary to study Latin, as well as for boys of the merchant classes, teaching methods did not rely on a prior knowledge of Latin grammar. With this new learner in mind, Baretti believes that in the early stages a student should not be bogged down by a myriad of rules that would hinder progress. The learner will profit more by returning to finer grammatical details once sufficient vocabulary and phraseology have been acquired through reading. In *La Frusta letteraria*, Baretti fictionalizes the seventeenth-century grammarian Buonmattei, as he argues that vocabulary and phraseology are the foundation of a language, not grammar, and concludes that a foreign learner ought first to acquire bricks and stones (i.e. common words and phrases) in abundance and then, and only then, to study grammar in order to cement them both in place. In this way the learner will see the edifice of his/her language 'alzarsi bello e presto, e star saldo e durevole incontro agli anni' (Baretti 1932a: 270).

Learning Conversation through Dialogues

Baretti's text for speaking the language stems directly from his teaching experience in the family of Henry Thrale, where he had been employed as private tutor to Thrale's children Harry and Hetty since 1773. The *Easy Phraseology for the Use of Young Ladies, Who Intend to Learn the Colloquial Part of the Italian Language* (1775) collects fifty-six bilingual dialogues of varying lengths, preceded by a Preface and a 'Dedicatory Letter to Miss Hetty' in which Baretti sets out the pedagogical principles underlying his view of language learning. It begins by stating the divide between written (literary, cultivated) and spoken (colloquial) language:

> Of every learned and elegant people the language is divided into two parts: the one lax and cursory, used on slight occasions with extemporary negligence; the other rigorous and solemn, the effect of deliberate choice and grammatical accuracy. When books are multiplied and style is cultivated, the colloquial and written diction separate by degrees, till there is one language of the tongue, and another of the pen. (Baretti 1775: 1)

Baretti proceeds by emphasizing the need to acquire an understanding of the language both in writing and in speaking, and calls on a tutor to create opportunities for practising the latter:

> No language can be said to have been learned till both these parts are understood: but to reach the colloquial without the opportunities of familiar conversation, is very difficult. By reading great Authors it cannot be obtained, as books speak but the language of books; and those, who in England intend to learn Italian, are seldom within reach of Italian conversation. (Baretti 1775: 1)

Bilingual dialogues therefore provide a role-play scenario, creating direct exposure to listening and the input for speaking practice through reading and repetition.[10] Baretti claims his dialogues exceed any previous work of this kind by 'copiousness of language, variety of topics, and power of entertainment' (Baretti 1775): in language learning manuals it is a constant topos to claim one's work to be better than the predecessors', but Baretti's dialogues are indeed imaginative, wide-ranging and entertaining, often humorous, while presenting a great variety of vocabulary in context. In principle, they aim at a spoken register, the author wanting 'only to teach Italian; to teach those words and phrases, which are appropriated to trifles; but of which, as life is made of trifles, there is frequent use' (Baretti 1775: iv). These dialogues are based on Baretti's teaching of the ten-year-old Hetty Thrale and some reproduce authentic communicative situations, particularly those 'Between Hetty and the Master', which emulate their tuition context. Others are less realistic and take place between Hetty and other unusual or abstract entities, such as her Birthday or Aurora; then we find dialogues 'Between the Box and the Snuff' (Baretti 1775: 147–51), 'Between the King of Prussia and the Republic of San Marino' (Baretti 1775: 244–52), 'Between Saturn and the Moon' (Baretti 1775: 172–87). These may in fact reproduce children's make-believe games and fantasies, in which objects and animals talk and imagination mingles with reality; and they often make fun of the young pupil Hetty. For example, in Dialogue 8 'a certain Peacock and his two Hens' discuss the latest news in the newspapers. The Peacock tells them that 'a cat has scratched' Miss Hetty, from which a hyperbolic dialogue ensues:

> Cock: The consequence has been, that a hundred hogsheads of blood issued out at her wounds.
> 2nd Hen: That must have looked like a river!
> C: Exactly like the Nile when it overflows all Egypt.

1st Hen: How many wounds has she got?
C: They are innumerable: think of a she-cat's paw!
2nd H: Are the wounds very deep!
C: A surgeon's wife says, that some of them are three leagues deep, particularly one close to her elbow.
2nd H: Alas! where did her blood run?
C: Down into the cellar and has drowned in an instant all the rats that were there.
[...]
2nd H: As I take it, her poor arm must now look like a field newly plowed.
C: You never saw furrows so deep!
[...]
C: The surgeon says, that during twenty years she must eat twenty pounds of roast-beef every morning, to repair her great loss of blood or she never will recover. [...] The surgeon has likewise prescribed another remedy. [...] That she must read a dialogue seven times over every day in the week, except Sunday. (Baretti 1775: 27–30)

Such humour and auto-referentiality underpins Baretti's pedagogical approach, and in one of the dialogues he has a 'certain Gentleman' claim: 'My view is to make her learn Italian whether she will or not; [...] Let her laugh, I say: provided she learns, I don't care whether she laughs at me, or you, or any other body living' (Baretti 1755: 87). The first dialogue also offers a glimpse into Baretti's teaching methodology as the Master and Hetty go over what has been learnt so far. In terms of grammar: conjugation of auxiliaries *essere* and *avere*; memorization of half a dozen regular and a dozen irregular verbs; word formation (of adverbs from adjectives and of verbs from adjectives); articles; adverbs that do not stem from an adjective. As for vocabulary, Hetty has learnt: numbers, the names of trees, quadrupeds, birds, body parts, parts of buildings, utensils, arts, sciences, signs of the zodiac, days, months, fruits, insects, reptiles and feelings. The method advocated is memorization ('imparare a memoria') of vocabulary lists by the tutor, as Hetty says: 'I know the names of almost all the things I see, thanks to your long lists, which look like an auctioneer's catalogues' (Baretti 1775: 2); and 'I learnt by heart, and in two days, that long list of verbs, together with their participles' (Baretti 1775: 8). Basic grammar and vocabulary lay the foundations for progressing to the point of practising 'some dialogues in order to give me an idea of the colloquial part of the Italian language' (Baretti 1775: 4). Memorization of rules and words is achieved through written, rather than oral repetition: 'I will not overburden your memory, and will be satisfied, if you do but copy with diligence and attention' (Baretti 1775: 4). Dialogues provide speaking practice: 'by reading [Italian] loud, I am sure that in a short time you will be able to speak it with some facility' (Baretti 1775: 11). Further observations on grammar points, such as the use of formal you, *Lei*, diminutives, suffixes, on the value of language learning, and the qualities inherent in various languages are interspersed in the dialogues, but overall emphasis is laid on learning by heart a large quantity of vocabulary, almost equivalent to that of the learner's native language: 'In sixty dialogues I am confident I shall introduce ten or twelve thousand words; that is to say, as much, or very near as much, of the Italian tongue as you already know of your own' (Baretti 1775: 10). Just as in *An Introduction to the Italian Language* the corpus of literary texts could be seen as amounting to 'a simple vocabulary', so too are the dialogues in *Easy Phraseology* conceived as a bilingual lexical collection of a very large corpus of words in context. In addition they rely on humour, irony, hyperbole and fantasy to create a memorable, entertaining and hence effective tool for learning new words, practising grammar patterns, reflecting on linguistic matters and on Italian culture as well as on language.

Conclusion

Baretti advocates, implements and experiments with an eclectic learning and teaching method based on extensive reading of the best authors, emphasis on vocabulary acquisition, a flexible approach to grammatical rules, explanation by means of translation, reference to other European languages, memorization, transcribing, reading aloud and repetition. Perhaps what made Baretti such an enthusiastic practitioner of teaching Italian was also his belief in the value of language learning, his own passion and urge to learn foreign languages, his experience as a learner as well as that of a teacher. On his journey from England to Italy through Spain and Portugal in 1760, he described how eagerly and committedly he had embraced his learning of Portuguese:

> I am studying Portuguese like a dragon, and am about it three or four hours every day. A fortnight or three weeks before I left London I did very nearly the same; and all along the road from Plymouth to Falmouth never did cease in my chaise to peep into a Portuguese book. (Baretti 1770: 102–04)

Both as learner and as teacher, such eagerness, dedication and intensity, coupled with direct teaching experience, would inform Baretti's views of language learning, and resurface in a transfigured, humorous autobiographical depiction of the Master featuring in his *Easy Phraseology*: as the young Hetty laments, 'He will have me do nothing else during this month, but eat, drink, and study Italian' (Baretti 1775: 19).

Bibliography

ALTIERI, F. 1726. *Dizionario italiano ed inglese. A Dictionary Italian and English Containing all the Words of the Vocabulary della Crusca And several Hundred more taken from the most Approved Authors; with Proverbs and Familiar Phrases. To which is Prefix'd A Table of the Authors Quoted in this Work. By F. Altieri, Professor of the Italian Tongue in London* (London: William and John Innys)

———. 1756. *A new Italian grammar, which contains a true and easy method for acquiring this language. With many useful remarks, which are not to be found in any other grammar of this kind, by Ferd. Altieri, professor of the Italian Tongue in London, now diligently corrected, and much enlarged, as well for the amusement as utility of all learners* (Leghorn: John Paul Fantechu and Company)

BARETTI, J. 1753. *Remarks on the Italian Language and Writers from Mr Joseph Baretti to an English Gentleman at Turin, written in the year 1751* (London: [n. pub.])

———. 1755. *An Introduction to the Italian Language. Containing Specimens both of Prose and Verse: Selected from [...]. With a literal Translation and Grammatical Notes, for the Use of those who being already acquainted with Grammar, attempt to learn it without a Master.* By Giuseppe Baretti (London: A. Millar)

———. 1757. *The Italian Library. Containing An Account of the Lives and Works of the Most valuable Authors of Italy. With a preface, exhibiting The Changes of the Tuscan Language, from the barbarous Ages to the present Time.* By Giuseppe Baretti (London: A. Millar)

———. 1760A. *A Dictionary of the English and Italian Languages. Improved and augmented with above Ten Thousand Words omitted in the last edition of Altieri. To which is added, An Italian and English Grammar,* 2 vols (London: C. Hitch and L. Hawes et al.), I

———. 1760B. *Dizionario delle lingue italiana ed inglese di Giuseppe Baretti. Più di dieci mila Vocaboli si sono aggiunti che l'Altieri aveva lasciati fuora. Questa edizione contiene una Grammatica della* [sic] *due Lingue*, 2 vols (London: C. Hitch and L. Hawes), II

———. 1762. *A Grammar of the Italian Language, with A copious Praxis of Moral Sentences. To which is added An English Grammar for the Use of the Italians.* By Joseph Baretti (London: C. Hitch and L. Hawes et al.)

———. 1770. *A Journey from London to Genoa through England, Portugal, Spain, and France.* By Joseph Baretti, Secretary for Foreign Correspondence to the Royal Academy of Painting, Sculpture, and Architecture. *In four volumes* (London: T. Davies [...] and L. Davies)

———. 1775. *Easy Phraseology for the Use of Young Ladies, Who Intend to Learn the Colloquial Part of the Italian Language* (London: G. Robinson and T. Cadell)

———. 1779. *Scelta di lettere familiari fatta per uso degli studiosi di lingua Italiana. Da Giuseppe Baretti, Segretario per la Corrispondenza della Reale Britannica Accademia. In due volumi* (London: Da Giovanni Nourse Librajo di Sua Maestà)

———. 1912. *La scelta delle lettere familiari*, ed. by Luigi Piccioni (Bari: Laterza)

———. 1932A. *La Frusta letteraria*, ed. by Luigi Piccioni, 2 vols (Bari: Laterza), I

———. 1932B. *La Frusta letteraria*, ed. by Luigi Piccioni, 2 vols (Bari: Laterza), II

———. 1933. *Prefazioni e polemiche*, ed. by Luigi Piccioni, 2nd edn (Bari: Laterza)

———. 1941. *Lettere familiari a' suoi tre fratelli Filippo, Giovanni e Amedeo*, ed. by Luigi Piccioni (Turin: Società Subalpina Editrice)

COLLISON-MORLEY, L. 1909. *Giuseppe Baretti, an account of his literary friendships and feuds in Italy and in England in the days of Dr. Johnson* (London: John Murray)

GAMBERINI, S. 1970. *Lo studio dell'italiano in Inghilterra nel '500 e nel '600* (Messina–Florence: D'Anna)

GRAF, A. 1911. *L'anglomania e l'influsso inglese in Italia nel secolo XVIII* (Turin: Loerscher)

FAITHFULL, G. 1962. 'Teorie filologiche nell'Italia del primo Seicento con particolare riferimento alla filologia volgare', *Studi di Filologia Italiana*, 20: 145–313

IAMARTINO, G. 1994A. 'Baretti maestro d'italiano in Inghilterra e l'*Easy Phraseology*', in *Il 'passaggiere' italiano: saggi sulle letterature di lingua inglese in onore di Sergio Rossi*, ed. by Renzo S. Crivelli and Luigi Sampietro (Rome: Bulzoni), pp. 383–420

———. 1994B. *Da Thomas a Baretti: i due primi secoli della lessicografia anglo-italiana* (Milan: ISU — Università Cattolica)

LAWRENCE, J. 2011 [2005]. *'Who the devil taught thee so much Italian?' Italian Language Learning and Literary Imitation in Early Modern England* (Manchester; New York: Manchester University Press)

LEPSCHY, G. 1978. 'La pronuncia dell'italiano', in G. Lepschy, *Saggi di linguistica italiana* (Bologna: Il Mulino), pp. 95–100

LUBBERS-VAN DER BRUGGE, C. J. M. 1951. *Johnson and Baretti: Some Aspects of Eighteenth-Century Literary Life in England and Italy* (Gröningen: Wolters)

MARTINO, M. G. 2009. 'L'interesse glottodidattico di Giuseppe Baretti durante gli anni londinesi', *Studi di Glottodidattica*, 3: 44–59

MATARRESE, T. 1993. *Il Settecento* (Bologna: Il Mulino)

MENGALDO, P. V. 2012. *Attraverso la prosa italiana: analisi di testi esemplari* (Rome: Carocci)
Motivation and Second Language Acquisition. 2001. Ed. by Z. Dörnyei and R. Schmidt (University of Hawai'i: Second Language Teaching & Curriculum Centre)
NIBBI, A. 1968. 'Il dizionario Italiano–Inglese e Inglese–Italiano di Giuseppe Baretti', *Lingua Nostra*, 29: 40–46
O'CONNOR, D. 1990. *A History of Italian and English Bilingual Dictionaries* (Florence: Olschki)
PEDRIALI, F. 1993. 'Una fama da non recuperare? Baretti e la *Grammatica della lingua inglese* (1760)', *The Italianist*, 13: 97–138
PICCIONI, L. 1912. 'Nota', in Giuseppe Baretti, *La scelta delle lettere familiari*, ed. by L. Piccioni (Bari: Laterza), pp. 423–34
PIZZOLI, L. 2004. *Le grammatiche di italiano per inglesi (1550–1776): un'analisi linguistica* (Florence: Accademia della Crusca)
RICHARDSON, B. 2010. '"Varie maniere di parlare": Aspects of Learning Italian in Renaissance Italy and Britain', in *Ciò che potea la lingua nostra: Lectures and Essays in Memory of Clara Florio Cooper*, ed. by V. De Gasperin (= *The Italianist*, Special Supplement, 30): 78–94
ROSSI, S. 1969. *Ricerche sull'umanesimo e sul Rinascimento in Inghilterra* (Milan: Vita e Pensiero)
SAVOIA, F. 2010. *Fra letterati e galantuomini: notizie e inediti del primo Baretti inglese* (Firenze: Società Editrice Fiorentina)
SWEET, R. 2012. *Cities and the Grand Tour: The British in Italy, c. 1690–1820* (Cambridge: Cambridge University Press)
VICENTINI, A. 2015 [2012]. *Anglomanie settecentesche: le prime grammatiche d'inglese per italiani* (Milan: Mimesis)
The Monthly Review, or Literary Journal. 1763. Vol. 27: 74–75
YATES, F. A. 1934. *John Florio: The Life of an Italian in Shakespeare's England* (Cambridge: Cambridge University Press)

Notes to Chapter 10

1. On Baretti in England, see Collison–Morley (1909); Lubbers-Van Der Brugge (1951); Savoia (2010).
2. Baretti seems to confuse the thirteenth century with the Italian *Trecento*, i.e. the fourteenth century, or be mistaken as to the dates of Boccaccio's life, when he claims that Boccaccio 'lived towards the end of the thirteenth century', whereas Boccaccio lived between 1313 and 1375 and his major work, the *Decameron*, is dated between 1349 and 1353.
3. See Matarrese 1993: 21-40.
4. For examples of his stylistic and linguistic criticism, see Baretti, *La Frusta letteraria*, no. I, 1 October 1763 (repr. in 1932a: 9–13); n° III, 1 November 1763 (repr. in 1932a: 380–81); n° IV, 15 November 1763 (repr. in 1932a: 85–102).
5. On the ways in which Italian grammar manuals dealt with the thorny issue of pronunciation rules, see Pizzoli 2004: 175-272.
6. The *Vocabolario della Crusca* was the monumental lexicographical work of the Accademia della Crusca (literally, The Bran Academy), which began informal gatherings between the 1570s and 1580s and was formally established with the aim of separating the good language (flour) from the bad language (bran). It followed the model of literary Florentine vernacular of fourteenth-century authors, as advocated by Pietro Bembo and later Lionardo Salviati. The first edition of the vocabulary appeared in Venice in 1612. The history and current activities of the Accademia can be seen at <http://www.accademiadellacrusca.it>.
7. On Baretti's *Grammatica della Lingua Inglese*, see Pedriali (1993); and on Baretti's and other eighteenth-century grammars of English in Italy, see Vicentini (2015).

8. On Baretti's *Dictionary*, see Nibbi (1968) and Iamartino (1994b). For a detailed analysis of grammars of Italian in England, including Baretti's, see Pizzoli (2004).
9. On the role of motivation, see for example Dörnyei and Schmidt 2001.
10. On dialogues in Italian language learning, see Gamberini 1970: 76-94; Pizzoli 2004: 65-77; Richardson 2010: 85-89; Rossi 1969: 110-28. On Baretti's *Easy Phraseology*, see Iamartino (1994a); Martino (2009).

CHAPTER 11

Londres et les britanniques dans l'ancienne grammaticographie du Portugais Langue Étrangère (XVIIe–XIXe siècles)

Maria do Céu Fonseca

When we analyse the corpus of grammars of Portuguese as a foreign language (between the seventeenth and nineteenth centuries) it becomes quite clear that London was an editorial capital of the Portuguese grammatical world and the British people (merchants, translators, men of letters, noblemen and noblewomen, students) a prime target group. As far as it is possible to know, the first manual of Portuguese as a foreign language was printed in London on the occasion of the marriage of Catherine of Bragança to Charles II of England: *A Portuguez Grammar: or. Rules shewing the True and Perfect way to learn the said language* (La Mollière, 1662), aimed at serving 'two sorts of Persons in England: to people of Traffique and Commerce [...] And to Persons of the Court' (La Mollière 1662: A$_2^v$). The production and circulation of grammars of Portuguese as a foreign language, written in English and printed in London, increased during the eighteenth and nineteenth centuries for commercial, cultural and political reasons. From there, grammars by Jacob Castro (1731), António Vieira (1786), Richard Woodhouse (1815), Luís Francisco Midosi (1832), Alfred Elwes (1876), Charles Henry Wall (1882) and others were commercialized and exported. The present article analyses this Portuguese–British grammatical movement, particularly regarding the quantity of this printed material and its impact. It also gives a brief overview of the ancient grammars of Portuguese as a foreign language and their connection to others European 'vulgar' languages, aiming to contribute to the study of the history of linguistic thought.

Portugais Langue Étrangère (PLE)

La tradition de grammaires de langues vivantes étrangères s'insère dans un mouvement de continuité de ce que Sylvain Auroux appela le '"processus massif de grammatisation" à partir de la Renaissance' des langues du monde (Auroux 1992: 11-13), qu'elles soient européennes, qu'elles soient extra-européennes (langues orientales, africaines et amérindiennes, étrangères au paradigme gréco-latin et même à la famille indo-européenne). Selon le même auteur, 'le besoin d'*apprentissage d'une langue étrangère* [...] est potentiellement la première cause de grammatisation' (Auroux 1992: 21), les motifs qui provoquent un tel besoin étant variés et chronologiquement différenciés.

Des situations comme 'travels and pilgrimages', 'military and political purpose' et 'missionary activity' (Bischoff 1961: 217, 221, 222) sont déjà retenues comme pertinentes dans l'étude médiévale des langues étrangères. Dans le même cadre de la grammaire de la Renaissance et l'après-renaissance, l'importance de telles situations est maintenue. En matière de 'missionary activity', les domaines des portugais furent, dès le début du XVIe siècle, l'Afrique, l'Asie et le Brésil, territoires où, au cours du siècle, la mise en règles des appelées langues exotiques (Salmon 1985: 50) se faisait en portugais pour aider 'the advanced learners who wanted to improve their knowledge of the native languages, or for the beginners who arrived from Europe' (Zwartjes 2011: 11). Et en supplément, ces grammaires missionnaires portugaises (cf. Zwartjes 2011: 1), décrites selon le modèle de la grammaire latine (indépendamment du type de langue), étaient un outil d'apprentissage de la langue vulgaire européenne efficace 'à l'usage des étrangers'. Les deux premiers grammairiens du portugais — João de Barros (1496-1570) et Fernão de Oliveira (1507-1581) — ont aussi participé à ce programme d'enseignement de leur langue maternelle dans les territoires conquis, au moment où ils initièrent la codification grammaticale du portugais et l'établissement de sa norme.[1]

En plus de l'activité missionnaire, nous pouvons signaler qu'en Angleterre, au XVIIe siècle, 'Portuguese was useful for the purposes of exploration and commerce in "the *Eastern* and *South-west* Parts of the World"', comme le soutient Salmon (1985: 50), citant l'auteur semi-anonyme A. J. (1701) de notre corpus (voir ci-dessous). D'autres auteurs de la même période s'appuient sur cet argument des relations commerciales avec l'Orient (ou l'Asie)[2] et l'Occident (ou le Brésil); c'est le cas du portugais António Vieira[3] dans la préface de sa populaire *A New Portuguese Grammar in four parts* (Londres, 1768): 'As the usefulness of the Portuguese language is so well known to all English merchants, who carry on a general trade with the different parts of the known world' (Vieira 1768: Preface).

Mais il semble consensuel qu'à l'ère de l'après-renaissance, ou dès la fin du XVIe siècle selon Suso López (2009: 116), s'ajoutent de nouveaux intérêts liés à des fins académiques et d'enrichissement intellectuel. Ce n'est certes pas un hasard au regard de ces fins académiques si le public cible étudiant fut explicitement mentionné dans des textes préambulaires de plusieurs grammaires de PLE.[4] Les traducteurs, les poètes, les nobles, les grammairiens, les philosophes (Suso López 2009: 116-17) constituent des lecteurs lettrés, un public érudit (Schäfer-Prieß 2012: 127), compétents dans le domaine de la langue maternelle et critiques vis-à-vis de la description grammaticale des langues étrangères, une fois conscients d'une grammaire contrastive ou, au moins, plus sensibles aux comparaisons linguistiques L1/L2 (cf. Thomas 2004: 92). Donc, comme le soutient Thomas (2004: 76), un nouveau regard sur l'étude de L2, qui est traversé par les idées d'universalité et de rationalisme de la grammaire universelle du XVIIe siècle.

La perspective qui ici nous intéresse tout particulièrement n'est pas vraiment celle de la linguistique appliquée à l'enseignement des langues étrangères, matière dont l'histoire, les méthodes d'apprentissage, les matériels didactiques (grammaires, manuels scolaires, guides de conversation) utilisés dans une période déterminée, furent déjà fort bien étudiées par des auteurs comme Howatt (1984), pour l'anglais, Sánchez Pérez (1992), pour l'espagnol, Glück (2002, 2013), pour l'allemand. Nous étudions de notre côté l'enseignement grammatical d'une autre langue vernaculaire européenne — le portugais — professé au service d'étudiants étrangers, donc en-dehors de la communauté de ceux qui l'utilisent comme langue maternelle. Comme l'ont fait ces auteurs plus récemment et plus brièvement (cf. McLelland and Smith 2014), nous visons plutôt le domaine de l'histoire des idées linguistiques, c'est-à-dire, des aspects historiographiques de l'enseignement grammatical du portugais aux non natifs de cette langue, à supposer que les grammaires de langues étrangères constituent un chapitre de l'histoire de la connaissance linguistique. Plus spécifiquement, nous visons ici le contexte de PLE restreint en presque totalité à l'Angleterre et avec un essor particulier en ce qui concerne la grammaticographie, entre 1662 (moment *a quo* de la publication des premiers manuels de PLE) et 1898 (*terminus ad quem* de la dernière publication du XIXe siècle). Quel fut le rôle de l'Angleterre dans l'édition et la mise en circulation d'imprimés grammaticaux de PLE? Dans une étude antérieure concernant ces œuvres dans le contexte anglophone (Fonseca, Marçalo and Silva 2012: 21-55), nous nous étions déjà aperçu que leur présence dans le panorama de l'édition à Londres était importante. Que dire de cette tradition portugaise par rapport à l'espagnol (dans l'espace ibérique) et à l'histoire d'autres langues (en tant que langues étrangères)? Quels présupposés épistémologiques, cadres théoriques et motivations comporte-t-elle? Dans le travail référé ci-dessus (Fonseca, Marçalo and Silva 2012), nous avons remarqué que ces grammaires étaient surtout conçues comme un ensemble de règles utiles aux étrangers qui désiraient apprendre la langue. En ce sens, plus que des grammaires spéculatives et théoriques, elles sont en majorité de nature pratique et normative, adéquates à l'approche communicative. Mais ces deux perspectives grammaticales — celle spéculative et théorique *vs* celle pratique et pédagogique — se trouvent au moment même de la conception de la grammaire, ayant toujours un soutien doctrinaire, pour plus petit que soit le tableau théorique des définitions et du métalangage grammatical. Des grammaires qui s'annonçaient dès le titre comme 'raisonnée'[5] ou 'philosophical' (cf. Midosi 1832) nous donnent de bonnes raisons pour invoquer Port-Royal et le modèle des grammaires générales, universelles et philosophiques du XVIIe, qui visaient simultanément les règles particulières de chaque langue et les principes généraux, valables pour toutes les langues, sans qu'il y ait de conflit entre ces deux tendances: 'the genius of languages serves to explain phonetic, morphological and semantic peculiarities, and this is possible not *in spite of* but *because of* their underlying unity' (Formigari 1988: 49).

Londres: capitale éditoriale des publications de Portugais Langue Étrangère

C'est à partir du mouvement de la Renaissance que l'enseignement hégémonique du latin cède le pas à la défense et à l'illustration des langues vulgaires et vivantes, en simultané avec la diffusion de ces mêmes vernaculaires dans la perspective des langues étrangères. Dans l'espace linguistique roman, le français et l'espagnol sont des cas paradigmatiques. D'un côté, '[t]he earliest grammars of French were written in English' (Percival 1975: 249) et ce fut en Angleterre que, depuis environ 1400, naquit la grammaire française dirigée à des étrangers (Kukenheim 1962: 19).[6] Quant à l'espagnol, d'un autre côté, l'œuvre de référence dans le domaine reste la *Gramática de la lengua castellana* (1492) de Antonio de Nebrija, dont le Livre V — 'De las introduciones de la lengua castellana para los que de estraña lengua querrán deprender' — s'adresse, ne l'oublions pas, à l'usage des étrangers (cf. Gómez Asencio 2006: 117-42), même s'il a eu très peu de succès (Aquilino Sánchez 2014: 63). Cela signifie que la promotion des vernaculaires nationaux (à savoir, leur règlementation et leur normalisation linguistiques) provoqua la curiosité et l'intérêt linguistiques pour des idiomes non maternels, incitant par conséquent le développement de la production éditoriale européenne de grammaires et de manuels orientés pour l'enseignement/l'apprentissage de langues étrangères.

Voyons maintenant le cas de la langue portugaise dont le processus de 'grammatisation' (Aurox 1992: 28) commença également au XVIe siècle, accompagnant le contexte linguistique européen.[7] Les grammaires de Fernão de Oliveira et João de Barros (cf. note 1 ci-dessus), congénères de la grammaire de Nebrija et de *Le tretté de la grammère françoèze* (1550) de Louis Meigret, donné comme première grammaire du français, les suivent dans le mouvement d'illustration et de codification des langues vulgaires de la Renaissance; et dans la seconde moitié du siècle, la codification du portugais passe par la fixation de son orthographe avec des textes normatifs[8] d'une écriture de base étymologique (non sans une certaine controverse entre l'orthographe étymologique et l'orthographe phonétique). La normalisation du portugais, par action de grammairiens de la Renaissance, et la priorité de l'enseignement grammatical de la langue maternelle marquent cependant le discours linguistique portugais de l'époque. Bien que ces textes de caractère normatif soient des instruments pédagogiques au service de l'activité missionnaire en dehors de l'Europe, nous ne pouvons parler de façon rigoureuse de matériels linguistiques de PLE qu'à partir de la seconde moitié du XVIIe siècle.

Ainsi, dans le contexte ibérique, l'enseignement grammatical du PLE a une tradition un tant soit peu modeste et tardive en comparaison avec celle de la langue castillane. Selon ce qu'il est possible de savoir, cette tradition portugaise remonte à 1662 et naquit, à la similitude de la grammaire française pour étrangers, en Angleterre, plus précisément à Londres. Au-delà de cette origine, la ville de Londres se détache dans la construction et l'évolution de cette tradition grammaticale jusqu'à la fin du XIXe siècle, compte tenu du nombre d'imprimés portugais ici produits en anglais par des auteurs de nationalité britannique, française et portugaise (pas toujours notables en matières d'études philologiques).

Analysant le corpus de grammaires de PLE jusqu'alors recensé (depuis la seconde moitié du XVIIe siècle jusqu'à la fin du XIXe siècle), écrites en anglais, en français, en espagnol et en italien,[9] nous constatons que Londres fut la capitale éditoriale de la littérature grammaticale portugaise et les britanniques (étudiants et commerçants, comme nous l'avons exposé ci-dessus) un public cible privilégié. Entre 1662 et 1898 furent publiés à Londres, en premières éditions, quatorze titres sur la grammaire portugaise, configurant une moyenne nettement supérieure à celle du reste de la publication dans d'autres endroits. Voyons le Graphique 1 concernant le nombre et les endroits de la production éditoriale de grammaires de PLE:

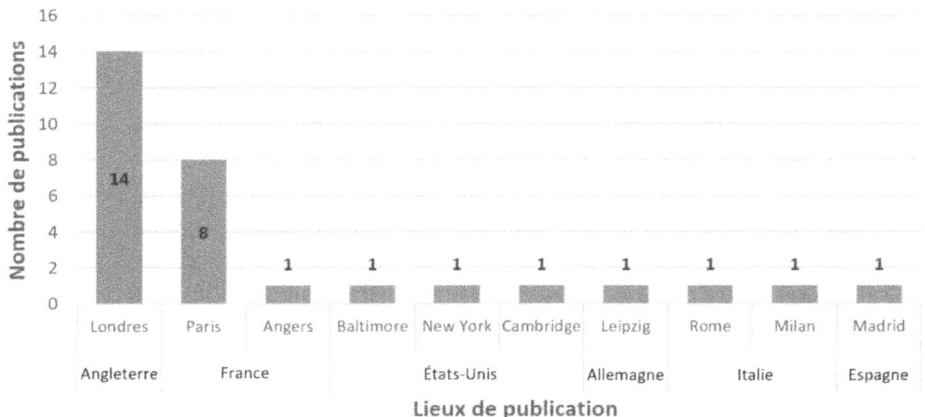

Graphique 1: Production éditoriale de grammaires de PLE (1662-1898)[10]

Londres et Paris, qui occupent des positions de pointe, se spécialisèrent sur un marché éditorial de PLE, soit en anglais, soit en français, respectivement, de manière à ce que, en règle générale, le lieu de publication soit associé aux locuteurs natifs et à la langue de rédaction de la grammaire (élément qui influence la qualité de l'*input* linguistique (cf. Gómez Asencio 2006: 124)). Il y a cependant des exceptions à cette règle générale. À Leipzig est publiée la grammaire rédigée en français *Nouvelle méthode pratique et facile pour apprendre la langue portugaise composée d'après les principes de F. Ahn* (1883), du philologue portugais Francisco de Sales Lencastre (1839-1916), qui revendique une filiation à la méthode pédagogique de l'allemand Franz Ahn. Une autre exception est la *Gramatica Portoghese ad uso d egl' Italiani per apprendere la lingua portoghese per mezzo dell'a Italiana* (Paris, 1869), de Vittore Felicissimo Francesco Nabantino, qui est ici comptabilisée parmi les publications de Paris. La lecture de ce Graphique 1 montre que, si l'Angleterre est en tête en termes de nombres de publication, l'anglais domine également cette production avec dix-sept titres grammaticaux (sur l'espace anglo-américain[11]), contre neuf en français (publications à Paris, Angers et Leipzig). Nous enregistrons encore, sur le graphique, la pénurie de matériels didactiques dirigés à un public cible espagnol (cf. Ponce de León 2009: 185-96)[12] et la chronologie tardive des deux premières grammaires éditées en Italie,[13] pays dont la langue et la culture furent, depuis la Renaissance, source d'auteurs portugais.

En ce qui concerne l'Angleterre, le nombre de publications augmente considérablement au long du XVIIIe et XIXe siècle, si nous comptabilisons également les rééditions et réimpressions londoniennes,[14] ce qui prouve l'intérêt porté par le public lecteur, au-delà du développement du marché éditorial. Les valeurs de ces comptages, concernant uniquement les grammaires (excluant, par conséquent, les dictionnaires et les manuels d'exercices[15]), mettent en relief l'importance du rôle de la capitale anglaise dans la production et la circulation d'imprimés grammaticaux portugais; et, dans ce commerce du livre portugais, qui inclut la diffusion, la distribution, la consommation et la lecture, s'engagèrent aussi des éditeurs, des imprimeurs et des libraires britanniques, dont le rôle fut important en ce qui concerne les transferts culturels entre l'Angleterre et le Portugal. Cette conjoncture éditoriale n'eut pas un caractère occasionnel. Au contraire, elle répond à un tableau historique d'alliances politiques et de relations commerciales anglo-portugaises qui favorisa le rapprochement linguistique et par conséquent sa production éditoriale, surtout à partir de la seconde moitié du XVIIe siècle.

Des circonstances politiques font de 1662 une année-clef. Selon Taylor (2002: 186), '[t]he matrimonial alliance between Charles II and Catherine of Braganza was the occasion for what may well be the first piece of Portuguese printing in London', thèse que l'auteur défend se référant à une publication littéraire datée de 1663. La même affirmation de Taylor vaut pour deux manuels grammaticaux de PLE — les premiers connus, d'après ce que nous savons — lesquels auraient été une motivation politique dans le cadre d'alliances matrimoniales entre l'Angleterre et la *casa de Bragança* de Portugal.[16] Le français Monsieur de La Mollière et le britannique James Howell publièrent à Londres deux travaux pour célébrer le mariage royal entre Charles II d'Angleterre et l'infante portugaise Catarina de Bragança. Selon le même raisonnement de Taylor, nous comprenons que ce sont ces deux travaux qui inaugurent en Angleterre les études grammaticales du portugais:

   1662   La Mollière. *A Portuguez Grammar: or Rules shewing the True and Perfect way to learn the said language* (London: Printed by D. Maxwel)

   1662   Howell, James. *A New English Grammar prescribing as certain rules as the languages will bear, for forreners to learn English: Ther is also another grammar of the Spanish or Castilian toung, with some special remarks upon the Portuguese Dialect, &c.* (London: Printed for T. Williams, H. Brome, and H. Marsh).

Le manuel trilingue de La Mollière (portugais, anglais et français, en trois colonnes), qui se destine à 'two sorts of Persons in England: To people of Traffique and Commerce [...] And to Persons of the Court', présente un texte préambulaire avec dédicatoire au roi Charles II (1662: A$_2^{r-v}$) et quelques allusions au marriage royal, répétées d'ailleurs à un autre moment de l'œuvre (La Mollière 1661: 33). Il s'agit d'un petit manuel didactique (pas d'une grammaire) pour débutants, une espèce de 'conversation manual' (Gallagher 2014: 26-27)[17] ou de miscellanées grammaticales sur les rudiments d'orthographe/phonétique, morphologie et lexique, présentés sous forme de dialogue entre le maître et l'étudiant, à la manière de la tradition médiévale de l'enseignement du latin. Nous le savons, il s'agit d'une technique surtout orale qui, à travers une méthode de questions/réponses successives, permet l'exposition d'une nomenclature grammaticale et sa description, ayant parfois recours aux tableaux traditionnels, aux schémas et aux paradigmes de déclinaisons et de conjugaisons. A titre d'exemple, voyons un extrait de l'œuvre de La Mollière (1662: 10-11), qui introduit la matière morphologique, en commençant par l'étude de la déclinaison nominale (avec la variation en genre, nombre et cas):

S. Ensine me agora, o modo que eu he de ter, por bem declinar os Nomes, e conjugar os verbos M. [...] os Nomes saõ de dos Generos, o Masculino, e o Femenino. Examplo. hum Mosso, he Masculino. huma Moça, he Femenino. o banco, he Masculino. a Ginella, he Feminino. Comessamos entaó a declinar os Nomes [...].	S. *Teach me now the way that I must hold for to decline well the Nouns, and conjugate the Verbs.* M. [...] *the Nouns are of two Genders, the Masculine, and the Feminine.* *Example* hum Mosso, *one Boy, is a Masculine.* huma Moça, *one Maid, is a Feminine.* o Banco, *the Forme, is a Masculine.* a Ginella, *the window, is a Feminine* *Let us then begin to decline the Nouns* [...].	S. Enseignez moy maintenant le moyen que je dois tenir, pour bien decliner les Noms, & conjuger les Verbs. M. [...] les noms sont de deux Genres, le Masculin, & le Feminin. Example. un Garçon, est Masculin. une Fille, est Feminin. le Banc, est Masculin. la Fenestre, est Feminin. Commençons donc a decliner les Noms [...].

La description morphologique, au-delà d'être élémentaire, n'est pas toujours rigoureuse, comme l'a déjà bien souligné Ponce de León (2012: 66-67) à propos de la réduction du système verbal du portugais présenté par La Mollière, qui confesse l'exercice de simplification grammaticale (1662: 16), de la même manière que d'autres auteurs le font. Nous pourrions rajouter, encore dans le cadre de la description élémentaire, le silence en matière des classes de mots invariables (comme les prépositions et les conjonctions, paradigmes de délimitation plus complexe), le manque de systématisation concernant les unités grammaticales comme les pronoms, l'absence de normes basiques de morphosyntaxe au niveau de phénomènes de concordance et de régime. L'œuvre de La Mollière vaut ainsi non pas tant pour les informations grammaticales mais pour le mérite d'avoir été le premier abordage du portugais selon la perspective de langue étrangère.

Bien que le manuel soit basique, son importance surélève cependant l'œuvre du britannique James Howell, dont la contribution pour l'historiographie de PLE se restreint à quelques observations contrastives entre les deux langues romanes (le portugais et l'espagnol). Dédié aussi à Catarina de Bragança, la nouvelle reine d'Angleterre, le travail de Howell est effectivement constitué par deux grammaires juxtaposées ayant une pagination indépendante (une grammaire de l'anglais et une autre de l'espagnol), suivies, sous forme d'opuscule, d'observations phonétiques et lexicales sur le portugais, vu comme dialecte ou variété du castellan:[18] 'Of the Portuguese language, or sub-dialect, &c.' (1662: [81]-84) et 'A short dictionary or, catalog of such Portuges words that have no affinity with the Spanish' (1662: [85]-95). En vertu des affinités linguistiques entre le portugais et l'espagnol, l'auteur se concentre sur des aspects phonético-phonologiques distinctifs, qui gagnent en pertinence dans le cadre de l'apprentissage des deux langues étrangères. Les différences signalées se situent uniquement au niveau synchronique, sans considérations diachroniques qui, dans le cas de l'exemple transcrit ensuite (Howell

1662: 82), aideraient à comprendre le phénomène de la palatalisation des groupes latins *cl-*, *fl-* et *pl-* en *ll-* (en espagnol) et en *ch-* (en portugais). Ainsi, présentons les cas de: LAT. *clamare* > ESP. *llamar*; PORT. *chamar*; LAT. *flamma* > ESP. *llama*; PORT. *chama*; LAT. *pluvia* > ESP. *lluvia*; PORT. *Chuva*:

> when *ll* beginns a word in *Spanish* the Portuguès turns them to *ch*; As, *Llamar* to call *chamar*; *Llama* a flame, *chama*; *Llaga* a wound, *chaga*; *Lleno* full, *Cheo* wherby [sic] the *n*. alloo is lost; *Luna* the Moon, *lue*: *Llegar allegar* to com or approach, *chegar achegar*; *Llave* a key, *chiave*; *Lloro* weeping, *choro*: *Luvia* [sic] Rain, *chuva*.

L'enseignement ou, du moins, la divulgation du portugais en Angleterre, visé directement ou indirectement par l'ensemble des deux ouvrages ci-dessus, est alors déclenché par la circonstance politique du Portugal recourant à une alliance matrimoniale luso-britannique à un moment de restauration de son indépendance, après soixante ans d'union politique avec le royaume d'Espagne (1580-1640).

Le XVIIIe siècle

Il paraît que le XVIIIe siècle aurait contribué à promouvoir ce rapprochement linguistique, que ce soit en continuité des relations politiques et commerciales anglo-portugaises, que ce soit par les nouvelles valeurs culturelles associées au mouvement européen de l'Illustration. Si Caravolas note que 'Le portugais reste au XVIIIe siècle une langue peu étudiée par les Anglais' (2000: 39), c'est pour souligner en termes relatifs, nous le croyons, l'extraordinaire production grammaticale française au siècle des Lumières.

En accord avec le corpus recensé, trois grammaires de PLE furent publiées à Londres pendant cette période, puis successivement rééditées / réimprimées jusqu'à la fin du siècle (et même au-delà de celui-ci, c'est le cas de la grammaire d'António Vieira):

1ère édition	Rééditions / réimpressions (XVIIIe siècle)	
1701	1702[19]	A.J. *A Compleat Account of the Portugueze Language. Being a Copious Dictionary of English with Portugueze, and Portugueze with English. Together With an Easie and Unerring Method of its Ponunciation, by a distinguishing Accent, and a Compendium of all the necessary Rules of Construction and Orthography digested into a Grammatical Form* (London: Printed by R. Janeway)
1731	1751, 1759, 1767, 1770	Castro, J[acob]. *Grammatica Anglo-Lusitanica & Lusitano-Anglica: or, a new grammar English and Portuguese and Portuguese and English* (London: Printed for W. Meadows)
1768	1777, 1782 1794	Vieira, António. *A New Portuguese Grammar in four parts* (London: Printed for J. Nourse)

TABLEAU 1: Publications londoniennes de grammaires de PLE (XVIIIe siècle)

L'ensemble dictionnaristique-grammatical intitulé *A Compleat Account* (Londres, 1701) fut déjà étudié par Kemmler quant à son semi-anonymat,[20] considérant l'importance de l'œuvre 'pour l'historiographie de la linguistique anglo-portugaise'[21] (Kemmler 2012: 214). De cette œuvre sera faite une réédition bilingue (anglais et portugais), en 1702, seulement de la grammaire, ayant 'beaucoup de matériel qui serait utilisé dans l'intégrité par des grammaires aussi bien de portugais que d'anglais publiées plus tard, ce qui était facilité par la nature bilingue des textes présentés' (Torre 1988: 43).[22]

Le XVIIIe siècle sera encore marqué par les éditions variées des œuvres de Jacob Castro et d'António Vieira, deux portugais émigrés en Angleterre et actifs promoteurs de l'enseignement du PLE, fait confirmé par la répercussion de leurs grammaires dans toute la grammaticographie postérieure du genre. Dans le cadre de l'enseignement du portugais aussi bien aux Etats-Unis qu'en France et Angleterre, la grammaire de Vieira, ou est citée comme titre de référence bibliographique,[23] ou est mentionnée comme source directe,[24] ou est traduite en français,[25] ou encore est adaptée pour des manuels d'exercices pratiques.[26] La grammaire de J. Castro, 'a double-grammar published in London in 1731' (Howatt 1984: 66), est nommée par Howatt à propos du statut du Portugal 'as "our oldest ally"'; un allié dans les relations politiques et commerciales, négociées au travers d'accords qui impliquaient la circulation des biens, des personnes et des idées. Un des plus célèbres de ces accords, signé au début du XVIIIe siècle, fut le traité de Methuen (1703), qui, permettant le libre-échange des anglais au Portugal, en échange de protection, aura fonctionné comme catalyseur du processus de grammaticalisation bilingue (en portugais et en anglais) afin de servir l'un et l'autre les publics. La préface 'To the reader' de la grammaire bilingue de Castro est une défense des plus-values de l'apprentissage de la langue portugaise, en commençant par son 'great use in Commerce' (Castro 1751: [iii]). La popularité et la divulgation des deux grammaires de J. Castro et A. Vieira sont aussi la conséquence de la conjoncture du mouvement européen de l'Illuminisme, duquel ces auteurs, ainsi que plusieurs portugais, furent les porte-paroles directs; leurs séjours prolongés en Angleterre (et en France, en Italie, en Espagne) leur permirent d'être perceptibles *in loco* à d'autres réalités culturelles et de les comparer avec la situation du Portugal. Nous appelons ces intellectuels portugais des auteurs 'éclairés' (*estrangeirados*), dans le sens où, étant protagonistes de la modernisation culturelle européenne, ils accélérèrent le rythme des mentalités dans l'ambiance intellectuelle de leur pays.

Il est nécessaire de souligner que, du point de vue macrostructural (Swiggers 2006: 169-70), l'organisation des matières grammaticales dans ces œuvres du XVIIIe siècle explique aussi sa bonne réceptivité. La structure canonique de la division de la grammaire en parties (orthographe / prosodie, étymologie, syntaxe) se répercute dans la façon dont les auteurs de grammaires de PLE organisèrent les matières: une section grapho-phonétique, une autre normalement large de traitement des classes de mots et une troisième de nature textuelle qui aborde l'*oratio* ou la construction de la phrase, l'étude syntactique plus ou moins systématisée des parties de la phrase. Commun à pratiquement toutes les grammaires, c'est l'existence d'une section

Auteurs	Textes préambulaires	Partie I	Partie II	Partie III	Partie IV	Appendices
António Vieira, 1768	• To Robert Orme, Esq. • Preface (pp. v-vi)	• Part I. Of the Portuguese Alphabet; Of the Manner of Pronouncing the Portuguese Letters; Of the Articles; Of the Nouns; Of Pronouns; Of Verbs; Of the Participles; Of the Adverbs; Of the Prepositions; Of the Conjunctions; Interjective Particles; Some abbreviations used in the Portuguese Language (chaps. I-VIII) (pp. 1-21)	• Part II. Of the Division of Syntax • Of the Syntax of Articles • Of the Syntax of Nouns; and first, of the Substantives • Of the Syntax of Adjectives • Of the Syntax of Pronouns • Of the Syntax of Verbs (...) (Chaps. I-IX) (pp. 122-221)	• Part III. The most elegant phrases of the Portuguese Language (pp. 222-48) • A vocabulary of words most used in Discourse (pp. 253-310) • Collecçaõ de Adagios Portuguezes / A collection of Portuguese Proverbs (pp. 310-19) • Diálogos Familiares / Familiar Dialogues (pp. 320-35)	• Part IV. Containing several useful and entertaining passages, whereof the greatest Part is collected from the best Portuguese writers, such as Andrade, Barros, Camoens, Lobo, &c. (pp. 336-76)	

TABLEAU 2: Macrostructure des grammaires (A.J., Castro et Vieira)

Auteurs	Textes préambulaires	Partie I	Partie II	Partie III	Partie IV	Appendices
A.J., 1701		• The first Letter A is pronounced with a full and open Mouth, as in the word Aqua or Agua, water [...] (fól. 200ʳ)	• As for the Nouns, as in all our modern Languages, so in this the first and common Division is into Substantive and Adjective [...] (fols 200ʳ-214ʳ)	• The next thing of use will be to take notice of the Importance is due of the Accent and Mode of Syntax, or the Composition of Pronunciation of Words [...] Speech, as is ordinary in all Languages [...] (fols 214ʳ-214ᵛ)	• Prosodia. The last thing of use of the forms to be of writing, commonly used in correspondence The last thing among them in of use to be the following mentioned in the manner Portugueze is (fols 219ʳ-224ʳ) concerning its Orthography [...] (fols 214ᵛ-218ᵛ)	• An Appendix
J[acob] Castro, 1731	• To the Reader • Advertisement (pp. iii-x)	• Of the Letters, and their Pronunciation (Chap. I) (pp. 1-9)	• Of the Parts of Speech (Chap. III) "The Portuguese, as well as the Latins, have Eight Parts of Speech [...] Noun, Pronoun, Verb, Participle, Preposition, Adverb, Conjunction, and Interjection" (pp. 10-109)	• The Syntax. Some General Remarks, (pp. 110-50) • Of the Orthography of the Portuguese Language (pp. 150-53) • The Etymology (pp. 153-57) • Of the Prosodie, or Accentuation of the Syllables (pp. 157-62)	• A Vocabulary in English and Portuguese (pp. 163-201) • Familiar Dialogues in English and Portuguese (pp. 202-40)	

indépendante de vocabulaires (organisés en dictionnaires ou par thèmes), de phrases, de dialogues, de lettres et de textes divers traduits ou à traduire. Ce sont des matériels linguistiques qui constituent des stratégies de contextualisation syntagmatique et, dans ce sens, peuvent être vus comme un prolongement de l'apprentissage de la matière syntactique, n'ayant pas toujours un traitement grammatical identique aux autres sections.

Le Tableau 2 permet une vision synoptique de la structure et de l'organisation des contenus grammaticaux des œuvres d'A. J., J. Castro et d'A. Vieira.

Le XIXe Siècle

L'institutionnalisation au Portugal de l'enseignement des langues vivantes étrangères (dans le sens de l'engagement de monarques, de politiciens et d'hommes de lettres du XVIIIe siècle) fut propice à la consolidation linguistique du PLE en contexte anglophone au XIXe siècle, période à laquelle furent publiées à Londres, en premières éditions, neuf grammaires: notamment, les œuvres de C. Laisné (1811), Richard Woodhouse (1815), John Laycock (1825), Luís Francisco Midosi (1832), L. P. R. F. De Porquet (1840), A. J. D. D'Orsey (1868), Alfred Elwes (1876), Arthur Kinlock (1876) et de Charles Henry Wall (1882)[27].

L'enseignement apprentissage de langues romanes en contexte anglophone est mis en avant dans l'œuvre de Richard Woodhouse, *A Grammar of the Spanish, Portuguese, and Italian Languages* (1815), à travers la comparaison linguistique entre l'espagnol, le portugais et l'italien. Bien que parfois l'anglais vienne à propos, la description contrastive privilégie ou les trois langues de la famille romane ou la confrontation entre les deux langues péninsulaires. A titre d'exemple, voyons, dans la description des noms, l'expression de l'accusatif de personne et de chose présentée par l'auteur (Woodhouse 1815: 21):

> In the Spanish and Portuguese, the accusative case of a personal noun is always marked by the preposition à, both with and without an article, whilst the accusative case of nouns not personal is like the nominative case; as,
>
> Span. Pedro ama à Pablo.   El hombre ama la virtud.
> Port. Pedro ama a Pablo.   O homem ama a virtude.
> Ital. Pietro ama Paoli.   L' uomo ama la virtu.
> Engl. Peter loves Paul.   Man loves virtue.
>
> In the Italian, the accusative and nominative cases of nouns are, as in the English, similar.

Du point de vue macro-structurel, la majorité de ces grammaires présente l'organisation de contenus suivante:

1. Un titre long, où parfois sont mentionnées la méthode d'enseignement suivie par l'auteur et les sources consultées.

Les grammaires de langues non maternelles reçoivent l'influence de grands pédagogues du XVIIe siècle dans le domaine de la méthodologie (William Bathe et Comenius), elles sont sensibles aux effets de l'école linguistique de Port-Royal (plutôt par voie des 'méthodes' de Claude Lancelot) et, au XIXe siècle, elles adoptent les nouvelles méthodes d'apprentissage d'idiomes étrangers qui arrivaient surtout d'Allemagne (méthodes de Franz Ahn et H. G. Ollendorff).[28]

2. Préfaces, Prologues ou Introductions: ce sont des textes préambulaires importants en ce qui concerne les informations sur le destinataire principal et sur la méthodologie grammaticale.

Il y a des affirmations qui sont significatives d'une conception de grammaire comme instrument utile à la pratique de la langue. Celle-ci est l'aspect de la grammaire pédagogique ou didactique où les usages linguistiques sont exposées et présentées comme norme à un public (ou culte, ou constitué de marchands, ou pas même défini), intéressé à connaître le système linguistique pour communiquer. Ainsi, '[t]he common terms of grammar are supposed to be known by all who attempt the acquirement of a foreign language; no definition of them is, therefore, entered into in the following work' (Woodhouse 1815: vii-viii). La grammaire philosophique du portugais Luís Francisco Midosi — *A New Grammar of the Portuguese and English Languages, in two parts; adapted to both nations, arranged on a philosophical system* (1832) — est également de façon assumée pratique:

> The work, when minutely examined, will be found, though small, quite sufficient for the learner to get a thorough grammatical knowledge of the language, without the tediousness of travelling through the labored definitions, and sometimes unintelligible subtilties. (Midosi 1832: v-vi)

Dans la mesure où une grammaire philosophique n'a rien de normatif, étant strictement descriptive et spéculative, nous comprenons que l'objectif philosophique de la grammaire de Midosi ne peut signifier qu'une tentative d'application des principes de la grammaire philosophique du XVIIIe siècle aux méthodes didactiques et à des publics de niveaux d'enseignement plus élémentaires. C'est depuis la seconde moitié du XVIIe siècle que la France et l'Angleterre (où vécut Midosi pendant quelques années) connaissent les grammaires générales, universelles ou philosophiques dont l'influence de cette grammaire de PLE est sensible en trois points fondamentaux (Midosi 1832: 79-80):

(i) Le concept de *sentence* ou le principe de combinaison des classes de mots en une unité plus grande appelée proposition: 'an assemblage of words, forming a complete sense';

(ii) La définition des trois composantes nécessaires à la phrase (sujet, attribut et objet): 'The subject is the thing chiefly spoken of; the attribute, the thing or action affirmed or denied; and the object, the thing affected by such action';

(iii) La conception de la phrase complexe ou composée: 'a compound sentence consists of two or more simple sentences, connected by relatives or conjunctions'.

Il existe plusieurs auteurs anglais de ce corpus du XIXe siècle qui, en préfaces, en prologues ou en introductions, montrent une connaissance considérable de certaines des plus paradigmatiques grammaires portugaises de l'époque, citées à titre de sources bibliographiques. Par exemple:

(i) La grammaire portugaise *Arte da Gramática da Lingua Portuguesa* (Lisboa, 1771), d'António José dos Reis Lobato (cf. Laycock 1825: iii);

(ii) Deux grammairiens portugaises de la première moitié du XIXe siècle, notamment Francisco Solano Constâncio et Carlos Augusto de Figueiredo Vieira (cf. Kinlock 1876: x);

(iii) L'œuvre du grammairien portugais Francisco Solano Constâncio et la très connue *Grammatica philosophica da língua portugueza* (Lisboa, 1822), de Jerónimo Soares Barbosa (cf. Wall 1882: ix).

3. Une section grammaticale qui suit la structure canonique gréco-latine de la division en trois parties relativement stables (cf. Auroux 1994: 112):

a) Contenus graphophonétiques (alphabet, prononciation et signes orthographiques comme l'accentuation);

b) Morphologie: les classes de mots traditionnelles (en premier les variables — les articles, les noms, les adjectifs, les pronoms, les verbes — et puis les invariables — les adverbes, les prépositions, les conjonctions et les interjections);

c) Syntaxe: matière présentée sous forme plus brève et pas toujours en section indépendante du traitement des classes de mots.

Remarquons que la structure grammaticale de manuels ollendorffiens ou adeptes d'Ahn est étrangère aux structures bi-, tri- ou quadripartites de la grammaire classique.

4. Vocabulaires, dialogues, lettres et textes divers: ce sont des matériels orientés vers des aspects plus fonctionnels de la communication, tout comme aujourd'hui nous le comprenons dans le champ de la didactique des langues étrangères.

En guise de conclusion

Nous considérons, ayant pour base Swiggers (2006: 168), que l'analyse des grammaires de PLE — ou des grammaires de langues non maternelles, en général — implique nécessairement trois éléments basiques qui contribuent à la définition d'un genre grammaticographique: le public cible étranger; la forme de description qui inclut une composante théorique et une composante appliquée/pratique; et l'auteur, entité qui peut correspondre ou non à un locuteur natif de la langue décrite. Ce sont ces trois instances qui permettent de situer les grammaires de PLE dans un contexte d'édition, de rédaction et de conception spécifique, de portée théorique, historiographique et culturelle, différent de la grammaticographie restante en langue maternelle.

En ces termes, les premières descriptions grammaticales que les grammairiens portugais (Fernão de Oliveira et João de Barros) firent de leur langue maternelle, dans le contexte de ce que l'on appelle 'question de la langue' (Buescu 1983), ne doivent pas être confondues avec les premiers abordages grammaticaux du portugais dans une perspective de langue étrangère pour un public anglophone, qui ont eu lieu en 1662. Un siècle plus tard, ces descriptions ne sont plus de simples abordages et commencent à constituer des *grammaires*, dans le sens d'un corps doctrinal d'idées et de méthodes de réglementations de la langue. A.J., J. Castro et A. Vieira sont les grammairiens de cette période; ils ont traité de forme indépendante 'the Letters, and Pronunciation', 'the Parts of Speech', 'the Syntax' et 'A Vocabulary' ou 'Familiar Dialogues' (Castro 1731). Au XIXe siècle, le nombre de publications londoniennes de grammaires de PLE augmente et la vitalité du marché de rééditions continue.

Pour revenir au point de départ de ce travail, nous cherchons à rendre les œuvres et les auteurs qui permettent une plus grande compréhension des lignes dominantes du mouvement grammatical de PLE en contexte anglophone. C'est donc pour cela que nous avons cherché à faire un relevé précis — prétendu complet — de l'édition de grammaires de PLE à Londres, entre 1662 et 1898.

Bibliography

Primary sources

A. J. 1701. *A Compleat Account of the Portugueze Language. Being a Copious Dictionary of English with Portugueze, and Portugueze with English. Together With an Easie and Unerring Method of its Pronunciation, by a distinguishing Accent, and a Compendium of all the necessary Rules of Construction and Orthography digested into a Grammatical Form* (London: Printed by R. Janeway)

CASTRO, J[ACOB]. 1731. *Grammatica Anglo-Lusitanica & Lusitano-Anglica: or, a new grammar English and Portuguese and Portuguese and English* (London: Printed for W. Meadows)

D'ORSEY, [ALEXANDER JAMES DONALD]. 1868. *Practical grammar of portuguese and english. Exhibiting in a series of exercises in double traduction the idiomatic structure of both languages as now spoken* (London)

DE PORQUET, L[OUIS] P[HILIPPE] R. F[ENWICK]. 1840. *The Portuguese Tresor; or, the Art of translating easy English into Portuguese, at sight* (London: Printed and published by Fenwick De Porquet)

ELWES, ALFRED. 1876. *A Grammar of the Portuguese Language in a simple and practical form with a course of exercices* (London: Crosby Lockwood)

HOWELL, JAMES. 1662. *A New English Grammar prescribing as certain rules as the languages will bear, for forreners to learn English: Ther is also another grammar of the Spanish or Castilian toung, with some special remarks upon the Portuguese Dialect, &c.* (London: Printed for T. Williams, H Brome, and H. Marsh)

KINLOCK, A. 1876. *Compendium of Portuguese Grammar, from the Portuguese (eleventh edition) of C. A. de Figueiredo Vieira, and the Grammars of Constancio, Vieyra, and others*, revised by A. J. dos Reis (London: Williams and Norgate)

LA MOLLIÈRE. 1662. *A Portuguez Grammar: or Rules shewing the True and Perfect way to learn the said language* (London: Printed by Da. Maxwel)

LAISNÉ, C. 1811. *A grammar of the Portuguese language, in which the rules are illustrated by examples, selected from the best authors* (London: Printed for the Author, and sold by Dulau and Co)

LAYCOCK, JOHN. 1825. *A Grammar of the Portuguese Language, compiled from the best sources, and chiefly designed for the use of Englishmen studying that tongue without the help of a master. In three parts, to which 18 added, a copious mercantile vocabulary together with sundry commercial letters* (London: Leeds)

MIDOSI, LUÍS FRANCISCO. 1832. *A New Grammar of the Portuguese and English Languages, in two parts; adapted to both nations, arranged on a philosophical system, containing a list of Verbs and Nouns spelt alike, but differently pronounced, and also an useful Appendix, Part I. — Portuguese* (London: Printed for A. A. Beça)

VIEIRA, ANTÓNIO. 1768. *A New Portuguese Grammar in four parts* (London: Printed for J. Nourse)

WALL, CHARLES HENRY. 1882. *A Practical Grammar of the Portuguese Language on Dr. Otto's conversational System* (London: David Nutt)

WOODHOUSE, RICHARD. 1815. *A Grammar or the Spanish, Portuguese, and Italian Languages, intended to facilitate the acquiring of these sister tongues, by exhibiting in a synoptical form the agreements and differences in their grammatical construction* (London: Printed for Black and Co.)

Secondary sources

AQUILINO, SÁNCHEZ. 2014. 'Spanish as a Foreign Language in Europe: Six Centuries of Teaching Materials', *Language & History*, 57: 59-74

AUROUX, SYLVAIN (ed.). 1992. *Histoire des idées linguistiques* (Liège: Mardaga), II

———. 1994. *La Révolution technologique de la grammatisation* (Liège: Mardaga)

BISCHOFF, BERNHARD. 1961. 'The Study of Foreign Languages in the Middle Ages', *Speculum*, 36: 209-24

BUESCU, MARIA LEONOR CARVALHÃO. 1983. *Babel ou a ruptura do signo: a gramática e os gramáticos portugueses do século XVI* (Lisbon: Imprensa Nacional–Casa da Moeda)

CARDIM, LUÍS. 1930. *Portuguese-English Grammarians and Eighteenth-Century Spoken English* (Porto: Emp. Indust. Gráfica do Porto)

CARAVOLAS, JEAN A. 2000. *Histoire de la didactique des langues au siècle des Lumières: précis et anthologie thématique* (Montreal: Presses de l'Université de Montréal; Tübingen: Narr)

CARDOSO, SIMÃO. 1994. *Historiografia Gramatical (1500–1920): Língua Portuguesa — Autores Portugueses* (Porto: Faculdade de Letras)

DUARTE, SÓNIA. 2009. ' "Of the Portugues language or subdialect" (1662): a consideração do Português como dialecto do Castelhano na obra gramatical de James Howell', *Diacrítica. Ciências da Linguagem*, 23: 209-21

FONSECA, MARIA DO CÉU, MARIA JOÃO MARÇALO and ANA ALEXANDRA SILVA. 2012. 'O português como língua estrangeira em gramáticas antigas: aspetos do contexto anglófono', in *Lusofone. SprachWissenschaftsGeschichte I*, ed. by Rolf Kemmler, Barbara Schäfer-Prieß and Roger Schöntag (Tübingen: Calepinus)

FORMIGARI, LIA. 1988. *Language and Experience in 17th-Century British Philosophy* (Amsterdam: Benjamins)

GALLAGHER, JOHN JAMES. 2014. 'Vernacular Language-Learning in Early Modern England' (unpublished doctoral thesis, University of Cambridge)

GLÜCK, HELMUT. 2002. *Deutsch als Fremdsprache in Europa vom Mittelalter bis zur Barockzeit* (Berlin: de Gruyter)

———. 2013. *Die Fremdsprache Deutsch im Zeitalter von Aufklärung, Klassik und Romantik* (Wiesbaden: Harrassowitz)

GÓMEZ ASENCIO, JOSÉ J. 2006. 'La gramática castellana para extranjeros de Nebrija', in *El Castellano y su Codificación Gramatical*, ed. by José J. Gómez Asencio, 3 vols (Burgos: Fundación Instituto Castellano y Leonés de la Lengua, 2006-11), I: *De 1942 (A. de Nebrija) a 1611 (John Sanford)*, pp. 117-42

GONÇALVES, MARIA FILOMENA. 2006. 'El portugués como dialecto del castellano: historia de una teoría entre los siglos XVII y XVIII', in *Caminos actuales de la Historiografía Lingüística*, ed. by A. Roldán et al. (Murcia: Universidad de Murcia), pp. 729-41

HOWATT, A. P. R. 1984. *A History of English Language Teaching* (Oxford: Oxford University Press)

KEMMLER, ROLF. 2012. '*O Compleat Account of the Portugueze Language* e a primeira *Grammatica Anglo-Lusitanica* (Londres, 1701): a discussão da autoria de 1859 até 1970', *Agália*, 105: 213-31

KUKENHEIM, LOUIS. 1962. *Esquisse historique de la linguistique française et de ses rapports avec la linguistique générale* (Leiden: Universitaire Pers Leiden)

MCLELLAND, NICOLA, and RICHARD SMITH (eds). 2014. Special issue of *Language & History*, 57.1, *Building the History of Language Learning and Teaching (HoLLT)*

PERCIVAL, W. KEITH. 1975. 'The Grammatical Tradition and the Rise of the Vernaculars', in *Historiography of Linguistics*, ed. by Thomas A. Sebeok, Current trends in Linguistics, 13 (Paris: Mouton), pp. 231-75

PONCE DE LEÓN, ROGELIO. 2009. 'Los inicios de la enseñanza-aprendizaje del portugués en España: breves consideraciones sobre el *Primero y segundo curso de portugués* (Madrid 1876) de Francisco de Paula Hidalgo', *Documents pour l'histoire du français langue étrangère ou seconde*, 42: 185-96

——. 2012. 'O primeiro manual do português como língua estrangeira? Breves considerações sobre *A portuguez grammar* (Londres 1662) de La Mollière', *Limite*, 6: 53-74

SALMON, VIVIAN. 1985. 'The Study of Foreign Languages in Seventeenth-Century England', *Histoire Epistémologie Langage*, 7(2): 45-70

SÁNCHEZ ESCRIBANO, FRANCISCO JAVIER. 2006. 'Portuguese in England in the Sixteenth and Seventeenth Centuries', *Sederi*, 16: 109-32

SÁNCHEZ PÉREZ, AQUILINO. 1992. *Historia de la enseñanza del español como lengua extranjera* (Madrid: Sociedad General Española de Librería)

SCHÄFER-PRIESS, BARBARA. 2012. 'A descrição da pronúncia portuguesa nas primeiras gramáticas para alemães', *Limite*, 6: 125-37

SMITH, ROBERT C. 1945. 'A Pioneer Teacher: Father Peter Babad and his Portuguese Grammar', *Hispania*, 28: 330-63

SUSO LÓPEZ, JAVIER. 2009. 'Conception de la langue et l'enseignement/apprentissage des langues au XVIe siècle', *Le Langage et l'Homme*, 44: 109-19

SWIGGERS, PIERRE. 2006. 'El foco "belga": las gramáticas españolas de Lovaina (1555, 1559)', in *El Castellano y su codificación gramatical*, ed. by José J. Gómez Asencio, 3 vols (Burgos: Fundación Instituto Castellano y Leonés de la Lengua, 2006-11), I: *De 1942 (A. de Nebrija) a 1611 (John Sanford)*, pp. 161-13

TAYLOR, BARRY. 2002. 'Un-Spanish Practices: Spanish and Portuguese Protestants, Jews and Liberals, 1500-1900', in *Foreign-Language Printing in London, 1500-1900*, ed. by Barry Taylor (Boston Spa and London: The British Library)

THOMAS, MARGARET. 2004. *Universal Grammar in Second Language Acquisition: A History* (London and New York: Routledge)

TORRE, MANUEL GOMES DA. 1988. 'O interesse pelo estudo do inglês em Portugal no séc. XVIII', in *Actas do Colóquio Comemorativo do VI Centenário do Tratado de Windsor* (Porto: Faculdade de Letras da Universidade do Porto), pp. 41-54

——. 1996. 'Who wrote *A compleat account of the Portugueze language*?', *Revista de Estudos Anglo-Portugueses*, 5: 33-47

VERDELHO, TELMO. 2009. 'On the Origins of Modern Bilingual Lexicography: Interaction between Portuguese and Other European Languages', in *Perspectives on Lexicography in Italy and Europe*, ed. by Silvia Bruti, Roberta Cella and Marina Foschi Albert (Cambridge: Cambridge Scholars Publishing), pp. 121-50

——. 2011. 'Lexicografia portuguesa bilingue: breve conspecto diacrónico', *Lexicografia bilingue. A tradição dicionarística português — línguas modernas*, ed. by Telmo Verdelho and João Paulo Silvestre (Lisbon and Aveiro: Centro de Linguística da Universidade de Lisboa/ Universidade de Aveiro), pp. 13-67

ZWARTJES, OTTO. 2011. *Portuguese Missionary Grammars in Asia, Africa and Brazil, 1550-1800* (Amsterdam: Benjamins)

Notes to Chapter 11

1. La *Grammatica da Linguagem Portuguesa* (Lisboa, 1536), de Fernão de Oliveira, et la *Gramática da Língua Portuguesa* (Lisboa, 1540), de João de Barros, sont les deux premières grammaires de la langue portugaise.

2. Où le portugais fut *lingua franca* pendant les XVIe-XVIIIe siècles, tant dans les relations avec les populations locales que dans l'intermédiation des contacts entre ces populations et les européens (notamment, des anglais et hollandais). Cf. Castro (1751: vii): 'I will only observe that the Portuguese being near akin to the Lingua Franca, it is current upon all the Coasts of the East Indies and Africa'.

3. António Vieira (1712-1797), un des plus importants grammairiens de PLE, est aussi l'auteur d'un célèbre *Dictionary of the Portuguese and English Languages in two parts: Portuguese and English: and English and Portuguese* (Londres, 1773), déjà étudié (cf. Verdelho 2011: 26-30; 2009: 121-50). Du point de vue biographique, il n'y a aucune information très sûre. Quelques données disponibles sont: la poursuite de l'Inquisition; l'exil en Angleterre; la conversion au protestantisme; la vie à Dublin (entre 1779 et la fin du siècle), où il fut membre de la *Royal Irish Academy* (donnée non confirmée) et enseigna l'anglais, l'espagnol, l'italien, l'arabe et le perse au *Trinity College* (donnée non confirmée). Voyez les informations de Smith (1945: 339) et de Taylor (2002: 191).

4. Cf., par exemple, la grammaire de l'italien Pietro Bachi, *A Comparative View of the Spanish and Portuguese Languages, or an easy method of learning the Portuguese tongue for those who are already acquainted with the Spanish* (Cambridge, 1831), dirigée 'To the students of Harvard University'.

5. Vd. la *Grammaire Portugaise Raisonnée et Simplifiée* (Paris, 1871) de Paulino de Souza.

6. C'est depuis 1400 que la grammaire française fut décrite par des nationaux et des auteurs anglais intéressés par l'enseignement du français aux étrangers. John Barton, John Palsgrave, Jacques Dubois et Gilles du Guez (ou du Wez) sont les grammairiens parmi les plus cités de ce mouvement. Entré dans le XVIIe siècle, l'importante *Grammaire et syntaxe françoise* (Orléans, 1607), de Charles Maupas, maintient le flux des œuvres 'en faveur des estrangiers qui en sont desireux'.

7. Sur le processus de codification grammatical du portugais, il existe la large bibliographie de Maria Leonor Carvalhão Buescu (1983).

8. Notamment, *Regras que ensinam a maneira de escrever e orthographia da lingua portuguesa* (1574) de Pêro de Magalhães de Gândavo et *Orthographia da lingoa portuguesa* (1576) de Duarte Nunes de Leão.

9. Nous excluons de ce travail les grammaires de PLE rédigées en allemand, pas encore analysées par manque d'opportunité. Schäfer-Prieß (2012: 125-37) s'est déjà occupé de ce sujet en étudiant la description de la prononciation portugaise dans les trois premières grammaires allemandes (une d'elles bilingue, rédigée également en portugais), publiées en Allemagne à la fin du XVIIIe siècle. Un recensement non exhaustif de ces grammaires se trouve chez Cardoso 1994: 215-18.

10. Rappelant la note antérieure, il convient de clarifier que ne sont pas comptabilisées ici les grammaires allemandes de PLE, vu que les données disponibles ne sont pas encore définitives.

11. Voyez les trois publications aux Etats-Unis: à Baltimore fut publiée *A Portuguese and English Grammar, compiled from those of Lobato, Durham, Sane and Vieyra, and simplified for the use of students* (1820), du français Pierre Babad, qui, selon Smith (1945: 330), 'might today have a recognized place among the pioneer professors of the Iberian languages in the United States'; *A Comparative View of the Spanish and Portuguese Languages, or an easy method*; *A Comparative View of the Spanish and Portuguese Languages, or an easy method of learning the Portuguese tongue for those who are already acquainted with the Spanish* (Cambridge, 1831), de l'italien Pietro Bachi; et *A new method for learning the Portuguese language* (New York, 1863), de E. F. Grauert.

12. D'où le caractère pionnier du manuel de Francisco de Paula Hidalgo, *Primer y segundo curso de portugués* (Madrid, 1876).

13. Nous nous référons à: *Ristretto di Grammatica Portoghese ad uso dei Missionarj di Propaganda* (Roma, 1846), de Paolo di Gesu Maria Giuseppe; e *Grammatica della Lingua Portoghese ad use degll'Italiani, sulle traccie della Grammatica Filosofica della Lingua Portoghese dell'illustre signor Jeronimo Soares Barbosa* (Milan, 1859), de Antonio Bernardini. Rappelons que la grammaire de Nabantino (1869) fut publiée à Paris (cf. *supra*).

14. En somme: la grammaire du portugais Jacob Castro (1731) fut rééditée en 1751 (London: W. Meadows); 1759 (London: W. Meadows); 1767 (London: F. Davis); 1770 (London: F. Davis); de l'historique grammaire d'António Vieira, *A New Portuguese Grammar in four parts* (1768), huit éditions sont connue (deux du XVIIe siècle et six du XVIIIe siècle): de 1777 (2ème éd., London:

J. Nourse); 1794 (3ème éd., London: F. Wingrave); 1809 (7ème éd., London: F. Wingrave); 1811 (8ème éd., London: F. Wingrave); 1813 (9ème éd., London: F. Wingrave); 1827 (10ème éd., London: J. Collingwood); 1858 (12ème éd., London: W. Cloves); 1890 (London); la grammaire de l'anglais Alfred Elwes (1876) eut une 4ème édition en 1892 et une 6ème édition en 1903 (les deux à Londres: Crosby Lockwood).

15. Il existe plusieurs œuvres du genre de ces manuels d'exercices pratiques: John Emmanuel Mordente, *Exercises Upon the Different Parts of Speech of the Portuguese Language: Referring to the Rules of Mr. Vieyra's Grammar; to which is Added, a Course of Commercial Letters in Portuguese* (London, 1807); C. Laisné, *Practice exercises, intended to facilitate the speedy acquisition of the Portuguese language* (London, 1810); C. Laisné, *A Copious Collection of Instructive and Entertaining Exercises on the Portuguese Language: With the Different Parts of Speech and Rules of Grammar Prefixed to Every Article* (London, 1815).

16. La *casa de Bragança* ('maison de Bragança') était une famille noble qui régna au Portugal de 1640 (date de la restauration de l'indépendance au Portugal après soixante ans d'union politique — 1580-1640 — avec le royaume d'Espagne) jusqu'en 1910 (date de l'implantation de la République au Portugal).

17. Nous remercions Nicole McLelland de nous avoir envoyé l'étude de Gallagher (2014).

18. La conception n'est pas nouvelle, ayant déjà été étudiée comme théorie et historiée dans la pensée linguistique portugaise et castillane du XVIIe et XVIIIe siècles (Gonçalves 2006: 729-41; Duarte 2009: 209-21). La théorie, sans fondement linguistique, se base sur les circonstances historiques de l'union politique entre le Portugal et l'Espagne pendant ce que l'on appelle la période de l'Union Ibérique (1580-1640).

19. L'ensemble composé du dictionnaire et de la grammaire fut publié en 1701; la publication individualisée se succède en 1702, sous le titre de *Grammatica Anglo-Lusitanica: Or a Short and Compendious System of an English and Portugueze Grammar* (London: Printed by R. Janeway).

20. À la suite d'autres auteurs (cf. Torre 1996: 33-47).

21. 'Para a historiografia linguística anglo-portuguesa' (author's translation).

22. 'Muito material que haveria de ser utilizado na íntegra por gramáticas tanto de português como de inglês mais tarde publicadas, o que era facilitado pela natureza bilingue dos textos apresentados' (author's translation).

23. Cf. Pietro Bachi, *A Comparative View of the Spanish and Portuguese Languages, or an easy method of learning the Portuguese tongue for those who are already acquainted with the Spanish* (Cambridge, 1831), p. viii.

24. Cf. Pierre Babad, *A Portuguese and English Grammar, compiled from those of Lobato, Durham, Sane and Vieyra, and simplified for the use of students* (Baltimore, 1820), p. vi; ou Kinlock (1876).

25. La *Nouvelle Grammaire Portugaise, suivie de plusieurs essais de traduction française interlenéaire, et de différents morceaux de prose et de poésie. Extraits de meilleurs classiques portugais* (1810), d'Alexandre Marie Sané, est une traduction française de la grammaire anglaise d'António Vieira.

26. Voyez le cas de l'œuvre de John Emmanuel Mordente, *Exercises Upon the Different Parts of Speech of the Portuguese Language: Referring to the Rules of Mr. Vieyra's Grammar; to which is Added, a Course of Commercial Letters in Portuguese* (London, 1807).

27. Cf. 'Sources primaires' dans la Bibliographie.

28. Voyez les œuvres de Wall (1852), de E. F. Grauet, *A new method for learning the Portuguese language* (New York, 1882) et de Francisco de Sales Lencastre, *Nouvelle méthode pratique et facile pour apprendre la langue portugaise composé d'après les principes de F. Ahn* (Leipzig, 1883).

INDEX

This is a composite index to the three volumes of the History. References are to volume and page number: e.g., '3.116' refers to page 116 of volume 3. Where a locator refers to a chapter in French rather than English text, it is italicized.

Abdel-Fattah, Françoise *3.236*
Abel-Rémusat, Jean-Pierre 3.148
Académie Française (French Academy) *2.48*
Académie Roumaine (Romanian Academy) *2.68*
Ade, George 3.116, 3.117
Agence Universitaire de la Francophonie (Francophonie University Association) *2.72–73*
Agnihotri, R.K. 3.257
Ahn, D. F. *2.48*
Ahn, Franz *1.177*, *1.185–86*
Ahn, Johann Franz 2.24, 2.25
Aksoy, Ekrem *3.237*
al-Miṣrī, Khalīfah ibn Mahmūd 3.116, 3.118–19, 3.130
Albero, Michel *3.242*
Albitès, Achille 2.7–8
Alcalá Galiano, Antonio 2.181
Alcibiade (Alcibiades) *2.53*
Alegre, Teresa 2.123
Alembert, Jean le Rond de *2.42*
Algeria *2.70*
Allemagne *see* Germany
allemand *see* German language
Alrabadi, Elie *3.236*
Altieri, Ferdinando 1.157, 1.161, 1.164
Ammon, U. *2.98*, *2.110*
Anderson, B. *2.99*
Andō Hikotarō 3.177, 3.185
Andreolli, Maria Giovanna 2.251, 2.252, 2.255, 2.255–56
Andrews, George 3.46–49
Andrews, John 2.12
Androchnikova, Galina M. 2.203
anglais *see* English language
Angleterre *see* England
Anstett, Philipp 2.122
Antoniou, David *2.48–49*
Anwykyll, John, *Compendium totius grammaticae* 1.58, 1.62, 1.63
Apell, Alfredo 2.122, 2.123
APHELLE (Associação Portuguesa para a História do Ensino das Línguas e Literaturas Estrangerias) 1.27
Arabic *3.238*, *3.240*
  popular instruction books for travellers 3.115–31

Arnold, Theodor 3.6–9, 3.10–11
Arnott, M. 2.283
Arturovna, Magda 2.201
Astell, Mary 2.1
Atherton, Mark 2.129
audio-lingual method (ALM) 2.260, 2.267–69, 2.273
  Modern Spanish (MS) 2.267–69, 2.272
Auroux, Sylvain *1.173*, *1.176*, *1.186*, *2.99*, *2.103*
Austria, language policy 1.113
Ayoub, Ibtisam *3.238–39*
Ayuso, Francisco García 2.116

Baker, J.H. 1.38–39
Balassa, Jószef 2.157
Ball, S.J. 2.280
Barbosa, Jerónimo Soares *1.186*
Barbusse, Henri 3.22, 3.24
Baretti, Giuseppe 1.156–69
Barros, João de *1.174*, *1.176*, *1.186*
Barrow, Reverend William 2.12
Barrows, Sarah 2.162, 2.167–68
Barsi, Monica 2.238
Barth, A. *2.104*
Barthélemy, Auguste Marseille *2.41*
Barton, John, *Donait françois* 1.42–43, 1.44
Bathe, William *1.184*
Bauch, Reinhold 3.79
Bauman, Zygmunt 3.69–70
Baumann, Henry 3.198
Baur, Arthur *2.106*
Bausenwein, Josef 3.79
Bauzée, Nicolas *2.42*
Bayer, Gottlieb Siegfried 1.138
Bayley, Susan 3.30–31
Beale, Dorothea 2.138
Beauvalet, Scarlett *2.55*
Bell, Alexander Graham 3.164, 3.167
Bell, Alexander Melville 2.153, 3.164, 3.167, 3.171
Bellère, Jean *1.88*
Bellot, James 1.71–72, 1.77
Benot, Eduardo *1.147*
Benson, Malcolm J. 2.23

Bentinck, William 3.247–48
Béranger, Pierre-Jean de 2.36
Berec, L. 1.76
Berg, C.M. 2.110
Bergeron, Christine 3.242
Berlaimont, Noël de 1.28, 1.70, 1.84–90
   Dictionarium quator linguarum 1.67, 1.70–71, 1.72–73, 1.74
Besse, Henri 2.53
Betskoy, Ivan 1.141, 1.142
Bibbesworth, Walter de, *Tretiz* 1.38, 1.43
Bibliothèque Nationale de France (National Library of France) 2.52, 2.61n1
Bidault, Murielle 3.242
Biller, Pierre-Paul 1.151
Bischoff, Bernhard 1.174
Bland, Maria Theresa 2.56
Blégny, Étienne de 1.147
Block, J. 3.40–41
Boccaccio, Giovanni 1.158–59, 1.160
Bodarenco, Ana 2.71
Bodmer, Johann Jacob 2.105
Bohlen, Adolf 3.87, 3.88, 3.100, 3.103–05, 3.107–09, 3.110, 3.112
Boia, Lucian 2.70
Boileau, Nicolas 2.41
Bonomi, Mauretta 2.251, 2.252–53, 2.255, 2.256
Bordas, Luis 1.147
Borg, Erik 2.151
Bossuet, Jacques-Béningne 2.41
Bouchez, Maurice 3.60, 3.61
Bouge, Xavier de 2.49
Bourland, C.B. 1.71
Boyer, Abel 2.5
Bragança, Catarina de 1.178–79
Braun, Juan Jorge 2.116
Breitinger, Johann Jacob 2.105
Breul, Karl 2.182
Brevissima institutio 1.53–54, 1.55, 1.56–57, 1.63
Briod, Vaudois 2.104
Brissaud, Eugène 2.49
Brunot, Ferdinand 1.20, 1.24–25
Bryce, James 2.10, 2.20n10
Büchi, C. 2.98, 2.108
Buescu, Maria Leonor Carvalhão 1.86
Buettner, Elizabeth 2.130
Burde, A.S. 3.248
Burstall, Claire 2.299
Burstall, Sara 2.14
Butler, George 2.130, 2.131
Butler, Reverend H. M. 2.9
Butler, Nicholas Murray 3.218
Butterfield, Ardis 1.45
Byram, Michael 3.39, 3.87
Byrne, Donn 2.233
Byron, George Godron (Lord) 2.36

Calabria, Antonio Maria 1.87
Caliberti, Anna 2.249
Calvet, Louis-Jean 2.72
Camaesca, Emma 2.251–52, 2.253
Camargo, Martin 1.40
Camariano-Cioran, Ariadna 2.67
Cambiol, C. 2.49
Cameroon, teaching and learning German 3.133–43
Campos, Agostinho Celso de Azevedo 2.122
Cannon, Christopher 1.44
Caradja, Nicolas 2.48, 2.50
Carassoutsas, Ioannis 2.34–37, 2.45n3
   Chrestomathie française 2.35, 2.40–43, 2.49
   Dictionnaire des synonymes de la langue française 2.35, 2.42–43
   Grammaire de la langue française 2.35, 2.37–40, 2.43–44, 2.46n15
   poésie (poetry) 2.36–37, 2.43
Caravolas, Jean 2.47
Caravolas, Jean-Antoine 1.20, 1.27, 1.71–72, 1.180
Carcano, Francesco 1.163
Carlson, R.A. 3.215
Carlyle, Thomas 2.13, 3.81
Caro, Annibal 1.163
Carrington, Christina 2.123
Carroll, E.J. 2.185
Casotti, L. 1.146
Cassal, Charles 2.14–15
Castro, Jacob 1.180–84, 1.186
Castroverde, Fernández de 2.116
Catach, Nina 1.85
Catechetical method 2.29
Caxton, William 1.71–72
   Cy commence la table 1.44, 1.45
Chalfont, Frank C. 2.172
Chambaud, Lewis 2.4–5
Chapsal, Noël de 2.39, 2.46n10, 2.48–49
Charlet, J.-L. 1.71
Charlet-Mesdjian, B. 1.71
Chartier, Alain 1.34, 1.45
Chateaubriand, François-René 2.36, 2.40, 2.42, 2.46n18, 2.48
Cheneau, Francis 2.4, 2.5
Chénier, André 2.41
Chervel, André 1.140, 2.41
Chevalier, J.-Cl. 1.68, 1.69
China, teaching German and cultural values in China 3.194–208
Chinese
   teaching of Chinese pronunciation 3.164–74
   Westerners learning Chinese languages 3.147–59
Choïda, Kondylia 2.41
Christ, Herbert 1.25, 2.93
Christaller, Theodor 3.138, 3.146n14
Ciliberti, Anna 2.235
Ciobanu, Stefan 2.68

CIRSIL (Centro Interuniversatario di Ricerca sulla Storia degli Insegnamenti Linguistici) 1.27
Clarendon Commission (1864) 2.1, 2.6, 2.9
Clarkson, Malcolm 2.298
classical method 2.21–22
CLIL (Content and Language Integrated Learning) 2.77, 2.78–83, 2.95
Coesmans, Hans *1.88*
Coles, James Oakley 2.163
Colet, John, *Aeditio* 1.53
Collier, Price 3.80
Comenius, Johannes Amos 1.96, 1.98, 1.99, 1.101, 1.103
Communicative Language Teaching (CLT) 2.231–42, 2.260–61, 2.273
  Cambridge English Course 2.269–72
Condillac, E. *2.39, 2.42*
Congo *2.70*
Congrès de Vienne (Congress of Vienna) *2.109*
Constâncio, Francisco Solano *1.186*
Cook, Guy 2.26–27
Coray, Adamance *2.37–38, 2.41*
Corble, Archibald Harrison 3.127
Corcuera Manso, F. 1.71
Cordes, Richard 3.197
Cortez, Maria Teresa 2.123
Coste, Daniel *2.69*
Coubertin, Pierre de *2.58*
Courville, Antoine *1.145, 1.147–48*
  Explicación de la gramática francesca 1.147–52
Crawford, J.P.W. 3.215, 3.226–27
Critten, Rory G. 1.33–47
Cuevas, Bruña *1.83, 1.89*
cultural content 3.1–19
Cutter, Victor 3.227
Czech language 1.110–22

D'Addio, Wanda 2.233–34, 2.248–49
Dahmen, Kristine 1.137
Dahrendorf, Malte 3.110, 3.111–12
Dalrymple, Caroline Lucy *see* Prendergast, Caroline Lucy (née Dalrymple)
Daru, Pierre *2.41*
David, Jules *2.51*
Davies, Emily 2.10
Day, Thomas 2.14
De Belges, Jean Lemaire 1.34
De Devitiis, Guido 2.252, 2.253–54, 2.255–56
De Gasperin, Vilma 1.156–69
De Mauro, Tullio 2.2448
De Meun, Jean 1.34
De Porquet, Louis Philippe R. Fenwick 2.7
de Worde 1.44
Decoo, Wilfried 2.23
deductive approach, language teaching 1.23, 1.28
Delavigne, Casimir *2.41*
dialogues, language teaching 1.67–79, 1.166–69

Dibelius, Wilhelm 3.74–75
Dictionnaire des synonymes de la langue française 2.35, 2.42–43
Diderot, Denis *2.42*
Dietze, Hugo 2.83
direct method, language teaching 1.138
Dixon, Revd William 3.256
Dobrovský, Josef 1.111, 1.115, 1.116–17, 1.119, 1.121
Doff, Sabine 3.38
Dolet, Estienne 1.70
Dorfeld, Karl 1.22–23
Doughty, H. 2.277
Doukas, Georges *2.43*
Doyle, Henry 3.230
Drury, Henry 2.131
Du Wes, Giles 1.46, 1.71–72
Dubois, Jacques *1.190n6*
Dufief, Nicolas Gouin 2.7
Dumas, Felicia *2.66*
Dürrenmatt, Friedrich *2.107*
Dutch language *2.62n19*
Duval, Frédéric *2.65*
Duvivier, Girault *2.49*
Dygon, John 1.37–38

Ebeling, Christoph Daniel 3.10–11
École Athénienne (The Athenian School of poets) *2.35–36, 2.45n2*
Edgeworth, Maria 2.14
Effendi, Khalīfah 3.118–19
Egypt *2.70, 3.236*
  popular instruction books for travellers 3.115–31
Ehrenthal, Heinrich 3.46, 3.50
El Fakhri, Sonia *3.235*
Elliott, Brian J. 3.25, 3.29
Ellis, A.J. 2.153
Ellison, Grace 2.163, 2.165, 2.167, 2.169, 2.174, 2.178n2
Elmiger, D. *2.100*
Elwes, Alfred *1.184*
Engels, Friedrich 3.123
England *1.146, 1.175–78, 1.180–81, 1.185, 2.56–57, 2.59*
  attitudes to speaking French 2.1–16
  changing notions about national character 2.1, 2.3, 2.13
  cultural 'other' represented in German classrooms 3.88–90
  development of French language teaching 2.293–305
  English language *1.146, 1.175–81*
  French didactics in late medieval and early modern England 1.33–47
  German-language teaching 3.57–58, 3.62–64, 3.67–69
  GOML (Graded Objectives for Modern Languages) 2.298, 2.301–302
  international correspondence scheme 3.37, 3.41–42
  internationalism in foreign language policy after First World War 3.22–33

Leathes Report 3.22, 3.29–33
medieval manuscripts 1.35–39
Oxford *dictatores* 1.33, 1.39
representations of 'the English' in German cultural readers 3.74–82
Englische Studien [English Studies] 2.148, 2.149
English language *2.38, 2.57, 2.59, 2.64, 2.69–72, 2.98, 2.101–02, 2.108, 3.236, 3.243*
  education policies in post-Independence India 3.246–58
  EFL textbooks used in Germany in 1800s and 1900s 3.1–19
  ELT in Italy 1980s and 1990s 2.231–42
Enlightenment, Age of *2.38, 2.48, 2.66*
Entwistle, William James 2.191
Erasmus, Desiderius 1.98
Espagne *see* Spain
Espagnol *see* Spanish language
Esperanto 3.31–32
États-Unis *see* United States
European Union *2.73, 2.108*
Extermann, Blaise *2.99, 2.101–02, 2.104–05*

Falke, K. *2.104*
Fauchon, James 2.4
Fehlen, F. *2.109*
Felbiger, Johann Ignaz 1.112, 1.117–18
Fell, Arthur 2.187
Fénelon, François *2.41, 2.48, 2.50–53*
Fernández Fraile, María Eugenia 1.28
Ferretti, Lorenzo *1.145*
Fidlerová, Alena A. *1.110–22*
Finland, Latin schoolbooks in late seventeenth century 1.96–104
Finocchiaro, Mary 2.233
Fischer-Wollpert, Heinz 3.91–92
Fisher, H.A.L. 3.28–29, 3.31
Fisher, Michael H. 2.132
Fitz-Gerald, John D. 3.214, 3.218, 3.223, 3.224
Fjodorovna, Emma 2.201
Florian, Jean-Pierre Claris de *2.41*
Florinus, Henricus Matthiae 1.98, 1.99, 1.101
Florio John 1.71, 1.78–79
Fonseca, Maria do *1.175*
Foote, Samuel 2.11–12
Fordyce, David 2.13–14
foreign language teaching *see* language teaching
Formigari, Lia *1.175*
Formula syntactical treatise 1.58–60, 1.61, 1.62
Forster, S. *2.100*
Forsyth, Michael 2.280–83, 2.286–87
Français *see* French language
France *2.35, 2.42, 2.54, 2.57–58, 2.66, 2.68–69, 2.71, 2.104–05, 2.110, 3.236–37, 3.239, 3.242*
  German-language teaching 3.57–62, 3.64–67
  international correspondence scheme 3.37, 3.41–42
  role of French culture and language 1.24–25
Franke, Felix 2.91
French language *2.2, 2.10–11, 2.99–100, 2.105, 2.108–09, 2.179–80, 3.235–43*
  didactics in late medieval and early modern England 1.33–47
  feminization of 2.2–3, 2.6, 2.16
  as a foreign language *2.35, 2.37–44, 2.47–55, 2.57–59, 2.63–73*
  gender of nouns and adjectives 2.7–9
  historiography in European context 1.20, 1.22–23, 1.26, 1.28–30, 1.132, 1.137–38
  opposition to teaching spoken or 'colloquial' French 2.1–16
  oral proficiency 2.1–16
  phases of French language teaching in England 2.293–305
  spoken French 1.40–42
  textbooks 2.6–9
Frigols, María Jesús 2.79, 2.80
Frisch, Max *2.107*
Froude, James Anthony 3.78
Fry, Rev. Thomas Charles 2.138
Fuchs, Eckhardt 3.26
Fuentes Morán, Teresa 2.123
Fullonius, William 1.34–35
Furno, M. 1.71
Futerman, Zinoviy Y. 2.203

Gabelentz, Georg von der 3.148
Galán, Gaspar 1.1, *1.85*
Gallagher, John James *1.178*
Gallina, A. 1.71
Galy, Laurent 3.153
Gardt, A. *2.99, 2.103*
Gatbonton, Elizabeth 2.269
Gellner, Ernst 3.22–23
Gensini, Stefano 2.248
German language *2.38, 2.48, 2.66–67, 2.69–70, 2.99–110, 3.243*
  concept of the Other in German-language teaching 3.57–70
  GAP (German for Academic Purposes) textbooks 2.119–21
  as language of science 2.116–17
  subject knowledge and language integration 2.76–84
  teaching German in context of Americanization (1914–1945) 3.212, 3.216–17, 3.220–21
  teaching German and cultural values in China 3.194–208
  teaching language at girls' secondary schools 2.87–96
  teaching and learning German in Cameroon 3.133–43
Germany *1.146, 1.177, 1.185, 2.101, 2.104–05, 2.110*
  concept of the Other in German-language teaching 3.57–70

conceptualizing the 'Other' 3.88–90
cultural representations of 'the English' in 1920s
  3.74–82
culture in English language teaching in post-war
  Germany 3.85–94
Deutschkunde 3.76
English language teaching 2.88–90
English language textbooks in 1800s and 1900s 3.1–19
German language *1.145–46*, *1.175*
international correspondence scheme 3.37, 3.42–43
Kulturkunde 3.74–82, 3.85–94
literature as part of French-language teaching
  3.99–112
'Pisa shock' report of education system 3.99, 3.100
Richert'sche Richtlinen 3.77–78, 3.82, 3.87
school system 2.76–84, 2.88–89, 2.90–91
Sozialkunde-Lehrplan 3.92
teaching German and cultural values in China
  3.194–208
teaching and learning German in Cameroon 3.133–43
Gesenius, Friedrich Wilhelm 3.12
Gezelius, Bishop Johannes, The Elder 1.96–104
Gezelius, Bishop Johannes, The Younger 1.97
Giacolone Ramat, Anna 2.251
Gianninoto, Mariarosaria 3.202
Giles, Herbert A. 3.155, 3.156, 3.157–58, 3.173
Gillespie, Vincent 1.37
Girard, Gabriel *2.42*
Girard, Marcel *2.69–70*
Girau, Lewis 2.263, 2.264–66, 2.269, 2.272
  Método de Inglés 2.264–66, 2.272
Girault-Duvivier, Ch. P *2.39*
Glück, Helmut *1.175*, *2.113*, *2.113*
Godin, André *2.68*
Gómez, Suárez *1.89*
Gonçalves, Joaquim Afonso 3.148, 3.151–53, 3.200–01,
  3.202
Gorlova, Natalia A. 2.205–06
Gouin, Francois 2.129
Govdelas, Dimítrios *2.51*
Gove, Michael 2.30
Grammaire de la langue française 35, 37–40, 43–44,
  46 n. 15 & 2.19
grammar-translation method 2.21–30, 2.91, 2.231–32,
  2.260–61, 2.273
Grammont, Maurice 2.162
Grant, Sir Charles 3.247, 3.248
Gratte, Henri 2.11
Grave, Louvain Bartholomy de *1.86–87*, *1.89*
Gray, Thomas 3.48, 3.49, 3.50
Greece *2.34–36*, *2.38*, *2.40*, *2.42–43*, *2.48*, *2.50–51*,
  2.55–56, *2.58–59*
Greek language 2.9, 2.21–22, 2.23, *2.38–39*, 2.43, *2.46n8*,
  2.50–51, *2.56*, *2.59*, *2.66*, *2.102*
Green, Major Arthur Octavius 3.126–27
Greiffenhehn, Johann Elias 3.8–9, 3.10–11

Greyerz, O. von *2.104*
Grigorievna, Maria 2.202
Grimm, Jacob 2.147
Gröber, Gustav 2.149
Grüneberg, Emil 2.122
Guarini, Battista 1.62
Guizot, François *2.41–43*
Gümüs, Hüseyin *3.237*
Günther, V.H. 2.27
Gutu, Ion *2.69*
Gwosdek, Hedwig 1.53
Gyr, U. *2.102*

Haertel, Martin H. 3.46
Hallet, Wolfgang 3.100
Halliday, Fred 3.24
Hanna, Ralph 1.37, 1.38
Hartig, Paul 3.81
Hartmann, Martin 3.37, 3.38, 3.39, 3.40, 3.42–43, 3.44,
  3.46, 3.50
Harvey, S. 3.269–70
Hase, Charles Benoît *2.50*
Hassan, Anton 3.115, 3.116, 3.121–26, 3.131
  Arabic Self-Taught 3.121–26, 3.127, 3.130
Haug, Martin 2.116
Haughton, Graves Chamney 2.132, 2.143n14
Hausknecht, Emil 3.16
Hawkins, Eric 2.300
Heath, S.B. 3.215
Hein, Henry 3.227–28, 3.229–30
Helvicus, Christophorus 1.97–98
Henry Sweet Society 1.27
Herkoulides, Anastasios *2.50*
Herman, D.M. 3.231
Herrig, Ludwig 2.151–52, 3.17
Hiley, R.W. 2.15
Hindié, Negib 3.125
historical societies 1.26–27
Hobsbawm, Eric J. 3.22–23
Höfer, Albert 2.147
Hofmann, Fritz 3.106, 3.107
Holbraad, Carsten 3.23–24, 3.25, 3.39
Holford Bottomley, H. 2.184–85
Holmes, Bernadette 2.302, 2.303
Hoover, Herbert 3.219, 3.230
Howatt, Anthony P.R. 3.40
Howatt, A.P.R. 1.26, 1.39, 1.46, 1.71–72, *1.175*, *1.181*,
  2.21, 2.23–24, 2.28, 2.77, 2.127–28, 2.129, 2.150,
  2.235, 2.236, 2.240, 2.255
Howell, James *1.178–79*
Hoy, Peter H. 2.295
Hugo, Victor *2.35*, *2.37*, *2.41*
Hüllen, Werner 1.28, 3.107
Humanist educational reform 1.52–63
Humes, W.M. 2.283
Hurd, Richard 2.12

Iberian Peninsula *see* Portugal; Spain
Ido 3.31
Ikonomos, Konstantinos 2.51
illuminisme (illuminism) *1.181*
India 2.70
   English-language education policies post-Independence 3.246–58
Indonesia 2.70
Informacio syntactical treatise 1.1, 1.58–60, 1.61, 1.62, 1.65n18
Inge, William Ralph 3.80, 3.81
Ingham, Richard 1.42
Inoue Midori 3.188
international correspondence scheme *see* Scholars' International Correspondence
Introduction ('Lily's Grammar') 1.53–58, 1.63
Irving, Washington 3.80
Isawa, Shuji, use of 'Visible Speech' in Japan 3.164–74
Italian language 1.156–69, *2.69*, *2.100–02*, *2.105*, *2.107*
Italy *1.146*, *1.151*, *1.177*, *1.181*
   English language teaching in 1980s and 1990s 2.231–42, 2.246–57
   grammar texts for EFL students 2.246–57
   language teaching at time of communicative turn 2.247–51

Jackson, E.J.W. 2.189
Jacotot, Joseph *2.50*
Janeway, R. *1.180*
Japan, Chinese language teaching 3.164–74, 3.176–91
Japanese language, education in New Zealand secondary schools 3.261–71
Jeffries, David 2.252, 2.255
Jespersen, Otto 2.150–51, 2.153, 2.161
Johnson, Francis 2.132
Johnson, Samuel 1.156, 1.164
Johnson, Dr Samuel 2.128
Johnston, R.C. 1.36
Johnstone, Richard 2.295
Joinville, Jean de *2.48*
Jones, Daniel 2.162–63, 2.165, 2.171–75
journals, language teaching 2.145–58
Joynson-Hicks, William 2.188
Julien, Stanislas 3.148, 3.154–55, 3.156

Kallifronas, Dimitris *2.49*
Kanehiro, Masao 2.165, 2.166
Kantelinen, Ritva 2.206
Karascutas, Georges *2.49*
Karascutas, Ioannis *see* Carassoutsas, Ioannis
Kelly, L.G. 2.23, 2.29
Kelly, Louis 1.20, 1.25
Kemmler, Rolf *1.181*
Keynes, John Maynard 3.24–25, 3.32, 3.33
Khanna, A.L. 3.257
Kibbee, D.A. 1.69

Kidd, Samuel 3.148
Kindermann, Ferdinand 1.115
King, Joseph 2.183
Kingsmill, William 1.40, 1.41, 1.42, 1.43, 1.44
Kinlock, Arthur *1.184*, *1.186*
Kirk, Sonya 2.128
Kleczkowski, Michel 3.153, 3.156
Klimentenko, Anna D. 2.203
Klinghardt, Hermann 2.91
Klippel, Friederike 2.80, 2.81
Klobás, Antonín Prokop 1.113
Kloss, H. 3.215
Klöter, Henning 3.147–48
Koenig, Rudolph 2.169
Kölbing, Eugen 2.148, 2.149
Koller, W. *2.102*, *2.105*
Kolodny, Emile *2.35*
König, Hans 2.89
König, Johann 2.25–26, 3.5, 3.6–9, 3.10–11, 3.18
Kontopoulos, N. *2.49*
Kontpgeorgis, D. *2.49*
Kramerius, Václav Matěj 1.115
Kramsch, Claire 2.299
Krause, Karl Christian Friedrich 2.117
Kreshchanovskaya, Anna I. 2.209
Krishnaswamy, N. 3.248, 3.249
Kristol, Andres Max 1.36–37, 1.41, 1.42, 1.43, 1.46
Krüper, Adolf 3.81
Kuehl, Warren F. 3.23
Kühn, Julio 2.115, 2.116
Kumar, K. 3.254, 3.257
Kuraishi Takeshiro 3.180
kymography 2.163, 2.164–68, 2.172, 2.178n5
Kyprios, Th. *2.49*

Lacavalleria, Antoni *1.90–92*
Laclotte, Fauste 2.168, 2.169, 2.171
Lafaye, Pierre-Benjamin *2.42*
Laisné, C. *1.184*
Lamartine, Alphonse de *2.36*, *2.40*, *2.41*, *2.45n5*
Lambley, Kathleen 1.23
Lancelot, Claude *1.184–85*
Landais, Napoléon *2.49*
language teaching
   anthologies 3.10–11
   at pre-school age in Russia 2.196–212
   cultural content of teaching material 3.1–19, 3.57–70
   deductive approach 1.23, 1.28
   dialogues 1.67–79, 1.166–69
   didactic perspective 1.22
   direct method 1.138
   diversification of learner profiles 1.29
   gendered approach 2.87–96
   grammar-translation method 1.28, 1.29, 1.33, 1.35, 1.39, 1.46–47
   historiographical development 1.20–30, 1.134–36

Humanist educational reform 1.52–63
imitative approach 1.23
interlinear method 3.12–13
international research 1.24–25, 1.27–28
internationalism in FLT policies after First World
    War 3.22–33, 3.35n1, 3.57–70
journals 2.145–58, 2.233–34
language lotto technique 2.207, 2.208–11
linguistic perspective 1.22
'marketplace' and 'monastery' traditions 2.87–90
'marketplace' tradition and 'monastery' tradition
    3.2–3, 3.18
modern languages decline in Scottish schools
    2.276–90
monolingual and bilingual instruction 1.44
social context 1.21, 1.22, 1.24
subject knowledge and language integration 2.76–84
syntactical theory 1.52–54
textbooks 3.1–19
traditional Latin grammars 1.52–53
use of idioms 1.162–63
see also audio-lingual method; Communicative
    Language Teaching (CLT); grammar-translation
    method; pronunciation teaching
Larsen-Freeman, Diane 2.269, 2.271
Latin *2.38, 2.48, 2.62n10, 2.66, 2.99–102, 2.110*
    teaching of 2.3, 2.4, 2.9, 2.14–15, 2.21–22, 2.23, 2.25
Lauwers, P. *2.103*
Lawrence, E. Annie 3.39, 3.40, 3.42, 3.44, 3.50
Lawrence, T.E. 3.126
Laycock, John *1.184*
Le Breton, Philip 2.5
Le Roy, Pierre Louis 1.138
League of Nations 3.25–26, 3.32, 3.76
Leathes, Stanley Mordaunt 3.22
Leber, Eugène *3.241*
Ledel, Jacques, *Vocabulario de los vocablos 1.85, 1.89–92*
Lediard, Thomas 3.6
Leech, Geoffrey 2.253–54
Legge, M. Dominique 1.40
Lencastre, Francisco de Sales *1.177*
Lennox, Charlotte 1.156
Lens, S. 3.217
Lenz, Rudolf 2.157
Lépine, Louis de *1.146, 1.151*
Lépinette, Brigitte *1.86, 1.88,* 2.113–14, *2.113–14*
Lescaze, Genevois *2.104*
Levadeus, Joannis Nikolaidis *2.48*
Levin, Lawrence M. 2.173
Lévizac, J.P.V. Lecoutz de 2.11
Leylond, John 1.60–61
Lhomond, Ch.-F *2.48*
Li Xianglan 3.185
Liaño/Ledel, Iaques de 1.71
    Vocabulario 1.67, 1.71, 1.73–74
Liesuelt, Jacob van *1.84*

Lily, William 1.52, 1.53
Lindemann, M. 1.71
lingusitics
    diachronic explanations 1.21
    synchronic explanations 1.21
Littlewood, William 2.297, 2.298
Lloyd, R.J. 2.156
Lobato, António José dos Reis *1.185*
Locke, John 2.128
Logeman, Willem Sijbrand 2.155–56
Lombardero Caparrós, Alberto 2.113–14
Loonen, Petrus Leonardus Maria 2.25, *2.52, 2.58*
López, Javier Suso 1.28, 1.67–79, 2.49
López, Suso *1.174*
Lovera, Romeo 2.157
Lucas, Charles 3.78, 3.80
Lucena Pedrosa, Lorenzo 2.181
Ludwig, Carl 2.165
Ludwig, Christian 3.6
Luhtala, Anneli 1.52–63
Lukina, Marina M. 2.211
Luna, Jean de 1.71
Lundell, J.A. 2.153–54
Luquiens, Frederick Bliss 3.212–13, 3.226
Luxemburg *2.108–10*
Lyttelton, George 2.11

Mably, Gabriel Bonnot de *2.41, 2.46n17*
McArthur, Tom 3.2
Macaulay, Thomas B. 2.136–37
Macaulay, Lord Thomas B. 3.247, 3.248
McCarthy, Helen 3.25
Mackey, William 1.25
McLelland, Nicola *1.175, 2.52,* 2.113, 3.208
McPherson, A. 2.283
Magill, Edward Hicks 3.37, 3.43–44, 3.46, 3.50
Maistre, Xavier de *2.41*
Malabari, B.M. 3.256
Malthus, Reverend Thomas R. 2.132
Manesca, Jean 2.24
Manso, Corcuera *1.85*
Manutius, Aldus 1.61
Marçalo, Maria João *1.175*
Marcel, Claude 2.129
Mariani, Luciano 2.232, 2.233, 2.234, 2.236, 2.239,
    2.240, 2.252
Markosian, Aida S 2.205–06
Marmontel, Jean-François *2.41*
Marquard, Odo 1.21
Marqués, Salomón *1.90*
Marriott, Major R.A. 3.125–27
Marsh, David 2.79, 2.80
Martei, S. *3.241*
Martin, Edward *1.146,* 1.166
Martin, William A.P. 3.155–56, 3.159
Martín-Gamero, S. 1.71

Martini, Martino 3.148
Masani, Z. 3.248
Mateckaya, Elena I. 2.203
Mateer, Calvin W. 3.158–59
Matheson, Thomas B. 3.130
Matteucci, Riccarda *1.146*
Matthiae Gothus, Johannes 1.102–03
Matthias-Kramer Society 1.27
Mauroy, Sandrine *2.50*
Mauger, Claude 1.163
Mavrocordato, Nicolae *2.64*
Maz von Braidenbach, Nicolás 2.121
Meadows, W. *1.180*
Mehisto, Peeter 2.79, 2.80
Meidinger, Johann Valentin 1.28, 1.29, 2.24, 2.25–26, 2.28, 3.12
Meigret, Louis *1.176*
Mengaldo, P.V. 1.159
Merrilees, Brian 1.38, 1.39, 1.40
Meurier, Gabriel *1.88*, *1.91*
    Family Colloquy 1.67, 1.71, 1.72, 1.74–75
    La Guirlande des jeunes Filles 1.67, 1.75, 1.77
Meylan, J. P. *2.101*
Michaëlis de Vasconellos, Carolina 2.122–23
Michaëlis, Henriette 2.122–23
Midosi, Luís Francisco *1.175*, *1.184–85*
Mieg, Johann 2.115
Miège, Guy 2.3, 2.4
Mieille, Paul 3.37, 3.38, 3.40, 3.41–42, 3.44, 3.45, 3.50
Mill, J. S. 2.10
Miller, John 3.256
Miller, Rod 3.264
Milton, John 1.160
Minerva, Nadia 1.26, *1.146*, *2.52*
Minsheu, John 1.71, 1.78
Mirel, J.E. 3.214
Miyajima Daihachi 3.176, 3.180–88, 3.189, 3.191
M'Lintock, R. 2.156
Moiseevna, Ida 2.202
Moldova *2.63–75*
Moles, Enrique 2.117
Mombert, Monique 3.38
Mommaert, Jean *1.88*
Moniz, Jaime 2.122
Montaigne, Michel *2.48*
More, Hannah 2.6
Morelle, José López de *1.147*
Morlang, Wilhelm 3.106, 3.107
Mormile, Mario *1.146*
Morrell, J.B. *2.146*, *2.149*
Morris, Rev. John 2.131
Morrison, Robert 3.148, 3.149–51
Müffler, Francisco Xavier Humberto 2.122
Müller, Max 2.14, 2.15, 2.135
Munde, Carl 3.13–14
Mytaloulis, Constantin *2.54*

Nabantino, Vittore Felicissimo Francesco *1.177*
Nabokov, Vladimir 2.198
Nakhlah, Yacoub 3.115, 3.123, 3.130
    New Manual of Arabic 3.119–21
Napoléon, Bonaparte *2.100*
Natal'ina, Svetlana A. 2.203
Nava, Andrea *2.252*
Nebrija, Antonio de *1.176*
Negnevickaya, Elena I. 2.203–04
Nehru, Jawaharlal 3.249
Nejedlý, Jan 1.119, 1.121
New Zealand, Japanese language teaching in secondary schools 3.261–71
Niederehe, H.J. 1.71
Nikolaeva, Marina N. 2.205–06
Nissille, Christel 1.37, 1.38, 1.42, 1.46
Noël, François *2.41*, *2.46n10*, *2.48–49*
Nonnote, C. *2.49*
Núñez, Hernán 1.74
Núñez, L.P. 1.71
Núñez, Pablo *1.89*

Odeh, Akram *3.242*
Odeh, Nasser 3.116, 3.126
Ody, Hermann Josef 3.8
Oikonomidis, G. N. *2.49*
Okenfuss, Max J. 1.139, 1.141
Oliva, Marilyn 1.37
Oliveira, Fernão de *1.174*, *1.176*, *1.184*
Ollendorf, Heinrich Gottfried 2.7, 2.24–25, 2.264, 2.265
Ollendorff, H.G. *1.185–86*
Olvarría Martínez, Cesáreo 2.118–19
Orme, Robert *1.182*
Orsey, A. J. D. de *1.184*
Oshima, R. 3.269–70
Osorio, Ignacio *1.151*
Ottoman Empire *2.36*, *2.51*, *2.56*, *2.64*
Oudin, Antoine *1.145*
Oudin, Cesár 1.71, *1.145*
Ozga, J. 2.283

palatography 2.163, 2.168, 2.172
Pallini, Lelio 2.252, 2.255
Palmer, Harold 2.2, 2.162
Palsgrave, John 1.33–35, 1.45
    Esclarcissement 1.33–34, 1.35, 1.39, 1.44, 1.45–46
Panconcelli-Calzia, Giulio 2.171
Panopoulos, P. *2.49*
Papa, Mario 2.233
Papadaki, Maria *2.44*
Paraschos, Cléon *2.35*
Parkes, William Riley 2.267
Partzoulas, Stéphanos *2.48*
Passy, Paul 2.150–51, 2.152, 2.155, 2.158, 2.161
Patterson, Paul J. 1.37

Peeter Heyns Society 1.27
Peeters-Fontainas, J. 1.71
Pelcl, František Martin 1.119
Pellandra, Carla 1.26, *2.49*
penfriend correspondence scheme, *see* Scholars' International Correspondence
Percival, W. Keith *1.176*
Percy, Lord Eustace 3.28–29
Pereira, João Félix 2.122
Pérez, Sánchez *1.175*
Perle, Friedrich 2.149
Perottus, Nicolaus 1.61, 1.62
Petrarch 1.159
Petrie, Sir W.M. Flinders 3.117, 3.125, 3.131
Peyton, V.J. 2.12, 2.15–16
Phanariotes (Phanariots) *2.64–66*
phonetics, experimental 2.161–75
Phonetische studien [Phonetic Studies] 2.145, 2.146, 2.147–48, 2.151–57, 2.161
Piccioni, Luigi 1.163
Picht, Georg 3.99, 3.109–10
Pinnock, William 2.29
Pizzoli, Lucilla *1.146*
Plate, Heinrich 3.12, 3.14, 3.15
Pleskalová, Jana 1.118
Plötz, Karl 2.24, 2.25, 2.33n3
Pluche, Noël-Antoine 1.28
Pochard, Jean-Charles *3.241*
Pohl, Jan Václav 1.113, 1.118
Polevchtchikova, Elena *2.67*
Politis, Linos *2.36*
Porquet, P. R. F de *1.184*
Porter, Barbara 2.300
Portugal, German language teaching 2.113, 2.121–23
Posselius, Johannes, The Younger 1.97–98
Prague Normal School 1.114
Prat Zagrebelsky, Maria Teresa 2.249–51, 2.255
Prendergast, Caroline Lucy (née Dalrymple) 2.134, 2.143n20
Prendergast, Fanny Elizabeth 2.134, 2.144n21
Prendergast, Henry North Dalrymple 2.134
Prendergast, Hew Lindsay 2.134
Prendergast, Sir Jeffrey 2.129–30, 2.143n6
Prendergast, Thomas 2.127–39, 2.142n5, 2.144n29, 3.206
Prescott, Daniel 3.26, 3.28–29, 3.32, 3.33
Presle, Wladimir Brunet de *2.50*
Preussner, Oskar 3.49
Primer, Sylvester 2.157
Procházka, František Faustin 1.114–15
pronunciation teaching 2.161–75
Protassova, Ekaterina Y. 2.206
Protopapa-Bouboulidou, Glykeria *2.36*
Provata, Despina *2.40*, *2.44*
Prussia *2.109*
Puren, Christian 3.158

Raab, C.D. 2.83
Racine, Jean *2.41*, *2.48*
Raddatz, Volker 3.38
Radhakrishnan, Sarvapalli 3.249
Radtke, E. 1.73
Raggett, Michael 2.298
Rajalenius, Barthollus Thomae 1.98, 1.99, 1.100, 1.101, 1.103
Ramírez, Ricardo 2.181, 2.195n3
Ramus, Petrus 1.96
Randén, Suvi 1.96–104
Rang, Hans-Joachim 1.25–26
Rapaport, Barbara 2.295, 2.297, 2.300
Ratke, Wolfgang 1.96, 1.103
Ratti-Kámeke, Richard 2.119–20
Raudnitzky, Hans 2.150–51
Rees, D.J. 3.198
Reform Movement 1.22, 1.26, 1.28, 1.30, 2.21, 2.77, 2.88, 2.91–92, 2.128, 3.14–16, 3.40–41
Regule 1.61–62
Reimer, Georg 2.147
Rein, Wilhelm 1.22
Reinfried, Marcus 1.20–30
Reinwad, Charles *2.48*
Reisner, Edward H. 3.35n5
Reixac i Carbó, Baldiri *1.90*, *1.91–92*
Restaut, P. *2.39*
Rey, Alain *2.65*
Reynold, G. de *2.104*
Rhenius, Joannes 2.26
Richards, Jack 2.5–6, 2.128
Richardson, H.G. 1.40
Richelieu, Armand Jean du Plessis de *2.67*
Richert, Hans 3.77, 3.78, 3.99, 3.100, 3.101–04, 3.105, 3.110
Riemens, Kornelius-Jacobus 1.23, 1.24
Rippman, Walter 2.16
Risager, Karen 1.30, 3.3, 3.4, 3.11, 3.18, 3.101
Rival, Sébastien 3.38
Rizzardi, Maria Cecilia 2.232, 2.237, 2.238, 2.241
Rjéoutski, Vladislav 1.129–42
Robins, R.H. 2.150
Roby, Warren B. 2.172–73
Rodgers, Theodore 2.5–6, 2.128
Rodina, Natalia M. 2.206
Rodríguez, Redondo 1.70
Roiss, Silvia 2.123
Rokkaku Tsunehiro 3.165, 3.176–77, 3.191
Rosembach, Hans 2.114, 2.121
Rosenthal, Lorch 3.206
Rosenthal, Richard S. 2.139
Ross, Sir Edward Denison 2.172
Rosset, Théodore 2.162, 2.178n11
Rosterre, Esteban *1.147*
Rostrenen, Grégoire de *1.147*
Rothwell, William 1.37, 1.40, 1.44

roumain (Romanian) 66–8, 70–71, 74 n. 9 & 2.12
Roumanie (Romania) 63–64, 75 n. 2.11
Rouse, Dr W.H.D. 2.33n1
Rousselot, Pierre-Jean 2.162–63, 2.165–66, 2.168–69, 2.171
Rouyer, H. P. Boumoussa 3.241
Rück, Heribert 3.109
Rudbeckius, Johannes 1.102, 1.103
Ruddiman, Thomas 2.26
Russell, Bertrand 3.25, 3.26
Russia:
  language teaching 1.129–42
  teaching second languages at pre-school age 2 196–212
Russian Empire 2.64

Sadler, Sir Michael 3.28–29
Sainliens, Claude de (Holyband) 1.71, 1.71–72, 1.75–78
  The French Littleton 1.67, 1.75–76, 1.77
  The French Schoolemaister 1.67, 1.75–77
  Campo di Fior 1.67, 1.75, 1.77, 1.78
Salenson, Girard de 1.88
Salewsky, Rudolf 3.81
Sallwürk, Ernst von 2.155
Salmon, Vivian 1.174
Salvini, Anton Maria 1.162
Samaha, Joseph 3.240–41
Sampson, Thomas 1.40, 1.41, 1.44
Sánchez, Aquilino 1.176
Sanchez-Summerer, Karène 3.237
Sanz del Río, Julián 2.117
Saulnier, Jean 1.71
Sauveur, Lambert 2.129
Scapula, Johannes 1.103
Scarlotas, Dimitris 2.48–49
Schäfer Prieβ, Barbara 1.174
Schanen, F. 2.110
Schinas, Michael 2.48
Schläpfer, R. 2.103
Schlunk, M. 3.137
Schlupp, Friedrich 3.105–06
Schmid, Ernst August 2.121
Schmidt, Reinhold 3.79
Schneck, Erna H. 2.173
Schnellenberger, Otto 3.79
Scholars' International Correspondence 3.37–50
  historical background 3.38–40
Schonaeus, Cornelius 1.97–98
Schönfeld, Johann Ferdinand 1.114
Schopenhauer, Arthur 2.92
Schopenhauer, Johanna 2.92
Schrey, Helmut 3.108, 3.109
Schröder, August 3.108, 3.109
Schröder, Konrad 1.25, 2.157, 3.2, 3.4
Schwedtke, Kurt 3.81
Scotland, governance and teaching of modern languages 2.276–90

Scott, Jonathan French 3.26–28, 3.29, 3.32–33
Seely, John Robert 3.81
Segalowitz, Norman 2.269
Seguin, Jean-Pierre 2.65
SEHEL (Sociedad Española para la Historia de las Enseñanzas Lingüísticas) 1.27
Seidelmann, Christian Friedrich 3.1
Seidenstücker, Johann Heinrich Philipp 2.24, 2.25, 3.12
Seuren, Pieter A.M. 2.150, 2.156
Sherwood, Mary 2.6
Sievers, Eduard 2.149
SIHFLES (Société Internationale pour l'Histoire du Français Langue Étrangère ou Seconde) 1.26–27, 1.28
Silva, Ana Alexandra 1.175
Silvestri, Paolo 1.147
Šimek, Maximilián Václav 1.113, 1.118
Simone, Raffaele 2.248
Sinclair, Catherine 2.14
Siouffi, Gilles 2.65
Sismondi, Sismode de 2.41
Sitarz-Fitzpatrick, Beata 1.39, 1.40
Skiadas, Athanassios 2.51
Skytte, Johan 1.102–03
Smith, Richard 1.26, 1.46, 1.175, 2.16, 2.28, 2.77, 2.113, 2.150, 2.236, 3.40
Sorensen, Louise Munch 3.117
Sotomayor, Baltasar 1.73, 1.89, 1.92
source materials 1.25–26
Spain 1.89, 1.92, 1.147, 1.147–48, 1.149, 1.151, 1.151–52, 1.177, 1.180–81
  German as a Language for Special Purposes (LSP) 2.113–23
Spanish language 2.69, 2.107, 3.242
  in context of Americanization (1914–1945) 3.212–31
  Spanish language teaching in British schools 2.179–93
Spurný, Ales Jan 1.113, 1.118
Sriraman, T. 3.249
Staël, Germaine de 2.41–42
Stamati-Ciuera, C. 2.67
Stead, William T. 3.37, 3.38, 3.39–40, 3.42, 3.44, 3.45, 3.50, 3.55n12
Stein, Gabriele 1.46
Steiner, R.J. 1.71
Stengel, Edmund 1.22, 1.26, 1.29
Stephanius, Stephanus Johannis 1.97–98
Stephens, H. Morse 2.133–34
Stepney, William 1.71, 1.78
Stern, H.H. 2.23
Steuerwald, Wilhelm 3.17
Stich, Alexander 1.111–12
Stigzelius, Laurentius 1.103
Storm, Johan 2.153
Strauch, Raymundo y Vidal 2.115
Streuber, Albert 1.23

Sulin, Mihail A. 2.205–06
Surkamp, Carola 3.103, 3.107
Svartvik, Jan 2.253–54
Svenonius, Enevaldus 1.103
Swales, John M. 2.145, 2.151
Swan, Michael 2.263
Sweden, Latin schoolbooks in late seventeenth century 1.96–104
Sweet, Henry 2.148, 2.149, 2.150, 2.153, 2.154, 2.156, 2.161–62, 3.166
Swift, Jonathan 2.2
Swiggers, P. 1.71, *1.181*, *1.186*
Switzerland *2.98–111*
syntactical theory, language teaching 1.52–54
Syrigos, A. *2.49*

Tafel, Leonhard 3.13
Tanaka Keitaro 3.189
Taunton Commission (1868) 2.1, 2.6, 2.10–11
Taylor, Barry *1.178*
Teisonnière, Hippolyte *2.48–49*
Teodorovna, Maria 2.202
Teufel, Carl, *Grammatik für Chinesen* 3.194–208
Theocaropoulos, Georges *2.47*, *2.50–59*
Thimm, Carl 3.123, 3.124, 3.131
Thimm, Franz, *Self-Taught* series 3.121–27, 3.130–31
Thomas, Rev. Joseph Llewellyn 3.126–27
Thomas, Margaret *1.174*
Thomson, David 1.60–61, 1.63
Thornbury, Scott 2.78
Thrale, Harry 1.166
Thrale, Henry 1.156, 1.166
Thrale, Hetty 1.166–69
Thurot, Charles *1.92–93*
Thurston, Edgar 2.134
Tickoo, M.L. 2.129
Tien, Anton 3.116, 3.127–30
Tiheeva, Elizaveta 2.201
Timelli, Colombo 1.69–70
Titone, Renzo 2.233
Tobin, William 2.84
Toledano, Colombo Angelo 2.181–82
Tolstaya-Voeikova, Olga 2.201
Tompson, John, *English Miscellanies* 3.10, 3.11
Tomsa, František Jan 1.110, 1.114–22
Torre, Manuel Gomes da *1.181*
Trausch, G. *2.109*
Trautmann, Moritz 2.149
Trevisa, John 1.44
Trikoupis, Charilaos *2.61n5*
Turcan, Olga *2.73*
Tyack, David 2.84

Uchida Kōsai 3.188–89
Ukraine *2.63*
Ulbrich, Oscar 2.149

United States *2.71*
United States (US) 3.43–44
  advocacy for Spanish language teaching (1914–1945) 3.212–31
  cultural 'other' represented in German classrooms 3.88–90
  German language teaching (1914–1945) 3.212, 3.216–17, 3.220–21
  international correspondence scheme 3.37
  representations of US culture in German cultural readers 3.74–82
Ushinskiy, Konstantin 2.201
U.S.S.R. *2.64*, *2.69–71*, *2.75n11*
Utrecht, Cornille Valere de *1.87*
Utz, Richard 2.148

Valdés, J. de 1.70
Valois, Isabelle de *1.89*
Varyac, Jean de *1.147*
Vassal, Jeanne *3.242*
Vendotis, Georges *2.47*, *2.48*, *2.50*
Veneroni, Giovanni *1.146–52*, *1.164*, *1.166*
Verdussen, Hierosme *1.88*
Verlag, Max Niemeyer 2.149
Vermes, Albert 2.23
Vertovec, S. *2.110*
Verulanus, Sulpitius 1.61
Verwithagen, Jean *1.88–89*
Viehoff, Heinrich 2.151–52
Vieira, António *1.174*, *1.180–84*, *1.186*
Vieira, Carlos Augusto de Figueiredo *1.186*
Viëtor, Wilhelm 1.22, 2.26–28, 2.91, 2.92, 2.120, 2.148, 2.152–53, 2.161
Viëtor, Willhelm 3.40, 3.43
Villa, Antonio de 2.115, 2.121
Villalobos, Francisco López de 1.72–73
Villehardouin, Geoffroy de *2.48*
Villemain, Abel-François *2.41–42*
Villoria-Prieto, Javier 1.67–79
Vinet, Alexandre *2.41*
Vives, Juan Luis 1.103
Vlachos, Anghélos *2.35*
Vodovozova, Elizaveta 2.201
Vogel, Ezechiel 1.103
Voltaire *2.41*, *2.46n18*, *2.48*
Von Flüe-Fleck, H. P. *2.101*
Von Haller, Albrecht *2.105*
von Tettau, Abel Friedrich 1.134, 1.136, 1.138, 1.141–42
Vorsterman, Willem *1.86*
Vygotsky, Lev 2.202

Wade, Thomas Francis 3.157, 3.173
Wadsworth, Ian 1.71
Wagner, João Daniel 2.121, 2.122
Wailly, N-F. de *2.39*
Walch, Agnès *2.55*

Wall, Charles Henry *1.184, 1.186*
Walter, Catherine 2.263
Waltz, Ralph H. 2.173
Waquet, Françoise 1.140
Ward, Ida Caroline 2.173
Watkin, Ralph G. 3.166
Watzke, J.L. 3.228–29
Weller, Franz-Rudolf 3.109, 3.110–11, 3.112
Wendt, Gustav 2.91
Werner, Friedrich 2.81
Western, August 2.153, 2.155–56
Westgate, David 2.295, 2.297, 2.300
Wheeler, Garon 2.24, 2.28, 2.30
Whitney, William Dwight 2.154
Widdowson, H.G. 1.39, 2.235, 2.240, 2.255
Widmer, J. *2.105*
Wiedemann, Václav Michal 1.113
Wiley, T.G. 3.216
Wilkins, Sir Charles 2.132, 2.143n15
Wilkins, Lawrence A. 3.214, 3.218, 3.220–24, 3.229–30, 3.231
Williams, Isaac 2.131
Wilson, Pastor Joseph 3.139
Winter, Johan 1.97
Witt, Nicolas de *2.69*
Wogan-Browne, Jocelyn 1.42
Wolfenden, Peter 2.300

Wolff, Philipp 3.116
  Arabischer Dragoman 3.121
Wollheim da Fonseca, Anton Edmund 2.122
Wollstonecraft, Mary 2.13
Wood, Charles 3.247–48, 3.254
Woodhouse, Richard *1.184–85*
Woods, Edward Frederick Lindley 2.188–89
Wordsworth, Charles 2.130, 2.143n9
Wülcker, Richard Paul 2.149

Yates, James 2.147
Yu, Weihua 2.21, 2.23

Zades, Georgios *2.49*
Zalikoglou, Grigorios *2.50*
Zamenhof, L.L. 3.31–32
Zanchi, Carine *3.239, 3.242*
Zeitschrift für die Wissenschaft der Sprache [Journal of the Science of Language] 2.147–48, 2.151–52
Zellmer, Ernst 3.89
Zhang Tingyan 3.176, 3.180, 3.184, 3.187, 3.188–91
Zhang Yuling 3.190
Zimmer, J.F.W. 3.13
Zimmermann, Petra 2.123
Zlobický, Josef Valentin 1.113, 1.117, 1.118
Zwartjes, Otto *1.174*

www.ingramcontent.com/pod-product-compliance
Lightning Source LLC
LaVergne TN
LVHW061251060426
835507LV00017B/2007